ROUTLEDGE LIBRARY EDITIONS:
POLITICAL THOUGHT AND
POLITICAL PHILOSOPHY

Volume 35

STUDIES IN REBELLION

STUDIES IN REBELLION

E. LAMPERT

Routledge
Taylor & Francis Group

LONDON AND NEW YORK

First published in 1957 by Routledge & Kegan Paul Ltd.

This edition first published in 2020
by Routledge
2 Park Square, Milton Park, Abingdon, Oxon OX14 4RN

and by Routledge
52 Vanderbilt Avenue, New York, NY 10017

Routledge is an imprint of the Taylor & Francis Group, an informa business

British Library Cataloguing in Publication Data
A catalogue record for this book is available from the British Library

ISBN: 978-0-367-21961-1 (Set)
ISBN: 978-0-429-35434-2 (Set) (ebk)
ISBN: 978-0-367-23388-4 (Volume 35) (hbk)
ISBN: 978-0-429-27966-9 (Volume 35) (ebk)

Publisher's Note
The publisher has gone to great lengths to ensure the quality of this reprint but points out that some imperfections in the original copies may be apparent.

Disclaimer
The publisher has made every effort to trace copyright holders and would welcome correspondence from those they have been unable to trace.

STUDIES
IN
REBELLION

by

E. LAMPERT

D.Phil. (Oxon)

Routledge and Kegan Paul

LONDON

First published 1957
© by Routledge & Kegan Paul Ltd.
Broadway House, Carter Lane, E.C.4
Printed in Great Britain
by Butler & Tanner Ltd.,
Frome and London

For
ISAIAH BERLIN

Preface

ALTHOUGH the present work is a whole in its own right, it was designed as the first part of a trilogy devoted to the study of the history of revolutionary thought in nineteenth-century Russia in some of its outstanding representatives. I am aware that, even within the limits I set myself, I have failed to say everything that could be said on the subject. But I am struck by the fact that the subject is a living one —for the general reader no less than for the expert—and that its treatment ought to be alive rather than encyclopaedic. I am aware, too, that my sense of proportion and relevance will not be shared by everyone. I have done my best to make amends by supporting the text with a maze of references and notes, to show, *inter alia*, that whatever bias there may be, it is not belied by the available evidence. Despite the obvious inconvenience for the reader, the notes have been relegated to the end of the book to avoid a clotted and congested appearance as well as to reduce the price of the book.

I am grateful to many friends for valuable help and criticisms, in particular to Dimitry Obolensky and to Patricia Vereker who stood the formidable test of friendship by reading the book in manuscript, to Patrick Thompson, who made the verse translations on pp. 90, 93, 104 and 276, and to Nikita Lobanoff-Rostovsky, who put at my disposal the valuable and little known drawing of Herzen by Sprink reproduced on p. 176. Above all I am indebted to Isaiah Berlin, to whom this book is dedicated, although this debt is a less tangible one. I need only say that his own brilliant contribution to the study of nineteenth-century Russian thought provided the main impetus for embarking on the present work. I am, however, alone responsible for the views and judgments expressed here.

OXFORD
1956

vii

Contents

ix

Illustrations

Chapter One

Introduction

T HIS book deals with the history of Russian revolutionary thought in the second quarter of the nineteenth century, or, more accurately, it is a study of three particular revolutionary thinkers whose work began and matured during that period. Such a study—whether from a predisposition on the student's part or from necessity—fulfils Aristotle's canon of purging the soul through pity and terror, and purging the mind of complacency about the alleged purity, timelessness, or objectivity of ideas and convictions entertained by men. The life of ideas is a strange, submerged life of illumination and obfuscation, of insight and confusion, in which human exigencies, feelings and passions operate. Behind the tedium of ideological superstructure there are human beings who think and feel, who see life whole or in part, and who see it with understanding or presumption, seeking truth or betraying it. Ideas—religious, philosophical, social and aesthetic—are so intimately confused with the man who gives birth to them that to study them is to realize what it is to be human and, perhaps, to discover that the kind of philosophy a man adopts depends on the kind of man he is.

It is this which turns the attention of the student from the general to the particular, from the search for syntheses and the eliciting of platitudes, to an interest in human beings for themselves, and not simply either as protagonists of movements in history or as pegs on which to hang ideas and ideals. And as one leaves the arena of abstract ideological contentions, whether they be called theism or atheism, idealism or materialism, socialism or conservatism, one takes one's place in the human comedy—not as a mere onlooker, sympathetic or otherwise, but as its participant.

Partisanship, prejudice and hypocrisy have, admittedly, converged on many names in history and combined to obscure and distort the story of their thoughts and doings. A dry and sober statement of facts among the multifarious, disparate ideas and feelings may, therefore, be the only desirable procedure. But neither a conscientious compilation of annals, nor impartial generalizations will effect understanding; nor will they evoke the mood and state of mind in which people think and act. This can only be derived from what Dr. Johnson called "a just and imaginative scrutiny of the fortunes of persons levelled with the surface of life".

The history of Russian thought is there to show the relevance of such scrutiny, for its outstanding feature is the intensity with which Russian thinkers were involved in human ends. Indeed, many historians of Russian thought, both in Russia and in western Europe, have contended that, though Russians have had their full share of prophets, thinkers, critics, publicists and revolutionary conspirators, there have been no Russian philosophers worthy of the name, that is to say, no people engaged in a systematic enquiry into logical, epistemological or meta-physical problems; that very little, if anything, said by Russians on specifically philosophical topics has made any difference whatever to the fate of philosophy in the world; and that those Russians who did philosophize in the recognized, technical sense of the word present "a knock-kneed collection of provincial practitioners".[1] This contention seems almost irrefutable to any student of philosophy familar with the history of Russian thought. It is also very salutary, since it serves to restrain the inflated and misplaced philosophical claims made by some Russians.[2] It may, nevertheless, be argued that such an allocation of philosophical merit does not lead us very far, since all philosophical reputations tend to be short-lived and precarious. It may also be argued that, while it is true that Russian thinkers were quick to proceed from the certainties of pure philosophical knowledge into the restlessness of opinion or into prophecy which carried them irresistibly beyond the pale of "scientific philosophy", a certain, perhaps even considerable measure, of such restlessness and engagement with passionate and human ends would mitigate the pallor and lifelessness of so much modern specialized philosophy, and import some air into its unventilated corridors.

The fact remains, however, that Russian thinkers, with few and not very remarkable exceptions, felt uncomfortable in the remote ranges of abstract speculation and could not, or would not be, mere masters in the craft of pure philosophical reasoning. "We were searching in philo-sophy for everything under the sun except pure thought", remarked Turgenev, in an account of his own and his Russian contemporaries' study of Hegelian philosophy in Berlin. The world with its move-ments and ordeals obtruded with terrible persistence through every crack in their changing philosophical outlooks, and philosophical knowledge was to them a way of freeing man from the ugliness and meaninglessness of existence, from the power of the commonplace and of man's intolerable servitude to it. They were quite incapable

2

of adopting that humourless Cartesian posture which enables one to keep cool, disinterested, dispassionate and neutral. They were, on the contrary, easily provoked, stirred, swayed, inflamed, disillusioned and revolted, and their mental experiences were frequently expressed in violent and excessive language. It is sufficient to read the intimate descriptions in Herzen's Memoirs, or even Annenkov's milder and less perturbed Reminiscences, of the leading figures of the contemporary Russian intelligentsia, to be convinced of the dominant impulse which moral tensions and the conflict of deeply felt, passionately reasoned and strongly expressed ideas gave to their life and thought. This inevitably bred the intolerance, presumption and exclusiveness particularly evident among the intelligentsia of the 'fifties and 'sixties of the last century.

A superficial acquaintance with this intellectual climate may prove almost embarrassing, especially to an English student, who in his instinctive aversion from the display of agitation, and attachment to moral and intellectual proprieties, has a number of very effective defences against eccentricity, violent views and excessive opinions. But behind the appearance of turgid enthusiasm and singleness, or even exclusiveness, of mind there was a spontaneous search for truth, and a spirit of moral and intellectual integrity. The violent interrogations of the Russian intelligentsia ring true, not in virtue of their possession of an unassailable gospel or a sense of certainty of their own rectitude, but through their closeness to the sufferings, the perplexity and the hope of their fellow-men. They rebelled morally, hated politically, and despised socially, without retiring to the right hand of God to engage in the grinding of some huge moral and intellectual axe, or to putrefy within from bitterness and revenge; without intending to preserve a private world of their own; and, above all, without letting their imagination become paralysed. They had not only the proverbial courage of their convictions, but also the courage to attack these convictions, differing not merely from other men, but from themselves at other moments.

Although few Russians may have been original philosophers, hardly anywhere have philosophy and philosophical discussion assumed so commanding a position as among the Russian intelligentsia in the second quarter of the nineteenth century. This may explain to some extent why so many historians of Russian thought seem to be aware of no other pressures in that period save that of opinion. This applies particularly to the Russian historians of the conservative type. Their histories are as often as not pitched in a vacuum in which nothing goes on but the discourse of thinkers.[3] But it is not enough simply to tease out the doctrines of individual thinkers, even if they are approximations of the truth. Human ideas are not changeless, logical entities indifferent to time and space, and the human mind does not work except in so far as it both lives in historical processes and knows itself as so doing.

3

Many Soviet historians have succumbed to an intellectual disablement of an opposite kind. Their analysis often helps to discover the nature of the historical situation mirrored in ideas and ideals. We are constantly reminded that no understanding is possible in abstraction from social and historical relations, and that we cannot moralize, philosophize or compile statistics while tied down to one term or the other. But a narrow application of this method turns living historical figures into prisoners of coherent, logical and inevitable movements and structures, and only succeeds in exhibiting great geniuses in the light of great bores.[4] Can anyone really maintain that men, whether they be aristocratic, upper or lower middle class, or proletarian create, discover, gain knowledge, or are illuminated as solid, cohesive, continuous blocs? Men have a tiresome habit of stepping out of neat prisons and even of struggling so violently for release as to burst their bonds. The Russian thinkers of the nineteenth century provide striking examples of such unruliness. It is not necessary, therefore, to treat the history of thought as a parade of unique personalities, however dull or sparkling, in order to satisfy oneself that there must be more in heaven and earth than is to be found in rapacious Stalinist nets.

Social and political factors, however, did much to determine the character of nineteenth-century thought in Russia and could not fail to disturb the serenity of its matter and manner. Cool, analytical thought as it was, and still is to a lesser extent, practised in western Europe could only stand up in a world comparatively safe and harmonious, a world which lent support to the belief that there is in history and society an inherent balance and harmony of movement, that man grows steadily kinder, wiser and more civilized, and that one can, therefore, ignore those irrational forces which in fact so largely account for human conduct and thinking. The Russian thinkers with whom I am concerned in this book were in no desperate need of logic, of the abstract intelligibility of existence and tight metaphysical systems, for logic soothes and gives confidence, and tight metaphysical systems are rationalizations of resentment against man. It was hard for them to sustain the belief that things are divinely ordained in this world, or proceed rationally, mercifully and justly towards an appointed goal; they knew that the world in which they lived was, in fact, ungodly, immoral and inhuman. They had their hopes, dreams and illusions, which account largely for their explosive, restless and refractory ways. But these were difficult and uncertain hopes; and the dreams and illusions proved a danger both to themselves and to the familiar world around them.

2. THE BACKGROUND

The beginning of the story of Russian revolutionary thought is the end of the Decembrists in 1825. The facts are familiar. Alexander I, whom Berdyaev extravagantly described as a member of the intelligentsia on the throne, and who, to quote Metternich's Memoirs, "has played in his own kingdom so much into the hands of the Revolutionists, succumbed mentally and bodily in the fight". He capitulated before the two-headed ascendancy of Archimandrite Photius, the precursor of Orthodoxy's "Black Hundred", and Arakcheev, the Czar's "black watch-dog", and before Metternich himself, who turned Alexander's idea of an alliance of peoples into an alliance of princes against the people. The Decembrist conspiracy, which broke out against the succession of Alexander and in furtherance of a constitutional monarchy or even a republic, was suppressed. It ushered in the most stagnant and oppressive period in the history of post-Petrine Russia.

While it is, no doubt, easy for the controversial historian to magnify the odious countenance of Nicolaian Russia, it is, in fact, a time which almost depresses by a kind of ill-looking obviousness. Nicolas began his reign with an ardent if uneasy ambition to emulate Peter the Great. But the good intentions were soon forgotten and he turned into the superior sergeant-major that he was. "The notorious colonel"—"cause of all our misfortunes", Pushkin said of him. Uniforms became a mania with him: he prescribed them for professors, students, engineers, civil servants and even the gentry. He was virtuous up to a point, relentless, pedantic and commonplace. He liked, as Herzen says, to display "the inflexible firmness that is to be found in cashiers, bailiffs, post-office clerks and sellers of theatre tickets". He was not devoid of some sense of justice which moved him to dislike serfdom and even call it an evil; but, at the same time, he dreaded the idea of emancipation as a "threat to discipline" and "contrary to Providence", in whose decrees he saw the source of his sovereign mission to maintain the existing order. The most apparent evil of his reign was the all-pervading bureaucratization of Russia. It was effectively and efficiently typified by the Third Section of His Majesty's Chancellery, attended by the Corps de Gendarmes, and, less efficiently, by a judicial system whose codification under Speransky, one of the ablest bureaucrats Russia ever produced, did not prevent it from becoming a system of procrastination, bribery and intimidation of the lower classes. Though steps were taken in the direction of stabilizing the obligations of serf-owners towards their peasants, the gentry in fact retained, and after 1848 even strengthened, its unmitigated power over something like twenty-three million human beings (excluding, that is to say, the Crown peasants who, especially in the north and in Siberia, enjoyed a some-what greater freedom). By repeatedly asserting the rights of the gentry, Nicolas consolidated a system of slavery and the subjection of one human being to the will of another which served to demoralize both the one and the other.[5] Its analogy is to be sought in the plantations of Louisiana rather than in feudal manorial society, except that it did not at the time yield any comparable economic results.

5

Some have found it convenient to represent slavery as a pedestal of unspeaking stone to man's noblest cultural edifices, or to maintain that the great achievements and the great leaders of mankind can only flourish to the full on the dunghill of exploitation and hypocrisy. The sacrifices of human material involved in Russian serfdom was not even relieved by such "compensations". On its pedestal grew a kingdom of "dead souls" as depicted in Gogol's novel, and the "grey world" of Saltykov-Shchedrin's ruthless satire—untaught, servile, mendacious and prosaic. The spirit of the *bourgeois*, in the widest sense of the word, raged like a disease: its constraint, its bigotry, its prevarications and drab vulgarity continued intermittently to disfigure life in Russia until the end of the century.[6] This atmosphere helped to support, and was itself the effect of, the "official nationalism" fostered by Nicolas. It thrived on the forcible cultivation of submissiveness, devotion to the monarchy, immobility and obscurantism. Disobedience was listed as the eighth deadly sin, while any manifestation of the spirit of freedom, independence and originality of mind was equated with subversiveness. The national church was elevated to the honourable position of pro- moter and guardian of conservatism among the people. Its official ethics consisted, at best, in the injunction to man to remain always in the posi- tion in which providence had placed him; at worst, in allowing knowledge gained in confession to be used as an aid to the detection of political unreliability. The formula "Orthodoxy, Autocracy, Nationality" served as the slogan for the "Russian Idea", although it was, in fact, largely a Russian transcription of German bureaucratic and military absolutism.

When seen against the background of the situation in contemporary Europe as a whole, the state of affairs in Russia can, however, in no way be regarded as very exceptional. For western Europe, as indeed in some respects in Russia, the post-Napoleonic period was, admittedly, one of preparation of far-reaching changes in the social and economic struc- ture and political organization. But despite or because of the French Revolution most countries in Europe, and particularly those under the control of Austria, found themselves under ruthless *régimes*, which deprived their citizens of liberty and, choosing to treat the revolutionary events in France as though they had never happened, adopted a policy of restoration and repression. Even the subsequent political upheavals in western and central Europe did not succeed in undermining the policies of reaction, and these remained triumphant until well into the second half of the nineteenth century. The only model of relative free- dom in Europe under despotic rule was provided by the British political system. But even in England the benefits of political democracy were neutralized by the effects of the Industrial and Agrarian Revolutions which produced the most appalling social conditions and gave the country and its *bourgeoisie* wealth and power at the price of the depend- ence, poverty and degradation of a proletarianized humanity.

Water-tight and uniform though nineteenth-century Russia may appear, it was yet in many ways a highly differentiated country and people. The vast and soulless bureaucracy emanated from Petersburg. But it was Petersburg, rather than Moscow, which, with some notable interruptions, spelt culture, for what Moscow thought was regarded, by Petersburg at any rate, of as little consequence as what one's belly thinks. It was, in the words of a contemporary historian, a "detribalized" city—a melting pot of many classes and estates, more active, colder and more hostile than the warm-hearted, lazy and self-indulgent Moscow. Petersburg seemed disfigured by the strain of some deep-seated and unresolved conflict. From Pushkin's *Bronze Horseman* onwards it has become one of the most suggestive symbols in Russian literature of man's fate in a hostile universe.

Moscow, for the most part a metropolis of the gentry, unassailable in mind and body and infused with a generous humanity, was patriarchally at ease with herself and her devoted children. It was reinforced in its southern suburbs by a large community of wealthy conservative merchants who ruled despotically over their families, dependants and retainers. Less at ease, they offered bribes to God and the Church to whitewash their sins and fortunes, and fostered a stifling atmosphere of ingrown Orthodox piety. These, together with small townsmen (*mesh-chane*) and the clergy were, in Moscow as elsewhere, legally constituted estates (*sostoyania*). The only section to which no social label is strictly applicable were the *raznochintsy* ("men of various rank"). They sprang from all classes while belonging to none—sons of government officials, of priests, merchants and impoverished squires, as well as serfs who had been freed or run away. These people constituted the most refractory and explosive element of Russian society, and served as one of the principal sources of the modern intelligentsia.

As for the peasants, who constituted the vast majority of the population, it is natural to think of them as a community firmly fixed within the framework of a settled way of life. In fact, until the squirearchical order and the organization of the peasant for service duly crystallized—a process which lasted some two hundred years, beginning in the middle of the seventeenth century—the peasant was, in John Maynard's words, a "land-sailor".[7] He had, and continued to have, an innate dislike for authority, submitting to it against his will in virtue of his adaptability and flexible habits, and periodically rebelling against its alien pressure. His static condition was induced by the prevailing social and political order, and only served to emphasize his restless, wandering and rebellious spirit. His other enemy was Nature: hardly anywhere in Europe is Nature so recalcitrant, so unkind, injurious and less closely married to the soul as in Russia. Only in the vineyards of Neuchâtel is it possible to believe romantically, *à la* Rousseau, in Nature as a beneficent source of mankind's regeneration. In Russia Nature signified the terrible "power of the land" with its pitiless and inexorable demands on man.[8] The peasant's life was at best nothing more than unending labour, neither beautiful nor ugly, but—except when he rebelled—just to be accepted in the same spirit as one accepts the changes of the seasons. He ate his bread in the sweat of his brow, and this was not so much a curse as the only balm which reconciled him to existence. He was a member of a subject race, of a "nation within a nation", almost completely segregated from the "upper classes". His characteristic attitude, save in cases of great national emergency, was one of non-responsibility for the course of public events, about which, again like the seasons, nothing could be done. The State was a remote entity, beyond the horizon of his life, and its policy and administration were the affair of the appropriate and, ever since the middle of the seventeenth century, widely despised authorities. He was conscious only of allegiance to the village commune (*mir*) which allotted the land, fixed the time for the main agricultural operations, and exercised a certain amount of local self-government. Though born of practical needs, the *mir* expressed a spontaneous sense of solidarity, which sustained the peasant's occasional stubborn and very costly resistance to his masters.

3. THE THEOCRATIC ILLUSION

It has been propounded by many, ignored by some and denied by others that the Church has been the nursing mother of almost everything of value in Russia. The question whether and how far Russian cultural traditions and habits of thought are derived from Christianity, and from the Orthodox Church in particular, cannot be adequately discussed in an introductory chapter. But it would be useless to try to understand intellectual and cultural trends in Russia without reference to at least some aspects of the question.

It is, generally, very hard to maintain the specifically Christian character of any branch of European civilization, at least in regard to moral values, or to show what residue, if any, is entirely dependent on Christian doctrines. Nevertheless, for centuries the Church in Russia, no less than in western Europe, was the centre of cultural and intellectual life. While it absorbed—corruption apart—more than it could Christianize of the thought and culture of paganism, it has, at the same time, evoked many riches in spiritual life, in art and in conduct, which one would be at a loss to understand from outside the Christian tradition. This is true even after the Muscovite mind had ceased to be satisfied with the relatively stable, harmonious, hieratic culture of pre-Petrine Russia. Ever since Moscow began to emulate Byzantium, and especially since the emergence in ecclesiastical circles of the doctrine of "Third Rome" as the only Orthodox kingdom in the world, the Church and the secular order were regarded as different aspects of the same thing, governed by the same universal and eternal principles and dedicated to the same purpose. There could be no separation and hence no "concordat" between Church and State such as could exist between two extraneous institutions, and their relation depended in theory, if not always in practice, on the idea of organic unity and a unifying tradition. As the doctrine of the Orthodox kingdom determined the very conception of society, no Tsar could rebel against its authority or curtail its rights, though some of them tried to reduce monastic land-holdings, and to induce the clergy to share the burden of taxation. On the other hand, it would have been equally beside the point to talk of resisting the power of temporal authority in the name of some spiritual principle, even while the Church did oppose the Tsar—as, for instance, in the case of Metropolitan Philip of Moscow (1507–68)—since, according to this whole conception, the former hardly pertained to what one would call strictly the "secular order" which suffered resistance.

The Western Church, in its struggle to resist imperial pressure, developed a theory of the absolute supremacy of the spiritual over the temporal order which received its final expression, and at the same time entered on its practical decline, at the beginning of the fourteenth century. This theory, to which St. Thomas Aquinas explicitly subscribed, helped to shape the attitude of the Roman Catholic Church towards the world: it underlies its urge to absorb all social forces and to become the sole and exclusive director of society, to unify kingdoms, to promote institutions, to monopolize the rules and precepts of thought and behaviour, and to subject men to the observation of those rules. The Russian Orthodox Church scarcely ever desired to rule and claimed no monopoly or absolute assurance beyond the articles of faith.[9] That monks in Russia have proved themselves effective missionaries and have had a civilizing influence, especially in the early history of the Church, is a fact, but it does not entitle one to conclude that religion in Russia sought consciously to permeate or arrogantly to usurp the secular order. The Russian Church, as indeed the Orthodox Church in general, was pre-eminently the Church of adoration, remaining comparatively untroubled by time and not intent on either reforming or attacking the world. That is why it has seldom shown symptoms of clericalism, attended as this is by a spirituality of "appropriation" and the arrogance of those who possess the truth, by watchfulness, mistrust, by that "lying in wait" and mental reservation which the Roman Catholic Church displayed even, and especially, when it shone with the spirit contending with the world. It was equally devoid of the legal casuistry and statecraft of Ancient Rome which reasserted themselves in Christian Rome with the aid of new forms and coercive measure. Its inability to analyse even its own problems in terms of contemporary idiom or to appeal to the conscience of society by something more arresting than liturgical splendours has frequently proved fatal for its survival in history. Its

9

insensitivity to what may convincingly be said and appropriately done in a given situation is almost alarming. While the Western Church was excelling in a baffling variety of apologetics by confidently handling "ultimates", by appealing to Nature, history, science and civilization, by making use of everything and insinuating itself everywhere, the Russian Church was pitifully inapt to force recognition of itself or produce a single piece of convincing and original apologetics.

This failure, however, was in some sense the Russian Church's most important asset, for in the attempt at self-defence it would have quarrelled or pleaded itself into destruction. It seems to have been moved by the instinct that the undefiled Christian truth, like every absolutism, must not seek to justify itself. Christ was mute before Pilate. Nowhere did he speak of his truth as an advantage which bears fruit in the increase of power in the world or as a useful weapon in the interests of society and civilization; nor did he promise the survival of society as a reward for the return to a divine allegiance.

But the Russian State entertained theocratic claims, particularly since Ivan IV adopted the title of Caesar. The apocalyptic idea of Moscow the Third Rome was responsible for, or at any rate contributed to, the emergence of the haunting myth of absolute sovereignty—a monster all the more terrible for pretending to be Christian since it conjures up the image of Christianity as a living vision of slavery down the ages. The relation of Church and State began to be shaped by the increasing manifestations of the sovereign power of theocratic Tsardom, which saw in its own institutions a reflection of God's ordinances for the government of his creation. The organic unity of the secular and spiritual orders proved no more than the fatal illusion to which every theocracy, whether of the caesaro-papal or the papo-caesarist variety, falls victim, and which ends in idolatry and the abolition of freedom. The theocratic fallacy was born of, and fed on, the conception of a divine providential order which determines the course of historical events, or rather imposes an objective plan upon history irrespective of man's subjective purposes. Oblivious of the fact that the purposes of God are notoriously inscrutable and that it is better not to presume them, men were led to believe, for their own bemusement, edification or exoneration, that the decrees of providence were written in historical, social and political forms and institutions, which thereby acquired the prestige and authority of sacred things. But this also served to demonstrate the recurring and brute historical fact that Caesar never really agrees to tolerate God except on his own terms and as a means for the promotion of his own ends. There was no difference in practice in this respect between Ivan IV's emphatic claims in the matter of man's salvation[10] and Peter's conception of the unlimited "justice of the monarch's will" which reduced the Church to the rank of an administrative department of the State.

Such claims demanded credulity as well as obedience, and they could be effective only so long as the Church itself could be induced to serve the kingdom of Caesar. And the official Church did adjust itself, in theory as well as in practice, leaving the theocratic system a Leviathan without a conscience.[11] The difference between the atmosphere of moral and spiritual vitality, independence and integrity which marked the age of the great Russian saints before the centralization of the monarchy, and the spirit of conformity and servility which characterizes the life of the Church from the sixteenth century onwards is indeed astounding.[12] It would be difficult to envisage a more servile and pharisaic system of morals than that contained, for instance, in the *Domostroy*, compiled by the priest Sylvester, one of the chief advisors of Ivan IV, which lays down the principles of family life in sixteenth-century Russia. Its morality of punishment as a means to improve and to gratify him who punishes, its notion of well-paid virtues, its straining at gnats and swallowing camels of pride and tyranny, were evidence of a widespread petrification of heart, mind and conscience. The Church in its official aspect acquired the character of a solid, pious, conservative, ritualistic, workaday institution, ready to twist the faith in order to justify anything, and to shatter the body in order to save the soul. It offered security at the price of obedience, and expressed itself in a primitive theology of the flogging type, warping its idiom to permit of perpetual expediency.

To the Russian Slavophils who, like the German romantics, misused the notion of the "organic" and made it serve to cover everything they liked, pre-Petrine Russia appeared as a piece of hagiology or a fragment from an illuminated liturgical text; and they approved of it precisely on account of its "organic", patriarchal, traditional, domestic quality. Leaving aside the question whether this is a valid reason for approbation, Muscovite theocracy was, however, by no means as organic and harmonious as might appear. Even the century immediately following the accession of Ivan III (1462–1505) was a period of internal tensions, religious as well as political. This is borne out by the conflict between the official Church party (the "Possessors"), which upheld the theocratic claims of the Autocrat and its own right to vast possessions, and the "Elders from beyond the Volga" (or the "Non-Possessors") who repudiated the Church's economic and political privileges and cherished its spiritual freedom and independence. Though supported by the boyars, whose oligarchic aspirations made them oppose the autocracy and whose economic interests turned them against the Church as a privileged owner of the land, there is no doubt that the "Non-Possessors" rather than their rivals represented the authentic tradition of Orthodoxy in Russia. But they were soon suppressed. The "Possessors" proved victorious, and their victory prefigured in some sense the fate of the Russian Church in more recent history, and served as an augury of the ambiguous rôle it was to play in post-Petrine Russia.

This first important conflict marked a crisis within the body of the "organic" Muscovite theocracy indicating the future lines of cleavage. A new and greater crisis was revealed in the Schism of the Old Believers in the seventeenth century. Although it originated within the conservative core of the people and expressed the extreme tendencies of ecclesiastical nationalism, the Schism represented a challenge to, and a judgment on, the theocratic order. Modern historians seem to agree that the *raskolnik's* defence of time-honoured Russian ecclesiastical usages against liturgical innovations was but the occasion for a deeper opposition. The heavy artillery of obscurantism and rigid ritualism which he directed against the mind concealed a plebeian revolt against a gentry-ridden State and State-ridden Church. The opposition had a distinctly revolutionary character, and gave rise to or influenced the popular rebellions against the State in the second half of the seventeenth century and throughout the eighteenth century.[13] It was only much later, and after fierce persecutions by the Government which lasted intermittently well into the nineteenth century, that the Old Believers developed into a law-abiding community of conservative trading capitalists. What had, initially, gone from the minds of the Old Believers was the certainty that the Tsar and their feudal superiors held their authority from God and, in the last analysis, the belief in the sanctity of the secular order. They believed the Church to be at its best in the midst of hostile criticism and alien institutions, and at its worst when it had everything its own way; that it is least fallible when endangered on all sides; that it is not by persecution but by appropriation that the Cross is trodden under foot. For the Church to bolster up its divine claims by worldly means was an ecclesiological heresy, while its loss of spiritual integrity undermined its competence to interpret spiritual truth. Such in part was the burden of Avvakum's fierce teaching.[14]

The Old Believers lived in expectation of the day of judgment; they almost wished for the day of doom. But this and the somewhat savage eschatology in which they articulated their belief were neither merely a religious curiosity, nor an aberration, nor the outcome of persecution mania, but a way of experiencing history as a tragedy upon which the curtain was always about to fall. The fact that the curtain never did fall made the experience more tragic, depriving them of the satisfaction which the experience of the end might have afforded, and rendering them more impatient, more recalcitrant and more rebellious. The intense apocalyptism of the Old Believers, attended paradoxically by a clinging to old forms that have ceased to be relevant, has prompted some historians to describe them as "romantics" and "utopians" who endeavoured pathetically to wriggle out of history. This charge, however, should not be taken seriously. There is nothing sacrosanct about history, seeing that its ruined sites are crowded with broken idols, lost causes and abandoned gods. "Romanticism" and "utopianism", moreover, have proved useful weapons with which moralists, philosophers and even historians of thought have sought to justify themselves and to paralyse their opponents.[15]

I shall not dwell on the subsequent crisis, brought about in the second half of the seventeenth century by the infiltration of western European influence—in a latinizing ecclesiastical and theological form *via* Kiev and, to a lesser degree and on more secular lines, through the German, Dutch and Scottish settlements in Moscow itself. It proved to be a prelude to the westernization of Russia under Peter the Great and provided further evidence of the gradual loosening and eventual break-up of the water-tight, theocratic culture of Moscow. But until Peter's revolution few developments can be wholly dissociated from Christian ideas and traditions, within which their influence has for the most part been exerted, and the Church remained the social and cultural centre of gravity.

Peter, a strange figure, embodying something of the demonic genius and human charm of Pushkin's *Bronze Horseman* and *Poltava* respectively, as well as of the "drunken fool" of Tolstoy's projected and discarded novel, disliked intensely and actively the whole character and style of the Muscovite structure. His libertine grandeur, rude irreverence and profligate ways, his matter-of-factness and extraordinary flights of imagination clashed with the hieratic, solemn, impersonal Muscovite mentality, which served as a kind of check on even the most extreme manifestations of his predecessors' autocratic power. Reverence for tradition appeared to him as a mask behind which are concealed vast clerical aims to maintain a hierarchical but meaningless pattern of life. The Church secured, and provided the necessary sanctions for, this traditional order and its stable values, and the Church, therefore, became one of Peter's principal enemies. In his endeavour to reduce its place of honour he abolished the patriarchate and instituted, after the model of Lutheran ecclesiastical administration, the "Most Holy Synod", ruled by "a reliable field-officer" with the title *Ober-Prokuror*. But, though the Church thus became, with hardly any opposition, a mere administrative department of the State and, consequently, lost all vestige of independence, it retained in a new form—entirely innocuous as far as the State was concerned—the function of the representative of the State in spiritual matters. The lack of opposition on the part of the Church was partly due to its innate inability to assert itself *vis-à-vis* the world, partly because Christendom, as indeed all religious societies, easily succumbs and conforms to "historical necessity", and even proclaims such conformity a divine truth. The enslavement of the Church, as distinct from its mere disablement, was, therefore, and contrary to a widely held view, not so much the work of Peter as the result of the Church's own degeneration. It lost its freedom, or at least as much of it as it has lost, by spiritual failure to expose false sanctities and idols,

13

moral values, and man's very grasp of truth. Russian historians with vested religious interests tended to disregard the fact that the Church was by this attitude morally and historically implicated in bringing about the crisis which divided Russian culture.[16]

Much has been said about the drastic secularization and westernization of the body politic under the impact of Peter's revolution. This is no doubt true, especially of Peter's principal allies, the "serving people" of various origins, who assumed the character of a corporate gentry and swamped the remains of the old nobility. But, though revolutions claim to break with the past, they are also known to continue it. Tocqueville demonstrated long ago the continuity of French history despite the Revolution—an event of greater dimensions than Peter's reforms. Whether a tragedy or a saving grace so far as Russia is concerned, post-Petrine history points in the same direction. The social changes were in complete accordance with trends in the seventeenth century: they issued only in a more rapid division of the upper and lower classes, while the peasants acquired a kind of official status to allow them to pay exorbitant taxes and to become, under Catherine, the absolute property of the serf-owners. Peter did, admittedly, proclaim the killing of a slave (*kholop*) to be equal to any other murder and decreed, in 1721, "to discontinue the sale of people, or, if that is not practicable, to sell them in families, and not severally, like cattle, which is unknown anywhere in the world". But this did not prevent him from abrogating the law that forbade the squire to expel the peasant from the land. Except for these minor innovations and the important changes in the military sphere and in Church administration, however, the intricate and high-sounding administrative reforms were mostly short-lived and chimerical. As regards the secularization, the middle and lower classes remained largely unsusceptible of the influence of secular ideas, and traditional religious patterns of life continued to command their allegiance. Only the theological Academies and Seminaries provided a propitious ground for the growth of secular and even anti-religious thought, and produced many outstanding representatives of the "plebeian", non-noble intelligèntsia. At the same time, the State itself was far from having become godless: on the contrary, God was widely regarded as a help not only in the Church but in government. Peter's empire proved in fact a *reductio ad absurdum* of the whole theocratic conception, which, in practice, always means a coalition of priest and policeman for the maintenance of religion, virtue and political reliability.

4. THE REVOLUTION OF SECULARISM

It would be wrong to construe the Petrine revolution as merely an additional item in a text-book of Russian history. It did initiate a new epoch and, as every new epoch, threw new light on the past as well as creating new conditions and new channels for the flow of spiritual energy. Behind the sometimes lamentable practice of the Muscovite structure there was the theoretical unity to which the people generally assented, even if they rebelled against it from time to time. Whether, divorced as it so often was from practice or merely enforced at the price of enslavement, such a conception made much difference, may be questioned, but its disappearance brought new problems and created a new climate, which lends itself less to definition than the more tangible continuity between pre-Petrine and post-Petrine Russia.

It is important in this connection to analyse more closely the significance of the secularization and westernization of Russia—two factors which gave a new orientation to her spiritual development and issued in a culture of greater liberty and hence of greater diversity.

What did secularization in Russia mean and how did it happen? Few go beyond stating the bare fact that, to quote a recent historian, "secular culture (as represented by the advanced classes of society) moved with elemental force in the direction of excluding the Church from life".[17] Those who have attempted to go further have, as a rule, confined themselves to generalizations about the superannuation and disintegration of the pre-Petrine order, or about the tensions and conflicts which issued in an opposition between progressive social forces and reactionary elements upheld by religion and ecclesiastical authority,[18] or simply about the pride and wickedness of self-seeking man. None of these explanations seem satisfactory. They ignore the fact that the conflict underlying the process of secularization takes place on no material ground where boundaries may be drawn and victories or defeats marked by extraneous tangible criteria. It is a manifestation of a struggle which man has been waging with himself, with the world, with God throughout history, and its arena is closely and constantly related to the deepest questions which can move the heart and mind of man. I cannot, therefore, forgo a few remarks of a general character.

Secularization became evident in Europe when man began to lose his faith in, or at least to question, both the way of life which Christendom has endeavoured to institute since Christianity's entry on the open stage of history, and the authority which sanctioned this endeavour. It involved rejection of the function of religion in history, society and civilization as well as of religious belief as such. Goethe has said that the only real and profound theme of the world and of human history remains the conflict between belief and unbelief. In this conflict both sides have, historically, shared the same deficiency of regarding their opponents as stunted men. Neither side was able to visualize the opposing half of this struggle in terms of human beings, and so both lost the sense of the magnitude of the common predicament. But, at least during the period of the ascendancy of belief, it is the believer who has throughout displayed the greater lack of vision. Had he been less imperious, less didactic,

15

less scornful, less voluble and sanctimonious he might have prevailed. It is not unbelief but belief which shatters by the hurricane of spiritual arrogance, encourages pride, infatuates. There is no greater spiritual ruthlessness than the ruthlessness of the meek who know God. The believer creates hell for the triumph of righteousness and the punishment of the unrighteous, and he is prepared to see all humanity writhe in torment so long as the principle of salvation is maintained. But as a preliminary to this he creates a world in which man exists as a means to the accomplishment of God's ends, for God has created him in order to work out his purpose through him. Unbelief turns against such a world and is, therefore, primarily concerned not with what the faith affirms of God, but with what it implies or fails to imply of man. It is the inhumanity of the believer's universe or his inhuman God, rather than God himself, which offends man and rouses him to revolt.

In some sense history may have gained by the view of human agency as a vehicle of God's purpose, since human agency became thereby historically important. But, at the same time, it has led to an isolation of divine ends from human ends: it has diverted the believer's vision from man himself, by impelling him to look for a divine purpose irrespective of man, by urging him to bow the knee before the necessities and exigencies of history, which claim to possess a sacred meaning, but which in fact pursue their non-human or inhuman ends. What chance, indeed, remained for individual man in face of the *civitas dei* of the western European medieval order or of the Muscovite theocracy, which fared no better? In such a confrontation he virtually ceased to exist, even though both "cities" ensured him the honour of being burnt for the good of his individual soul. The trouble was that for some time, with certain interruptions, enslaved man easily accepted his lot on the assurance of a better life to come: which, though perhaps laudable on his part, was not creditable to the order which enslaved him. He may have hated his guardians and his persecutors, but he had to accept their authority; he may even have voiced from time to time the unhappiness of his own life or that of his fellow men, but he could turn against that life itself only at the price of his very existence.

In this connection it is impossible to disregard too lightly the deep moral and spiritual responsibility which the Church must accept in the provocation of the crisis brought about by secularization. Its policy of interdict, coercion, pitilessness and injustice, its greedy seizing of opportunities for becoming the rallying-point of every kind of reaction, and its hostility to attempts to liberate man were a betrayal of man, in fact and to some extent in principle, for it enjoyed the great advantage of having God to endorse this policy. A great deal may have been due to the errors and blindness to which the members of the Church, together with the rest of fallible humanity, are liable. But the devil has so oddly shuffled the cards that it becomes impossible to affirm anything with certainty about the "pure" and "holy" as against the "impure" and "unholy" image of the Church or about intentions in the Church's alliances with the world. The fact remains, however, that the long-established conformity of the Church with the world's exigencies resulted in its allowing policy to dictate thought. The most typical instance of this is St. Augustine's step, momentous in its consequences, at least for the Western Church. Obsessed as he was with the idea of providence, which fixed his attention upon the function of "tyrants" in the historical process, he appealed to the secular arm, not merely to maintain law and order in society, but to enforce orthodox views. A similar attitude was adopted much later in the Russian Church by Joseph of Volotsk, the leader of the "Possessors". Coercion produced the desired result, and therefore it was justified.

The betrayal of man kindled the fire of secularism and played a great part in alienating him from the Church and eventually arousing him to revolt against it. The "exclusion of the Church from life" developed in various directions, but it consistently involved an affirmation or self-affirmation of man. He affirmed his manhood as a creature of passion and impulse in the Renaissance, with the Faust figure as its characteristic symbol; as a problematic being, recognizable in his diverse and variable characteristics, in romanticism; as social being, whose creative function is not to explain the word but to change it, in Marxism.

It has been argued in many quarters and on frequent occasions that these and other forms of man's affirmation of himself contained a self-destructive dialectic in which the creative human impulses revealed a core or foundation of the purposelessness and despair of man; that the further European man rolled from the centre, from the divine sources of his existence, from his Christian heritage, the more he found himself reduced to a fragmentary, natural condition, and thereby lost his unique character, his dignity and wholeness, with all the disaster that this involves even for his natural life.

No doubt, just as Prometheus broke on his *non serviam* after having measured all the heights and depths, so broke and will break thousands of other men. No doubt "anthropocentric humanism" has created idols of its own and its own thraldom. Even man's rebellion, with no limits but historical expediency, can induce unlimited slavery. A break with God does not abolish the need for God. If there is no God we worship one or other of various fragmentary men; and the fragment turns out to be in conflict with all the rest of man, which it is expected to obliterate or to absorb. But it is not the dethronement of man which is likely to redeem his humanistic search. The tragedy of humanism is not that it has overstressed the dignity of man, but that it has not stressed it enough, that it has fatally underestimated him. Short of affirming man in God, or to use an apocalyptic idiom, short of an absolute manhood on the right hand of God, there can be no manhood. This is a fundamental truth of the Christian revelation. Has Christianity freed Prometheus from his fetters, or has it chained him still more heavily? It would seem that it had freed him, since he was chained not by God but by the demons of Nature with whose powers he was wrestling.

But, as Christendom never was in historical fact the reality which it was supposed to be, and which romantics and apologists like to think that it was, Christian life and thought has variously and consistently belied the truth about man. The lie was of such magnitude that whenever man, caught up as he was in a stream of inhuman historical purposes in which God's presence was presumed, became alive in his human right, whenever he endeavoured to recover his human inheritance, he found himself denying God. What man could not bring himself to accept and believe was the omnipotent, external God—the utmost extension of man's enslaved condition. The dice were admittedly loaded against man—the dice of all kinds of historical and social agents claiming absolute divine authority—but he had the courage to go on playing; and, when he felt he had lost, he committed acts of crazy defiance.

The defiance, however, proved a true liberation of man, even in his defeats and suicidal manias. The Church, meanwhile, continued to regard the process with dismay, and either to find heresy in the thought of rebellious man, or try to chase this heresy without ever quite catching up with it. A new world was coming into being, ordained for the purpose of portraying man. It had become released from the stern discipline of the theocentric scheme. European mankind was moving out of a static society towards modern civilization, undermining the walls which held the old society together and breaking up the unchanging symbols, images and idols of truth. If previously man was scarcely able to draw any moral beyond ascribing his fate to the fickleness of fortune and seeing in that fate the reflection of the workings of eternal justice, he now became conscious of historical development, of the strangely unpredictable passing of time and of that masterpiece of tragic irony which is progress. His social structure became more differentiated, with a rapid widening of the gap between the various strata of society and a greater individual, social, national and cultural disparity. There ensued a greater proclivity to action, a heightened experience of love, friendship, family and social relations. In applying his unaided powers to the world, into which he is cast no one knows why, and to the observable and unobservable phenomena of his environment, man became more curious and more searching in his knowledge, more eager to break his way through the servitude imposed by natural and supernatural necessity towards freedom.

This process of secularization proceeded in Russia not gradually, as in western Europe, but suddenly and impatiently. Its deeper effects, however, were not fully realized until almost a century after Peter the Great. It touched the greater part of the Russian people later still, or touched it at first only by offending its susceptibilities. But, as in western Europe, it spelt the end of a world created with the fixity of the iconographic canon. It released individual energy and a quest for self-discovery. Man made a bid for independence, with all the danger that threatened from such presumption. He began to ask questions and could no longer take on trust the old and current mythologies. This begot a critical and individual rationalism which was incompatible with the previous stabilized order of things and served the Russian well in his subsequent rebelliousness. It expressed itself to begin with in harmless political satire, encouraged both by Peter and Catherine II, who herself founded a number of satirical journals, and especially in the work of Nicolas Novikov (1744–1816) and Alexander Radishchev (1749–1802), the first spokesmen and martyrs of the Russian intelligentsia.[19]

The political structure remained authoritarian, and its leaders were harsh and inclement. But the breaking down of old barriers produced a different outlook on life. A universe of experience and discourse of which the frame of reference was God gave way to a universe of which the frame of reference was man: perhaps a belated Renaissance, but without its relish and naïveté. For, by breaking up the unity, the process of secularization in Russia, more than in western Europe, uprooted and isolated those who were genuinely affected by it, and cut them off from their natural environment. They were quite incapable of entertaining the pious hope that Christianity, rejected in point of truth, should be adopted as a social convenience, as an anodyne or conventional social and cultural cement. Secularization gave rise to a sense of conflict between absolute and relative values—conflict between man and God, man and history, man and the society he lives in, man and his own conscience. In literature the old "objective" forms were breathing their last, and soon the novel, embodying all these conflicts, was to be paramount. Post-Petrine man assumed the character of a divided being, unable to give allegiance to the objective world or recognize anything as everlasting, ordained by God, fate, nature, history or civilization. All these were but a source of pain and anguish to him, owing to their strange and merciless indifference to man and his fate. He ceased to be satisfied: that is why he came to speak with the incoherence of anger and of dreams, and why his interrogations have the shrillness of revolt. There ensued a sense of dualism underlying the whole of life, instead of the unity to which pre-Petrine man had tended. Although aware of his involvement in history, he could no more feel altogether at home in it. He was, except perhaps during the short-lived "Pushkin period" of Russian life and letters, a homeless, nomadic, and somewhat otherworldly figure, far removed from the creative, Rabelaisian *rire immense* of the western European Renaissance. Life was experienced as an exile rather than as a source of triumphant glee. And on entering the road of exile he gained a freedom unknown to him who has roots in this earth and lives in peace with the world and with himself. There is perhaps no more expressive symbol of the condition of post-Petrine man than Petersburg itself, the new capital without citizens, the city of the restive, uprooted, prodigal stranger—a world of nightmare enveloped in fog which drifts clear from time to time to reveal terrifying images and isolated moments of human loneliness and revolt.

The Russian Church, paralysed by secular power, was ill-adapted to come to terms with a world where the ideas of man's freedom was thus coming to birth. The fact that it retained its rigorist structure served only to create new problems and continued to add to their difficulties. The Church was looked upon and used as an all-too-willing safeguard of the existing social and political pattern against the possibility of radical change, as a means of mitigating that which without its influence might bring revolutionary destruction. Its rôle in post-Petrine Russia may, no doubt, be capable, at the price of considerable disingenuity, of some respectable interpretation. A few intellectual leaders, particularly in the nineteenth century, who were in contact with the genuine tradition of Orthodoxy, offered such interpretations, but even they were unable to dissociate their faith in the Orthodox Church from the political and nationalistic myths which were a major source of inspiration for the existing order.[20] By those whose conscience was uncorrupted the Church was interpreted in the light of the actual practice and the theory of the ecclesiastical *régime* and, so understood, its rôle was pernicious and degrading. The fact that the Church, through its outstanding spokesman, volubly justified resignation by giving hope of a better future in heaven and, notably, showed every hostility to measures likely to promote man's emancipation, even where serfdom was concerned, could not but drive men of good-will into opposition to itself. But, while a few determined ecclesiastical voices were raised against the appropriation by the State of the domains of the Church in the 'sixties of the eighteenth century, no such determination was displayed then or later in regard to serfdom. On the contrary, the Church proved in this matter at best a silent abetter, at worst an overt accomplice.[21]

But the Church itself became largely a victim of the order which it supported. It turned into an isolated domain, forming as Kluchevsky says, an "exotic growth in the midst of secular society", with a clergy acquiring the character of a closed caste, and resembling, in its lowest stratum, a kind of ecclesiastical peasant proletariat which shared all the disablement and servitude of the peasant population, and, significantly enough, supplied the Russian intelligentsia with its most radical and atheistic elements. It grew into, and continued to be until 1917, a thoroughly dependent and dependable institution, solid, lifeless, a little stony, pious and not without common sense, but, in general, fully justifying the verdict of such a loyal churchman as Khomyakov that "the Russian Church is in a state of paralysis".

What kept the Church spiritually alive, apart from its widely misused and misapplied sacramental functions, was only the recovery in some monasteries of the tradition of the "Non-Possessors". The revival of monastic asceticism in the second half of the eighteenth century by Paissy Velichkovsky (1722–94) and by his direct and indirect disciples, particularly in the Optina Hermitage, who devoted their lives to *starchestvo* or spiritual guidance; the manifestation of true spirituality in the pentecostal figure of St. Seraphim of Sarov (1759–1833), the numerous lay and monastic pilgrims bound for the great sanctuaries in Kiev, Moscow, Mount Athos or Jerusalem, were evidence that at some obscure and deeper level life in the Church was not extinct.[22] Some of these mystics and ascetics were men of great goodness and illumination, as well as of immense sympathy for their fellow-men, while others, according to certain eye-witnesses, were merely worthy or even dull representatives of traditional Orthodox monasticism.[23] Yet they were all beyond the pale: the Church had become, except as an instrument of oppression or as a heavenly or not-so-heavenly firmament arching over the established order, so much out of range for intellectually and morally awakened man that even these signs of life within the Church were not only not known but unrecognized. It is an ironic commentary on the situation that Pushkin, an exact if younger contemporary of Seraphim of Sarov, and endowed as he was with universal sympathies and responsiveness to the most intimate aspects of the life of the Russian people, should apparently not even have been conscious of his existence; and that Seraphim of Sarov, with all his miraculous power of understanding and insight, should in turn have been unaware of or unconcerned with his great contemporary.

5. "RUSSIA AND THE WEST". THE AMBIGUITY OF EUROPEAN DIVISIONS

The other factor which resulted in a re-orientation of Russia's historical development, her relations with western Europe, is a subject that has suffered from too much treatment and it is scarcely possible to say anything fresh on the matter. A current view, especially among those, Russians and western Europeans alike, who interpret history in the somewhat abstract terms of civilization, is that Russia represents a separate cultural entity; that until late in the seventeenth century she remained a self-contained country and people; that about a century later her ruling classes began to imitate Europe as the one paragon of civilization and succeeded more or less in attaching her to it; that she would have been better off without this attachment, according to some, and worse off, according to others; and that, to bring the story up-to-date by quoting the surprising statement of a modern Roman Catholic historian, she has been "lopped away from the trunk of Western culture and grafted into a new totalitarian organism which has grown up in Russia and Northern Asia during the last thirty years".[24]

As early as 1839, the Marquis de Custine, in his famous account of a visit to Imperial Russia, depicted the country as an Asiatic society too early forced into a European mould by Peter the Great and his successors who thus thwarted it of its proper growth. To the mind of Custine the scientific knowledge and power which it took so avidly from the "West" were only a veneer to serving the ends of barbarism and an alleged deep-seated, half-conscious purpose of world-conquest. In presenting his thesis he drew a haunting picture of Tsarist oppression and of the slavery with which, he thought, the Russian people were generally and severally intoxicated.[25] A few years earlier Peter Chaadaev, "the Decembrist turned mystic", published his *Philosophical Letters*, which, as Herzen put it, acted like a shot in the darkness of the night. It was a manifesto of revolt against Russian history, for in the first Letter he proclaimed that, though he loved Russia "as Peter the Great had taught [him] to love it", Russia does not "belong to any of the great families of the human race: we are not of the West nor of the East, and we have the tradition of neither . . ." "Founded entirely upon borrowing and imitation" Russian culture, in his view, was "absolutely devoid of internal development, of natural progress". "We belong to those nations which, as it were, are not part of the structure of mankind, but exist only in order to teach the world some important (negative) lesson." "We constitute a gap in the moral world-order." Chaadaev's indictment reached its climax when he wrote that "looking at us it might be said that the general law of mankind has been abrogated so far as we are concerned. Leading an isolated life in the world we have given nothing to the world; we have taught it nothing; we have not contributed a single idea to the sum total of human ideas; we have not in any way taken a share in promoting the progress of human thought, and every element of that progress which has come our way we have marred and distorted."[26]

Chaadaev's challenge initiated one of the most important debates in the history of Russian thought—the debate between the Westerners and the Slavophils concerning the place and function of Russia in European history. The Slavophils replied by voicing their belief in the distinctiveness, originality and superiority of Russia's ways issuing from her spiritual bond with the Orthodox Church. The conviction lying behind the attitude to history of a Konstantin Aksakov (1817–60), one of the most extreme if least gifted spokesmen of the Slavophil movement, was that Russia possesses a virtual monopoly of the values of freedom, spontaneity, love of peace, true nationhood, the family instinct and a just, "organic" society, all of which had roots in the Russian past, and of which the Westerners are ignorant or neglectful at their peril. He charged "Western" civilization with the exaltation of "formal reason", with abolition of the soul and erosion of personality until the human being has become a mere scientific or political mechanism, and he repudiated Petrine westernization as a betrayal of "Holy Russia".

Chaadaev's passionate confrontation with Russia, however, and the equally passionate conviction of the Slavophils that their case for Orthodox Russia had the best of it, as well as the fearsome incriminations of Custine and his many past and present successors, who make her appear as a monster unable to learn the wisdom of "Western" ways and to be guarded against as the Romans kept guard on the *limes* of civilization: all alike have greatly contributed to a confusion of historical perspective. The perspective is falsified by the very use of such notions as the "West", "Europe", "Western civilization" and, nowadays, "Western values", on the one hand, and of the "East", "Holy Russia", "Orthodox culture" and "people's paradise", on the other. These have fostered a picture of the respective regions as free and mutually exclusive worlds marred by minor blemishes and mutually threatened by evil foreign doctrines or unscrupulous organizations. The picture belongs to the realm of myths (in Sorel's sense), which have impelled men to action regardless of their truth; they have, in fact, largely proved to be mere battle-cries in a world shaped by fear and devoted to crusades, propaganda and liberating armies.

The confusion begins when we attempt to define "Europe", with which Russia is implicitly or explicitly contrasted by "Europeans" and Russians alike. For some, Europe stops at the Rhine; for others, it extends to the Oder, to the eastern frontiers of Poland or the Ural Mountains: but in most cases it must not be made sufficiently flexible to include Russia.[27] No doubt there are factors which draw Russia away from western Europe—not only and not primarily perhaps the "Byzantine tradition", to which Professor Toynbee attaches a separate cultural character, but which, nonetheless, he recognizes as springing from the same parent as "Western civilization", but the simple geopolitical fact that Russia's backdoor opens on to Asia. Western European pressure, moreover, from the first Catholic crusade against Russian Orthodoxy in the thirteenth century to Hitler's invasion, compelled Russia to turn her back on western Europe. But if the idea of European unity has, as seems to be generally held, two principle sources, namely, Judeo-Christianity and the Classical tradition, then Russia and the "West" must be regarded as sharing the same cultural background. Both are partners in the Graeco-Roman heritage (though Russia received more from the former than from the latter) and both combine to make Christendom. From this angle the conflicts and mutual estrangement which characterize the history of their relations no more invalidates their unity and interdependence than the unity of the Latin, Teutonic and Nordic worlds is invalidated by their divergent fortunes and by the increasing division on fundamental questions of belief and practice within them.

In stressing the disunity, on the other hand, one would have to conclude that the differences between the various cultural and ideological sections within the "West" go as deep as the differences between the "West" and Russia—differences to which, in the words of a modern historian, "the Socratic brain and the Christian heart could give no more than a veneer of unity". Indeed, such a conclusion might help to restore the historical perspective and, incidentally, make appear the assumption that the more people can communicate with and know one another, the more they will like each other as a piece of unwarranted optimism. Thus, speaking in concrete, psychological terms, Germany is to the mind of Frenchmen like Maurras, Massis, or even Valéry and the Anglo-French Belloc, the embodiment of the irrational, tenebrous, impenetrable and unintelligible East, and they could not look east without a shudder of fear and repulsion. The attitude of a Friedrich Schlegel and the German romantics to France, on the contrary, was in all essentials identical with that of the Slavophils to "Europe", including Germany: France's fate appeared to them as the *splendeurs et misères* of Reason, abstract and unreal, whose airless, surgical, litigious world infects Europe with pallor and lifelessness. Richard Wagner devised an "organic" theory of culture similar to that of the Slavophils which he contrasted with the culture of the French and Anglo-Saxon West. To Fourier England was the arch-enemy of liberty and to Victor Hugo, for whom Europe meant Paris, and Paris "the Mecca of civilization", England remained a cultural outsider so far as Europe was concerned. At the beginning of the last century a German geographer (Karl Ritter) stated that "when America was discovered the European Occident became an Orient"—a statement which to modern ears has a more than geographical ring, seeing that the "American way of life" is being seriously and solemnly equated with Christian civilization. Such and similar examples could be multiplied indefinitely, and they all go to show that "the West", "Western civilization", "Western values", and the rest, are symbols which hardly exist in reality and which have led many historians of culture, particularly in nineteenth-century Russia, into synthetic, artificial generalizations.[28]

There is, then, in the last analysis, no such thing as the unity of "Western culture": it would be more meaningful to speak of the unity of world culture, of universal human elements in culture which are transmitted by different channels and transmuted by different environments. There is more truth in the universalism of the Classical outlook which knew only of civilization or culture than in any rigid differentiation of a multitude of cultures and civilizations, although this universalism was, in turn, of a very limited if not parochial kind. In other words, culture exhibits a variety of individualized national destinies, following distinct paths, sometimes in collision, sometimes sheering away from one another, sometimes revolutionized by their mutual incursions: yet

24

they possess a universal human aspect and as such are valid and valuable for the whole of mankind. Their manifold character expresses, and responds to, the questions and anxieties, the needs and moods, the failures and achievements of man; and even if the expressions are uncongenial to some and the responses unacceptable to others, the questions and anxieties are real for all and applicable to all, in the west as in the east. Culture makes sense because it embraces Italy and Russia, England and Spain, Germany and Serbia, France and Norway, and all who are or are not part of Europe; because it signifies the excellence of sharing the experiences of, and belonging to, a world rent asunder yet one in its humanity, the excellence, that is to say, of treating the world's fortunes as one's autobiography.

Returning to the point at issue, one cannot fail to find, fully conscious though one may be of the element of wishful thinking in every historical interpretation, that "Europe" and Russia do not face each other extraneously and heterogeneously across the Oder or any other river, curtain or mosquito-netting, which might be chosen to mark their separate existences, but in the depth of their human and historical interdependence.

That Russia was really drawn into the main stream of western European history before Peter the Great may be disputed; and the extent to which even Peter's work brought her and kept her in that position may be open to argument. Yet no one could claim to understand the cultural and political development of Petrine Russia out of relation with western Europe, or to deny, not only that Russia has become in the last two and a half centuries a most conspicuous and dominant figure on the European stage, but also that her problems and preoccupations are applicable to western Europe and *vice versa*. Their relations may have been accompanied by mutual suspicion, panic or defiance, by the angry protests of the Russian against the suicidal manias of "Western civilization" and by the refusal of the western European to swallow his contempt for what he calls Russian barbarism, but they could and can now no more escape from one another than they can escape from guilt. They were at war with each other because they were at war with themselves; and it was their respective dis-ease that projected itself in their mutual opposition and repulsion. So far as Russia is concerned, the apparent arbitrariness and the force applied in her initial westernization, the sufferings it inflicted on the Russian people and the divisions it brought about among them do not invalidate the fact that it was enacted with the impetus of "manifest destiny". It showed Russia to herself by effecting her entry into the wide world and bringing out her partnership in universal culture. It did not so much add new components as it released those which were already there, and created new conditions for their development.

The first impact of western European civilization on Russia was of a mainly technical character, in accordance with Peter's pre-eminently practical ends. Under Elizabeth and Catherine II Russian society became conscious of the refinements and the intellectual joys of the civilized state. It has been said that in the eighteenth century gentlemen from Dublin to St. Petersburg built, thought, read and wrote in more or less the same manner. While it is true that among its representatives there were some of the most elusive and complex characters in the history of thought, this period is justifiably reputed for its smug sanity, its Augustan virtues of order, perspicacity and reasonableness, its easy and considerate ways, its libertine but well-mannered intellectual and sexual joys, its contempt of obtuseness even in the form of virtue and for lack of delicacy even in monks and ascetics. It was the expression of the mental and spiritual attitude most nearly appropriate to the prosperous, leisured upper class sections of society, which lived on capital, intellectual as well as commercial, that had been created in the preceding century. But, in addition to being confined to the privileged nobility, in Russia, more than in any other European country, this attitude remained purely imitative of the French model, although, later in the century, Adam Smith, Bentham and English philosophical empiricism found some faithful if not inspiring adepts in the University of Moscow (founded in 1755) and elsewhere.[29] And, on the whole, it was a bad imitation, lacking the talent and the taste of the French Enlightenment, despite the few serious attempts at assimilating Voltairianism and the French "natural law" school.[30] It gave "high society", art and the literary manner an insincere, even a pharisaical character. It was unspontaneous, spineless, full of dressing-gown thoughts and expressions, unpleasantly dissipated and devoid of any background, social or otherwise.[31]

There were exceptions to this rule, particularly in the person of the "Russian Pindar", the solitary figure of the peasant-born Mikhailo Lomonosov (1711–65), a scholar of genius and the founder of the Russian literary language. There was a mystical and philosophical movement derived mainly from Saint-Martin and Jacob Böhme (whose works appeared in a number of Russian masonic editions), with Grigory Skovoroda (1722–94) as its most original and unaccountable representative. There was, above all, freemasonry, which is particularly important from the point of view of the history of ideas: for it provides some of the most remarkable examples of the recrudescence of interest in the supernatural in unorthodox forms which were fairly wide-spread in Europe at that time.[32] In Russia, however, it was much less given to the occult and charlatan-ridden practices and speculations of magic and alchemy. For Novikov, the pioneer of Russian journalism, a leading freemason and a victim of Catherine's relapse into political reaction subsequent to the French Revolution, masonry was a means of pursuing enlightened moral and social aims, a way out of the unbearable realities of the social order in Russia, and a move against the artificial French-made way of life, which was narrow and ridiculous in its pretensions.[33] It also inspired and trained some of the Decembrists.

But the awakening of social conscience was particularly associated with the process of secularization which issued from Peter's revolution. Radishchev, the most outstanding representative of the secular mentality in eighteenth-century Russia, not a freemason himself, was the first to turn against and to expose, more radically and uncompromisingly than any of his contemporaries, the social and moral structure of imperial Russia.[34] His philosophical and quasi-philosophical views belonged to the stock-in-trade of the Age of Reason, fertile doubt and facile conviction. But he had none of the restraint and propriety which in other eighteenth century European writers banished ordinary expression of feeling, none of their insouciance, cheerfulness, conventional elegance and refinement. He was endowed with an extraordinary moral sensitiveness, which he betrayed on his journey through Russia: "I looked around," he wrote, "and my soul was rent asunder by the sufferings of mankind." The eighteenth century was full of travellers for whom the world began to appear too narrow: they returned from a distant country to enlighten on the absurdity of its customs, institutions and laws and, in so doing, indirectly to open their readers' eyes to the tyrannies and injustices in their own native land. Radishchev was bolder, and expressed his indictment in an account of a *Voyage from Petersburg to Moscow*, for which he paid with his tragic end.

While in western Europe the rationalism of the Enlightenment was being exploded in the irrational drama of the French Revolution, to be followed by the romantic reaction against the contented austerity of the one and the angry violence of the other, Russia was reaching the culminating point of the Petersburg period. It retained, in form and manner, the aristocratic culture of pre-revolutionary western Europe, but it was less insistent on the universal validity of reason, and imparted to that culture a new atmospheric intensity, vigour, spontaneity and freedom. There was a sense of national pride and achievement; a realization of Russia as a cultural and political force of universal significance; a sense of the joy of creative abundance and of living in beauty and light. Though short-lived and unique in Russian history, it constituted a complete epoch, a whole attitude to life; and it issued in the dazzling output of the classical artistic genius as reflected in the young Pushkin, Zhukovsky, Yazykov, Batyushkov, Baratynsky, and other poets of the Golden Age, as well as in the architectural monuments of Russian Renaissance classicism. But it also ushered in the revolutionary century, for the Pushkin phase in literature is closely related to the Decembrist movement, which marks the beginning of the story of Russian revolutionary thought.

6. THE INTELLIGENTSIA

The political and social background to the Decembrist rising has already been touched upon. It was a background of growing reaction, dominated by martinets, dotards and black archimandrites, a background of thraldom and infinitely dispiriting abdication of thought, which stood in flagrant contrast to the effervescent vitality and creative vigour of the glorious young cultural *élite*. The fact that the Decembrists were not a group of covetous and hide-bound have-nots, but consisted chiefly of officers of the Guards and represented a highly class-conscious gentry, provides one of the paradoxes in the history of the Russian revolutionary movement. It prompted Count Rostopchin, who had defended Moscow against Napoleon, to exclaim that he could "understand the French citizen with his revolution for the aquisition of rights, but what idea can a Russian nobleman have in starting a revolution in order to lose his privileges?" This paradox became, in fact, a constant feature of the Russian revolutionary mind throughout the first half of the nineteenth century, when the squirearchical structure reached such a state of moral degeneracy that the mere fact of possessing a certain moral and social conscience dissociated them from their own class, which had become immune against moral problems and disquietude.

Gershenzon, in one of the most illuminating works on the period, together with some other historians, contends, however, that the participants in the Decembrist movement and the man of the 'twenties in general were still relatively "complete", unruffled, confident and spiritually incurious characters.[35] They lacked, indeed, the constriction of experience, the dark chasm of doubt, the intensely searching mentality which formed the spiritual landscape of their ardent and tormented successors. Such was the semi-humorous society "Arzamas", whose members skimmed the polished surface of literary conversation and cultivated literary friendships; such were the kind, liberal and finally forsaken, but eminently sane and moderate Decembrist Mikhail Orlov, and the cynical, clever, "demonic" or Byronic Alexander Raevsky, Pushkin's friend and rival; such were the dry Jacobin colonel Paul Pestel, the strongest if most treacherous character and best brain among the Decembrist conspirators, and the courageous, idealistic and gentle captain Nikita Muravyev. Even their revolutionary mood was disciplined and did not cause them to lose their ease and distinction.

When the Decembrist rebellion failed, political disillusion came to deepen the dissatisfaction with the world in which the men of the 'twenties lived. "At first we craved frantically for light", wrote the liberal censor Nikitenko in his Diary. "But when we realized that it was no joking matter, that we were expected to hold our tongues and remain inert, that our talents and brains were condemned to petrify or putrefy at the bottom of the heart, which was to become their prison, that every fresh thought proved a crime against the social order; when, in short, we were told that educated men in our society were outlaws, that it can receive into its bosom only soulless compliance, and that military discipline is considered the sole principle on the basis of which action is permitted—then, suddenly, the whole young generation felt out of gear. All its lofty feelings, all the ideas which fired its imagination and inspired it to truth and goodness turned into dreams without practical significance: and for clever people to dream is ridiculous."[36]

One is not, however, left with the impression that gloom and misanthropy were widespread, as happened in western Europe after the failure of the French Revolution and the fall of the Empire, when, in Shelley's words, "disappointment found relief in the exaggeration of its own despair". There was no despair, no loss of vigour, but also none of the stability and balance of the Decembrists; there was great perplexity, a deepening attitude to life, and a tendency to introspection and contemplation. This latter tendency opened the door to a new, hitherto quite unknown interest in philosophical questions and philosophical speculation. The change in climate issued in a succession of decades, in which the development of philosophical and literary ideas is measured not in epochs or periods, but in years and even in months, involving not only changes of opinion but of human attitudes and types. It was an intensive rather than an extensive process, due to the lack of a broad enough cultural environment and tradition (to which Chaadaev had already drawn attention), as well as to the restless, impatient, questioning character of its representatives. They did not work, and could not work, within a framework of established convention, literary, religious and social. Post-Napoleonic western European society was able to count confidently on established if evolving tradition, on the permanence of a century of progress bolstered up by the English Industrial Revolution and by the growing exploitation of industrial areas all over western Europe. The first two generations in Russia after the Decembrist rising, on the contrary, could have no sense of cultural and social homogeneity, and they were deprived of all practical activity: they felt impelled towards a possible future, in which everything would be better but which they could never attain, and they knew their home in their homesickness. They were perpetually driven and deceived in their search, in their hopes and disappointed hopes, in their creative endeavours and disablement, in their service of ideas and theories, and their story is contained in this search and homesickness. While closely involved in the ordeals of the world around them, into which they put all their creative strength; while they offered, especially later in the century, extraordinary instances of self-identification and solidarity—growing, intense, in many cases despairing—with their fellow-men, their face was nevertheless turned against the world, and they called into question not merely a particular pattern of social life, a particular set of

29

social conventions, but the validity of the social and historical order as such. They were rising against the enslavement of man by the world of objects with its historical necessities, its universal laws and social tyrannies, its moral shams and fictitious sanctities. It was this revolt which revealed in Russia man's title to his universal inheritance which is his humanity. And it was this revolt which sustained the characteristic process of devaluation in which the Russian intelligentsia of the nineteenth century pursued its denials of every kind of absolutism that turns illusions into absolute truths and values.

The new intelligentsia was born and grew up in this revolutionary mood, in this almost instinctive impetus to revolt. It did not represent any distinct social class, and it does not, therefore, lend itself to any uniform sociological definition. This has provided its Marxist detractors with considerable difficulties and has prompted "populist" sociologists and historians (Lavrov, Mikhailovsky, Ivanov-Ruzumnik) to regard the intelligentsia as pertaining to "all estates and to no class" (*vsesoslovnaya i vneklassovaya*). It was balanced precariously between two forces: on the one hand, the autocratic Tsardom, upheld by a reliable quasi-militaristic bureaucracy and cashing in on the religious beliefs of the people, and, on the other, that people themselves, silent for a time, enslaved, uneducated, but stubborn, full of elemental strength and utterly unpredictable. It rebelled against the one and felt the fascination of the other. The unaffected but guilty sense of solidarity with, and fascination by, the people produced the historically unique but characteristic Russian theme of "the intelligentsia and the people" (*intelligentsia i narod*).

The definition of the intelligentsia offered by the populists, who were the chief promoters of this theme, correctly reflects the precarious and variegated character of the intelligentsia, but the further conclusion drawn by some of them, that it was living in a kind of vacuum, influenced solely by ideas and fighting, as Ivanov-Razumnik put it, for the ideal of "abstract man" against the *bourgeois* spirit blowing from the west, is one-sided and misleading, though not entirely irrelevant. In fact, the men of the intelligentsia were neither intellectually nor temperamentally averted from reality. Their attitude to "the people" was sufficient to ensure them against inhabiting ivory towers. Indeed, they would have been at a loss to declare their meaning without taking man's concrete historical, social and political situation into account. What they had to convey, even when they yielded, as will be seen presently, to the pressure of idealist philosophical influences, was conveyed in terms of the magnitude of human suffering and endurance. They had no inclination to fastidiousness or that distaste which leads to retirement into a private world.

And yet they were *déclassés*, rootless, with no solid ground beneath their feet. They were incapable of absolute allegiance to anything and quite unable to conform to their environment. Outcasts from the existing Russian world, they became outcasts from the world at large, leading a life, at home and abroad, of voluntary and involuntary separation, abnegation and dedication, which suggests comparison with a religious order rather than a sociologically definable body. They did not behave or think as representatives of a political group or party, defending their vested interests, but as individuals and innovators, without traditions and standing alone and isolated. It is this lack of attachment to any definite social form and organization which gave their outlook the quality of comprehensive humanity. *Gentilhomme russe—citoyen du monde!*

Those who came from amongst the gentry were guiltily conscious of springing from a class that had oppressed the people for centuries. Revolution for them, especially for those who, like Herzen and Bakunin, belonged to the radical and socialist wing, was a moral necessity and an emotional reaction against a hated old order. Others, like Turgenev, Annenkov, Botkin, were wistfully dissatisfied, altruistic, liberal, rich and idle. At the other extreme stood the plebeian *raznochintsy*, equally dissatisfied, but angrier, more impetuous, more iconoclastic, and neither liberal, nor idle, nor rich. The only social activity which was accessible to them and, at the same time, enabled them to earn their living, was literature and journalism, or in some cases teaching privately and in schools. The greatest single influence among the *raznochintsy* was Belinsky, and he was followed in the 'fifties and 'sixties by the "democratic intelligentsia", Chernyshevsky, Dobrolyubov and Pisarev who, however, marked a considerable change in the climate of opinion.

From the 'thirties onwards the intelligentsia lived in a kind of white heat of moral endeavour and a passionate search for truth. It became the experimental conscience of Russia, sacrificing everything on the altar of ethics: religion, art, culture, the State and, in the end, ethics itself. This gave the dominant tone to the Russian realistic novel, for, whatever the dissimilarity between the creative genius of Russian nineteenth-century literature and the tradition of the intelligentsia, in the narrow sense of the word, they share this intensity of moral concern, which in its greatest representatives had the power of transfiguring the world, and a common will to truth which was carried to the point of destroying all truths and calling truth itself into question.

It would be quite impossible to translate this moral concern into ethical generalities or propositions of morality. It was free from all moralic acid, as well as from that romantic moralism whose representatives, like the heroes of certain nineteenth-century novels, unfailingly go up in the world as they become more refined by moral struggle. It was as far removed from the ordinary bovine notions of prudence and duty as it was from that most disastrous alibi of moral man which is framed in the absolutes of moral doctrines, and consists in regarding behaviour as subject to general laws and susceptible of determinate explanations. The only general principle which could be ascribed to it was a belief in integrity and truthfulness, in the discovery and pursuit of truth which casts aside all external influence, and, more intimately, in the personal choice made anew by every human being. Conscience and moral sensitiveness was a source of vision, enabling them to see and understand the moral and religious shams and pretexts which cover an immoral and irreligious reality, as well as to desire the transformation of that reality. They were moralists with a message, not a doctrine; they set out not so much to convince as to provoke.

Their intellectual faults sprang from an eagerness to say everything at once, from an absence of humility of the mind. They went to extremes and jumped to conclusions without testing them by the methods of sober intellectual enquiry. They could never resist a philosophical theory, even though they were perpetually engaged in fighting and discarding theories. Their chief moral error lay in having deposited too much of their moral capital in politics, in having staked nearly everything on one card. Their fierce revolutionary element was ordained as an investment into the process of regenerating their country's spiritual resources: in breaking all moulds it pointed towards a new order of things, towards something universal in its aim and hitherto unknown. Instead, it was increasingly and persistently incorporated into political action. The sin was not, of course, in politics itself, but in a surrender to the vampiric quality of politics, which is as ominous as the vampiricism of aesthetics or of any other autonomous sphere of human existence. The fate of the Russian intelligentsia was thus finally played out in the figure of Lenin, the supreme example of the *zoon politikon*, whose human image was more closely approximated to his superhuman political task than that of any other man in history; just as the great Russian literature, imbued though it was with moral passion, came to an end in the vampiric, decadent aestheticism of the early twentieth century.

(a) Romantics

There is a widely held view that Russian nineteenth-century thought as a whole is ridden with romanticism, sentimentalism and utopianism, and that the moral preoccupation of the Russian intelligentsia in particular can be reduced to mere moral feeling and *Schwärmerei*. The most sustained and impressive indictment of these crimes has been made by George Florovsky in his work, already mentioned, on the history of Russian religious and theological thought. Florovsky writes from the point of view of a not easily accountable Byzantine Orthodox Christianity, which he contrasts with the supposedly adulterated but no more accountable Russian version of it; and the crimes in question are denounced as innovations and "Western influences", which, however, appear to be so all-inclusive as to lose any significant character. Similar charges, in a less impressive, milder and more diffuse form are made by Zenkovsky, who bases his case on the impact of secularization on Russian thought. Professor Carr, writing in a different vein, likewise draws a picture of romantic infatuation as represented by some typical figures of the Russian intelligentsia in exile, although, unlike the two previous authors, he does not allot praise or blame, and does not rationalize or weave doctrines in speculative circumlocutions, and this gives his book a special human and psychological interest.[37] Florovsky maintains that Russian thought, indeed Russian culture as a whole, was virtually ruined by too much susceptibility to the sorrows and sufferings of man, by excessive sensitiveness, by the strains and stresses of emotion, by moral unease and restlessness, by a surfeit of enthusiasm and imagination, all of which is subsumed in the romantic odium and ascribed to an alleged aversion from or indifference to historical reality. Although Florovsky's own strangely cramped, sinuous passion for ascetic theology and Orthodox antiquity betrays him as a victim of the *trahison des clercs*, even this cannot absolve the student from discussing the problem he raises in such a forceful manner.

Romanticism is a hydra-headed word: it cannot be equated with any one intellectual principle, however broad. The Calvinist doctrine of predestination, issuing in a sense of personal goodness and power; the desperate daring of a Byron who, as one of the elect, chooses to opt out of heaven; and Florovsky's own restless search through the past, which sends him, like many another disappointed intellectual, to the Greeks, arid heart in hand, begging a transfusion of ancient blood; all these and many others can be effective vehicles of romantic feeling in the most current and pejorative sense of the word.

It is, therefore, desirable, for the sake of intelligibility, to eliminate the category of romanticism from the vocabulary of religious, psychological and even aesthetic discourse. Nevertheless it invariably returns together with its anti-thesis or corollary, classicism, as a convenient means of indicating the nature of certain opposed points of view in moral and artistic experience. It is in the moral or psychological sense that romanticism must be rescued in order to understand the attitude of the Russian revolutionary thinkers. But it will be useful, in the first place, to eliminate a number of connotations carried by romanticism which cannot in any way be regarded as typical of these thinkers. They were at the furthest remove from that romantic mood which sees no landscape but that of the romantic's own mind, from the melancholia and world-weariness, the *ennui* and *Weltschmerz* so familiar as the epidemic illness of the Romantic Age—in Chateaubriand and Lamartine, in Constant, Shelley, Leopardi and others. They felt no inclination to hug their misery with pride and affection, to regard despair as a sublime passion and enjoy surrendering themselves to it, in order to feel less miserable and less desperate. They had, furthermore, none of that craving after solid and permanent social structure, that constant nostalgia for leadership, which, paradoxically, caused many German romantics, in their pursuit of freedom and utopia, to pay homage to, and in the case of Fichte even to worship, the autocratic Prussian State; or even to seek, like Novalis, firm foundations in a wider field transcending finite existence, in "a dark something", in "the blue flower", or in some general cosmic synthesis. There was, likewise, no movement for that worship of Nature in Russia which, to the English mind at least, is primarily associated with the romantic tradition; and, unlike Wordsworth, the only important Russian Nature poet, Fyodr Tyutchev (1803–73) produces the effect of what Mirsky has called a "profoundly pessimistic and dualistic—in fact Manichean" poetic experience.

Lermontov, it is true, in his early period began a cult of Byronic postures, which for a time infected a few other Russian authors and the Russian reading public in the 'thirties. But, as literary historians never tire of emphasizing, Lermontov's romantic poetry only serves to conceal his real importance as one of the originators of the realistic novel in Russia: as the author of *A Hero of Our Time* and of the series of realistic poems written during the last four years of his life. The Russian writers had, on the whole, too much pity and abnegation and, perhaps, too little egotism to wear for long the romantic Byronic mask of a "doomed" or "lost" generation. Neither was there the slightest tendency among them to worship the past, which romantics, to some advantage for the study of history, admired as something of permanent value in itself or as leading to still greater values which they contrasted with those of the present. Even the influence of George Sand in Russia has left no traces, except perhaps among some Russian women, of the psychology of those romantic characters who maintain an unending stream of words and invoke "virtue", "chastity", "honour" and "purity" as they plunge into an adulterous couch.

Nevertheless, it is legitimate to ascribe romantic elements to Russian revolutionary thought, for reasons which will transpire in the main body of this book, but which I should like to state at this point in more general terms. The distinction, hackneyed though it may be, between the men of the Enlightenment and the romantics in the period between the mid-eighteenth and the mid-nineteenth centuries, is perhaps the best starting-point from which to estimate these elements. Romanticism in this connection destroyed the would-be universalism of the Enlightenment and created a polarization of modes of thought which, to use another well-worn distinction, substituted the dynamic and the dialectical for the static and dogmatic. The real or imaginary timeless values of the medieval world and of the Enlightenment—based in the one case on a supernatural, divine plan, and in the other on a deified, supratemporal Reason—gave way to values which were recognized as rooted in time and space. It was a further step in the reaction against that phase of history in which each human destiny is decreed within a moral and social order sustained by divine authority.

The most significant expression of this new attitude was the German *Sturm und Drang* in the 'seventies of the eighteenth century, which embraced the early imaginative work of Goethe and Herder's brilliant philosophical intuitions. Herder was the central figure. It is the idea of man as an end, rather than as a means, formulated in Herder's *Ideen zur Philosophie der Menschengeschichte*, and subsequently adopted by Kant as the basis of his moral philosophy, which deserves particular attention, and which is more important than all the elaborate notions of Herderian *Naturphilosophie*. Romanticism stands and falls according to whether this idea is valid or not. Herder's influence in Russia was negligible when compared with that of other German romantic thinkers, but the Russian "romantics" shared with him the awareness of the unique image of man. It is from this awareness that emerged the supremacy of "character" in literature, and particularly in the novel, the interest in human motives and human eccentricities, the awakening to human absurdity and inconsistency, the exploration of human secrets, unforeseen thoughts and actions. Man no longer appeared as a mere object of divine providence or of universal Reason, or as a symbol of historical processes, and he was seen to be seeking the human, not the divine meaning, the irony, not the allegory of his relation with God.

In romanticism man emerged, from within his human condition, with several additional notes of interrogation and a will to question more than ever, more profoundly, more strictly, more sternly, more wickedly than he had ever questioned hitherto. He allowed himself the impatient and prodigious luxury of destruction, disorganization and negation. And this has become a constant trait of the Russian revolutionary thinkers. They attached great importance to social and political factors —even in their materialist interpretation—because to them they were the raw material to be shaped to express their vision and advocacy of man—a vision and an advocacy that demand for their embodiment the extreme and destructive situation of revolution. In this they stand out from the exuberantly youthful *Sturm und Drang*. They did not see life, in the manner of Herder, in terms of a teleological naturalism, as closely and securely tied to its setting in the natural world, but in a tension which reveals man's constant struggle to relate himself to the outside world. They saw human action and achievement against a background of social, cultural and spiritual ambiguities, in which each onset of human endeavour seems determined to shed one more comforting illusion. They refused to be impressed by and rejected the achievements of history, and rebelled against its hypostatized tyranny over man. Hence that characteristic leaning towards utopianism, the need to devalue the whole existing and established context of Nature and society in which they were implicated, the destructive gesture of nihilism and anarchism. Hence the hitherto insufficiently emphasized, entirely unromantic dualism pervading their more considered views and attitudes, a tendency to let in, unrecognized perhaps, the recurring and alluring nightmare of the Manichean, with its terrible explanation of the human plight—that the world was made not by God but by Satan. And Satan is no less real or less horrifying because he is seen to be the product of history and society.

A term like heresy (Florovsky's favoured weapon) is not applicable here, for it defines by negation: it cannot interpret. Neither does it suffice to concentrate on the allegedly false historical assumption underlying the "romanticism" and "utopianism" of Russian thought, however clear the moral may be for Florovsky and similar critics. For others the panorama of Russian revolutionary thought is a tragic, or tragicomic, witness to man's search for truth, a part, perhaps, of humanity's quest for the City of God, testifying to that "pain and weariness, yet hope of better things which is the experience of her children in every time". And above all it is an impatient judgment on history and on historical sanctities which claim to embody and possess divine truth but, in fact, prove to be its falsifications. No doubt it is impatience that makes the heretic, but it is their humanity, on the one hand, and the inhuman facts of the religious and social universe, on the other, that made the Russian revolutionary thinkers an ecclesiastically and socially destructive force.

It would be wrong to conclude from this that the tension reflected in the life and thought of the Russian revolutionary thinkers, and the opposition which they experienced against their environment, was a way of retiring from history. Romantics, it is true, have occasionally displayed the self-consciousness of their rôle as enemies of society. But this seems to be more typical of vain psychopaths congenitally incapable of loving (or hating) anyone, or of controlling their own aggression. No evidence can be adduced for such an attitude among these Russians. They hated a great many things and they loved even more, indeed so much so that they have been charged with being mournful romantics, obsessed by the thought of goodwill towards their fellow-men. But (*pace* some religious monopolists) this quality is neither a Christian invention, nor (*pace* Florovsky) a form of libidinous sentimentality, but an elementary human virtue. The opposition of the Russians was due in the last resort to the simple fact that they were human and had a conscience. They revolted, but they did not renounce; they rebelled, but kept nothing in reserve, and only in so far as they identified themselves with humanity; they destroyed because they had to break down the isolation which separates man from other men. The measure of this "romantic" opposition was not an alleged lack of a sense of historical reality, but, on the contrary, a heightened historical perceptiveness which saved them from regarding history as sacrosanct, and, by revealing history's inescapable relativity, renewed their awareness of the only true human condition, which is that of journeying in a world where there is no abiding city.

(b) Idealists. The Moscow "Circles"

The reaction against the philosophy of the Enlightenment with its concepts of reason, nature, scientific empiricism, progress, and the rest, exhibited, in Russia, tendencies which were also at work in western Europe. There were few new and startling doctrines. But these tendencies showed themselves in a more extreme form, and the context and accent were of a new kind. The reaction in Russia was most evident in the interest in philosophical idealism which in the middle of the 'twenties had already begun to influence Russian minds among the members of the first Moscow "Circle", suppressed after the Decembrist rising. They called themselves the "Wisdom Lovers" (lyubomudry), and included Prince Vladimir Odoevsky (1803–69), a man of immense philosophical and scientific erudition, of great charm and a very charitable disposition,[38] many of the older Slavophils and conservative publicists, and Dimitry Venevitinov, a cousin of Pushkin, whose death in 1827 at the age of twenty-two deprived Russian literature and possible Russian philosophical thought of one of their greatest hopes. Apart from Venevitinov, whose literary ideas and manner belonged to the brilliant "classical" tradition of the pre-Decembrist cultural élite, the Wisdom Lovers, and Odoevsky in particular, were apt to surrender to an unabashed ecstatic emotionalism and a dreamy desire for communication with a world unknown to experience, to a sense of fantasy and to nostalgia. It was a mood reminiscent of and stimulated by the contemporary western European mal de siècle, which found its most characteristic literary expression in the romantic contes fantastiques of Hoffmann, Gautier, Mérimée and the ultra-romantic Mrs. Radcliffe satirized in some of Jane Austen's novels.

Odoevsky's importance as a philosopher is negligible, although his Russian Nights, a collection of very nocturnal and very "Russian" philosophical conversations, published only in the 'forties, contain some original thoughts about the "intuitive" or "instinctive" nature of knowledge which prompted a number of historians of Russian thought to describe him as a precursor of Bergson or even as a Russian Bergson. He was one of the first Russian writers to speak of the "decline of the West" and of Russia's mission "to save the soul of Europe"—notions that were subsequently familiarized, with greater subtlety, by the Slavophils.

This early form of idealism, shadowy, complacent and blissful, was

37

short-lived and changed with the general drift of attitude and opinion in the 'thirties. What remained of it throughout this decade was an air of moral and artistic exultation and a taste for totality, for a universe of discourse, which is concerned with nothing less than the whole of knowledge, with the purpose and meaning of life, with God in the world and the world in God. The romantic residue in this attitude is unmistakable. While the life of European man was moving with increasing intensity towards the autonomous and atomistic age of modern history, the western European romantic idealists were making a desperate effort to recapture the spirit of medieval unity and wholeness. For medieval and romantic man alike original sin lay in separation, and unity spelt the lost paradise of the creature's pristine innocence. *"Alles vereinzelte ist verwerflich"*, wrote Hamann, an eighteenth-century German romantic philosopher and mystic who enjoyed some popularity in Russia. But the romantics turned their minds from the reflection on life in terms of conceptual *universalia*, which to the medieval scholastics possessed greater reality than any concrete individual existence, to a reflection on distinctive, particular phenomena in Nature and history, on the life of peoples and on the diversity of cultures and civilizations. They looked for a unity which is attained, not by the subsumption of time in eternity, but for one which reveals eternity in time. It was an idea of unity which appealed to the imagination as well as to the intelligence and provided symbols for those inner powers and perplexities, of which both the Middle Ages and the Enlightenment had taken little account.

Even the social question, which so forcibly engaged the attention of this generation in Russia, was treated, not so much in the manner of the pragmatic and scientific social theories of a Lasalle or Marx, as with reference to the perennial problems of the human mind. Something similar occurred in western Europe, where some purely political movements assumed a quasi-religious character, as in Mazzini's secret revolutionary society "Young Italy" with its motto "God and the People", as in the visionary schemes of Fourier and his apostle Considérant, or in early English socialism. With the Russians, moreover, the idea of a radical change in social relations served as a kind of eschatology, even while they persuaded themselves and others of the perfect soundness and applicability of their aims, an eschatology designed as a source of perpetual danger to every established order and every congested and petrified form of human existence.

The residue of moral exultation left over from the first initiation into idealism found a spectacular refuge in the cult of Schiller. It was not, of course, Schiller, the heroic mid-wife of the German *Bürger*, dressing up and sentimentalizing history for the benefit of his abortive aspirations to power, who attracted the Russians, but Schiller the author of "The Graceful and the Exalted" with its idea of the Beautiful Soul whose impulse to freedom clashes with the servile world around. They turned chiefly on Schillerian rebellion. Their hero was Karl Moor, the good man, tricked by a wicked society into sin, crime and punishment. But, though their environment could not but imbue them with a sense of the ambiguity of action, they were remote from Schiller's frustrated thirst for glamour and power.[39]

The next in the hierarchy of romantic infatuations were Goethe and Shakespeare—the latter often pathetically misunderstood in the manner of the German *Sturm und Drang*. An ecstatic worship of poetry, the theatre, music and friendship filled their lives, interrupted by violent debates in the course of which it was established or denied that Goethe was objective, but that his objectivity was subjective, while Schiller was subjective, but his subjectivity was objective. This, however, did not prevent them from going to dances, making love, and playing practical jokes. Their emotional reaction, particularly among women, and their love-affairs owed a great deal, sometimes with disastrous consequences for their private lives, to sentimental literature, in which George Sand occupied a position of honour—a mythologized George Sand, it is true, without her insensitiveness and her solid, hard, peasant shrewdness, but George Sand, nevertheless. Shakespeare's plays excited them to such frenzy that they returned home from the theatre with swollen hands from too much clapping and sore throats from too much shouting by way of applause.

The search for a comprehensive philosophy of life was stimulated by the many conflicting, or apparently conflicting, ideas of German idealism, which were also Schiller's source of inspiration and which he tried, monotonously and disastrously, to dramatize and versify. "Romanticism for the heart", as Herzen said, "and idealism for the head." Schelling's *Natur*, Fichte's omnipotent *Ich* and Hegel's *Weltgeist* gradually realizing themselves with an enormous display of speculative juggling within and without their respective minds, and finally reaching a state of complete harmony, stirred the imagination of many Russians. They learned and appropriated these ideas, despite the fact that they had plenty of their own, spluttering and half-formed though they were; they crushed them and eventually used the pulped remnant for their own purpose. Many acquired the idealistic jargon as their native tongue: they often wrote and spoke German—and what German!—put into Russian word for word. No one, as Herzen remarked, would have repudiated the illuminating proposition that "the congressionalizing of abstract ideas in the sphere of plastics represents that phase of the Spirit in search of itself, in which it, determining itself for itself, is potentialized from natural immanence into the harmonious sphere of imaginative consciousness in beauty."[40]

When, in 1840, after his exile, Herzen reappeared in Moscow, he found that Hegel had already entered, unknown to himself, upon his undisputed and brilliant career in Russia. Hegel's *Phenomenology* and

39

Logic reigned supreme. "They discussed [them] incessantly; there was not a paragraph . . . which had not been the subject of furious battles for several nights together. People who loved each other were parted for weeks at a time because they disagreed about the definition of 'transcendent spirit', or had taken as a personal insult an opinion on 'the absolute personality and its existence in itself'. Every insignificant treatise published in Berlin or other provincial or district towns of German philosophy was ordered and read into tatters, so that the spattered leaves fell out in a few days, if only there was a mention of Hegel in it."—"In all this there was a naiveté of a sort, because it was perfectly sincere. The man who went for a walk in Sokolniki went in order to give himself up to the pantheistic feeling of his unity with the cosmos; and if on the way he happened upon a drunken soldier or a peasant woman who got into conversation with him, the philosopher did not simply talk to them, but proceeded to define the fundamental substance of the people in its immediate and phenomenal manifestation. The very tear glistening on the eyelash was strictly referred to its proper classification, to *Gemüth* or to 'the tragic in the heart'.

"It was the same in art. A knowledge of Goethe, especially of the second part of *Faust* (either because it was inferior to the first or because it was more difficult) was as obligatory as the wearing of clothes. The philosophy of music assumed a foremost position. Of course, no one ever spoke of Rossini; to Mozart they were indulgent, although they considered him childish and poor. On the other hand, they made philosophical investigations into every chord of Beethoven and greatly respected Schubert, not so much, I think, for his superb melodies as for the fact that he chose philosophical themes for them, such as 'The Divine Omnipotence' and 'Atlas'. French literature, everything French in fact, and, incidentally, everything political has shared the interdict laid on Italian music."[41]

Despite the somewhat embarrassing and high seriousness with which the Russian idealists engaged in their metaphysical, ethical and aesthetic speculations, they were quite capable of smiling at themselves. Already in the middle 'thirties comic Hegelians, or "Hegelists" as they were called at the time, begin to appear on the pages of Russian literature both humorous and serious. A minor author of the name Pavlov (not to be confused with the professor of philosophy of the same name who was the first to inject German idealism into the University of Moscow) describes some typical figures in the streets of Moscow, among whom were to be found University students: "they walked in solitude, casting their eyes angrily, gravely, profoundly over the pathetic crowd where no one knew the things they had heard, where no one had read Hegel and everybody believed, breathed, walked, lived by God knows what philosophy". Panaev, Nekrasov's co-editor of the famous literary review *Sovremennik* ("The Contemporary"), makes fun of the infatuation with Hegel in a description in verse of a youth disappointed in the lady of his heart because "she was still too young and gaily surrendered her nature to *Entwicklung*". The youth admits, however, that it is easier to hit a dozen croquet balls than to realize how "great and fruitful Hegel is". He finds eventually relative comfort in the fact that the dialectic of being will bring her to her Hegelian senses.[42]

Nevertheless, as Herzen remarked, "exclusive preoccupation with theory is utterly opposed to the Russian temperament. . . . The Russian mind transformed Hegel's philosophy . . . and the vitality of our nature asserted itself in spite of all the tonsures of the philosophical monks. But at the beginning of 1840 the young people . . . had as yet no thought of rebelling against the letter on behalf of the spirit, against the abstract on behalf of life."[43] More will be said about these and other intellectual influences or, rather, attempts to gain the sanction of the then prevailing western European concepts for an intellectual experience which, in the end, proved wholly incompatible with the substance and purpose of these concepts.

The centre of philosophical debates were the "Moscow Circles", which met at the salons of various members of educated society, and which, after an interval of several years, succeeded the first Circle of the middle 'twenties. Turgenev, in *Rudin*, Herzen in his *Memoirs*, and Annenkov in his Reminiscences, have drawn a vivid and by now familiar picture of these Circles and of the whole atmosphere prevailing at the time. For a time Moscow became the nucleus of intense and inspired intellectual activity. Petersburg, on the other hand, was officially sinking into the swamp of obsequiousness, hollowness and mendacity, relieved by occasional debauchery, which issued from the heart of Nicolaian bureaucracy, and whose literary laureates and well-paid servants were the notorious critic Faddey Bulgarin, the journalist Nicolas Grech, and the professor of Arabic studies Osip Senkovsky. These writers were endeavouring, in the words of their *doyen* Bulgarin, to "lead the fair sex to the temple of virtue along a pleasant path strewn with flowers" and "accurately and zealously to execute His Majesty the Emperor's will whenever His Majesty may be pleased to use [their] pen for political articles". In the literary circles of Petersburg, where a few men had still some decency and taste, one's estimate of these gentlemen was sufficient indication as to whether one was honest or not, irrespective of any views on moral, social or political questions, which in any case it would have been impossible to express openly.

The Circles, known to the Secret Police as "gangs of liberal bandits", recruited most of their participants amongst the junior members of the University of Moscow, which became, as Apollon Grigoriev said, "the University of secret Hegelism". But they exercised a considerable influence outside it, and included, with a few exceptions, all the creative elements of educated Russian society. There were a great many of these

41

Circles, each having its own individual character, but pursuing, until the middle of the 'forties, similar philosophical, literary and historical interests. They constituted loose associations of gifted, imaginative intellectuals, whose energy was devoted to a passionate pursuit of ideas as a means of discovering truth, and to personal relationships, which were, respectively, fostered and jeopardized by their common ideological aspirations and disagreements. The principle Circles were led by Stankevich (who was later succeeded by Bakunin), with Belinsky, Granovsky and Vassily Botkin, a gifted and jovial tea-merchant's son who dabbled in philosophy, literature and musical criticism; by Herzen, with Ogarev, Satin, Sazonov and Ketcher, the well-known translator of Shakespeare into Russian (this Circle, as will be seen in the chapter on Herzen, stood somewhat apart); the Slavophil Circles at Madame Elagina's (the mother of the brothers Kireevsky) and at Khomyakov's, and others.

Their members found themselves estranged and isolated from the "official" cultural environment. But the charge made against these Circles of being an artificial, heterogeneous, exotic growth, and the view that they were formed under alien French and German influences, that they professed badly translated German and French philosophical views, and lay outside the pale of the deeper aspirations of the Russian people, is wholly unjustified. Such accusations apply properly to those fringes of the nobility ("the Russian Germans", as Herzen called them) who were implicated in the ascendancy of the all-powerful imperial bureaucracy. This milieu had no vital interests or convictions, and it remained a stranger to all creative cultural traditions. It came into being as a result of Peter's rupture with "the people", and its representatives were the true outsiders and eccentrics—profoundly cynical and divorced from national life. The men who were able to convey that life in terms of its deeper movement and of the magnitude of suffering, endurance and achievement were precisely those queer "Russian boys" who made up most of the Moscow circles, and who were so relentlessly impelled by dissent and denial and lived in mental and physical exile. It is not by chance that the Slavophil section of these circles reached, as Herzen put it, "the height of ultra-Slavism with Hegel in hand", that Herzen himself became in his London exile the father of Russian populism, and that Bakunin relied on the destructive energies of the Russian peasant for the attainment of world-revolution. They laid no claim to producing tangible changes in their surroundings, for they belonged, on their own showing, to "a generation in transition", destined only to forge the instruments for such changes. And their controversies converged on the question of the nature and efficacy of these instruments.

The Circles resembled, as Annenkov says, "brotherhoods of knights" in search of truth, or "fighting orders", though there was nothing wilfully exclusive, nothing self-conscious, deliberate or ostentatious about this. No one expected the Circle members to display brilliant gifts or overwhelm with volubility. Only stunted minds and hearts were barred. What they expected from their companions was a certain intellectual awareness and nobility of character. "All that sounded false and artificial, every manifestation of insincerity, empty phrases, spurious protestations were immediately detected" and "provoked a storm of derision, irony and ruthless exposure".[44] No one dreamt of devising statutes or of imposing rules of behaviour and thinking; and yet the Circles developed a distinct ethos of their own and proved instrumental in changing the whole cultural climate in Russia. To those who took part in them they appeared as a vehicle of nothing less than a spiritual revolution. *"Das alte stürzt, es ändert sich die Zeit, und neues Leben blüht auf den Ruinen"* quoted Botkin, in evidence of this revolution. "What we have been taught," wrote Belinsky in 1840, "has deprived us of religion; the conditions of life . . . have failed to provide us with education and debarred us from all contact with knowledge; we are at odds with the reality around us and rightfully detest and despise it, as it rightfully detests and despises us. Where could we take refuge? On a deserted island which, for us, was our Circle."[45]

There was indeed no other place where free intellectual enquiry could occur. The universities, both before and after the reforms of higher education, were to a great extent seats of enforced patriotic obscurantism rather than learning, especially where philosophy was concerned.[46] The fate of philosophy and of philosophers under Nicolas I was indeed a tragic one. They were continuously under suspicion, ostracized, anathematized, persecuted and finally (in 1850) forbidden altogether. The only place where philosophical tradition of a kind, a rather truncated and timid kind, survived were the Theological Academies. Philosophical idealism was viewed with particular disfavour, as the greatest source of danger and unreliability. It was, oddly enough, sometimes easier to profess rationalistic and positivistic opinions, owing, no doubt, to their clear and unequivocal nature, than the more ambiguous, cryptic and unpredictable ideas of metaphysical philosophy. The teaching of the natural sciences met with least adversity: it had its practical use and material advantages which obscurantists naturally hold in greater esteem than the useless and risky flights of speculative imagination.

In these conditions the Circles became the only resort where one could breathe freely. Their initiator and guiding spirit in Moscow, until his departure abroad and early death, was Nicolas Stankevich (1813–40). From all the evidence it appears that he was a most attractive character, and his influence on all his Circles friends and companions was very great, though perhaps out of proportion with his actual intellectual power. Turgenev, who gave what he called "a pale reflection" of him in the figure of Pokrovsky in *Rudin*, Annenkov, Herzen, Belinsky and others are unanimous in recognizing his moral strength, his ability to inspire, his perceptiveness and, above all, his sympathy. "Stankevich", wrote Turgenev in a biographical note to Annenkov, "exerted such an influence over others because he was genuinely interested in every human being, and, without being conscious of it himself, carried him off into the sphere of the ideal."[47] Despite the romantic uplift reflected in his language "he has not the trace of a phrase in him; even Tolstoy would not have found one".—"Sickly in constitution and gentle in character, a poet and a dreamer, Stankevich was naturally bound to prefer contemplation and abstract thought to living and purely practical questions; his artistic idealism suited him; it was 'the crown of victory' on his pale, youthful brow that bore the imprint of death."[48] His philosophical and literary importance, however, has been greatly exaggerated, especially by Chizhevsky.[49] Of all the influential Russian thinkers of this generation he is the only one who can be legitimately regarded as a typical romantic—a victim of high sentiments for their own sake, of emotional moisture and virtuous enthusiasm, of inanition and imprecision, coupled with a complete absence of any rebellious feelings, and a forced hopefulness and optimism, which outran even his intellectual mentors Schelling and Hegel.

Nevertheless, Stankevich, bemused though he was by German idealism and romanticism, was, at least biographically, very much a part of the new cultural environment which was emerging in succession to that wholly other world of Lomonosov, Novikov and Pushkin. It was a period which, especially in its later stages, i.e. roughly from 1836 to 1848 (the "remarkable decade", as Annenkov called it), for richness, complexity and dynamism, would be hard to parallel in any other decade of European life and letters.[50] What surprises is that with the social and political conditions obtaining during Nicolas's *régime* of officialdom; with the systematic repression of all thought and initiative; with the enforcement of "obedience without discussion", of "moderation and accuracy"; with a censorship issuing and applying innumerable stifling regulations and compelling the intelligentsia to write, read and even speak "between the lines"; with prison, exile and administrative discipline becoming a matter of regular policy for what were called "intellectual offences" and a point of honour for the actual or potential victims of that policy; with the general public lying in a state of torpor— what surprises is that with all this pressure and all the bitterness and frustration it had caused there was no stifling of imagination and talent, no disablement of critical faculties among the leading minds. They seemed, on the contrary, to display all the qualities of vitality and vigour —rebellious, curious, eagerly seeking, enthusiastic over some new discovery that might provide just the key which had been wanting to problems of the universe, and tossing off hastily and carelessly a spate of chaotic, prophetic works. Turgenev, meek, delicate, ready to compromise as he was, and not given to intense convictions, though not without proneness to hysteria, accused them in one of his *Sketches* (*A*

44

Hamlet of the Shchigry District) of being "ridden with reflectiveness", of fruitless volubility, idleness, and mutual back-scratching. "You may not, perhaps, know", remarks the hero of the Sketch, "what a Circle is! Do you remember Schiller saying somewhere:

> Gefährlich ist's den Leu zu wecken
> und schrecklich ist des Tiger's Zahn,
> doch der schrecklichste der Schrecken
> ist der Mensch in seinem Wahn!

I assure you he meant to say something quite different: he meant to say: *das ist ein* Circle . . . *in der Stadt Moskau.*" In point of fact, Turgenev's second thoughts on the matter (in *Rudin*) show that there was not the slightest suggestion of striking intense attitudes, for they were completely genuine. They may leave the impression of clowns of the imagination, whose comic effect is obtained by the pursuit of impossible aims with passionate seriousness. But they would not be true to themselves and to the historical situation if they had, instead, become *belles-lettristes* listening to the sound of their golden voices. Urbanity and indolent charm, or polish and catholicity of taste would have been out of tune with, and out of place in, their situation. Some of them belonged to the leisured, wealthy, and independent educated class, but they were all rebels against the ruthless and suffocating order in which they lived. Extreme and violent views alone counted.

But they were not only alive and stimulating. They made a remarkable and twofold contribution to the history of the Russian mind. They have, in the first place, embodied to a high degree the revolutionary as a kind of permanent form of human existence—not in the sense of some general "Russian idea" overlaid by the products of accidental biographical or historical occurrence, but in the sense of living, tangible characters, appearing again and again on the stage of Russian history, characters in whom something profoundly human acquires shape and substance. It is with this revolutionary quality rather than with its specific political expressions that I shall be mainly concerned in this book. They have, in the second place, and inseparable from this, created the spiritual conditions for the birth and development of the Russian novel, which proved to be of such great importance for the understanding of the nature of man. They changed the relationship between literature and life, between thought and the world. The permanent significance of this change arose from an alliance between spiritual and artistic insight and intense feeling, on the one hand, and, on the other, a realistic grasp of the outer world, in which their inner promptings served both as a destructive and a creative force.

Chapter Two

Vissarion Belinsky

(1811–1848)

1. ORLANDO FURIOSO

"I HAD been so impressed by the passionate tone of Belinsky's philosophical essays, and especially by his polemical ardour", records Annenkov in his Reminiscences, "that I naturally imagined him to be a person of extreme opinions, impatient of any views contrary to his own, always striving to lead and outshine others in conversation. I must confess, therefore, that I was rather surprised when at A. Komarov's party somebody pointed Belinsky out to me. I saw a short, stooping, flat-chested man, with large, pensive eyes, who very unassumingly and simply, with a kind of spontaneous friendliness, returned the greetings of those who were introduced to him. There was certainly no sign of haughtiness or pose, no trace of the dictatorial manner I had feared; Belinsky betrayed, on the contrary, a certain shyness and timidity . . . He was quiet and thoughtful, and, even more surprising to me, sad."[1]

Belinsky's dejected mood, which struck Annenkov on this first occasion of meeting him, was due, as Annenkov himself surmised, to some important events shortly before Belinsky's arrival in Petersburg in 1839 from Moscow. He was twenty-eight at the time, and he came to the capital on the invitation of Kraevsky, the owner of the review *Otechestvennye Zapiski* ("Annals of the Fatherland") to be its principal but, as it turned out, grossly underpaid and overworked literary critic, although Belinsky's collaboration made Kraevsky himself a very rich man. The literary scene in Petersburg in the 'thirties, as we already know, was dominated by the unsavoury figure of Bulgarin and his associates, and the coming of Belinsky was awaited as a breath of fresh air: he was welcomed as "the strong hand" alone capable of "undermining, or at least of weakening, the alliance of literary factotums who

46

deeply despised Russian society in all its aspirations, hopes and claims to determine its spiritual life".[2] But to the great surprise of his Petersburg friends and readers Belinsky's first contributions to Kraevsky's review were an open and almost enthusiastic advocacy of the reactionary Tsarist *régime* and its "official nationalism".[3] No one realized at first that this unexpected attitude was evidence of a profound intellectual crisis which Belinsky was undergoing, and which resulted in a painful break with his Moscow friends. According to Herzen he had left Moscow, partly at any rate, on this account, and he did so in a state of extreme depression and irritation. In addition, the suppression (after the Chaadaev affair) of the *Moscow Telescope* in which he collaborated for less than three years, and the unsuccessful editorship of the *Moskovsky Nablyudatel* ("Moscow Observer"), left him penniless, and he was in no position to refuse Kraevsky's offer.

The crisis which Belinsky underwent, the mood which resulted from it, and the effect it had on relations with this friends, are an important chapter in the history of Hegelianism in Russia and, more generally, in the history of Russian revolutionary thought. But before discussing the ideological background, context and outcome of this crisis it is important to say more about Belinsky's character—not merely in order to bring colour to what appears to be a chimerical conflict in the remote and recondite sphere of metaphysical speculation, but because few conflicts of this kind have their key as recognizably in the character of their protagonist as in the case of Belinsky.

Belinsky's early development may be said to be typical of the section of the Russian intelligentsia (the *raznochintsy*) to which he belonged. Born in 1811 in the family of a poor country doctor, he grew up in the small town of Chembar (since 1948 renamed Belinsky) in the department of Penza, against the background of the stolid, narrow, and bigoted environment of provincial Russia. The religious, social and domestic atmosphere of this environment has been described by Kavelin as "the bombination of squalid devils in a pit". He had no reason, therefore, to keep any grateful memories of this childhood. His parents were brutal and ignorant, as most people of this *milieu* were. He was ten or eleven years of age when his father, returning home one day, began to scold him. The boy made signs of justifying himself, whereupon his father struck him and threw him to the floor. Then something happened within him. He rose to his feet completely transformed: the wrong and injustice seemed suddenly to have broken all ties with his family. For some time the thought of revenge gnawed at him, and gradually, with new and painful impressions from his surroundings, changed into an aversion from all relations of kindred, against the principle of family life and domesticity, and into an overwhelming sense of living in an alien world. Such was the beginning of Belinsky's education. "The family emancipated him by unjust treatment, and society by penury." Highly-strung and ailing, he was scarcely fit for strenuous academic work. But there was also something in his character which unfitted him for any institutional education. He was quite unable to "assimilate" knowledge, to submit his mind to routine instruction. He remained self-taught throughout his whole life, because he could not acquire knowledge except by way of struggling for it himself and spontaneously pursuing his own lines of enquiry. Although he developed intellectually earlier than is usual, and read omnivorously and indiscriminately books which no youth of his age would consider reading, he had a most undistinguished career at a local school and at a "gymnasium" in the provincial capital of Penza. In 1829 he went as a "state-boarder" to the University of Moscow, where he did nothing, and from which he was expelled, avowedly "on account of ill-health and limited abilities" but, at least in part, on account of a drama he wrote, entitled *Dimitry Kalinin*. It was worthless from the literary point of view, as he himself subsequently admitted, but expressed in a somewhat rhapsodically romantic manner his first considered protest against injustice, in particular against the injustice of serfdom, as well as a pledge not to rest, so long as a single human being is suffering. He had the misfortune and the naïveté to submit his work to the censorship committee, consisting mainly of the professors of Moscow University who were, as was to be expected, shocked and disgusted by such a piece of shameless rebelliousness, especially "against the rights of noble birth" as the report solemnly exemplifies.[4] Sent away from the University with an attested copy of a humiliating certificate of expulsion, he found himself in the streets of Moscow with nothing to eat and no prospect of survival. It was then that Stankevich and his friends took him up, and he soon embarked on his journalistic career by joining the *Telescope*, whose editor, Nikolai Nadezhdin, an old literary enemy of Pushkin, happened to be another *raznochinets*.

From the maze of contemporary reminiscences[5] Belinsky emerges as a lovable man, awkward in life, a little coarse, and knowing that he was coarse, avid, single-minded, at the mercy of life and yet defying it, endowed with an extraordinary absorbing power, absolutely genuine, candid, and physically impeded by early symptoms of consumption. His was, in Turgenev's phrase, "a central nature", bringing the whole of himself to bear at whatever point he was engaged. He never thought with a part of himself, but altogether, and all his thinking and being was urged from within. He could not think without feeling or feel without thinking: "For me", he remarked, "to think, to feel, to understand and to suffer are one and the same thing." He was certainly not of the breed which believes that a thinker can wriggle out of his skin and construct a system of depersonalized or dehumanized thought. Nor did he wish to do this if it had been possible. Knowledge for him was an approximation to truth wrought of personal experience. And yet, this personal,

48

Belinsky's death-mask

[face page 48

Belinsky at the age of 32

emotive attitude in thought as well as in behaviour had nothing self-indulgent, sentimental, gushing, or "dionysiac" about it. His element was neither earth nor water, but fire. His very passions were predominantly moral passions, passions of the will rather than of the heart, even, and especially perhaps, when he turned against the norms and conventions of morality: they were concerned with man and were directed against the assault upon the dignity and personality of man.

Modesty or pride made him extremely shy and reticent in matters concerning his private life, although a few scattered allusions in letters to his intimate friends are revealing. He married a very unromantic lady, comparatively late in life, in what appears to have been a very unromantic mood. His wife imported her equally unromantic sister, and they lived together. Such arrangements were widely practised in Russian households, with the male or female partners in the majority, although in Belinsky's case it was not a *mariage à trois*. Neither lady appears to have been very bright, and Panaev's wife (another, and more alluring, practitioner of *mariage à trois*, in which she was in the minority) describes them as positively imbecile: they looked at life uniformly and consistently through the prism of a boarding-school for respectable damsels which they had attended in their youth, and gossiped in French about people and domestic trifles. Belinsky's place in this picture was strangely incongruous. He was, however, deeply attached to his only child, a daughter (another child, a boy, died soon after birth), and he used to play with her on all fours for hours, or run about their small Petersburg flat with the little girl on his back.

The words Belinsky chose were quite inadequate to describe his thought. Language itself seems to have been for him the failure to say exactly what he meant, and he tried unsuccessfully to create a new language: he wrote the worst Russian of any contemporary writer of his stature. It was obscure, confused, long-winded, untidy and crude, although glowing and pungent at the same time.[6] Nor did he have any words to express his feelings, and to relieve them he would utter an obscene jest. Together with many of his Russian contemporaries he had a passion and a wildness of spirit that seem to have gone out of the world for ever. It is difficult to imagine a modern thinker of anything like his importance capable of such reckless thoughts.

Belinsky was *homme revolté* first and foremost. No doubt, the state of Russia in the throes of serfdom and Nicolaian oppression might have made any decent man a rebel, although it was possible openly to denounce it only at the price of exposing oneself to the rigours of censorship (fortunately not always an efficient or intelligent one) and of the Third Section.[7] But Belinsky was a rebel by temperament as well as by conviction. Some have seen fit to describe this rebelliousness as just a private romantic bee in Belinsky's bonnet, stirred to buzzing point by

E   49

the reading of German literature; others as another instance of the equally romantic revolutionary utopianism typical of the Russian intelligentsia. Quite apart from any literary influences, however, or even from his own specifically romantic tastes, which marked the earlier period of his intellectual development, Belinsky was indeed a romantic, in the sense in which romanticism never ceases to express something profoundly human. Even while involved in contemporary conflicts, he preserved something of a Promethean attitude, and chose to see life in terms of man invaded by hostile forces and embattled against God and the universe. He was quite unable to assume the existence of a static, perpetuated, organic order of life, because he saw in such an order a source or instrument of tyranny over man, and because for him any attempt to contain life in intellectual or religious norms meant idolatry and a betrayal of the unique image or man. He proved a true rebel because he never ceased to question this order (even when, for a brief time, he forced himself to accept "Russian reality") and to aim, in his erratic fashion, at a revolution of an unparalleled kind, more radical than any social revolution can ever be—a revolution on behalf of the human person.

More will be said about this revolutionary aspect of Belinsky's thought in another context. What strikes one in Belinsky's character is that with him the revolutionary attitude was as much a passion as love is for those who are captured by its ecstasy. It marked him by expelling him from the categories of any permanent historic structure, of all that has roots in the earth and lives in peace, relieved, assured and stupefied. He was, in this at least, typical of the whole Russian intelligentsia, which had few roots, and of the *raznochintsy* in particular, who had none at all. But he was typical only in being extreme. He was the first, though not the greatest, in the long gallery of Russian rebels to embody the image of the eternal revolutionary, to bear, like Cain, the indelible sign of man's unfinished wayfaring, of disquiet, reproach and perpetual interrogation—not as a romantic malady of the will, but as an index of the will to truth.

With the ferocity of an avenging angel he sought out truth and fulminated against falsehood, especially where it appeared as a grave made invisible under a heap of flowers. This landed him and his friends frequently in embarrassing stituations in which he appeared to display all the qualities of a prig. Herzen relates how one day in Holy Week he went to dine with a literary acquaintance of his. They were served with Lenten dishes. " 'Since when have you become so devout?' asked Belinsky. 'We fast', replied the host, 'on account of the servants.'—'*Of the servants?*' retorted Belinsky and turned pale. 'Of the servants?' he repeated and flung down his dinner napkin. 'Where are your servants? I am going to tell them that they have been tricked. . . . And you imagine you are free-minded people? You are in the same boat with all the tsars, priests and slave owners! Good-bye, I do not eat Lenten fare for edification. I have no *servants!* ' "

Whether or not he was a prig, he was a man made furious by injustice and prevarication, by sham and moral pretexts, by the sufferings and unallayed pain of the human lot, rather than a philosopher or even a literary critic in the accepted sense of the word. It earned him the epithet of "furious Vissarion", or *Orlando furioso*, as he was called by his Moscow Circle friends; and the school of thought and of literary criticism issuing from him had all the qualities of a "furious" school. Strictly speaking, however, he founded no school and left no body of disciples to carry on some specific line of thought or investigation. Yet he was largely responsible for the dominant concern with moral problems and moral conflicts in Russian writers. Goncharov, who disliked extremes and whose attitude remained fairly consistently and somewhat disconcertingly at a low ebb, scarcely exaggerated when he said that "Belinsky was not only a critic, a publicist, a *littérateur*, but a tribune, the voice and conscience of Russia, the herald of life's new foundations." Belinsky's own heart-searchings were so severe that literature became a scourge rather than an aesthetic pleasure for him, and he was virtually burnt out, mentally as well as physically, by the time of his death.

Annenkov speaks of Belinsky's "inability to admit any bad faith, falsification, subterfuge in the world around him as in his own life, even when these things served to soothe wavering minds, and he felt an irresistible aversion from connivance with shallow and insincere judgments . . . even when they became apparent within his ranks". His own judgment was both hampered and deepened by a sense of the brutality and indifference of the world, by a sense of being in the midst of things, too close to things, pressed upon by reality. If he had succeeded in standing aside from himself, he would have achieved greater balance and clarity of vision and, certainly, better control, but he would have lost in freedom, spontaneity and closeness to humanity. In fact he wrote best and most spontaneously when the pressure was hardest to bear. One has learned to expect outbursts of blustering, sentimentality and melodrama from those in great bitterness and frustration. With Belinsky they freed his imagination and produced vividness, pathos and a certain melancholy which many of his friends detected in his otherwise austere and angular face. But there was no resolute cheerfulness in him, and he lacked that sense of humour which comes from detachment, from weighing up things and circumstances against the absolute of the imagination. It is, perhaps, an inevitable deficiency where history has produced a state of mind in which everything is in terms of either-or, and life is always felt to be the realization or the betrayal of some primordial dream. He had, however, a trenchant if somewhat coarse irony; he laughed readily and would occasionally break out into self-critical mockery. His great seriousness never led him into pomposity. In praise and blame he was extravagant, fiery, pugnacious, biassed and courageous. Turgenev recalls a conversation in Prince Odoevsky's drawing-room in the course of which Belinsky announced in everyone's hearing that "our disorders will be redeemed by our holy mother the guillotine", and, on a similar occasion, he shouted furiously that all the Montenegrins ought to be massacred. His enemies seized on such freak remarks, and it is not surprising that, despite his highly developed and disciplined art of writing "between the lines", he had a full dossier at the Third Section. But he died just in time, that is, before the reaction which followed the Revolution of 1848, and Dubbelt, the head of the political police, regretted bitterly that it was too late, remarking that "we would have left him to rot in the Fortress".

The Third Section was not alone in showing its cloven hoof. The first two or three years after his arrival in the capital Petersburg society viewed him with unmixed horror as an "upstart" and "plebeian". He was referred to as "the semi-literate frog expelled from the University for immoral behaviour". People who had never set their eyes on him described him as a monster in appearance, a carper, a "bull-dog" used by his editors for the purpose of running amok among their enemies. They were indignant about his "impertinence" and resented his "unwashed commonness"; they denounced him to the police and spread libels.[8] In point of fact this "ugly customer" had a heart of almost bashful purity, tender, compassionate and noble to the point of chivalry; he also happened to live the life of an ascetic, and moral integrity provided the chief tone to everything he said and did.

There was, however, a streak of vindictiveness in him: it was a disinterested vindictiveness, not for any outward reason or from wounded vanity, but because he was an idealist in the true sense of the word, an idealist even in his hatred. He hated in his enemies the deepest, most vital possession they had—their ideas. It was in this way that he broke with the Slavophil Konstantin Aksakov, his erstwhile friend and a most gentle if wholly uncongenial person, with Herzen for a time, with Bakunin and others. In some cases the break was a result of conflict with other angry minds. Belinsky's relationship with Dostoevsky is of special interest in this respect. Few young writers evoked such profound wonder and rapturous admiration in Belinsky as Dostoevsky with his first novel *Poor Folk*. Belinsky's artistic insight enabled him to perceive Dostoevsky's first vision of man outlined against "the mystery of compassion". "Do you understand *what* you have written?" he said to Dostoevsky, who remembered the incident thirty years after Belinsky's death as one of the happiest days of his life. But Dostoevsky's struggle against his own past, as well as a residue of pride and wounded vanity from the cool reception of his subsequent early work, which Belinsky considered immature and sentimental, compelled him to destroy the spell of the teacher whose teaching, as he himself admits, he had adopted with passion. He depicts Belinsky as an "under-sized, feeble-minded liberal", "buoyed up in his self-satisfied, narrow mind": "a stinking gnat, impotent and with little talent". "He would have finished", Dostoevsky prophesied retrospectively in his *Diary of a Writer*, "as an *émigré*; he would by now be wandering, a tiny feverish dotard . . . from congress to congress somewhere in Germany or Switzerland, or would have joined some German Madame Goegg . . . running her errands on account of some little question concerning the emancipation of women." Yet three or four years later, while still engaged in fighting the "liberals" and, at the same time, probably himself undergoing an inward crisis, he begins to refer to Belinsky as "the noblest, most high-minded, chivalrous of men", and to speak of his "remarkable intelligence" and "great search for truth".

In one of his most brilliant polemical articles against the Slavophils[9] Belinsky himself expressed his bewilderment at the inability among Russians "to divorce a man from his thought", at their having "to lose time, to ruin their own health and make enemies from attachment to some deeply felt opinion, from love for some lofty, disinterested thought".[10] Enmities of this kind were by no means confined to philosophical discussion. Literary movements, which, in the conditions prevailing in nineteenth-century Russia, became the battlefield of ideas, were an equally propitious ground for discord, and issued in isolation and mutual estrangement amongst even the greatest writers: Pushkin, Gogol and Lermontov remained solitary figures; Dostoevsky jeered at Turgenev for his knock-kneed liberalism; Nekrasov and Shchedrin abominated Dostoevsky for his reactionary mystery-mongering; Tolstoy was nauseated by Turgenev's insincerity and Turgenev condemned Tolstoy for betraying literature—to mention only a few well-known examples. Goncharov recalls how Belinsky reproached him with indifference towards his characters: " 'You don't mind whether you get a scoundrel, an idiot, a monster, or a decent and honest man: you depict them all alike, without hatred or love for one another.' He said this", Goncharov continues, "with a kind of good-natured malice, and then put his hands tenderly on my shoulders and whispered into my ear: 'it is fair, it is just what we need, it is the sign of a true artist', as though he feared to be overheard and accused of sympathy with an untendentious writer."[11]

At times Belinsky seemed unable to do without a foe: and sometimes the foe had to be made first in some way or other in order to become an object of his destructive onslaught. "He could not preach or lecture", wrote Herzen, "what he needed was disputation. If he met with no objection, if he was not stirred to irritation, he did not speak well; but when he felt stung, when his cherished convictions were touched upon, when the muscles of his cheeks began to quiver and his voice broke, then he was worth seeing. He pounced on his opponent like a panther, he tore him to pieces, made him ridiculous, made him a piteous object, and incidentally developed his own thought, with extraordinary force and poetry. The discussion would often end in blood which flowed from the sick man's throat; pale, gasping, with his eyes fixed on the person with whom he was speaking, he would lift his handkerchief to his mouth with shaking hand and stop, deeply mortified, crushed by his physical weakness. How I loved and how I pitied him at those moments!"

Herzen goes on to describe an incident at a dinner party where Belinsky met an insignificant and pedantic scholar, an "inveterate German", who embarked on a solemn disquisition about Chaadaev's nefarious influence on the minds of His Majesty's loyal subjects, about the need to uphold the unity of the nation, about sacred traditions which ought not to be endangered. Belinsky listened in silence. Suddenly "he leapt up from his sofa, came up to me as white as a sheet and, slapping me on the shoulder, said: 'Here you have them, they have spoken out— the inquisitors, the censors—keeping thought on leading-strings . . .' and so he went on and on. With savage inspiration he spoke, interspersing grave words with deadly sarcasms: 'We are strangely sensitive: people are flogged and we don't resent it, sent to Siberia and we don't resent it, but here Chaadaev, you see, has picked holes in the national honour, he mustn't dare to speak; to talk is impudence, a flunkey must never speak! Why is it that in more civilized countries where one would expect national susceptibilities to be more developed than in Kostroma and Kaluga words are not resented?'—'In civilized countries,' replied the gentleman . . . with inimitable self-satisfaction, 'there are prisons in which they confine the senseless creatures who insult what the whole people respect . . . and a good thing too.' Belinsky seemed to tower above us; he was terrible, great at that moment. Folding his arms over his sick chest, and looking straight at his opponent, he answered in a hollow voice: 'And in still more civilized countries there is a guillotine for those who consider that a good thing.' On saying this he sank exhausted in an arm-chair and ceased speaking. At the word 'guillotine' our host turned pale, the guests were uneasy and a pause followed. The . . . gentleman was annihilated . . . [but] continued uttering feeble trivialities, addressing himself rather to the rest of the company than to Belinsky. 'In spite of your intolerance', he said at last, 'I am certain that you would agree with me. . . .'—'No', answered Belinsky, 'whatever you might say I shouldn't agree with anything!' "

When there was no provocation from without, Belinsky just hacked away at the foundations of life, debunking idols and sanctities, twisting the girders of established values, shattering the dwelling-places of illusions, and building up out of the ruins his case for man's freedom and personality. All this was suffused with his customary restlessness, mixed with human warmth and irony, and reaching at times a hectic, almost feverish pitch.

Belinsky's powerful imagination made him transfer his hatred to people and events belonging to a distant past, and when these emerged in some connection or other he behaved as if he were their contemporary, facing them in some imaginary personal contest. He seemed then like an ungovernable Quixotic exile in a court of shadows. It cannot of course be said that his prepossessions ensured fairness towards other people and their ideas. They served to isolate him beyond the closed circle of intimate friends, and this in turn proved a source of bewilderment, perplexity and irritation to him. His real foes and opponents were, however, even less inclined to practice the virtue of fairness, and, in the context of Belinsky's battles, it would have been strangely abstract to make on him exaggerated demands of tolerance and "good manners". Nothing was further from him than the cautious compromise which leads to nothing being said at all. He was never able to consider the arguments for and against or admit, especially in a fit of denunciatory passion, that his opponents might in any way be right. He repudiated their views wholesale and as indignantly as he repudiated his own views whenever he found them untenable. "I am a Jew by nature", he wrote to Herzen, "and cannot eat at the same table with Philistines. . . . Granovsky wants to know if I have read his article in the *Moskvityanin*. No, I am not going to read it; tell him I am not fond of meeting my friends in improper places, and I don't make appointments with them there."[12]

Some of his friends (Turgenev among them), however, noticed a temperamental change in him after his return from abroad, that is, shortly before his death: he became gentler, humbler and even more tolerant of other people, and made concessions more readily in matters which previously drove him to distraction. Still, as Turgenev aptly remarked, "even in cursing he *understood*" (italics in the original): indeed, while easily blinded by what he loved, he saw what he hated with the greatest clarity, and since he could see what he hated when it was inside what he loved (as in his repudiation of Gogol's great betrayal) he was able to exceed mere "propaganda" and special pleading, of which he has been accused by his critics.

It was Turgenev also who once suggested, to Belinsky's great amusement: "one can break through you". Truth was too precious for him, and when he recognized it he could not resist it. When he saw his error he used to say with perfect candour and undissembling modesty: "I say, I did talk a lot of drivel!" It is characteristic of him that with all his ferocity and absolute awareness of his own intention he was, as many of his friends testify, neither obstinate, nor high-handed, nor doctrinaire, and he laid no claims to infallibility for himself.[13] His writings had an enormous success, though they brought him little material reward, and he eventually became undisputed leader of the creative elements in Russian society. Young people in Moscow and Petersburg awaited the appearance of his reviews with breathless impatience and read them with voracity. "Half a dozen times", writes Herzen, "the students would call in at the coffee-houses to ask whether the *Annals of the Fatherland* had been received; the heavy volume was snatched from hand to hand. 'Is there an article of Belinsky's?'—'Yes', and it was devoured with feverish interest, with laughter, with argument . . . and three or four cherished convictions and reputations were no more." There were, therefore, laurels for Belinsky, as well as a great deal of abuse. Yet he never rested on them. He was never satisfied with his performance. He did not even look back unduly. It would never occur to him to add up compliments—or vilifications either, for that matter. Only truth mattered to him in the long run. In his advocacy of truth he would not count the cost, the harm which might result from upholding it, or the benefits which might fall to his lot if he withheld it. And when truth was really at stake he would be thrown into a ferment, and woe to him who fell into his hands.

He did, it is true, quite frequently alter his opinions on most of the questions which held his interest. This laid him open to a charge of volatility. "How do you like it?" he once remarked about Goncharov, who had made fun of his inconstancy, "he thinks I am a weather-cock: I admit I change my views, but I change them as one changes a kopek for a rouble!" In point of fact, as will be seen presently, however divergent the conclusions he reached at different times, his underlying attitude was very much the same throughout.

"He worked", Kavelin writes, "as befits as true Russian—by leaps and bounds; and when he was able to rest, that is, when necessity did not drive him to work, he readily idled his time away, chattered, played cards, just for the sake of doing nothing." But even to playing cards he imparted all the antics of passion, despair and rejoicing, as though he were enacting some shattering historical drama. On such occasions he displayed all the naïveté, simplicity and abandon of a child. As soon as he returned to his books, articles and ideological disputations his attention was immediately riveted to the matter in hand, and he would show all the usual excitement from intellectual enterprise. "How often", recalls Annenkov, "did we find him wandering through the three-roomed flat which he inhabited after his marriage, straight from finishing a book, a chapter, an article, with all his customary symptoms of agitation. He immediately proceeded to impart his impressions of what he had just read—it was a glowing, unencumbered improvisation. I found these improvisations even better than his articles. . . ." But his articles, too, were largely improvised: he wrote them in the last days of the month, standing over his escritoire and throwing sheets of paper covered with his sprawling handwriting on the floor. He had no time, or even inclination, to polish his style, to weigh up or think over every statement and expression and lapsed continually into verbosity.

The squandering of prospects introduced a general note of knight-errantry into Belinsky's life and thought. Sometimes, especially during his Moscow career, he seemed utterly at the mercy of ideas and of the people who provided him with ideas, entering into their inmost springs and recesses with a generosity which was like an effacement of his own personality. "He identified himself to such an extent with the authors whom he studied," says Annenkov, "that he constantly revealed their secret thought, corrected them whenever they betrayed it or deliberately withheld it, and spoke out their last word, which they were afraid or unwilling to utter. This kind of exposure was the strongest side of his (literary) criticism. Such was his estimate of George Sand, in whom he perceived a greater attachment to the ideas and principles which she repudiated than she herself admitted. Pierre Leroux he called a catholic priest turned rebel. As to the Russian writers, he almost unerringly foresaw their whole future from their very first literary production."

He was never squeamish about contradicting himself on different levels, or even on the same level. Ideas fascinated him and well-nigh obsessed him. Turgenev relates how for a time Belinsky was preoccupied with an important religious question. In the course of eight days, until he had hammered out what appeared to him as a solution of his perplexity, he was in a feverish state, unable to talk, or to understand how it is possible to talk, about anything else while a question of such consequence remained unanswered. He reproached Turgenev with flippancy at the slightest sign of wavering attention. "I was affected by his sincerity and enthusiasm", says Turgenev, "and I was carried away by the importance of the subject; but after spending two to three hours in conversation, I began to flag, the lightheartedness of youth took the upper hand, I longed for respite, I thought of a walk, of dinner; even Belinsky's wife implored him and me to leave off for a while, reminded him of the doctor's orders. . . . But it was not easy to manage Belinsky. 'We have not yet solved the question of the existence of God', he said to me bitterly and in earnest, 'and you want to eat!' " Turgenev himself, it should be noted, had flirted with philosophy for a time: it was, after all, a popular game in the 'thirties and 'forties. But he dropped it very soon, and it was as if the flirtation had never been. He was, therefore, scarcely able to understand Belinsky's solemn preoccupations, and tended to regard them, in his worldly and sybaritical fashion, as hair-splitting and sophistry. Despite his great admiration for Belinsky, the latter must have struck him on occasion as a pathetic consumptive prophet.

Belinsky's attitude towards his ideas and ideals was that of a Don Juan to his ladies: he was lured and infatuated by them, grew indifferent towards them, and then felt ashamed on their account. "As with the admirers of feminine beauty, Belinsky's past ideals became pale in the light of new ones, which sometimes proved quite insignificant but possessed all the charm of novelty" (Goncharov). He was indeed easily blinded by the intoxication of intellectual discovery, of new ideas which seemed to him to resolve his mental conflicts, but which often resulted in slap-dash statements and naïve simplifications.

As has already been mentioned, all his life he remained an autodidact with second-hand ideas and first-hand insights and intuitions, and a strange medley of general knowledge acquired or picked up with unbounded verve and versatility on his intellectual wanderings: from friends and a maze of books—including cookery manuals, dream-books and works on mathematics, about which he knew nothing whatever but which he was obliged to review under the *régime* of his exploiting editors.[14] The extent of his reading was indeed colossal. Turgenev, Goncharov and Odoevsky considered him the most educated man in the Russia of his time[15]—"with the exception of Herzen" (Goncharov); and Herzen himself had a very high opinion of Belinsky's intellectual abilities. Turgenev likened his place in Russian letters to that of the great German literary critic Lessing, whose criticism, like Belinsky's, made itself felt throughout the whole range of thought and feeling—in religion, in science, in philosophy and literature, and whose polemic overcame every adversary and waxed stronger with every victory. But if he was educated, he certainly was no scholar, either in matter or in manner. Scholarship was scarcely what Russia needed at the time. Senkovsky was infinitely more erudite and accomplished than Belinsky, yet nothing survives him but the ill odour of servility and baseness. There were, of course, a few of Belinsky's contemporaries, more reputable than Senkovsky, Bulgarin and Grech, who surpassed him in learning, brilliance and subtlety of mind, but hardly anyone possessed his intense feeling for and understanding of the human situation and, above all, his responsiveness and intellectual vitality. Even Pushkin, whose lucid, classical mind and Parnassian, "aristocratic" tastes could not but recoil from Belinsky's loose, turbid, frantic and "plebeian" universe of discourse, even Pushkin called upon those who attacked Belinsky to learn from him.[16] He may not have been able to distinguish between Lord Chatham and William Pitt: Pushkin's epigram "We Russians get our information on something, somehow—and so-so" is wholly applicable to Belinsky. Having grown up in the midst of mental and material poverty and obscurantism, Belinsky had himself tasted to the full all the bitterness of ignorance, which also inclined him, with a great section of the Russian intelligentsia in his wake, to overrate the beauties and blessings of enlightenment. But, as Turgenev pertinently remarked, while "the German strives to redeem the faults of his people by convincing himself of their harmfulness, the Russian suffers and will suffer long afterwards on their account".

Belinsky's real schooling began with his initiation into philosophy through his Circle friends. The Circles, where, as we have seen, young minds pursued a fearless search for truth, served him better than any professorial pulpit or Athenian Academy complete with portico and Zeno in cap, gown and spectacles could have done. Though ignorant of any foreign language, except for a smattering of pedlar's French, he thought out or, more precisely, lived through all the recesses and dead-ends of German philosophical idealism—from passages of translated texts prepared especially by his friends, from hints and suggestions, through sheer guess-work and conjecture. Odoevsky, a liberally-minded if somewhat stilted erudite well-versed in philosophy, speaks of him as of "one of the greatest philosophical minds [he] ever came across in [his] life. [Belinsky] embodied a synthesis of Kant, Schelling and Hegel: and a very organic synthesis it was, for he had not read any of them. . . . Belinsky's opponents try in vain to convince him that he does not understand Hegel. No! He did not know him, but was drawn towards him in the same way in which one mathematician arrives at the conclusions of another without knowing anything of his work, by merely elaborating a given theorem."[17] In point of fact, however, it is difficult to discover any consistent philosophical view in Belinsky. His strong emotional attitudes and inward conflicts—many of them the characteristic attitudes and conflicts of the Russian intelligentsia—prevented him from finding a permanent resting-place for his ideas and insights under a single roof, save for the overriding concern with man, with the unique value, freedom and personality of man.

2. "GOD—MANKIND—MAN"

The main source for the study of Belinsky are his letters, which are valuable not so much for the light they shed on his life in its external aspects as for their revelation of his mind. One must, indeed, place them higher than his formal writings, for, quite apart from the fact that the latter were composed under the shadow of the censorship, here the vitality, forcefulness and versatility—together with their obverse quality, a slipshodness of thought and expression—which was characteristic of everything he wrote, can find free rein without provoking the reader's resistance. Their value, moreover, consists in that they serve to show his intellectual attitude and experience as a model of "prophetic" thinking, which, as we already know, appears to have been the only type of thinking congenial to the Russian mind. It is defined by two interdependent factors. One is the use of philosophical and literary ideas for mediating a view of life, a *Weltanschauung*, not logically and systematically, but, as it were, by contact: by communicating a vision and staking one's whole personality on the issues involved. The other is the turning of every argument into an *argumentum ad hominem* or *pro homine*, having for one's task not the abstract comprehension of the concrete (in terms of "essences", sums of properties, or of "things in general"), but an understanding of the abstract concretely, an experience and representation of truth in terms of human existence and human ends. In doing this the Russian thinkers addressed the imagination as well as reason and used a language which of its nature leads to action, to "changing the world" rather than "explaining" it. It is for these reasons that their thought expressed itself more readily in novels, in incidental writings, in letters and literary criticism than in dogmatic and academic works.

It is the peculiarity of theorists, doctrinaires and academic pundits that they never change, that their mental and emotional make-up is fixed at an early stage and moves only to attain a greater mental rigidity. Belinsky was not a theorist, nor a doctrinaire, nor an academic pundit, and his mental and spiritual development moved through crises and contradictions: indeed, the contradictions were such as to baffle his contemporaries, and they are equally baffling today, even though their philosophical terms of reference are no longer likely to arouse the same passions. The points at which Belinsky's crises were most evident are diversely defined and even diversely numbered. Plekhanov suggests four such points, roughly corresponding to the various philosophical allegiances which Belinsky chose.[18] Others, on the same principle, count three phases; modern Soviet writers distinguish only two, namely a pre-socialist, idealistic phase and a "revolutionary-democratic", materialist one. It is, however, more fitting to follow Belinsky's own account of the matter, for he wrote briefly a short time before his death, in 1847, that "God was my first thought, mankind—my second, man—my third and last one". Whether, in fact, it would have been the last one may be doubted; since at each turn he tended, with characteristic vehemence, to regard his new "thought" as final. At any rate these "thoughts" transcend all the philosophical theories which Belinsky adopted in the course of his intellectual development: the theories served only as a means to their articulation, and more often than not proved a Procrustean bed for them. It is important to emphasize that the "thoughts" themselves represent Belinsky's striving to resolve a fundamental and acutely experienced conflict between the world around him, with its inhumanity, its inexorable and crushing determinations, and another world which does not cheat man of his identity, his freedom and creativity. Torn as he was out of time and space, Belinsky strove to relate himself to the world and to relate the world to himself. It may be said that the inconsistencies and contradictions of his changing outlook were evidence of a conflict within him, and, perhaps, of a conflict which lies at the very heart of human existence: they could not and did not, therefore, render him guilty of betraying himself. This makes nonsense of any rigid chronological interpretation of his thought, of any attempt to force his intellectual development into defined periods; and the three elements of "God", "mankind", and "man" of which Belinsky speaks constituted throughout, and in some sense simultaneously, the essential motives and attitudes of his mind, the groundwork of his scale of values and the consistent pattern of his sentiments.

Belinsky's first literary attempt, the tragedy *Dimitry Kalinin*, which was partly responsible for his expulsion from the University of Moscow, leaves the impression of a taut drumskin of melodrama stretched over a frame of profound insight. Behind its grandiloquent shadows is concealed the real experience of a world of malice, cruelty and injustice, in which major horrors are found side by side with little commonplace iniquities—with all Belinsky's youthful anger upon them. The question he raised was not only a social one, namely that of serfdom; the indignation, anguish and perplexity which besets his hero Kalinin refer to the power which moral and metaphysical evil exercises in human life. He speaks of "the tyrant man" and "the tyrant God", who has "surrendered our unhappy earth as a ransom to the devil". The complaint, as old as the world, that God has deserted man, turns into rebellion against the "divine tyrant" and his providential order, against a God who drinks in the blood shed in man's fight for existence and laughs because the wretched creature, fainting, staggers ridiculously. "To suffer", says Kalinin, ". . . to endure here so as to rejoice there in all eternity. Such then is the truly excellent as well as comforting philosophy!. . . Can it really be true that eternal bliss must necessarily be bought at the price of the most frightful sufferings? It comes rather expensive!" Almost half a century later Dostoevsky's Ivan Karamazov was to reject God in almost identical terms and "return his ticket to world harmony", acquired at the price of the innocent sufferings and tears of a single tortured child. Belinsky himself was to revert to the same subject in his final confrontation with Hegel.

Such attitudes have, of course, been widely regarded as instances of romanticism, self-dramatization, weakness, or mischief-making. Philosophers, writing with the assurance of bookworms crawling into the world of human pain and sorrow, explained that evil is necessary, so that man may know God; or that the Absolute is richer for every discord and for all diversity which it embraces. At any rate it appears from their metaphysical, not-so-metaphysical and anti-metaphysical writings that it is bad form to attach any great importance to evil, and though its existence must be admitted, it is unreasonable to make a fuss about it. It is, however, only fair to point out that the range of painful experience with which their lives and imaginations appear to have been afflicted, and which evidently prompted them to adopt these comforting convictions, did not extend beyond the twinges of tooth-ache, the qualms of sea-sickness, flea-bites and pin-pricks, to mention only a few of the most current and favourite misfortunes which philosophers tend to consider in discussing the problem of pain. On the other side are the theologians who cheerfully revere "God's great gift of pain" and rejoice in the blood of the Lamb as well as in that of their fellow-men; who bring to bear the heavy artillery of divine wrath on passionate, weak, stupid and pitiful humanity; who even find delight in contemplating the triumph of God's glory and justice in the pains of sinners in the hell of this life or of life to come.

Belinsky's intellectual development begins with reflection on the problem of the justification of God in face of the measureless pain in the world. His "first thought" was one of compassion for man and revolt against the idea of an almighty omniscient punitive deity beholding this stricken world of ours. Yet what Belinsky stood for was not a heart-wringing and lachrymose sentimentality, but a stern, almost a cold ethic of compassion, despite the dramatic fog of rhetoric which he employed, particularly in his early writings. It is, after all, the cruel who are the true sentimentalists, for cruelty is resentful, weak, hide-bound and self-loving, whereas compassion is strong, generous and free. Belinsky could not bear cruelty, though in his struggle for freedom he was capable of cruelty towards those who preach and practise it, and desired hell for those who advocate and prepare it for others. He had a horror of the thought of salvation apart from the whole human kind. He was not so much troubled by the intellectual difficulties attendant on faith in God, as by the state of mind that finds its faith justified by belief in a divine providential agency, which picks its favourites and saves a few while millions perish. "Providentially," said the gentleman wrecked in a coach in a thunderstorm, "providentially, the lightning struck the box-seat." "Who is guilty?"—such, from Belinsky onwards, is the dominant question which torments the Russian mind throughout the nineteenth century. Belinsky's compassionate philosophy, however, was not due to any virtuous disposition on his part, though his vices were few, but rather to his rebelliousness and non-conforming, lawless spirit. He could not admit then, and still less when he broke away from Hegel, the domination of the "whole", "the general", the "commonplace"—even where it assumed the shape of a closed and all-pervasive divine providential order—over the "particular", the "singular", the "individual", seeing that the former spells a world in dependence and subjection, a world of harmony, reasonableness and bliss at the expense of the anguish, desolation, solitude and freedom of the latter. What separated him at this early stage from religious belief was not an inability to discover God in human life: he repudiated the God revered by man, a God whom he estimated, not as divine, but as false and pernicious. He denied "God" as God. The existence or presence of such a God signified to him the *tour de force* of man's self-justification, of man's attempt to bolster up a miserable state of affairs by attaching a divine quality to it and, in the last analysis, the *tour de force* of justifying evil.

To that extent Belinsky was an atheist even then. His atheism, however, was no thesis or proposition of unbelief to be proved or disproved, but an attitude of refusal, an anti-theism. Beyond the verifiable and, therefore, beyond that which can be denied there lay a reality for him. He was still inclined to justify God and to incriminate man in the perennial contest between God and man.

In 1834 Belinsky's first important essay, *Literaturnye mechtanya* ("Literary Musings") appeared in *Molva* ("Rumour") which marked a new epoch in Russian literary criticism and made him Russia's foremost literary critic. It contained a survey of Russian literature and, in particular, an appraisal of the playwright Griboyedov and the poets Krylov and Pushkin. But it also reflected his first philosophical preoccupations and his adoption of Schelling's philosophy of Nature. There is no doubt that the temporary enthusiasm for Schelling, just as the other successive enthusiasm for Fichte, and especially for Hegel, were an echo of his own deepest thoughts and experience, rather than an indication of easy subservience to his Circle friends, who filled his philosophically untutored mind with more or less digested tenets of German idealism. He was, in fact, not easily influenced by anybody, not even by Stankevich and his associates, although he depended on them for his philosophical information. Whenever he felt like challenging the formidable quagmire of idealistic notions supplied by his German-reading mentors, he did so by relying on his own intellectual resources.[19]

It is not easy to disentangle Schelling's somewhat nebulous speculations about Nature.[20] It is not even quite clear what he meant by the concept of Nature: the sum total of things or facts which exist in the world, or something inherent in these things, which is the source or principle of their existence. He probably meant both, but the emphasis was on the second meaning, and it is this which interested Schelling's Russian adepts. Their thoughts turned, in particular, on two principles which are, according to Schelling, inherent in the natural world: namely that, on the one hand, whatever exists is the embodiment of rationality and intelligibility, or, to use his language, a manifestation of the Absolute, and, on the other, that the regular or conflicting relations between the things or facts that exist are subsumed in the Absolute.

To Belinsky's mind the idea of the Absolute as the identity which resolves all opposites appeared, provisionally, as an answer to Kalinin's question concerning the unhappy lot of man. It appealed to his imaginative mind by its range and totality: it seemed to include everything, to give a place for the world with its beauty, sorrow and unimaginable variety. Since he was far removed from the view of some contemporary philosophers that philosophy is the activity of curing people of the desire to ask philosophical questions, he did not find it discreditable to look to philosophy for an answer to the problems of the value of life, of how one should live and what sense one could ascribe to the universe. Schelling provided all the answers. They seemed perfect in their comprehensiveness. They had, indeed, as Belinsky was soon to find out, but one defect—they were unbelievable. Meanwhile, however, he adopted unreservedly the conviction of metaphysical idealism that "idea" or "value" is a constituent of the universe, and that therefore things are fundamentally good, or will be so in the end, or, even if they are not so nor ever will be, certain other things and ideas exist which make up for it. He even repeated Schelling's dictum "*es herrscht eine allweise Güte uber der Welt*", which was Stankevich's favourite motto and which, as Stankevich confessed, "appeased [him] in regard to everything". Yet all the while Belinsky pursued his business of advocating the cause of humanity. Unlike most idealists, including his optimistic friend Stankevich, he was scarcely moved by a desire to escape from the prison of human existence into the experience of some greater transcendental unity in which the only real objects were ghosts loving one another. On the contrary, he desired to find a place for human existence within that unity. He even succeeded in discovering "dynamic movement" and the conflict of good and evil in Schelling's monistic universe. He could not be satisfied with the mere abstract intelligibility of Nature. He seized on Schelling's idea that Nature as the intelligible demands of man that he should know it and, Belinsky would add, should as it were make Nature's intelligibility effective. His emphasis was on what he called "the eternal idea enacted in the moral life" of man, on "the divine capacity for moral activation" (*bozhestvennaya sposobnost nravstvennoy dvizhimosti*).[21] "For this 'idea' ", he wrote at the time, "there is no repose; it lives perpetually, that is to say, it creates in order to destroy, and destroys in order to create. It is embodied in the blaze of the sun, in the magnificence of the planet, in the movement of the star; it lives and breathes in the restless ebb and flow of the sea, in the violent storm of the sandy desert, in the rustle of leaves, in the rushing stream, in the roar of the lion, in the tears of a child, in the smile of woman, in the will of man, and in the shapely creations of genius. . . . The wheel of time turns with ineffable speed, the heavenly bodies eclipse like burnt out volcanoes in the unbounded space of heaven and new ones are kindled; generations pass on earth in constant succession, death destroys life and life destroys death; . . . but harmony reigns in this perpetual turmoil."[22]

Belinsky's language remained rhetorical and expletive and bore all the marks of magniloquent romantic and idealistic circumlocution. Were it not for his courageous inconsistency and untiring interrogations he would no doubt have turned into a metaphysical slicing machine, as happened with so many followers of Schelling and Hegel in Germany. But his mind was fitful and erratic. He could not think except in the "open air", which imports imagination, phantasy and irrationality—in fact all those things which cannot stand the philosopher's test.

In 1836 Belinsky is carried away by a temporary infatuation with Fichte. But it is neither delight in philosophical speculation nor mere subservience to his new friend and mentor Bakunin, who was at the time himself addicted to Fichte and dictatorially imposed his views on all and sundry. What Bakunin succeeded in doing was to help to create in Belinsky's mind the illusion that Fichte's solipsistic idealism provides an adequate account of the freedom and moral endeavour of man. It was in keeping with Belinsky's search for the "justification of man". It was less eloquent and more ethical than Schelling's poetic metaphysical naturalism, and for that very reason more congenial to Belinsky's moral preoccupations.

One cannot be an idealist without becoming involved with solipsism, and idealism is always trembling on the brink of it. The form in which solipsism is usually arrived at is the conclusion that since knowledge is dependent on the mind of the knower all we know must be our own mental states. Life becomes a dream in which man creates the objects that come before him, and when he ceases to dream the world ceases to be. Fichte's theory of knowledge opens with the abstract tautology "I $=$ I": man creates the world (the not-I, in Fichte's language) out of the recesses of his mind. The mind retraces its steps over the road it had travelled towards abstraction until it regains the world of phenomena, and subsequently declares the phenomenal world to be a necessary condition for its activity. That idealism, pursued to its ultimate consequence, should end by denying the world seemed to philosophers and laymen alike to be carrying the joke too far. People grew rather merry over the Fichtean Ego which produced by its mere thinking the whole external world. It is not surprising, therefore, that his philosophy has always had to endure much from satire.[23] Some asked with understandable annoyance if the Ego of Johann Gottlieb Fichte implied a negation of all other existences? Fichte's lady friends are said to have enquired anxiously whether he does not at least believe in the existence of his wife: and if not, whether Frau Fichte puts up with this?

But to Belinsky, who was little inclined to examine philosophical theories on their own merit, Fichte's solipsism seemed to have given a peculiar sense of liberation. It became to his mind a weapon for man's assumption of control over his fate, for the assertion of the independence of human destiny. It fitted into the pattern of his intellectual and emotional attitudes, in which the conception of man as the antagonist played such an important part: man within the world yet against the world; man as a world-denying principle, as the standard of the value of things, as judge of the world, who puts existence itself on the scales and finds it wanting. For a time the emphasis remained entirely on the rejection of the world, to the point of driving him away from "reality" (a term which was to produce such havoc in this subsequent intellectual development) into the sphere of the "Idea". "Ideal life", he wrote, "is the only real, positive, concrete life, whereas so-called real life is negation, illusion, unmeaning and emptiness." He begins to suspect all empirical knowledge and attempts to compromise sense experience. "We cannot understand and know anything", he wrote at the beginning of this Fichtean phase, "which does not lie as a possibility within our mind. . . . Science only develops what is given to us by nature, and we recognize outside ourselves only that which exists within ourselves."

The enthusiasm for Fichte, however, lasted for little more than a year, and in 1837, when Bakunin embarked on his wild proselytizing campaign in favour of Hegel, Belinsky plunged into the profundities of Hegelianism. It proved, of course, very much a procession from the frying-pan into the fire, but it had all the virtues of the transient, the sudden and the momentous; and it showed that for Belinsky at any rate, all philosophies and philosophical solutions had no more than an interim character, despite the tenacity with which he was wedded to his philosophical opinions while actually professing them. Philosophy for him was never to come to an end, but to persist in its search for wisdom and truth. It leads now into another world, different from the world of the commonplace, which enables man to run on in a groove and dissemble ease. While Stankevich with his steadier and smoother mind expressed his misgivings concerning Belinsky's new philosophical allegiance, not knowing whether to deplore or rejoice at it, Belinsky admitted that he could not "be partly convinced". "There are thoughts that live in me for only half an hour," he said. "How do they live? In such a way that when they leave me they must tear away my blood and nerves."[24]

The idealism of Fichte acquired all the appearance of extreme metaphysical pride, by deifying man and setting him over against the world. Fichte was even accused of atheism, though he did not understand what was meant by the accusation and remarked, inconsistently but not without some degree of justice, that the question whether a philosophy is atheist or not sounds to a philosopher as extraordinary as the question whether a triangle is green or red would sound to a mathematician. The trouble was, as Belinsky soon realized, that this idealism was inhuman rather than atheist. Fichte's Ego is indeed neither divine nor human, or at any rate less human than divine. It represented the evil genius of German thought: *Bewusstein überhaupt*, vampiric yet completely void. The ruthlessness with which Fichte endeavoured to eliminate from the being of God all concrete attributes, until nothing remained but an abstract universal law, was only matched and surpassed by his savage squeezing of human existence through the filter of every possible abstraction, until at last no human residue was left, save for the blank and faceless "I" pouring itself into the pint-pot of the "I".[25] Having parted company with Fichte, Belinsky wrote to Bakunin that he had "seen through him". "I respect thought and value it, but only thought which is concrete. . . . Man who lives in awareness of the real is superior to him who lives by cerebration, among spectres. . . . Peter the Great, who was a very bad philosopher, understood reality more and better than Fichte. Every actor on the stage of history understood it better than him."[26]

It is of some importance that it was at the time when Belinsky first became acquainted with Fichte's system that he met Bakunin's sister Alexandra at their parental estate, Pryamukhino, where he was invited to study the German philosopher under the guidance of Bakunin. Belinsky fell in love with Alexandra. It was a kind of forced, cheerless, and tortured love. I have already mentioned the romantic theory of love prevalent in Russia in the 'thirties, fostered mainly by Russian women. Love was seen and felt as a form of religious ecstasy, an object and a source of unending psychological analysis, reflection and vacillation, even while the partners were infatuated with one another to the point of distraction. Woman appeared as a ministering angel on earth, who must be worshipped as an incarnation of "the beautiful" and the "unmittelbares Gefühl". Stankevich, Botkin, Belinsky, and, for a short time, even Herzen and Turgenev conformed to this erotic pseudo-religion, in which sublime imaginings became the repository for love affairs which had not been, and in the circumstances scarcely could be, satisfactorily consummated on earth. Russian novels, even the greatest among them, abound in female characters, sometimes known to their advocates as "Russian Women", who are incredible and insipid angels, swooning and sexless dream-creatures in one dimension; although, by way of nemesis, they likewise abound in female gargoyles, termagants and masterful wives. Belinsky seems to have suffered most from this romantic deception. Being, as she thought, a "beautiful soul" wedded to absolute archetypes, Alexandra, on the other hand, excited desires which she was not prepared to satisfy. Belinsky despaired, "fell", "died" and "rose again". The "falls", however, proved the saving grace which eventually extricated him from the swamp not only of "absolute love", but also of "absolute philosophy".[27] Meanwhile he surrendered with all his customary "fury" to the Titan of German idealism, Hegel, whose influence in Russia persisted intermittently and in a variety of interpretations throughout the nineteenth century and after.[28]

In the present climate of philosophical opinion it is not easy to appreciate how and why Hegel could have come to be considered, as he tended to consider himself and as he was considered in Russia, the supreme dispenser of human thought. Berdyaev observed that Hegel had the same importance for Russian thought as Plato had for patristics and Aristotle for scholasticism.[29] Until chastened by Khomyakov, the Slavophil Yury Samarin affirmed solemnly that the fate of the Orthodox Church was contingent on that of Hegelian philosophy. Stankevich exclaimed that he "had no desire to live in the world until [he] found happiness in Hegel". To Bakunin, Hegel became for a time the object of a quasi-religious mania. The spectre of Hegel turned up in the most unexpected connections. Some members of the Moscow Circles, meeting by chance at a charity ball, decided to drink to Hegelian categories. Kryukov (a young professor of Roman studies at the University of Moscow) began with a toast to "pure being". Granovsky, who recalls the incident, left the ball while a toast to "substance" was being announced. Botkin ventured further into the Holy of Holies by drinking to the supreme and last category of Hegel's logic—to the "Idea".[30]

Whether it be a sign of philosophical confusion and disability, or on the contrary of vigour and excellence, Russian thinkers knew nothing of the narrow and rigid worlds of contemporary philosophical controversy, with its logoid formalism and its blunt missiles of logical detection. Philosophical procedure for them pertained to the domain of wisdom, where philosophy is not a "subject" like physics or chemistry, not just a method of logical argument, but a means of deepening consciousness, a search for the reconciliation of knowledge and the ultimate reaches of human existence. They discussed whether a philosophy was relevant, whether it held some important truth: not whether it was correct or conformed to the conditions under which it is correct to say that someone knows something correctly.

About Hegelianism, then, which during the last century commanded a larger measure of agreement among philosophers than has been accorded to any philosopher since the Middle Ages, there seemed to be a sense of metaphysical finality. Hegel's system claimed to embody and to conclude all the principal tendencies and problems of European philosophy. Nothing less than a full account of the Hegelian system could substantiate this claim, or, indeed, do justice to Belinsky's part in the philosophical discussion which took place in Russia in the late 'thirties of the last century. Unfortunately I have neither the space nor the ability to do so. Moreover, I am not sure if Belinsky, either by temperament or by training, was able to make the most of the exceedingly technical arguments with which Hegel supported his position. His attempts to restate some of these arguments were rather cumbersome and ineffectual. This in no way implies, as Chizhevsky tries to suggest, that Belinsky's misfortune was to have lived in an age rent by intellectual disputes without even suspecting his unfitness to take part in them, and that he had nothing but fervent feelings, and only supposed that he had something to say. On the contrary, in his hands the common coin, the small change of Hegelian metaphysical speculation, which was of no real use to him, turned to gold. It reaches us through the filter of his imagination, which enabled him, especially in his critique of Hegelianism, to state for the first time some of the most important problems in the history of Russian thought. Herzen, whose sensitivity to ideas and philosophical insight were greater than Belinsky's, said that in his life he had met only two people who really understood Hegel's thought, and neither knew a word of German. One of them was Proudhon, the other Belinsky. Even the opaque inventory of Hegelian speculation, terms like "Absolute", "Relative", "Life", "Spirit", "Being", "Non-being", were words to denote a conflict which, to Belinsky's imaginative mind, was real enough to motivate his search for truth. His thought was, no doubt, emotive; and it should be assessed not for its promotion or obstruction of the grammar of science, but for its power to generate creative vision.

It must be admitted that, though one of the most outstanding examples of sustained speculative ratiocination, the Hegelian edifice furnishes an almost unparalleled instance of the enduring potency of a system of unintelligible words. It appears to be possessed by the specifically German devil, the Demon of obscurity, as Nietzsche once called it. It is this obscurity, magnifying and distorting both the familiar and the unknown, which nearly killed philosophical thought in Russia. But it is not only the obscurity of style with its welter of abstract nouns, all of them charged with ineffable significance; it is above all the dimensional constriction which almost stifled the mind of Belinsky. And yet, as will be seen presently, in one respect at least the encounter with Hegelianism was immensely fruitful for his intellectual development and, as Plekhanov rightly points out, kept him a Hegelian even when he came to repudiate Hegel.

There is a sense in which Hegel's system does not differ much from that of Fichte and Schelling, even though Hegel was attacked by them. For they professed all alike a monistic metaphysical doctrine which asserts that the universe is a single whole or unity, involving all that occurs in Nature and history; that this whole expresses an ultimate reality or principle which they usually termed the Absolute; and that this Absolute takes the form of experience in finite human minds. But Hegel adopted a distinct logical method of his own, the dialectical method, to which, unlike some later Hegelians, he himself, as well as his Russian disciples, attached a very great importance. Since, according to Hegel, the distinction between knowledge and its object, and, therefore, between logic and metaphysics, is unreal, he claimed that his theory of method, though primarily a theory of logic, is also a theory of reality. He claimed, furthermore, that this method implied not merely a description of reality, but actually helped to constitute that which it described, so that reality itself was seen by him as behaving according to this method.

Hegel's theory of dialectics denotes, to begin with, the necessary relation in which any concept, idea, or doctrine stands to its own opposite. This, however, is not something merely to be substituted for its own opposite, because it is no less prone to self-contradiction. The truth is seen as lying in a third term (synthesis), which unites on a higher plane the essential features of the original term (thesis) as well as of its opposite (antithesis). But the third term, though embodying more truth than the first term and its opposite is found, on analysis, to generate in turn *its* contrary, and therefore to require a new synthesis on a still higher plane. The process of creating and overcoming oppositions continues indefinitely, and the mind is continually driven forward through conflict and opposition to ever wider and more comprehensive formulations of truth.

I shall not embark on a critical examination of this method. Hegel used it with apparent effect, although some have refused to regard the specifically philosophical problems to which he applied it as real problems. What is important is that Hegel did not use it to describe only conceptual relations, but life itself and individual phenomena in life which he regarded as instances of these relations. Hegel's whole philosophy of history turns on the principle that every historical process is a dialectical process, in which one form of life brings about its opposite and out of these there arise new forms of life, and so on. Unlike Plato's world of Forms, Hegel's dialectical system of concepts is neither purely intelligible and immaterial nor static and devoid of change and becoming: it demands realization in the concrete and is permeated by process and dynamic movement. Indeed, it is Hegel who is largely responsible for the recognition of the fundamental fact of change and development in life. He marks the final abandonment by European thought of the old idea of life as a static system. Without Hegel there would have been no Darwin, for it is Hegel who stopped at no logical usage or fastidiousness, who ventured to teach that the conceptions of kinds develop out of one another. With this theory European thought was prepared for the scientific movement of the nineteenth century with its idea of evolution.

But Hegel's doctrine of dialectical development went a great deal deeper than the evolutionary theory. For the evolutionary theory, whatever its applicability to purely natural processes, suffered from all the defects of naturalism when applied to human affairs. It conceived of change as dependent on environment, and, therefore, in the last resort as an effect of external influences. It ignored the inner factor in development and lead to the idea that selection by which farmers improve breeds of pigs provides an analogy for the progress of human life and history. For Hegel, on the other hand, change was not primarily a development in external Nature in which everything is outside everything else in space and time, and where change denotes a relation of distinction rather than opposition. He found change to be a dialectical movement of the spirit, which is not part of anything and cannot be reduced to anything in the world of the external—a movement chacterized by inward conflict which makes for revolution from within and is capable of producing creative newness. In his philosophy, therefore, explosive materials were in preparation: it was to lead to revolutionary conclusions and to change the measured tread of natural and historical necessity, despite the fact that Hegel himself was a reactionary in politics.

In the light of this aspect of Hegel's system the Russian revolutionary thinkers would have been Hegelians even if they had never encountered him, inasmuch as they instinctively attributed to "becoming", to movement, a deeper significance and higher value than to that which is, to "being". "Being" is the cause of stability and perpetuation, while "becoming" is the cause of destruction, and the philosophy of becoming is impelled by the desire for change whose only limit is more change, for renewal, for the future. "Becoming" imprints the image of the impermanence and the torture of time upon all things and endangers them. "We question time and put it on the rack." "Life consists in that it changes perpetually and is continually made anew; this is the basic principle of my life." "All that is alive is a result of conflict; all that arises and affirms itself without conflict is dead."[31] Belinsky's writings abound in such and similar utterances. Not only the closed cycle of Nature, but also the "closed cycle of being" cannot permit and explain the rise of newness, the essentially linear, unpredictable, forward-looking quality of life.

The immediate impact of Hegel's thought on the mind of Belinsky, however, did not produce any revolutionary convictions. On the contrary, it made him come to terms with a reality which eventually proved a challenge to his own rebellious nature. There were enough discrepancies in Hegel's own thought to warrant Belinsky's period of "reconciliation with reality". Hegel's thought was no less rationalistic and deductive than Fichte's; and yet his rationalism was of a curious kind because it assumed irrational elements in reason itself, and his dialectics were largely an expression of his awareness of history in its brute, irrational and irreducible quality. He was consciously working away from the abstract and static theory of human nature and history that prevailed in the eighteenth century, and it was this which helped Belinsky to tear himself away, not without considerable mental agony, from the abstract idealism of his preceding philosophical allegiance. It revived him and cleared his eyes with the re-discovery of historical reality, and made him avoid the brassy plugging of high sentiments which, in natures less candid and searching than Belinsky's, would have finally shut all doors and windows on the world and humanity outside. "I look at reality, which I used to despise so much", he wrote to Bakunin in 1837, "and feel strangely stirred by a sense of its rightness; I realize that nothing can be banished from it, that nothing can be imprecated and rejected." "Sensation itself, which issues from the fullness of life", he wrote in another letter, "appears to me as mysterious."[32] He planned to write a "Correspondence" between a "Beautiful Soul" and "Spirit",

71

to show that he had grown tired of *Schönseligkeit* and its heroic attitudes, and to charge its protagonists with insensitivity to the real conflicts and sufferings of human life. "For me there is no more exit into the *Jenseits*."[33]

Belinsky's constant and laborious use of the word "reality" was a source of considerable confusion. He intended it to have a Hegelian connotation. But in his hands it acquired a somewhat different meaning. Hegel's idea of reality is part of his monistic conception of the relation between the whole and its parts. The whole, according to Hegel is, as it were, there from the beginning, and being there, it expresses itself in parts whose nature it pervades and determines. The whole, therefore, is more real than its parts: reality is proportional to the mass and richness of the elements which go to make it. The model for Hegel's conception of reality is the all-inclusive whole which contains and gathers up into itself both the abstract universal of Platonic philosophy and the raw matter of sense experience. And it is in this sense that Hegel asserted in the Introduction to his *Philosophy of Right* "the rationality of the real" or "the reality of the rational". To regard something as real, and therefore as rational, was for him to regard it as an aspect of the whole.

Whether the assertion is a mere tautology or implies an identification of the real with the rational, whether, in other words, it amounts to no more than the Molièreian doctor's formula—*opium facit dormire, quare est in eo virtus dormitiva* or whether it means that "whatever is, is right" must remain a debatable point.[34] Belinsky at any rate, with Bakunin's help, drew this very conclusion, with rather disastrous consequences to himself. A rebel by nature, he forced himself into the straight-jacket of the most abject worship of history. The *Moscow Observer*, Belinsky's literary organ from 1838 until his departure to Petersburg, represented in the course of several months "a gloomy stage, where one could see a remarkable and original thinker in the humiliating position of a martyr pining and weakening under the impact of a cruel intellectual discipline which he obstinately persisted in imposing on himself, although it deprived him of his power, refusing to admit that it was a punishment" (Annenkov). "The word 'reality' ", Belinsky wrote at the time, "has for me the same significance as the word 'God'." "Now that I am in the position of contemplating the infinite, I begin to understand that everyone is right and no one is guilty, that there are no false, erroneous opinions, and that all things are different facets of the Spirit." His humanism becomes a homage to mankind at the expense of individual man. He claims to have found a standpoint from which he can view all things as parts of a comprehended whole. "Man is part of a living whole." In the true spirit of Hegel, who accords to wholeness and unity a higher ontological status than that which is partial and diverse, the "universal human spirit", "mankind", and even "society" became "always more in the right and standing above the individual person".[35] Such comparatively mild statements were soon followed by an overt apology for power. In a series of articles, of which the essay on the anniversary of the Battle of Borodino was one, he proclaims the idea that right is might and might is right; he tries to persuade his readers of the necessity of submitting to the "universal agencies" in history; he advocates a special morality for conquerors, for "great men" and "geniuses" and pays tribute to the "sacred quality" of Tsarist autocracy. "Do you know", Herzen asked him, "that from your point of view you can prove that the monstrous tyranny under which we live is rational and ought to exist?" "There is no doubt about it," replied Belinsky, and "proceeded to recite to us Pushkin's Anniversary of Borodino".[36]

In the absence of any evidence of Belinsky's disposition to conform to the demands of his environment, or to pursue any vested interests of his own, one explanation suggests itself for this startling and abrupt change of attitude. It is not connected with philosophy, although Hegel helped to formulate and to rationalize it. It lies in Belinsky's awakened sense of commitment to or implication in the world outside. He was reacting against the romantic mood which left man suspended in mid-air, isolated, and powerless against the world. He felt impelled to give this world a meaning. He was, temperamentally, quite unable to look at life for long obliquely and extraneously: he had to choose it as his own, to re-create it in his imagination, through compassion or hatred, through understanding and a sense of wonder, even when this meant incorporating into his outlook facts that were manifestly indigestible. A desire took hold of him to be in the world with ears alert: not, like the romantic ear, to delicate cadences, to lofty feelings, and to what, until now, he had been fond of calling "the poetry of life", but to the abruptness of human speech and behaviour, to the life-giving reality at hand. He did not cease to impose his vision, but "to see things as they are" came to define for him more and more the philosopher's task. He shows increasing interest in empirical knowledge, in restoring meaning to things in time and place and hence to truths that are relative and contingent.[37] Yet even so, and at the very extreme of his acceptance of "reality", he went on experiencing it as a "terrible phantom urging its claim on man", as a "monster armed with claws of iron and colossal iron jaws: whoever does not give himself freely, the monster will take by force. . . . Sooner or later it will devour anyone who stands opposed." There is only one way out and "that is to become conscious of its reality".[38] "Reality" which, he said, became his "God" seemed to threaten his inmost self: in his struggle with it the God proved victorious, if only for a time, but this victory too had to be accepted from within.

In this mood he embarked on a fruitless course of identifying himself with the Russia of his day. Herzen broke off all relations with him.

Even Bakunin refused to follow. Belinsky "reproached him with weakness, with making concessions, and went to extremes which frightened his own friends and followers" (Herzen). The Moscow Slavophils, on the contrary, unaware of Belinsky's mental struggles, were triumphant. At times he seemed to long for objections to the Hegelian orthodoxy which had led him to such straits. He "flared up and became sullen and angry just when he met with unquestioning agreement with his own propositions" (Annenkov). Nevertheless he continued to reject all compromise, even in the form of the lulling and pleasing opium of scepticism. He could not wait or comfort himself with waiting. Scepticism at this point would have been a euphemism for inability to choose—self-defence, a luxury, an ornament for a diseased will. He seized Hegel by the throat and extorted from him what Hegel himself scarcely dared to proclaim, although it was implicitly contained in his philosophical system, and constituted Hegel's fatal legacy to German historical thinking. What Belinsky found in Hegel was the worship of the power of history, which turns every actual historical moment into an idol, and which modern man has vulgarized in the delectable practice of "adapting himself to circumstances".[39] If whatever happens is inevitable in virtue of "dialectical necessity", and every event in history shows the victory of logic or the Idea, then down on your knees and let every step in the dialectical ladder have its appropriate devotion.

Belinsky soon realized how thoroughly he had been fooled by this theory and by the reality which he chose to accept with its help. Annenkov speaks of the bewilderment produced among friends by the ambivalence and inconsistencies of Belinsky's attitude at this critical moment. "But we longed for Belinsky's heresies, for Belinsky's contradictions, for his betrayals of (Hegelian) propositions and for his violations of philosophical dogmas: they seemed to give us back our old Belinsky of 1834–5, when, Schelling notwithstanding, he had his independent thought. . . ."[40] Still, he continued to embrace out of spite what always had been and at bottom always remained for him the ugliest of realities. "I am more ludicrous than Don Quixote", he wrote to Bakunin: "he, at any rate, believed himself to be a knight, fighting with giants and not with windmills, possessing a true beauty, and not a fat and ugly Dulcinea; I know I am no knight but a madman. Even so I go on being a knight-errant. I know I am fighting windmills and still continue to fight them; I know my Dulcinea (life) to be unseemly and vile, and yet I love her, in the teeth of commonsense and all the evidence." Belinsky hated the idealist in himself—the idealist who recoils from embodiment, from the identification of the idea of the fact with the fact itself. Or, as Plekhanov says, "he tried to come to terms, not with reality, but with the sad fate of his abstract *ideal*". His ferocious deliberateness in embracing "reality", and the bitterness and irritation arising from this, were evidence of the revolt of his mind against a deep-rooted instinct of wanting to be somewhere else, and things to be otherwise; against his own need to discover a lost or unheard-of reality; and, in the end, perhaps, against his own imagination—since to imagine is to fail, to acknowledge defeat in the encounter with reality.

That Belinsky was profoundly unhappy about his own position is evident from his behaviour and attitude towards his friends at the period in question, and especially from the letters written at the height of his Hegelianism in Moscow. The "reconciliation" did not work, for it left him with a vivid awareness that, however much he might try to include everything in the "universal Idea", there would always remain loose ends, uncomposed contrasts, elements of brute fact and, above all, the irreducible and unique reality of the human person. It may be, historically speaking, of the very essence of philosophical thinking to explain and to mediate in the conflict between the finite and infinite, the particular and universal, the active and passive, sense and thought, and so on. But there is one conflict which no philosophical bridge-building can eliminate: the conflict between the human person and every impersonal, anonymous force or system which would absorb or annul it. It was the almost desperate realization of this conflict which brought Belinsky to his senses and, incidentally, made him (together with his in other respects so very different younger contemporary Søren Kierkegaard, of whose existence he knew nothing) the first and most radical critic of Hegelian monism.[41] The theme which Belinsky unfolds in passionate antithesis to Hegel constitutes his greatest contribution; it is also, from Belinsky onwards, the most insistent and persistent theme of Russian thought.

The question of the nature and reality of life in its eminently particular and individual aspect, the question, that is to say, of the nature of personality, has always been a stumbling block for philosophy, especially for philosophy of the essentialist and conceptualist type. Neither the eternal, immortal essences of the Platonic intelligible world, nor the Aristotelian and Thomist claim to attain knowledge through abstraction from the diversity and particularity of existence, nor Baconian "simple natures" and Cartesian "clear and distinct ideas", nor, indeed, the general laws by means of which science analyses behaviour in the life of man and of Nature, are favourable for the evaluation of the human person. The attitude of philosophical empiricism proved even less propitious, for, since Hume's polite but insistent reduction of the Ego to a bundle of different perceptions in a continual ebb and flow, it has turned into a philosophy of impersonality. It has gone so far as to declare all disputes concerning the identity of the person to be merely a battle of words, and the very idea of the human Ego to be a misleading creation of the grammarian. Hume's certainty that he had no Ego may have been a philosopher's modesty, but he

75

ventured to suggest that the majority of mankind, apart from a few misguided metaphysicians, were mere bundles. The most astonishing thing in this connection, however, is the fate of idealist metaphysics. It began as a philosophy of the Ego and autonomous reason, and ended by reducing them to an instrument of the impersonal universal Mind. Hegel reached the summit of essentialist depersonalization and finally sacrificed the individual on the altar of the Absolute. Even religion was resolved into the "self-consciousness of God in man". And, although Hegel understood the dynamic of life and history better than most philosophers before him, his dialectics implied primarily not conflict between human agents, nor a struggle of free human beings with the external necessities and exigencies of the world order, but a conflict in which men are moved by universal forces and the "cunning" of historical Reason, and in which freedom turns out to be the child of necessity.[42]

Belinsky's attack on the Hegelian through-and-through universe was not due to his detection of any logical or academic incorrectness in Hegel's philosophical procedure. His appeal, in this as in so many other matters, was human and was, if anything, directed against logic, which knows no respect of persons, and aims at making the unwilling believe. It was, similarly, directed against the academic halo and professorial quality of the Hegelian structure. Professorial fetichism is a specifically German phenomenon which, watched over by the academic pontiffs of idealist philosophy, became, in the nineteenth century at any rate, the German substitute for religious, cultural and social values. It moved Nietzsche, in an attempt to save philosophy from ridicule, to propose that all philosophers should be left to run wild, forbidden any thoughts of office and academic status, deprived of all bribes, or even be persecuted and ill-treated. He expected admirable results from this, and prophesied that the unworthy would become parsons, schoolmasters or editors, the vainest go to court and, like Hegel, become court philosophers; but the wisest would remain unemployed and unemployable. Belinsky, too, expressed the gravest misgivings about professors and, like Kierkegaard, came to regard them as professors of the fact that another has suffered, professors of the subjugation of man to the hypostatized exigencies of a philosophical, or religious, or social universe.

Belinsky's most powerful indictment is contained in a much quoted letter to Botkin written about a year after his arrival in Petersburg. "Hegel", he says, "has turned living things into shadowy skeletons hooked together by their bony arms, and dancing in the air over the cemetery. For him the subject is not an end in itself, but a means to the momentary expression of the Universal; but in relation to the subject the Universal is like Moloch, who makes a show of himself in the subject, and then throws it away like an old pair of trousers." "To the devil with all your higher strivings and purposes!" "All Hegelian doctrines about morality are pure rubbish, for in an objectified world-order there is no sense of moral values, as there is no morality in objectivistic religion. . . . I have particularly serious grounds for being angry with Hegel, because I feel that it was my belief in him which made me come to terms with Russian reality." "Do as you like, but I shall persist in my conviction that the fate of the subject, of the individual, of the person is more important than the fate of the whole world and the well-being of the Chinese Emperor, that is to say, the Hegelian *Allgemeinheit*. I am told: develop all the treasures of your spirit for free delight in its realization; weep that you may be comforted, grieve that you may rejoice anew; strive after perfection; flounder and fall but climb to the highest rung of the ladder of development, and the devil take you. . . . I humbly express my gratitude to Egor Fedorovich [Hegel]; I bow down before your philosophic nightcap. But, with all due respect to your philosophic philistinism, I have the honour of informing you that if I were enabled to reach the highest rung of that ladder, even there I would ask to be rendered an account of all the victims of life and history, for all the victims of chance, of superstition, of Philip II's Inquisition, and so on and so on. Otherwise I prefer to fling myself headlong from the highest rung. I do not want happiness, even as a gift, unless I have peace of mind about every one of my brothers by blood, bone of my bone, flesh of my flesh. It is said that disharmony is a condition of harmony. That may be very profitable and pleasant for lovers of music; but it is hardly so for those whose lot it is to suffer disharmony in actual experience. . . . I am one of those people who see in everything the tail of the devil, and this, it seems, is my final outlook on life, and will probably remain so until I die."

Belinsky's peroration to Botkin strikes one by its similarity in content and formulation to the words of Dostoevsky, in the mouth of his hero Ivan Karamazov.[43] Already in his *Notes from Underground* Dostoevsky depicted man as an irrational creature who refuses to acquiesce in being a mere "cog in the world mechanism" and repudiates the "crystal palace" of universal harmony, towards the achievement of which the human individual would be nothing but a means. In the same way Ivan Karamazov revolts against compulsory happiness, against a world and a Paradise without freedom. "In the last resort", he says to Alyosha, "I do not accept God's world, and although I cannot but admit its existence, I do not in the least degree permit it. The world may attain the highest degree of harmony, a universal reconciliation, but this will not atone for the innocent suffering of the past." "I absolutely repudiate the highest harmony; it is not worth the tears of this one tortured child."

Dostoevsky, though he was never able to integrate his Christian faith into his creative vision of man, found a reflection of, and answer to, the misfortunes and perplexities of human existence in the Cross, that is to say in God who takes upon himself the sufferings of man. But Belinsky

77

was very much of this world: he probably never attempted to make his journey to the end of the night which, for the initiate, if for no one else, is filled with illumination. An experience of human tragedy similar to Dostoevsky's led Belinsky to an avowed atheistic conviction, which was enhanced and deepened by his impression of the Church, whose defence of the Christian faith served to sanction the enslavement of man in mind and body, and enforced a belief in compensation in supernatural glories for miseries endured in this world. Suffering for Belinsky had no redemption; it just served the purpose of the devil—an idea which was too frightening even for Dostoevsky to face.

The sense of evil is, of course, in a large measure, a religious prerogative. While suffering proved a source of disbelief in God and men lost faith in the divine meaning of the world because they found evil victorious in it, suffering and evil have also created religion. In some sense the "problem of evil" only exists in relation to the conceivability of salvation. If no thought of a world wholly other than this arose, evil would cease to be a problem, and man would be an animal content, like other animals, with life as he finds it. And yet the very search for deliverance pervading religious experience served to soften, slur or even whitewash the sharp and cold edges which unsoften and pierce the conscience of the godless. It is, therefore, more significant to speak of the sense of evil and the resulting preoccupation with moral conflict as a part of the human heritage, as belonging to the whole drama of the human condition. And it is the recovered awareness of this drama that made Belinsky's experience of evil so poignant.

There is not sufficient evidence to establish with any precision when Belinsky became an atheist (and later a materialist). It appears to have been a gradual process. As late as November 1842 he wrote to Bakunin that he could not live without God. But early in 1846 he says in a letter to Herzen that he sees "in the words 'God' and 'religion'—bad faith, darkness, chains and the knout", and "likes these two words as he likes the four which follow them". At a still later stage he contended in approbation that the Russian people were "by nature a profoundly atheistic people" and "far removed from every kind of mystical exultation". The motive of Belinsky's atheism, however, was moral, not intellectual. He was no sceptic or agnostic mildly pleading for the incredibility of a theistic universe. "To believe and not to know", he said, "—this may still have some meaning for man; but to know and not to believe does not mean anything at all." [44] The atheistic motive was linked with his central preoccupation with the human person. He was moved by a passion for human freedom, which has led others beside Belinsky to despise the attitude, servile, frightened and egotistical as it is, of believers who look for God and find only such reflections of their own self-will as God the potentate, the guarantor of social values and civilization, the receiver of petitions, the domestic servant, the sergeant major, the general supply and welfare officer, or, for that matter, the gratifying object of a vague and sloppy pursuit of eternity. It was his re-awakened sense of the human person, exposed to and almost narrowed by a savagely impersonal world, that deprived Belinsky of all the teleological delight which feeds on the real or imaginary traces of God's hand in all its worldly manifestations. It brought him to the realization of a deep-rooted duality between man and the external object-world—a world claiming its monstrous power over man and evoking a vast quantity of illusions as a safeguard for its existence and survival. He saw this object-world as a source of triumph of the common over the particular, of the species over the individual person, and of society over man. Its illusions assume the form of established beliefs and sanctities which inspire man with idolatrous awe, with what Belinsky calls the "terror of the objective world". The terrorizing power of objectification is exercised through the conventional falsehood, the concepts and laws of society and civilization, of religious institutions and family life, of creeds and sanctuaries which shape human life in accordance with an inhuman and faceless world. To this power of objectification, however, Belinsky did not oppose, as did Rousseau, the romantics or Tolstoy, the abstraction "Nature", which is supposed to undo evil by making man abandon civilization, but which, as Belinsky put it, in its "deadliness and unconsciousness . . . treats man worse than a savage step-mother". He confronted it, once again, with man in the "mysteriousness" and "immediate absoluteness" of his personal character—at a point, that is to say, which external influences cannot altogether determine, and which provides the element of creativity and originality inexplicable by any mechanistic or naturalistic theory.[45]

In this confrontation Belinsky returned to the sources of his rebellion in his youthful drama *Dimitry Kalinin*, except that now the attitude of revolt had little of its specifically religious connotation, and eventually made him abandon all concern even with philosophical speculation, and attend almost exclusively to literary and social questions. The gesture of revolt turns into one of total denial, of nihilism, which was to become a most important theme in the subsequent history of Russian thought. "The dark spirit of doubt and negation" instils into Belinsky a readiness to "destroy without reflection and without excuse, wherever and however [he] can". "He who believes in truth will not be afraid of any denial." "Negation is my God. My heroes in history are the destroyers of the old: Luther, Voltaire, the encyclopaedists, the terrorists, Byron (*Cain*), and others."[46] The values approved by human society are henceforth a dead letter for him and, what is more, the suspicion enters that the world is not built on any superior order and that man, like Lermontov's Pechorin, about whom Belinsky wrote some of his most inspired and penetrating literary criticism, is abandoned to an eternal and senseless exile.

A certain symbolic significance in this connection is attached to Belinsky's change of residence. For, on moving to Petersburg, the "rational reality" assumed the appearance of a "purposeless" and "irrational" world. It showed its real face to him—a staring, grinning face, scowling and disfigured by the strain and brutality of the world as it was, and not as he had imagined it to be against the background of the soft and complacent Muscovite pattern. The Muscovite myth (or as Belinsky expressed it in the untranslatable *moskvodushie* and *kitaizm*) was routed by the tragic and austere fate of Petersburg man. "I use the word *man*", he wrote in 1843 to his future wife, "as an antithesis to a Muscovite". In Petersburg he became conscious of the "devil's tail behind all things", of the night beyond and beneath his life, of the illimitable, the purposeless, and of the evil which surrounds and pervades human existence. The confidence in dialectical progress which subsumes all things in a harmonious totality, and which inclined Belinsky's mind to an optimistic contemplation of the world, gives place to a pervasive disillusionment. It is noteworthy that he begins to drop all those soul-stirring words which are the well-known pedals of the romantic organ, and which he had been so fond of using in his less gloomy and less dejected mood. His language becomes (especially in his letters) sober, matter-of-fact, almost abrupt, and at the same time more unmistakably his own. Behind it there lay, no doubt, a deeper experience than the intellectual and emotional uplift of his idealist days. Evil acquired for him the character, not of a special misfortune, but, as we have seen, of a ubiquitous rift, a condition of human life, a lack of one of the essential threads which bind experience into a coherent whole and give it consistent meaning. "Life is a trap; and we are all mice. Some succeed in tearing away the bait and running from the snare, but most are caught. Life is a stupid farce: to the devil with it! We will drink and be merry if we can; today is ours, but there is no redemption in our grief." "Life deceives me horribly: it is unscrupulous, treacherous. In the past, fantasy; in the present, slow death; in the future, decay and stench. Why couldn't I have pegged out six months ago, when I could still dream about reality?"[47] Disillusionment led to "orgies" (as he put it in a letter to Bakunin), in which he sought momentary oblivion. He speaks of "miserable and sordid dissipation", which to his chaste and almost puritanical heart and mind must have been particularly miserable and sordid, of "adventures on the Nevsky, in the street, in the ditch and devil knows where". "Anyway, no one anywhere has responded to our cry! I say, my dear! . . . but pray no tender ceremonies. . . ."[48]

There was, besides "Petersburg reality", another cause of Belinsky's failure to discover any secure and comforting values that could relieve his nihilistic mood. It was his encounter with death on losing his two greatest friends, Stankevich and Koltsov. Death, the thief, the taker away of what is most valued, the evictor from the human image of the spirit which made it an individual, brought him against the futility of his metaphysical optimism. It appeared before him as the ultimate dead-end, the pre-eminent disaster, the mark of the "objective mean-inglessness of the human lot", from which no religious, philosophical or scientific smoke-screens can hide man. "No", he wrote to Botkin on hearing of Stankevich's death, "I shall not let this Moloch alone, whom philosophy has named the Absolute; I shall question it: what have you done with him, what has become of him?"—and he goes on to speak of the horror of the irrevocability of death. Though for a while he was still inclined to look for comfort in the idealistic doctrine of immortality, he came to realize that no immortal powers, of which man would be a function or instrument, or a fleeting transitory manifestation, can be substituted for concrete, individual man. It is only for the human person and from the point of view of the human person that death is a tragedy. Death which reigns in Nature or in the ghost-ridden universe of the metaphysicians is but an element of change and transformation, of decomposition and recomposition. Only man, in facing death, has the experience of the end, of the void, of non-being. No conceivable tragedy can be attached to the displacement of divine souls released from their bodily condition, of abstract concepts, or of the impersonal, transitory phenomena of Nature. The only agonizing and unendurable thing about death is that it should threaten to destroy the unique and unre-peatable image of man. And it is this image of man which, as Belinsky himself confessed, became for him "the point at which I fear to lose my reason".

3. MAN IN SOCIETY. THE SLAVOPHIL ILLUSION

Every lamentation has its measure of revenge. The very fact of be-wailing one's lot may lend such charm to life that one is ready to endure it on that account alone. But only those who inhabit ivory towers can surrender to the luxuries of deliberate doom, make of disillusion a matter of speculation and lament, or take advantage of the curious power of weakness. The Russian intelligentsia found ivory towers unin-habitable, and among its ranks there took place a gradual elimination of emotional luxuries: it was a result of their closeness to reality as well as of their realization that the ugliest truth is as often as not the only truth. Belinsky in particular had neither the gift nor the will to relish failure and desperation. The experience of hell within made him prepared for the hell without. The very violence of his kind of repudiation taught him to think and speak, not through the possession of an unassailable truth, but through closeness to man in time and space. Life for him was very much a *hic et nunc*, to be split up, quarried out, remade and carried away into the future. He was completely inside life—yet not comfort-ably, but uncomfortably. This should be kept in mind when trying to understand Belinsky's adoption of socialism and the attitude to Russia which he formulated in his conflict with the Slavophils. I propose to devote this section to a discussion of these two topics.

For reasons already stated any strict division of Belinsky's intellectual development into periods is unhelpful, and, with regard to his post-Hegelian phase, positively misleading. We have seen that, while insisting that he never felt moved to adopt a finished philosophy which solves and shelves the problems of life, and while abandoning many of his previously cherished opinions and acquiring new ones, he nonetheless remained throughout true to himself. Indeed, the value of Belinsky's thought lies not in the whole, in the structure (if any), but in the material with which it is built, in the fact that the structure may be destroyed and yet have value as material. What seems to have survived all his intellectual permutations is his revolt on behalf of living man and in the name of human personality. It is significant that at his most personalistic, in a letter to Botkin in 1841, where he speaks of a "wild, frenzied . . . love for the freedom and independence of the human person that has taken hold of [him]", Belinsky confesses to "cruel hatred towards anyone who desires to separate himself from his brotherhood with mankind". "I have now reached a new extreme", he continues, "—it is the idea of socialism . . ., the way of all ways of living, the problem of problems, the *alpha* and *omega* of belief and knowledge. . . . More and more I become a citizen of the whole world. More and more a mad longing for love devours me . . ., a yearning which becomes increasingly urgent and intractable. . . . I am beginning to love mankind in the manner of Marat. To make the smallest part of it happy, I think I would exterminate the rest with fire and sword." And he concludes by exclaiming: "the social spirit (*sotsialnost*) . . . or death!" In a letter to the same correspondent and in the same year he contended that "people are so stupid that you have to drag them to happiness. And, in any case, what is the blood of thousands in comparison with the humiliation and sufferings of millions?" These and similar statements, recurring as they do with increasing frequency in Belinsky's writings (to be more precise, in his letters) during the Petersburg period, have all the appearance of the familiar tale of "the lesser evil", of idealism turned cynicism, and of rebels transformed into iron-fisted masters. While little disposed to turn his mind to any sustained reflection on political problems, he showed signs of that politomania which became a characteristic feature of the later intelligentsia.[49] At any rate he was, in some moods, quite prepared to approve proceedings on behalf of "mankind" which his conscience would certainly not allow him to undertake on his own behalf, and which appear to contradict his passionate advocacy of the human person. He came to understand those contradictions in human nature which can deem death cheap as the price of an act of defiance, or which can deliberately seek the scaffold as a means of salvation for his "brothers by blood".

The precise revolutionary element in Belinsky has drawn the attention of students of his thought least of all.[50] Annenkov, who combined a great gift for friendship with great adaptability, and who, in spite or because of his liberalism, succeeded in sailing unscathed and untouched through all the pressures and adversities of Nicolaian Russia, prefers to minimize or to ignore Belinsky's revolutionary convictions. So does Turgenev. The view has taken root that Belinsky believed in economic and political evolution, in the idea of non-interference with the "natural laws" of industry and commerce, and in the policy of economic and political *laissez faire*; that even when he became a socialist, his socialism was a mild gradualist affair. He differed, it is true, from the Slavophils (or, for that matter, from Herzen) in regarding the Russian peasant commune as a transitory form of land tenure in a primitive feudal society: it was, in his view, destined to be uprooted by the advent of capitalism, which would make Russia ripe for the socialist revolution. He even suggested of Louis Blanc's *History of the French Revolution* that "the process of social development in Russia will not begin until the whole of the Russian gentry is transformed into a *bourgeoisie*".[51] But, in the first place, he was too much of a personalist not to see that the mechanics of capitalist production disintegrate and dehumanize man's personality.[52] In the second place, nothing was further from Belinsky than a *bourgeois* outlook, as will be seen presently from his reaction to Gogol's "apostasy". He clearly distinguished a triumphant *bourgeoisie*, "the syphilitic wound on the body of France", which he abominated no less than Herzen, from its temporary revolutionary rôle ("the *bourgeoisie* in conflict", as he says). Indeed, according to Herzen, he was "the most revolutionary character of the Nicolaian age". Even Annenkov admits that Belinsky, as well as Herzen, welcomed the destructive forces of revolution: "they were far from dogmatizing socialism, yet they did not shy away from its real or imaginary threat to the values of civilization. On the contrary, they were inclined to welcome the socialist cataclysm that was to shake all the beliefs, convictions, habits, ideas and historical principles acquired by Europe with such effort in the course of centuries. Herzen and Belinsky alike looked straight in the face of all the symptoms of disintegration which, in their opinion, endangered Europe from the socialist quarter: they did not ask for, yet were not afraid of, the ruins which socialism was to bring."[53]

Once he had succeeded in tearing himself from what he calls "the German book" and stopped spinning "the German web", revolutionary thought attracted more and more of Belinsky's attention and eventually became uppermost in his mind. He embarked on a study of the French Revolution, of which he seems to have become enamoured, of Proudhon, Fourier, Saint-Simon and Louis Blanc, who, like Schelling and Hegel before them, had an increasing number of followers, protagonists and, later, even martyrs in Russia. But for Belinsky revolution was not just a piece of social doctrine or a political entanglement; neither did he accept it with nostalgia and regret, shrinking with distaste from the violence that was its most powerful expression: it was a form of freedom in its very threat to "civilized" values, a way of setting free the lives and thoughts of man, embodying them in the most hazardous realities, crushing with its thyrsus the most exquisite flowers, invading old sanctuaries, and overthrowing hierarchical orders that seemed everlasting. It is true, he believed, not without some relish, that "a liberated Russian people would not go to Parliament, but would hurry to the pub to have a drink, to smash windows and hang the gentry". But he also wrote to Botkin in 1841 *à propos* of the creation of new social relations, "that it is ridiculous to think that this can produce itself of its own accord, with time and without violent upheavals". He realized that, as a matter of fact if not of principle, revolutions never are made with orange blossom, to the accompaniment of delicate tunes; that they are full of ferocity, intolerance, passion, baseness and grandeur.

Nevertheless, Belinsky's revolutionism is far from implying that he embraced the ethics of the underworld or that he came to think in terms of the struggle for power in which men believe themselves beyond good and evil and regard truth, mercy and individual loyalty as proofs of weakness. His revolutionary socialism is, in fact, unintelligible without reference to his personalistic ethics. It was directed *against* the power derived from coherence and consistency, against claims to see everything as part of one logical and inevitable movement. When he denounced the prevailing social and political order in Russia he did so, not because it was obsolete and had come to fetter the further development of society, but because it was morally evil. He spoke of this order as of a "Chinese kingdom of bestial, material life, of servility, of Mammon worship, nepotism, irreligion and moral prostitution, of the absence of all spiritual concern and the triumph of shameless stupidity: a kingdom of the commonplace and mediocrity, where everything that is remotely human and noble is condemned to be trampled upon and tormented, where censorship has become a military discipline for deserters, where freedom of thought is abolished, . . . where Pushkin perished a victim of perfidy, while the Bulgarins and the Grechs manipulate literature by informing and have a wonderful time. . . ." [54] He refuses to accept a social order unless it is founded on "right and chivalry". He was too much of a rebel and too much of a personalist to be able to acquiesce in any form of slavery on the grounds that it may have been or is a great advance in its day. With all his newly acquired relativism and rejection of "absolute" truths he establishes his case for socialism on the basis of the moral values of human freedom and personality. To that extent he was no doubt a "utopian" socialist, still showing his capacity for enthusiasm and still somehow asking what, if not illusion, gives man a sense of freedom? In an almost pathetically high-flown manner, once again reminiscent of Dostoevsky's vision of perfect society, he looks to a time "when no one will be burnt, no one brought to the block, when the criminal will beg to be made an end of as an act of saving mercy, and there will be no punishment, but life will be left to him as a punishment, as death is now; when there will be no senseless codes and conventions, when no terms or conditions will be imposed on feeling, when there will be no duty and obligation, and when will yields not to will but to love alone; when there will be no husbands and wives, but lovers, men and women; when the loved one will come to her lover and say: 'I love another', and he will answer: 'I cannot be happy without you; I shall suffer my whole life long, but go to him whom you love.' And he will not accept her sacrifice, if through magnanimity she desires to remain with him, but like God, he will say to her: 'I will have mercy and not sacrifice.' There will be no rich and no poor, neither kings nor subjects; but there will be brothers, there will be men and women, and in the words of the Apostle Paul, Christ will yield his power to the Father, and the Father . . . will ascend to the throne anew, but now over a new heaven and a new earth."[55]

It is of some interest that Belinsky's socialism was in a sense bound up with his attitude to woman, and this in turn had something to do with his new interest in the French utopian socialists and, perhaps, particularly in George Sand. The theme crops up as early as 1840. "A prostitute", he wrote then, "is better than a wife who does not love; and Saint-Simon's views on marriage are better and more human than those of Hegel (that is, those I thought were Hegel's). What does it matter that the State is maintained by the abstraction called marriage? It is, after all, equally maintained by the hangman with knout in hand." George Sand becomes for him an "inspired prophetess", although on other occasions he did not discount in her a certain conscious or unconscious hypocrisy. Few writers have produced such divergent effects on their contemporaries as Sand did.[56] In Russia she was on everybody's lips, and more especially on every woman's. Many tried, with alarming literalness, to apply in their lives emancipatory principles, which without her would never have entered their heads, or would have found their way, as usual, without the head. Thus Botkin married after the fashion of George Sand, but forthwith left his wife after his own fashion.

To us George Sand seems to sum up almost everything we find contemptible and reprehensible in nineteenth century mentality, all its romantic wishful thinking and self-delusions. What captivated Belinsky in her, however, was not the romantic sublimations of her gluttony of desire, but the idea of moral freedom which he, legitimately or not, detected in her advocacy of woman's right to love whom and how she pleases. In the conflict between love and marriage or family as social institutions he saw but another manifestation of the conflict between personality and society, between freedom and necessity. He knew from childhood of the tyranny with which the institution of the family can be associated, and which may be still more enslaving than the tyranny of the State. There was no other love for him except free love; and love which is unwilling, obligatory or binding he regarded as an absurd and meaningless notion. To whatever extent society denied free love to that extent it turned man into an instrument of its inhuman operations and acted in accordance with its impersonal, i.e. immoral morality. Socialism was, paradoxically, to induce a complete and radical desocialization of love, since love is fundamentally not a social but a personal relationship.

Belinsky's real problem, once he had succeeded in shedding his various idealistic skins, was the idea of society standing on one side, an organism with its own laws of growth and self-preservation, while the individual stands on the other and is used by society for its own ends, trampling upon him if he thwarts it, rewarding him with its medals, pensions, honours, when he serves it faithfully. He refused to attribute goodness to actions which are to the advantage of society and evil to these which are to its disadvantage. In other words, he opposed the exteriorization of society, the notion of society as a hypostatized entity, as some kind of absolute "not-self". Social life in general, and socialism in particular, he saw as expressive primarily of relations between persons. Despite his anxiety to applaud the French utopian socialists, there is no evidence in his writings of that schematic and theoretical utopianism which deduces a social order from some abstract theory of the nature of man, and of his capacities and needs. His sympathies in this respect were much more with English radical social and political thought. In as much as Belinsky had any positive social ideas, these are summed up in the notion of solidarity or in what he called, in criticizing Max Stirner's solipsism, the idea of the "continuance of the self in others". The "socializing" factor is the human person transcending himself and entering into communion with other persons, in freedom, in love and mercy. In fact, his views on this matter do not differ much from the Slavophil conception of *sobornost*, although they can only be inferred from a mass of fragmentary utterances. He did not, however, accept either the religious connotations of the Slavophils' ideas about society or, as we shall see presently, their "organic" interpretation of it. Yet his whole critique of Russian serfdom is based on ethical and personalistic grounds.[57] Even while preferring justice to charity, he did so because he felt charity to be only too often the half-open purse for the scavenger virtue, pity, depriving so many of its beneficiaries of half their dignity as human beings. And, in considering the effects of poverty on man, he was certain that if people were forced to live like debased sub-humans, they began to behave accordingly, and that ethics did not survive long in a society where every breath you drew was at the expense of "suffering brothers by blood". All this is, of course, easily explicable in terms of utopia, but for Belinsky, as for the other men of the "remarkable decade", utopianism meant awareness of the indubitable reality of the finite world, in which man has his being and which he finds wanting; it was the measure of the intensity of their search for truth. Belinsky pursued this search through all his ideological aberrations.

He pursued it even when he began to voice materialistic views of the crudest kind, according to which the thoughts and actions of each individual can be determined by the fixed laws of bodily functions. In one of his last articles Belinsky invited his readers to consider the human mind, "that cerebral mass where all mental functions take place and whence strings of nerves spread all over the organism through the vertebral column". "These [the nerves] are the organs of feelings and sensations charged with liquids so thin that they escape material observation and do not lend themselves to perception. . . . [If you fail to consider this] you will find yourself trying to account for effects apart from causes, or, what is worse, invent imaginary causes and be satisfied with them. A psychology which is not based on physiology is as faulty as a physiology which ignores the existence of anatomy. Modern science goes still further: by means of chemical analysis it seeks to penetrate into the mysterious laboratory of Nature and, by observing the embryo, to trace the physical process of moral development."[58] This piece of weather-beaten, provincial cerebralism, which may come as a solace to the most hardened of the behaviourists, was not, of course, very favourable to Belinsky's fundamental revolutionary attitude. And it is his revolutionary instinct, as well as his obstinate personalism, that prevented him from drawing the obvious conclusions from such propositions. He expressed these materialistic views while maintaining with disconcerting inconsistency that every development in human life depends on the "conflux of ideas", and while speaking of history as the history of the minds of men, swayed by chance, emotion, prejudice and occasional glimpses of truth, and often driven head on into opposition to material facts.

The conflict between the Westerners and the Slavophils is a perennial Russian conflict, a continuous civil war which far transcends in historical and cultural importance the particular dispute in the middle of the nineteenth century, and in which every Russian is to some extent divided against himself. Indeed, it may be argued that Russia herself is an embodiment of that tension in which she and the "West" find themselves face to face in the very depth of European mankind. Be this as it may, so far as the original controversy between the Westerners and the Slavophils is concerned, one finds it difficult now to take sides; and, though it has by no means been understood once and for all, and the divergencies neither can nor should be rounded off, time seems to have reconciled the disputants. If this is true of the ideas or doctrines which divided the disputants, however, the same cannot be said of the personalities involved, or of their respective spiritual and psychological attitudes, which are, in fact, not complementary at all but reflect a profound and fundamental opposition. This is not the place to analyse the origin or character of the dispute and I shall discuss it only in as much as it throws light on the three revolutionary thinkers with whom this study is concerned.

Every text-book on Russian history or literature will inform the student that the impetus came from the already mentioned Chaadaev affair. Chaadaev issued the challenge; but the disagreement deepened when Herzen's increasing influence on the members of the Moscow Circle, originally led by Stankevich, induced them to define their position *vis-à-vis* the other Circles led by Khomyakov, the Kireevskys and Aksakovs. The cleavage between the respective groups became more or less final when, subsequent to his renunciation of "Hegelian conservatism", Belinsky joined issue with the cause of Russian radicalism and, from the banks of the Neva, declared war on the Moscow Slavophils.

It is seldom realized that Belinsky, who in this war showed himself at his fiercest and most vituperative, knew the Slavophil "ideology" mainly as reflected in the articles of such eager but bigoted and primitive adepts as Mikhail Pogodin (1800–75), the editor of the patriotic review *Moskvityanin* ("The Muscovite") and his associate Stepan Shevyrev (1806–64), a professor of Literature at the University of Moscow. Khomyakov's, Ivan Kireevsky's and Samarin's mature views did not see the light until shortly before and after Belinsky's death. What he knew of them was still largely shrouded in what he derisively called "metaphysical darkness". The only Slavophil whose mind he knew intimately was Konstantin Aksakov's, and though the Slavophil movement found its principal support in the Aksakov family, Konstantin and the whole atmosphere prevailing in his parental home were least of all likely to make the Slavophil creed palatable to people of Belinsky's mentality.

The Aksakovs were living examples of prayers promptly answered. They were sincerely believing Christians of good comfort and considerable wealth. They were happy, hospitable, and kindly. Their life was patriarchal. They were creatures of settled habits held fast to one place, but carried away upon enchanted journeys of the spirit through Muscovy. Aksakov father (the distinguished author of the superbly tranquil and airless *Family Chronicle*), after ten years in the Civil Service, spent his life in cultivating friendships with Slavophil intellectuals, fishing and writing (writing, amongst other things, about fishing). Aksakov mother was a dutiful matron presiding over a large family and a model of domestic virtues. Konstantin, the eldest son, embodied, in Panaev's words, "honesty, candour, steadfastness, nobility, kindness and obstinacy". His attachment to Moscow reached at times an almost

88

monotonous intensity. He loved mankind, but only Russian mankind, and even then only that part of it which was born on the river Moskva or on the Klyazma. "Those who had the misfortune to have been born on the shores of the Gulf of Finland he did not regard as Russians or, therefore, as human beings" (Panaev). As a symbol of his Muscovite allegiance he decked himself with an absurd traditional skullcap (*murmolka*) and homespun peasant coat (*zipun*) which, pathetically enough, made him liable to be taken by his lesser and more simple-minded compatriots for a Persian or even a German. He also wore, for the same reasons, a luxuriant beard, which he considered in his Hegelian days a matter of dialectical necessity: bearded Russia of old (thesis)—beardless Russia "of new" (anti-thesis)—rebearded Russia of the future (synthesis). He wanted, in Belinsky's parody, to "stuff pies with the substance of the Russian soul and to bottle it up in a pot of cabbage soup and buckwheat porridge". But it is palpably untrue that, as Turgenev alleges, he sent denunciations to the police. His whole life was spent under the comfortable family wing: he was carefree and unable to envisage existence apart, alone, deprived of the warm, heavy, abundant home. The death of his father (in 1859), and still more the changes resulting from this in the domestic arrangements, undermined his hitherto impregnable health, and he died a year later from sheer domestic dislocation.[59]

A similar, stern if less pathetic sense of the traditional informed the life of Khomyakov, about whom more will be said in the chapter on Herzen. He was, of course, a greater man than Konstantin Aksakov, with a greater ingenuity of imagination, a greater shrewdness and a more dangerous pride in his extraordinary dialectical abilities; but he, too, lived the untroubled life of his class, with its opulence grown on the rich soil of serfdom, with its traditional rhythm, its gargantuan meals, troops of servants (*dvornya*) and endless leisure, enjoying every moment of it and absorbed almost as much in dogs and horses as in the ultimate destiny of Slavdom.

Anyone less rebellious than Belinsky would have had no wish to disturb this patriarchal pattern, which had a character and completeness that gave it beauty and which was infinitely preferable to the habits of a compulsively busy, mechanical, *bourgeois* world, where everybody goes his own way and gets under everybody else's feet. But even Belinsky's stringent, "plebeian" objections were concerned with the moral and mental attitude of the Slavophils rather than with the admittedly uncongenial peculiarities of the Slavophil way of life. What he could not accept was the glorification of "organic" immobility, the certainty which the Slavophils wore like armour, their *esprit profondément et totalement certitudien*.[60] All Belinsky's own affirmations and negations were wrested, not from the secure consciousness of a divinity and an ensuing clear conscience, but from the unrest which remains within the limits of the world, from a feeling for that which is always striving to outdistance itself and which lay at the root of his eternal disquiet. The Slavophils had no doubts, and their orthodoxy was to Belinsky's mind an illusion, a source of frustration and insincerity. Their sensitive patriotism, with its mystical nostalgia masquerading as realism, had for him too much the air of being contrived and he was at a loss to relate it to the surrounding scene.

Russian history, as interpreted by the Slavophils, and in particular by Konstantin Aksakov, was indeed a piece of fiction in which a perfect future was identified with an imperfect past and an equally imperfect present. They conceived of that future as a life based on true religion and virtue, on ancestral tradition and spontaneous social relations proceeding from a sense of liberty and love. Their idea of organic society differed from the Spencerian theory, effectively criticized later in the century by Mikhailovsky as a comfort to the individualistic *régime* of *laissez-faire*, but a grave danger to the human person—the theory which is based on evolutionary concepts and envisages society as a scene where natural forces take their course. But it also differed from the reactionary and counter-revolutionary traditionalism of de Maistre and de Bonald, with its hierarchical idea of inviolable, sacred authority and the reign of law, which presents an even greater challenge to human personality. The Slavophils could adhere neither to the individualists nor to the authoritarians. They asked for what they thought to be the only truly human society—a society whose roots are to be found in the mystical life of the Church, resolving the conflict between freedom and authority and providing the effective framework for free and just relations that require no established rights and duties for their existence. They claimed to discover the social prototype of such relations in the life of the family, in the intimate ties of kinship and in the coherence of organic, patriarchal groups. They regarded the tendency for every type of political power to express itself in a legal system, instituted and perpetuated through the organs of the State, as a specifically "Western" phenomenon. No such relations obtain in a family, between father and children; and the Christian family was, in their opinion, the basis of social and political life in Old Russia, from which Peter the Great had torn the Russian people by forcing them into the godless, inhuman, legalistic and rationalistic western European mould.

> Historians most veridical
> Assure us that we lack
> That hell-inspired juridical
> Doubt whether white is black.
> In such a narrow border
> Broad natures find no scope:
> The Russian form of order
> Requires a lot more rope. (Almazov)

The facts, so far as Old Russia is concerned, were very different from what the Slavophils imagined them to be.[61] Organic societies do not arise idyllically and they have no less violent origins than social and political revolutions. The Kievian princes and Muscovite Tsars survived a murderous struggle for power. Behind their thrones were the gleaming pikes, the halberds and the axe. Even if "the organic life" existed in Russia before Peter the Great, it came into being as a consequence of, and attended by, conflict and human victims. It in no way precluded, as we have seen, the development of an omnicompetent theocratic order with all the overriding violence, hard vigilance and invasions of freedom involved in both its theory and practice. Neither were the earnest domestic recommendations of the *Domostroy* conducive to the development of human freedom.[62] The truth which the idea of "organic life" may have embraced was a myth, a transcendental representation that bore no relation to the human condition, and in the end could be maintained only by the forcible suppression of whatever was opposed to it.

There was something profoundly ambiguous about the position of the Slavophils. They were originally imbued with a genuine sense of freedom which they shared with their opponents, the Westerners. They did not like the Nicolaian (or indeed the whole post-Petrine) *régime*, nor did they pretend to like it. And the *régime* scarcely looked upon them as friends. They repudiated the coercive actions and compulsory membership by which all political power maintains itself and romantically awaited the return of the Russian State to its spiritual sources where they believed it to be free, popular, and organic. But they overlooked or refused to face the fact that behind the "will" of the State, whether before or after Peter, there stood force, not only as a defence but as a substitute for the "will" acting in its stead; that it was not a free, organic corporation, but a monster which left man scant room to breathe. And their very sufficiency and unquestioning moral and mental attitude tied them by loyalties to a world that was not their own, and in the end defeated their own ends. They were driven more and more to identify with symbols that which symbols may faintly shadow forth, but cannot possibly embody and, as often as not, can only betray. Thus it was that the Slavophil cause was lost through the incorrigible Slavophilism of its adherents.

The story of the degeneration of Slavophilism, of how its volume of inspiration was frittered away into a delta of dozens of conventional mouths where it lost itself in the sand, is a sad story, incomparably sadder than the analogous story of the decline of Westernism. What played a particularly fatal rôle in this process of degeneration was the Slavophil notion of humility. The Slavophils proudly believed the Russian people to be specialists in feeling humble. So did Dostoevsky. But, as Belinsky was quick to discern, whatever may be the religious, moral or intellectual value of this particular virtue, and notwithstanding all the Slavophil hymnologists, its advocacy presented a potential threat to the freedom and dignity of the human person: there was nothing particularly noble or even pleasant about humility against the background of nineteenth-century Russia, i.e. about the humility of the oppressed towards the oppressor, the serf towards the serf owner, the poor towards the rich or, indeed, *vice versa*. The epigoni of Slavophilism soon began to exploit this virtue as well as the whole devout, hieratic, religious pose of the Slavophils, by steering it, consciously and unconsciously, from its spiritual sources towards the less commendable traditions and practices of the Russian State with its jingoism and its usurpations. The Slavophil mystique thus turned into what was known among the "repentant" intelligentsia of the early twentieth century as the "State positivism" (*gosudarstvennyi positivizm*) of people like Boleslav Markievich, Victor Klyushnikov, and above all Mikhail Katkov (1818–87), who became the personification of the Slavophil creed without its idealistic and romantic halo.

Katkov's career can be described as a kind of progressive *mouvement à la baisse*, in which he was helped by an uncommonly acute brain, a persuasive tongue, self-confidence, and a complete indifference to the finer thoughts and spiritual intimations of man, notwithstanding all his piety. Belinsky called him "a bubble inflated with conceit and about to burst at any moment". As he grew older, he drifted into the most determined and cynical reactionary conservatism. He began as an active member of the Stankevich Circle, contributed to Belinsky's initiation into Hegelian philosophy, passed through a brief liberal, "constitutional" phase and eventually came to put his brilliant journalistic gifts at the disposal of the "official nationalism". There was, however, apparently no trace of opportunism in him and he acted throughout from conviction. In the 'fifties he joined, as their editor, the most influential conservative paper, *Moskovskie Vedomosti* ("Moscow Gazette"), and the affiliated review *Russky Vestnik* ("Russian Messenger"), and became the most outspoken enemy of the radical intelligentsia. When the government applied repressive measures it was he who asked for more. No other Russian journalist, not even Bulgarin, went to such lengths in identifying himself with the government and almost equally in making the government listen to his editorial policy. Dostoevsky, who later contributed to Katkov's review, called him *Faddey bulgarinstvuyushchy* ("Faddey the Bulgarinizer"); and Vladimir Soloviev, one of the initiators of the flight of all decent and creative men from the conservative camp, styled him even more pointfully the Nemesis of Slavophilism.[63]

Katkov's disciples and followers went even further: lacking his talent they lost all touch with Russia's spiritual and cultural traditions and reduced their literary activity to summoning the police. Only the great figure of Konstantin Leontiev (1831–91) stood solitarily aloof: the prophet of black reaction and aristocratic contempt for the herd proved too romantic and utopian, and quite useless for the purpose of practical, commonplace conservatism. Dostoevsky, too, may be said to stand apart. For, although the views expressed in his publicistic writings reflect all the banalities of nineteenth century Russian reaction, although his journalistic pronouncements on the radical intelligentsia read like officially inspired pasquinades, his case was infinitely more complex than Katkov's. His real meaning is conveyed not in the *Diary of a Writer*, but in the heroes of his novels, who have endured all the hell of humanity that lives in the soul of the eternal revolutionary; and all Dostoevsky's religious nationalism could not conceal his solidarity with the homeless, uprooted, prodigal and refractory Petersburg man who so appalled the Slavophils.

Belinsky, who even in his pre-Petersburg days was regarded, in Annenkov's words, as "the fermentor of life, appealing to the sword of his friends against his Muscovite enemies" felt the latent oppressive possibilities and influence of the Slavophil myth. In Petersburg he finally lost all capacity for breathing freely whenever it began to operate on him. His reaction became almost physiological. The Muscovite Slavophils in turn embarked on an anti-Belinsky campaign. They or their fellow-travellers issued a spate of pasquinades and epigrams. One of them accused Petersburg (meaning, of course, Belinsky) of "luxuriating on the easy Voltairian chair of protest and despair". Belinsky retorted that nowhere is it easier to sleep than "on the historical feather-bed of Moscow and to the boom of Moscow church bells". Petersburg sang a song which contained the following verse:

> As you would have it, Russia still
> Is as she was till Peter's day:
> Still stuffs her guts with meagre swill,
> Still belches the long night away.

Lashed into fury by polemics, Belinsky, according to Annenkov, became "intensely distrustful". "Between the Petersburgian and the Muscovite", he asserted, aiming at the more tolerant Muscovite Westerners no less than at the Slavophils, "there can be no community of views for long: the former is *arid* by nature, the latter is *unctuous* in all his thoughts and words. They play discrepant parts; they only get into one another's way and grate upon each other." Yet even at his most violent he was prepared to admit, in an essay entitled *Petersburg and Moscow*, that Moscow "is capable of thinking more and better than Petersburg" and to acknowledge all that was genuine and sincere in Slavophilism.

What were the constituents of Belinsky's Westernism, a Westernism of which he is usually considered to be one of the chief and most uncompromising protagonists? Belinsky denounced Muscovite Russia,

93

exalted Peter as a great citizen; he saw no other course but for Russians to become once more the pupils of modern western, progressive and scientific Europe: all this is true up to a point, but is nevertheless misleading. In the last analysis and in his more considered judgment, his criterion lay neither in the "West" nor in the "East", and he found it neither in ideas nor in institutions, but in that which moved him to attack the deathly abstractions of the metaphysical cult, in the fact of being human. "It is high time for us to stop admiring European things because they are not Asiatic. We ought to love, respect, and aspire to them because and if they are human, and to repudiate all that is European where it fails to be human, to repudiate it as energetically as we repudiate all that is Asiatic where *it* lacks humanity."[64]

Having wearied of the soul of nations and continents, he was no more anxious to discover the "Western" than the "Eastern" soul. He spoke, on the contrary, of the "absurd attempts to contrast nationality with humanity" and declared that he was prepared in this respect "to side with the Slavophils rather than to remain with the humanistic cosmopolitans, because if the former err, they do so like living human beings, whereas the latter speak of truth as if they had found it in a text-book on logic. . . . Fortunately, however, I hope to stand where I am and not to side with anybody."[65] Only that which is genuinely human, whether western or Russian, deserves approbation. Hence Belinsky's "biographical" interpretation of history, valuable perhaps in our mass-ridden civilization for its suggestiveness rather than for its empirical validity. "Historical development", he wrote in the same article, "is enacted always and everywhere through human personality; and this explains why the history of every nation resembles a combination of the biographies of individuals." "Great men" are those by whom an essential truth is expressed, a response which has universal historical importance because it is their own, unique and creative response, and which, on account of its very creativity, calls in question the existing order, or all attempts to turn "becoming" into "being". Belinsky's eloquent tributes to Peter the Great are largely a reflection of this attitude. Unlike the Slavophils, or at any rate, those with whose ideas he was familiar, he attributed to the Russians the virtue of being unable or unwilling to preserve and to absolutize anything, of believing truth to begin with the doubt of all truths, and moral valuations with condemnations and negations. He saw Peter's revolution as an act of national self-denunciation, which must be constantly renewed if it is to be fruitful and creative, but which his successors have betrayed by trying to keep Russia in the condition she had reached in 1800.[66] Peter was to his mind the huge question mark over all the partial achievements and betrayals of Russian history, the historical model for that daring venture, that cruel, prophetic Nay, that self-accusatory genius which informed post-Petrine Russian literature from Novikov to Gogol and, indeed, beyond Gogol and Belinsky himself, in Shchedrin and the Nihilists, in Tolstoy and Soloviev, in the Russian Symbolists and the "Landmarks" intelligentsia.

It is of some interest that Belinsky's reactions to western Europe, where he spent a few months in 1847 on account of his failing health, moved him to express views similar to those in Herzen's *Letters from France and Italy*. Kavelin recalls that, on his return from abroad, in a conversation with Granovsky in Moscow at which Kavelin was present, Belinsky spoke of the Russians as the people who would reveal the ways of undoing the evils of western European society and civilization.[67] "Did you like being abroad?" Goncharov asked him, to which Belinsky replied laconically: "Babylon!" "It is strange", wrote Annenkov, "that this admirer of the West and of western culture, on his way through the West, stood mute and listless before the monuments of that culture, as if absorbed in a wholly other, alien thought." The western European world, the "land of holy wonders" as it appeared even to the Slavophil Khomyakov and to Dostoevsky, left him with a sense of having been cheated or more, betrayed, and helped him to shed yet another illusion. Or was he, as Turgenev suggests, just "too much of a Russian, feeling like a fish out of water outside Russia", and, perhaps, scarcely differing in this respect from his erstwhile friend and later opponent Konstantin Aksakov? And yet it sufficed for the Slavophils to express their claim to have discovered a stable and secure foundation of life in some past or present idol to bring out all the intellectual and spiritual incompatibility of their respective attitudes. This brings me to Belinsky's last word, his famous letter from abroad to Gogol on the occasion of Gogol's book *Selected Passages from a Correspondence with Friends*, which appeared in 1847.

Gogol's *Correspondence* (or, more accurately, a collection of sermons and exhortations) is a strange document, whose strangeness becomes apparent when seen in the context of the even stranger personality of its author.[68] When he wrote it Gogol had already fallen a tragic victim to that haunted and perilous journey through darkness of which the grotesque figures of his artistic imagination have been the visual expressions. Shut up in the world of nightmares, which he himself had created, but which was directly related to the realities of Russian life—a world inhabited by men and women personifying a blend of demonism and vulgarity (Gogol's *poshlost*)—Gogol was driven to melancholia and obsession by guilt, from melancholia and guilt to a passion for self-improvement and the improvement of others, and from that passion to religious monomania. The *Correspondence* was a fruit of the middle phase in which his desperate straining after moral perfection moved him to declare his art wicked and to exchange it for a swamp of moralistic platitudes choking his diseased and entangled mind. But it was unmistakably bound up with the other experiences, since the theory and practice of self-improvement often proceeds from a sinister and malignant instinct for distortion, from squinting souls which love, as did Gogol, the hidden crannies and back-doors of human existence.

The moral emphasis of the *Correspondence* lay in the attribution of a divine right and quality to the existing order of things. Nothing that is is "in vain", Gogol insists again and again. It is not "in vain" that God has decreed some women to be beautiful and others ugly; that some men are Governors General and others their clerks, some slaves and others slave-owners; that some are oppressed and others their oppressors. "God would ask you for an account if you were to change your calling for another, because everyone must serve God in his allotted station." Gogol knows no limits in singing the praise of divine wisdom and enjoins his fellow-countrymen to behold its revelation, not only in the beauty and ugliness of female faces, but in the social, political and administrative dispensations of the Tsarist State and in the established rules and patterns of domestic life. Even the Table of Ranks of the Russian nobility and the Russian notabilities is pronounced of divine, providential order. Any office, Gogol argues, can be justified by the personal qualities of its holder, so that one ought to discuss (although Gogol does not actually do so) the handiness and dexterity of the public hangman. Serfdom and poverty are dealt with on the Dickensian *Christmas Carol* basis, with more and better cabbage soup for the deserving impoverished brethren in Christ. The invitation to fulfil the duty of conscientious conformity is accompanied by exhortations to repent of one's sin against God and the divinely planned order of life, and to acknowledge that the Orthodox Church possesses all the necessary remedies for solving the questions which preoccupy nineteenth-century mankind.

Gogol expected his book to be received "with awe and gratitude", but when it appeared even his best friends, the Slavophils, were outraged, although they accused him chiefly of pride, of assuming the rôle of a would-be prophet, and of being rude and pompous. "For the sake of Christ himself", he wrote to Aksakov on hearing about this reception, "put yourself in my place, so that you can gain some notion of what I am going through and tell me what am I to do? What and how am I to write now?" To Belinsky this was nothing less than treason to the cause to which he believed Gogol to have dedicated his art. The violence of his reaction was partly due to the painful memories of his own defection in the past; but, whereas for Belinsky "reconciliation with reality" was a circuitous way of being brought into life and of recovering his sense of humanity, for Gogol it proved a revenge on life and a way of utter dehumanization. By the time he was writing his letter to Gogol, that is, after having himself experienced Gogol's *inferno*, inhabited as it was by "dead souls", by the Khlestakovs and the Chichikovs, the Sobakevichs and the Nozdrevs, there was little left for Belinsky to idealize in the world in which he lived. There was no longer time or room to surrender to the dreams of paradygmatic Russia, or of any other paradygmatic world, not even that which opened up before him in his inspired Moscow Circle days.

"Russia needs no sermons (she has had enough of them!)", Belinsky wrote, "but an awakening among the people of the sense of human dignity lost in dirt and dust during so many centuries. . . . She presents the ghastly spectacle of a country where human beings are sold without even that justification of which American plantation lords cunningly avail themselves, by maintaining that a negro is not a man. . . . The most vital national questions in Russia now are the abolition of serfdom, the abolition of corporal punishment, the implementation of at least those laws which already exist. The government itself is conscious of the situation, knowing well what landlords do with their peasants and how many of them are massacred every year by the peasants; and it provides evidence of its knowledge by its own timid and fruitless half-measures in favour of the white negroes and by its comic substitution of a cat of one tail for a cat of three tails.

"These are the questions with which Russia is concerned in her apathetic sleep. And at such a time a great writer, who contributed so greatly to the recovery of awareness in Russia by his wonderful artistic and deeply truthful creations and who enabled her to look at herself as if in a mirror, comes forward with a book in which, in the name of Christ and the Church . . ., he teaches the tyrant-landlord to grow rich at the expense of the peasants. And this should not rouse me to indignation? . . . If indeed you had made an attempt on my life, even then I would not have hated you as much as for these lines you have written. . . .

"Preacher of the knout, apostle of ignorance, defender of darkness and oppression, eulogist of Tartar morals, what are you doing? Look under your feet—you are standing over a precipice. . . . I can understand that you should rely upon the Orthodox Church as a support for such tenets. It has always been a prop for the knout and a fawner upon despotism. But Christ: why do you drag him into all this? He was the first to bring man freedom . . ., and to seal and avouch his truth by suffering. . . . That is why some Voltaire, who, armed with ridicule, extinguished the fires of fanaticism in Europe, is, of course, more of a son of Christ, flesh of his flesh and bone of his bone, than all your priests, bishops, metropolitans and patriarchs. Can it be that you do not know this? It is, after all, no news to any schoolboy. . . .

"As I see it, you fail to understand the Russian reading public. Its character is determined by the condition of Russian society in which fresh energies are seething and striving to express themselves, but, crushed by heavy oppression, they succeed only in producing despair, weariness and apathy. Only in literature, is there still life and movement, despite the Tartar censorship. That is why the vocation of the writer stands so high in our esteem, why literary success comes so easily even to those who have little talent. The title of a poet, the status of a literary man have for some time already come to substitute the tawdry brilliance of uniforms and epaulets. That is why we reward every so-called liberal tendency with particular attention, even where there is poverty of talent, and why esteem for talent, however great, wanes whenever it surrenders, sincerely or not, to the service of 'Orthodoxy, autocracy and nationality'.

"Your conversion may, for all I know, have been sincere, but the idea of bringing it to the knowledge of the public was most unfortunate. The time of naïve piety has long since passed even in our society. It has come to understand that . . . only those people look for Christ in Jerusalem who have either never borne him in their hearts or have lost him altogether. He who is capable of suffering when he sees the suffering of another, he who is grieved at the spectacle of his oppressed brethren, is bearing Christ in his heart and does not need to go on foot to Jerusalem. The humility which you preach is, in the first place, not a new thing and, in the second, sounds like terrible pride and like a shameful degradation of human dignity. The idea of turning into some figure of spectral perfection, of becoming higher than everybody else by means of humility, can only be a fruit of pride or of idiocy: in both cases it leads to hypocrisy, bigotry and Chinadom. You have dared in your book to speak cynically and uncleanly not only about others (this would be no more than impoliteness) but about yourself, and this is just unsavoury: for if a man who hits another in the face provokes indignation, a man who hits himself in the face provokes contempt. No, you have not been illuminated: you are darkened. You have failed to understand either the spirit or the letter of Christianity in our time. Your book radiates not the truth of the Christian teaching but a sickly fear of death, the devil and hell. . . . Were it not for the fact that you speak of yourself as a writer, who would have thought that this far-fetched, dishevelled farrago of words and phrases is a product of the author of *Government Inspector* and *Dead Souls*. . . .

"I cannot hum and haw, I cannot avoid the issue—it's not in my nature. I leave it to you or to time to prove that I was wrong in my conclusions about you. I shall be the first to rejoice when the proof comes, but I shall not repent of what I have said to you. What is at stake is not my person or yours, but a matter which goes beyond me and even you: the matter of truth . . ."—"If you love Russia", Belinsky cruelly concluded, "you will rejoice with me in the disaster that has befallen your book."[69]

The greater the esteem in which Belinsky held Gogol, the deeper and more intense his indignation at Gogol's pious fraud was bound to be. He did not even spare him the charge of insincerity; and in view of the ghastly countenance of the very thing to which Gogol was paying homage, it cannot cause surprise that his sincerity was not accepted, although Belinsky did in fact realize how profoundly unhappy Gogol must have been when he wrote his book.

Belinsky's letter, which Herzen described as "a piece of genius", spread clandestinely throughout Russia, at the risk of imprisonment and exile to Siberia for those who were found in possession of it. But it was not merely a rebutter of the opinions of Gogol turned reactionary. As such it was effective but by no means remarkable. Its real importance lay in Belinsky's exposure of the utter emptiness and monstrosity of that ideal of the "good" which, in Gogol's own words, has lost its goodness, in his critique of the illusory value of those values with whose help Gogol, and with Gogol a major section of Russian society, attempted to sanctify a vulgar and ruthless world. He was warning Gogol that this "good" is a result, a symptom and a mask of a diseased body and a diseased soul, as well as a fetter for and drug against their regeneration. It is customary to see the point of disagreement between Gogol and Belinsky in their respective answers to the problem of the relation of the human person to society: whereas Belinsky is alleged to hold out to man the prospect of absorption in society, Gogol is said to defend the ideal of individual salvation. In point of fact, however, it is Gogol who wallows in the pleasures of "serving the State" (as he cheerfully admits in his *Author's Confession*). It is Gogol who preaches the salvation of man through comfortable submersion in society, in which the "common man" with his "common good", the dumb ox, the "we", the "all of us" are to reign supreme. Hence the incredibly banal and *bourgeois* utilitarian morality which pervades so many of his "prophetic" utterances. "My mind", he let out in his *Confession*, "had always been inclined towards the ponderable and the useful." He was at bottom devoid even of any true religious disposition: he forced himself into religion. He only had a pious and somewhat superstitious Ukranian's fear of death, and terror of hell strengthened by belief in the Devil. Indeed, Gogol's constricted and constipated hortative mentality, his tight confinement to finite certitudes, his nookishness, contrast strikingly with the angry and undismayed, but austere spirit of freedom which kindles Belinsky's rebuke. On Belinsky's atheistic lips Christianity meant danger to a world which seeks to strengthen its self-esteem by claiming divine origin and right for its compulsory affairs.

But at the time Belinsky wrote his letter to Gogol he was no longer the fighter of old. That letter, as Herzen remarked when he saw him in Paris for the last time, was evidence of rare moments of revived energy when the ebbing fire of his spirit glowed brightly. He was already burnt out by the intensity of his mental strains and the rapid dissolution of his consumptive body. He died in Petersburg on the 7th of June 1848.

4. THE FREEDOM AND COMMITMENT OF THE WRITER

Belinsky made no claims to be either a philosopher or a social and political thinker. His thoughts on philosophical, social and political matters, important though they were for him and important though they may be found to be for us, were haphazard, wayward and disjointed thoughts, reflecting the varying pressures to which he was constantly open from within and from without. But in one sphere alone Belinsky's preoccupations showed purpose and authority, and this was literature, to which his whole life was devoted; and it would be a complete travesty of Belinsky to omit a discussion of him as a literary critic. Even in the white heat of his infatuation with Hegelianism he wrote to Bakunin: "Whenever it is a question of art . . . I am confident and bold, and my confidence and boldness in this respect go so far as to defy the authority of Hegel himself." "Russian literature is my life and my blood", he said even while suffering under the *régime* of his exploiting editors. All his most distinguished older and younger literary contemporaries, Turgenev, Goncharov, Gogol, Nekrasov, Tolstoy, even Pushkin are unanimous in recognizing his "profound feeling for literary values" (Goncharov), his "infallible literary taste" (Turgenev). These and similar testimonies strike one by their contrast with the estimate of Belinsky's worth as literary critic current in more recent years. In the first two decades of this century it was, indeed, almost a matter of fashion to denigrate Belinsky; and this was followed, in post-revolutionary Russia, by conventional and dogmatic adulation of him. Victor Shklovsky, one of the most influential critics immediately before and after the Revolution, voiced a widespread attitude (not shared, however, by such leading Symbolists as Alexander Blok and Andrey Bely) when he said that he "detested Belinsky and all the other (fortunately unsuccessful) murderers of Russian literature" who have "swamped it with theory", while Soviet writers never tire of declining and conjugating the theme of Belinsky as "great", "illustrious" and "super-eminent", as the "father", "paragon" and "chief propagator" of "revolutionary-democratic aesthetics and criticism" who has successfully explained the mind of Russian writers and the development of their ideas.

There are reasons to believe that Pushkin, Turgenev, Goncharov, Blok and the Soviet writers are right, whereas Shklovsky, the Futurists, the Acmeists, the Formalists are wrong. It would serve a more useful purpose, however, to set forth the fundamental principles of Belinsky's literary activity than to join in the domestic dispute over reputations.

Belinsky's literary criticism, Turgenev says, "had no system: critical theories, arguments for or against different literary forms, and so on, did not greatly preoccupy him (it would have been out of season if they had). He was in this, as in other respects, very Russian, feeling a stranger in the world of abstractions. Literature for him was one of the most abundant manifestations of life. In this matter, no one was his teacher or guide. Most of his erudition was derived from the circle of his Moscow friends. He owed them a great deal, they gave into his hands the instruments, but no one could tell him how to use them: in this he remained profoundly individual, more individual than Stankevich. Not one of his associates and mentors was capable of taking his place, of doing his job, because he surpassed them all without exception in the power and sensitivity of his aesthetic perception, in his almost infallible taste."[70] He frequently fell a victim to extremes, to precipitate conclusions, to violent likes and dislikes; he was impelled to fight his truly decisive battles in other than artistic fields, while trying simultaneously to explain the intricacies of Pushkin's and Lermontov's poetry. Sometimes, when he disagreed on fundamental issues, he was ready to reject what a writer had to say before considering what was said, for it is the writer himself whom he rejected. Yet he did so not for lack of imagination, for lack of plurality of aesthetic experiences, but because he could not assume a multiple loyalty. And even in his denials he did not fail to preserve a sense of artistic discrimination and an ability to discern talent. His errors of literary judgment were few and far between, but then even such a perfect artist as Pushkin was subject to them, not to mention Tolstoy and Dostoevsky. Belinsky's verdicts on Lermontov, Gogol, Goncharov, Turgenev, Dostoevsky and many others provide evidence of his extraordinary instinct. He was endowed, above all, with the gift of sympathy and even more with that of empathy, which enabled him to feel himself into his authors, think their thoughts, suffer their emotions, rather than attend to his own reactions—a gift all the more surprising in view of the more than usually extreme and passionate character of these reactions. He knew, as Turgenev testifies from personal experience and as Dostoevsky somewhat grudgingly admits, how to encourage, with candour and generosity, the first literary attempts of young and inexperienced authors, when they showed the slightest sign of talent; and, with equal candour, how to criticize their subsequent performance if they showed signs of deterioration, mercilessly exposing errors in taste, conception or execution, and exploding literary presumptions.

Belinsky's best essays are those dealing with Russian rather than foreign literature, and they belong especially to the beginning and the end of his career as literary critic. He started by philosophizing about literature, his thought turning, as seems to have become customary among philosophers of art, largely upon the question whether aesthetic judgments are subjective or objective, whether they express the personal preferences and prejudices of the judge or refer to some intrinsic quality possessed by the work under judgment. In accordance with his early idealistic views, his own discussion of literary works was based on the assumption that art enables us to perceive a reality which lies outside that of which we are normally aware, that it arouses emotions which are not of this world. His first important article of literary criticism ("Literary Musings" in Nadezhdin's *Telescope*) began with the solemn statement: "God's entire, boundless world of beauty is the breath of the one eternal idea, the thought of the one eternal God."—"Art is the reflection, in sounds, words and colours, of the life of the one eternal idea." It is the "unconscious expression of the creative spirit", "a fruit of aesthetic intuition". In his literary criticism Belinsky was, in fact, professing and applying the faith which the world owes not so much to romantic idealism as to a somewhat battered Platonism—the faith in an Absolute Beauty throned above the earth like an Alabaster Lady on a cloud and, from time to time, coming down to earth to generate the heat of the artist's fancy. This moved him to almost unqualified hostility towards every kind of "tendency" in art: he even repudiated Schiller, to whom he was devoted in his youth, because he suspected him of being tendentious. Poetry became for him primarily a stream of indefinite suggestions, an expression of unencumbered inspiration, a way of saying nothing in particular.

> I know not yet what I shall sing
> I only know the song is there. (Fet.)

But even in his advocacy of "pure art" he was anything but "pure": he could only be partial in his very demand for objectivity, polluting purity and enjoying the privilege of sacrificing it to his own passionately held point of view.

The immediate predecessors of Belinsky were the critics Marlinsky, Polevoy, Nadezhdin and others, who prided themselves on a very lofty conception of art, on their philosophical idealism, on their contempt for a purely stylistic approach to literature. They scoffed at the old classical tradition, which in fact hardly ever existed in Russia, they reproached it for its insincerity, lifelessness and domination by tyrannical rules that reduce the creative writer to a pedant. It was an echo of the young French critical school of the Restoration period, and had as little in common with the authentic literary traditions in Russia as had the late eighteenth-century classical *belles-lettres* (*izyashchnaya slovesnost*). Its only importance lay in the account of a search for new pathways in literature.

Though still dependent on these influences, Belinsky was increasingly showing an appreciation of the purpose and the consequent limitation of mere fantasy. He began to apply his at the time favourite criterion of "sincerity" to the effusions of romanticism itself, to set aside inappropriate ideas and feelings in his aesthetic evaluations, to disapprove of what he called "romantic dishevelment". He sensed that fantasy is only justified and successful when it uses its freedom to discover a new logic in which the uses and abuses of our world are still mirrored. This enabled him to write at this early period some of the most illuminating criticism of Russian folklore (popular songs, *byliny*, tales, and the poems of the "Russian Burns", Aleksey Koltsov [1808–42]) all of which show that he was by no means assuming literary inspiration to be an automatic passport out of the tangible, human world.

In the long run "pure literature" proved to Belinsky as impossible as "pure philosophy", and just as he was not afraid to associate the practice of philosophy with the promotion of opinion, one sees him linking literature with the function of prophecy and witness. The principle of "art for art's sake" gives place to that of art for life's sake. He is led more and more to emphasize, sometimes almost to exaggerate, a grave and dedicated attitude to art of which the latter to Gogol provides the most outspoken example. This new attitude, evident in Belinsky's writings ever since he joined the Petersburg *Annals of the Fatherland* and which became the *leitmotif* of his literary criticism from the middle of the 'forties, was for him, after many evasions, a way of becoming human again. It was also Belinsky's contribution to the rise and growth of "realism", which dominated imaginative writing in Russia throughout the latter half of the nineteenth century, from Gogol to Chekhov, and even to Gorky, constituting Russia's great legacy to European literature. Indeed, he may be regarded as its true progenitor and prophet.[71] The main characteristics of this literary tradition are well known to the reader of Russian literature, and this is not the place to discuss its merits and limitations. The problem which Belinsky, and with or through him Russian nineteenth-century literature as a whole, brought to light was the problem of the freedom of the writer and his commitment in the world.

Fundamentally we can conceive of man's creative activity only as free and independent, and, therefore, as standing in no need of justification by anything outside itself. In creating man ceases to be satisfied, he rises above the world which demands his acceptance and changes it into a world he dominates: he brings about a world of new values, perspectives and attitudes. His activity is to this extent autonomous and may not be annexed. To regard it as existing for, or subordinated to, something else is but a natural impertinence of politics or a natural presumption of theology. It is not even immediately relevant to say that artists are known to see their work in the light of their religious or social allegiances, even though their work may be characterized by such allegiances. Whether art is art can only be determined by artistic standards. The only "Absolute" that can inspire an artist is the "Absolute" of his creativity, hidden within it, rather than persisting in some independent validity outside it. And it is through being vowed to this Absolute that his work has power to move us.

But to separate the creative act of man from extraneous pressures, from religious and social infringements, and the pulpits of human opinion is not to separate it from humanity. The "perfect creator", the "pure artist" are, as Belinsky observed, fictions leading to sterile dreams, which have been the opium and the undoing of so many artists.[72] Every creator makes something from the world in which he lives, even while rising above it or rejecting it. He must needs ask about his own attitude towards the world, towards history, towards his fellow-men, no less than towards himself. The sources of his activity are in life itself, whether that life be evil or good. Perhaps more than any other artist the imaginative writer is first of all a literary humanist. He creates human beings who suffer all that men are capable of suffering in a given situation, and his skill lets us know them as we know ourselves. He communicates the forces which move men to love and to hate, to act and to speak, to accept and to refuse.

Nowhere perhaps has this twofold character of creative activity been enacted with such intensity as in Russian literature of the nineteenth century, for Russia knew little of the world in which men could simply sit back and enjoy their freedom from anxiety and their unobtrusive and civilized pleasures of life, where literature and the arts themselves were a means of hiding the issue in question. Pushkin affirmed the creative freedom and autonomy of the poet. He rose against the "mob" with its behests and intimations. The mob which he resisted was not, of course, the Russian "people", the peasants, the "toiling masses", but above all the artistocratic society in which he lived and which submitted him to its pressures. It is in the "inane and hollow life" of the "worldly throng" that he experienced the poet's solitude until his awakened soul was stirred by "Apollo's word". The spirit of freedom impels him to turn away "from the idol of the day" and to resist its commonplace, vain and odious presence.

> We were not born to speed your bustling day,
> To swell your takings, or to drug your fears:
> We stir to winds that blow from far away,
> Hear secret music, speak to unseen ears.

Such sentiments, which in Pushkin were free from the romantic undertones ordinarily associated with them, do not, of course, exhaust his universal genius, but they are an important element in it. Belinsky was aware of their importance. The two processes, seemingly contradictory, but by the paradox of life interdependent, were constantly present to him, acting like a simultaneous flood and ebb in his own consciousness: the flood coming in solitude, the ebb going in the call to extend himself by sympathy, solicitude and watchfulness. Writing, in 1842, of romantic experience, he spoke of it as "a world of inwardness . . . , a world of moral sensibility and faith, the world of human hearts that strain after infinity". It is "the mysterious laboratory of inward man, where he is persistently brought face to face with the question of life and death, of his ultimate personal destiny, of love, happiness and pain. . . . Strong natures, on plunging into this world of inward vision, could turn into mystical dreamers, into inspired madmen, into living shadows among strange and alien surroundings. People with stunted and shallow minds grow pietistic . . . and moralistic. But woe unto him who is swept away by bustling extraversion (*vneshnost*), and turns into a man of outwardness (*vneshny chelovek*), with nothing left within him to withstand the storms outside; he is void of moral depth, void of resources to discern reality. All is cold, arid and unfeeling within him. He is incapable of love. He is a citizen, a warrior, a merchant, he is anything you like, but he is never a human being. Thus both . . . the inward and the outward are limiting worlds; . . . both stand in need of each other, and their intimate coinherence is the mark of the true stature of man. . . . Let it [romantic experience] take hold of our minds, let it stir our imagination and our fanaticism: for him whose nature is strong and sensitive it will be offset . . . by that other voice which calls him into the world of historical reality."

Belinsky's reactions to Lermontov are particularly significant in this connection. His first meeting with him (in the Caucasus in 1837) was very unfortunate. Lermontov made fun of his seriousness and referred to him as a "ponderous windbag" and a "jack-pudding", while Belinsky called him a "slick and cynical bully" and a snob. Two or three years later their antipathy turned into mutual admiration.[73] What finally converted Belinsky was Lermontov's vindication of man's singularity and revolt, which, in his "realistic" period, had none of the posturing and haughtiness of his earlier romantic days, and yet preserved all its irony and vigour. Lermontov became for him the embodiment of his own protest against the flattening and mendacious worldliness which invades human life and pervades what he described in curiously modern terms as "commercialized literature", the embodiment of his own search for freedom, which saves man both from effete solitude and from the compulsive mediocrity of the crowd.

In using literature for prophetic ends he was breaking down the isolation of the writer, and yet he could not refuse to look into the deep. A prophet turns his attention upwards and outwards, as well as inwards and downwards: he is in conflict with society, unacknowledged and ill-used by it, and, at the same time, he is committed to it, bearing the burden of the world outside, forecasting the world's future, bringing judgment and promise of renewal. The solitude of the prophet, alike as a witness of divine revelation and as a social reformer, an artist or a thinker, does not belong to the small and secure world of aesthetes, of select cultural *élites*, or of thinkers confined within their mental isolation. He is not hugging himself in his inner dreams, either violent or beatific. Indeed, he is not free to do anything separately or to be anything separately: his mission is to serve his fellow-men even while rebelling against them. Yet he fulfils, not the demands of his environment, but of truth, and receives his charge, not from society, but for it. It is in this sense that Belinsky spoke of literature as a means of spiritual communion between people, and that for him only those ideas could give true inspiration to the artist which promote communion between men.

What Belinsky found increasingly impossible to accept was a literature which cultivates the constriction of experience and shuts all doors to human distress. With all his profound admiration for and appreciation of Pushkin he could not, for instance, help being infuriated by certain passages in Pushkin's well-known poem *The Poet and the Mob*, which ends with the lines quoted above, referring to the mob's preference for "the pot in the oven" over Apollo's genius, because it gets its swill from it. "Of course, the pot is dearer", repeated Belinsky, winging his way from one corner of the room to the other and his eyes glistening, "of course, it is dearer. It's not my food, it's the food of my family, of the starveling round the corner, and before marvelling at the loveliness of an idol, be it even an arch-phidian Apollo, it is my right and duty to feed them—in the teeth of all the raging coxcombs and poetasters." Turgenev, who recalls the incident in his Reminiscences of Belinsky, remarks that all this went hand-in-hand with his "innate, almost physiological feeling for art". Belinsky stood in silence, apparently quite unmoved before the Sistine Madonna in Dresden because "he perceived in her expression a disregard for the wants and sufferings of this inglorious world of ours" (Annenkov). He could not bear literary men with stuffed ears, no longer listening to life, but only talking about it, and spinning intricate, delicate or even beautiful cobwebs; and his own literary criticism became more and more concerned with the value of literature for living.

He felt no need, therefore, to concentrate on technical discussion and would not allow aesthetic criteria where false moral choices have been made. This is not to say that he was incapable of pure literary analysis or that he was unaware of subtleties and complications beyond mere utility. His account of Pushkin's *Stone Guest*, or the later essay on Griboedov's *Woe from Wit* (which contains more about Gogol than Griboedov), particularly the analysis of the *Story of How Ivan Ivanovich Quarrelled with Ivan Nikiforovich*, is convincing evidence of Belinsky's extraordinary exploratory and interpretative gift. But as a rule, he looked first at what was being said, and only secondarily at how it was said. The criterion was: is it on the side of humanity and truth? If it was not, Belinsky tended to discard it and to give a vigorous exposition of what he considered to be the real need, with the ensuing temptation, least of all evident in his later criticism, to succumb to vagueness, dilating and unhelpful rhetoric. Yet any attempt to substitute "tracts for novels", as he put it, or "to make books instead of creating them", to rely on the title of a book for the book's literary value, met with immediate dissent on his part. What he expected was the building up of the meaning or the idea by the literary technique, the mode of argument, the use of language, character, scene, so that in the end the "teaching" is the presentation, and *vice versa*. He was looking in a writer, especially in a novelist, for an ability to create depth, to make a particular situation, a fragment, even a detail extend into a wider range and deepen until the horizon is no longer within sight, until the particular acquires a universal human significance.[74]

His articles of literary criticism provoke thought, but they do not, on the whole, irradiate our reading, or create an atmosphere in which literature can merely be pleasing. They are not an exercise in the free play of natural gaiety, in amusement and urbanity. To be that would have required a different world from the one in which he lived or, perhaps, different from any world inhabited by men—a world reduced to the manageable status of a still-life, with an abundance of beautiful things and human beings lounging amongst them. The world in which he lived provided no such opportunities, and even when it did, he could never forget "the nightmares of history". Life for him became more exacting than writing. And so it became for the whole of Russian nineteenth-century literature from Gogol onwards.

Gogol was in search of dedicated, redemptive art. He could never have affirmed, as Pushkin did, that we "stir to winds that blow from far away". While Pushkin's work, or a major portion of it, radiates an atmosphere of ease, delight, and effervescence, Gogol reproduced a world of farce and comedy which, with all his extraordinary power of imagination, was the saddest and most cruel poetry, and a revenge upon life, expressed with such absurdity in that ugliest fruit on the tree of Russian literature—the *Correspondence with Friends*. Gogol's tragic end showed him to be a victim of his own search to transcend literature, to presume a purpose for art which lies beyond or beneath it. His disquietude about the ultimate justification of art prefigured the persistent attempt by Russian writers to use art as a means for denying it. It underlies the spiritual experience and the literary development of Tolstoy; it can be seen in the artistic experience of the Russian Symbolists; it provides the impetus for the destructive onslaught on art and culture of the Russian Nihilists. Indeed, the social, political and religious varieties of nihilistic experience are recurring phenomena in Russia, and, as Dostoevsky has observed, with Berdyaev and others in his wake, all Russians are at bottom nihilists. So was Belinsky, "the apostle of negation, who", in Goncharov's words, "was destined to play in the realm of criticism the same rôle that Gogol played, by different means, in the realm of art, and that, in still different ways, was to be played out by Russian literature as a whole".

Chapter Three

Mikhail Bakunin

(1814–1876)

THE history of Russian thought knows few men who demand our involvement in their own mental universe to such an extent as Bakunin. As for his contemporaries and associates there is a great deal to pay and to endure if we are to listen to and understand, let alone to accept him. That is why his reputation was subject to such vicissitudes and why there are so many and such divergent estimates of him. Bakunin's eventful and entangled life has been explored in greater detail than that of almost any other Russian revolutionary of the nineteenth century.[1] The same cannot, however, be said of Bakunin's striking personality and outlook, and the study of his character and ideas is still capable of yielding many surprises.[2]

Bakunin was born and grew up in what was in many ways a typical "nest of gentlefolk". His father was a moderately cultivated man of mildly liberal opinions, and the Bakunin family was not only representative of all that was noble in the old ideals of the Russian gentry, but became also in due course a "nest" of intense intellectual activity carried on by the numerous young members of the family and by Mikhail Bakunin in particular. Belinsky described it as a hot-bed of "semi-philosophical and semi-mystical exultation".[3] Bakunin was fond of his "kind and indulgent" father, whose "conservative fanaticism of the frightened liberal" (as Bakunin characterized him) served as an excuse for out-manœuvring him and opposing his wishes whenever they clashed with his own. But he disliked his mother, whom he regarded, not without some justification, as "vainglorious and egotistical", and in whose despotic behaviour some biographers saw a source of Bakunin's congenital hatred of every restriction of liberty.[4] It is not surprising that his attitude towards his parents as well as his wilful and passionate relations with his sisters became a rewarding subject for psychoanalytical detection, although what follows will show perhaps that his inner and outer conflicts were both more concrete and deeper than any psychoanalytical case-history might indicate.

Bakunin's formal education began in a Cadet Corps, from which he was removed for slackness to an ordinary regiment, serving for a time in White Russia. But at the age of twenty-one he resigned his commission in order to escape from the "tedium and apathy" of military life and to devote himself to "science", which, in the then prevailing idiom, meant philosophy. Without informing his father of his decision, he betook himself to Moscow where he met Stankevich, Belinsky, Herzen and other members of the Moscow Circles. This meeting marked the beginning of an intellectual development whose pattern is already familiar from the story of Belinsky's philosophical pilgrimage, as well as from that of so many of Bakunin's contemporaries during the "remarkable decade". He embarked on a serious and determined study of philosophy, religion, mysticism, and even the classical languages. With an enthusiasm even more infectious than Belinsky's and, like Belinsky, demonstrating the significance of an intellectual effort which fails because its chosen standards have been too rigorously applied, he drove through the succession of the already known blind-alleys of German idealism—Schelling, Fichte and Hegel. Impelled by a kind of savage and passionate thirst for knowledge, he left no stone unturned until he succeeded in getting to Berlin—the Mecca of philosophy for so many Russians at the time—to drink there at the sources of Hegelian wisdom; which, on arrival in the Prussian capital in 1840, he proceeded to do, in the company of Turgenev, by assiduously attending University lectures, reading, and spending nights in philosophical discussion.[5]

A split, however, was revealed among the Hegelians in Berlin. Bakunin became acquainted with the works of Strauss, Feuerbach and other representatives of the Hegelian Left, and discovered the revolutionary implications of Hegelianism. It was at this time (in 1842) that he wrote for Ruge's Left Hegelian *Deutsche Jahrbücher* one of his most powerful and brilliant essays, *Reaction in Germany*, which produced a profound impression on Herzen and Belinsky, and created something of a sensation in European revolutionary circles.[6] Although still largely concerned with philosophical questions, it marked his conversion from an "abstract philosopher" to an "abstract revolutionary". From 1844–7 we find him in Paris, where he was still capable of spending whole nights in philosophical discussion (with Proudhon amongst others). But the revolution of 1848 finally revealed to him his true vocation of an active revolutionary. Thus began Bakunin's "years of wandering", in the course of which he roved from place to place, expelled, persecuted, hiding, escaping, starving, becoming the star, or rather comet, of Europe in revolt, and in particular of the revolt of Slavdom against Austro-

Hungarian autocracy. "Bakunin has become a myth", announced the *Dresdener Zeitung*. He successively took part in the risings at Prague and in the Saxon revolution in Dresden. He was arrested, chained, and twice condemned to death, in Saxony and again in Austria, but was finally (in 1851) handed over to the Russian authorities, who imprisoned him in the Fortress of St. Peter and St. Paul, where he was "to rot indefinitely". An attack of scurvy, which caused him to loose all his teeth, gastric diseases and constant tormenting headaches turned the once magnificent and somewhat dandified Bakunin into a "living corpse". It was in this Fortress that he wrote his notorious *Confession* to the Tsar—an account of his activities between 1840–9—and signed it "the repentant sinner Mikhail Bakunin".[7] The Confession was of no avail so far as his imprisonment was concerned. After three years he was transferred to the Schlüsselburg Fortress. Despair, unrelieved loneliness, and, above all, the haunting fear of complete degradation coupled with physical disintegration, brought him near to suicide. But only after the death of Nicolas I, and as a result of renewed attempts by his relatives (especially by his much reviled mother) and a second petition by Bakunin himself, was he granted in 1857 release from the Fortress and sent to perpetual exile to Siberia. In Siberia he married—from boredom rather than from love—a Polish merchant's daughter. He also became friendly with the Governor of Siberia, Nikolai Muraviev, a cousin of his mother; and for a time Bakunin entertained the odd belief that this Siberian Governor, who was admittedly quite exceptionally enlightened for his time, was called upon to lead the liberation of the Slavs from the Austrian yoke. But in 1861 he managed to escape from Siberia and its Governor. Making his way to England *via* Japan and the United States, he arrived in London, and henceforward undertook the direction of a vigorous revolutionary campaign, which was carried on throughout Europe. His impassioned quasi-religious convictions give place to an equally impassioned atheism, and revolutionary Slavism to anarchism, for which he was now fighting on both straight and crooked paths. Indefatigable and irreconcilable, he pursued the undoing of social and political authority and the destruction of all idols and sanctuaries of man's body, mind, and soul. He retired, however, from all activity in 1874 and died two years later in Berne, an almost forgotten, helpless, penniless, and doddering old man—as Turgenev put it, "an old and played out agitator".

The most familiar and by now well-established picture of Bakunin is provided in Herzen's *Memoirs*.[8] "As soon as Bakunin had looked about him and settled in London", Herzen writes, ". . . he set to work. To a passion for propaganda, for agitation, for demagogy, to incessant activity in founding, organizing plots and conspiracies, and establishing contacts, to a belief in their immense significance, Bakunin added a readiness to risk his life, and reckless daring in facing all the consequences."

He argued, preached, gave orders, shouted, decided, arranged, organized and encouraged all day long, all night long, for days and nights on end. In the brief moments he had left he rushed to his writing table, swept a little space clear of cigarette ash and set out to write five, ten, fifteen letters to Semipalatinsk and Arad, to Belgrade and to Constantinople, to Bessarabia, Moldavia and Belaya-Krinitsa. In the middle of a letter he would fling aside the pen and refute the views of some reactionary Dalmatian; then, without finishing his exhortation, snatch up the pen and go on writing. . . . His activity, his laziness, his appetite, his titanic stature and the everlasting perspiration he was in, everything about him, in fact, was on a superhuman scale. He remained as of old a blue-eyed giant with leonine head and a tousled mane. At fifty he was exactly the same vagrant student, the same homeless *bohémien* from the *rue de Bourgogne*, with no thought of the morrow, careless of money, flinging it away when he had it, borrowing it indiscriminately, right and left, when he had not, as simply as children take from their parents, careless of repayment; as simply as he himself would give his last shilling to anyone, only keeping what he needed for cigarettes and tea. This manner of life did not worry him; he was born to be the great vagrant, the great outcast. If anyone had asked him point-blank what he thought of the rights of property, he might have replied as Lalande replied to Napoleon about God: 'Sire, in my pursuits I have not come across any necessity to believe in these rights!'

"When carried away in argument, Bakunin poured on his opponent's head a noisy storm of abuse for which no one else would have been forgiven; everyone forgave Bakunin, and I among the first. Martyanov would sometimes say: 'He is only a grown-up Liza, Alexander Ivanovich, a child; you can't be angry with him!'[9]

"He preserved intact all the habits and customs of his fatherland, that is, of student life in Moscow; heaps of tobacco lay on his table like stores of forage, cigar ash covered his papers, together with half-finished glasses of tea. From morning onwards clouds of smoke hung about the room from a regular chorus of smokers, who smoked as though against time, hurriedly blowing it out and drawing it in—as only Russians and Slavs do smoke, in fact. Many a time I enjoyed the amazement, accompanied by a certain horror and embarrassment, of the landlady's maid, Grace, when at dead of night she brought boiling water and a fifth basin of sugar into this hotbed of Slav emancipation.[10]

"There was something childlike, simple and free from malice about him, and this gave him an extraordinary charm and attracted both the weak and the strong, repelling none but the stiff petty-*bourgeois*. His striking personality, the eccentric and powerful appearance he made everywhere, in the circle of the young in Moscow, in the lecture-room of the Berlin University, among Weitling's Communists and Caussidière's Montagnards, his speeches in Prague, his leadership in Dresden,

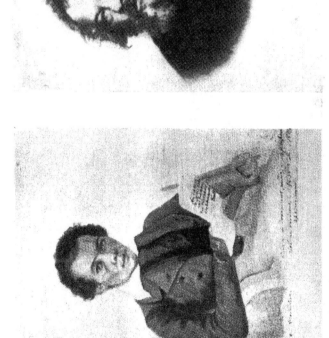

Bakunin at the age of 24
(For inscription see page 123)

Bakunin at the age of 54

[face page 112

his trial, imprisonment, sentence to death, tortures in Austria and surrender to Russia—where he vanished behind the terrible walls of the Alekseevsky Ravelin—make of him one of those original figures which neither the contemporary world nor history can pass by."

It should be noted that this skilful and brilliant portrait, which is amplified by Herzen elsewhere in a similar vein and which is, as so much in Herzen's *Memoirs*, *Dichtung* as well as *Wahrheit*, reflects no less of Herzen's grievances against Bakunin than of Bakunin himself. The grievances were legitimate, and they were shared by many others beside Herzen. One of Bakunin's most intolerable traits was to strike out for absolute domination in personal relationships. His attitude in this was dictated by something fundamental in his character and perhaps in his subconscious. It is true that in his progress through life he limited, or was forced to limit many of his demands, and to take such friends as he could find. But during his early years he seems to have reached a state close to megalomania, trying to subjugate and master his surroundings and give them the imprint of his personality with the imperiousness of a dictator. His first and principal victims were his family, and particularly his sisters. The letters from the Pryamukhino archive show how the private affairs of his sisters as well as their intellectual interests and pursuits were used by Bakunin as a means to establish his unbounded authority over their hearts and minds. "I send you my blessing", he wrote to them in 1842, already from abroad, "—my gift for the New Year; and you must accept it, because you know I have always been your spiritual father." There seemed to be no limit to adoration for Bakunin among his sisters, and they, together with most of his other women friends, competed in their worship of him. Life in Pryamukhino in the latter half of the 'thirties became an "orgy of mutual infatuation" (Carr). "*Michel* says" became a sort of *Roma locuta causa finita*. Bakunin himself admitted, with customary frankness, that he felt the "need to serve as a support to some beloved person". "I need someone who will put himself with confidence under my guidance."[11] "Despite my love of freedom", he wrote later to his brother Paul from abroad, "I had a great tendency to despotism, and often tormented and oppressed my poor sisters: ask Tanyusha about this. She was always the first to rebel and once even ventured to call me a despot." Frankness was Bakunin's characteristic trait. His attitude in this respect revealed a bewitching combination of naïveté and intelligence, and at times made him appear like an angel of innocence who rushes in where fools have feared to tread. But, as frequently happens on such occasions, he incurred the charge of many of his friends of not being innocent at all, but of being shrewd and calculating in a rather original way.

The sentiments, thoughts, passions, and dramas which accompanied relations in the Bakunin family expressed themselves as often as not in an extraordinary intense and hyperbolic language, and a special significance was attributed to them by means of philosophical and mystical speculations and quotations from the Scripture, from Fichte, Hegel, Goethe, Schiller and . . . Bettina von Arnim. The situation became quite intolerable as a result of a series of incidents, which became known in the Bakunin family as "the struggle for the liberation of Varenka", Bakunin's married sister, in the course of which Bakunin attempted to force her into a divorce, and contrived to bring about a temporary separation. Already then he showed symptoms of a tendency to intrigue wedded to a kind of unholy curiosity. He laid his plans to "liberate Varvara" from what he regarded as a "sinful", "animal" connection, and nearly succeeded in finally alienating his docile sister from her worthy, infinitely patient, if insignificant and "*bourgeois*" husband. His motives in this affair are as obscure as in that of his relations with his sister Tatyana. Varvara's marriage, encouraged by her father, no doubt, set a limit to Bakunin's control over her life. But he was also moved in this by a secret hatred of what he called "sinful earthly pleasures". He used to mock at asceticism, and yet could not forgive the body for having attached itself to the spirit, and was imbued with an almost Manichean aversion against natural processes—to compensate perhaps for some profound insufficiency, or for the sexual impotence which most biographers ascribe to him, although the Manichean streak expresssed itself in a different and wider context, as we shall see later. The reaction of outsiders to Bakunin's conduct towards his sisters can be gauged from Belinsky's charge against him of beginning with an indignant desire to liberate and ending in coercion and moral cruelty. "I will tell you quite frankly, briefly and clearly", he wrote to Botkin, "I hate *Michel*—not for his sake but for theirs, the sisters, for his attitude to them, for doing violence to their . . . natures."[12]

The impulses of domination deployed within his family were transferred by Bakunin to relations with his friends in the Moscow Circle, of which he became in the late 'thirties the acknowledged leader in succession to Stankevich. Unlike the latter, he expected from them absolute devotion and unqualified loyalty, and many of his letters to friends from this period read like philosophical speeches for the prosecution. Like most people who set out to order the life and thought of others, however, he finished by evoking violent opposition. The "blue-eyed giant with leonine head" had undoubtedly many qualities for taking Stankevich's place, but he had none of his graciousness and humility. Konstantin Aksakov describes in his Reminiscences how Bakunin proceeded to "sort out" all the members of the Circle *à la* Hegel and in accordance with their respective "stages of development". On Aksakov he bestowed the lowest degree of "*Schönseligkeit*" and promoted himself to the highest stage of the "illumined spirit". Most of the other members were placed in the region of "reflectiveness"; and all, with the exception of Bakunin himself, continued to dwell in "abstractness". Bakunin's intel-

lectual abilities and vitality, nevertheless, far surpassed those of Stankevich. There was an inner brutal force about him: it was like a cold
flame that burnt him with an unendurable fury and shed a glow on those
about him. He had, in Belinsky's words, "a demonic capacity for communicating ideas". His tongue, a tongue by which he had stirred his
hearers and from time to time charmed considerable sums of money out
of his credulous and not so credulous friends, swayed men's minds and
touched their hearts. "People listened to Bakunin with rapture", writes
Annenkov. "When Bakunin was inspired and spoke", Mikhail Shchepkin,
the great Russian actor, owned, "I listened, I hung on his lips, and never
grew tired of listening." Bakunin's friend, Natalie Beyer, said that she
did not know "why or how, but his presence produced on [her] an
effect for which [she] was unable to account: it was some chaos, some
whirlwind of ideas and feelings which had a shattering effect on [her]".
The most unexpected people felt enthralled in his company—Brazilian
diplomats, academic and non-academic philosophers, inveterate revolutionaries and just ordinary people who happened to cross his path.
"People", writes Annenkov, "flocked to Bakunin for advice and solutions in matters of abstract, philosophical thought, Proudhon for instance. An intelligent and cultivated Frenchman, who was conscious of
the deficiencies in his country's intellectual development, summoned his
acquaintances on Bakunin's account by saying: *Je vais vous montrer une
monstruosité par sa dialectique serrée et sa perception lumineuse des idées
dans leur essence.*" It was the sheer impact of Bakunin's powerful personality that brought about the defeat of Marx, and his initial overwhelming majority at the Congress of the First International in 1869;
but even Marx had previously admitted to having fallen under Bakunin's
spell. A young Russian woman, a revolutionary, describing the last days
of Bakunin, when he was already a sick and forgotten old man, knowing
and seeing no one except a few Swiss Italian workers, said that she had
"never witnessed, before or after, such a display of spontaneous and disinterested loyalty towards him by these simple people".[13] For Turgenev
Bakunin was in the end just a fool, "because he was such an involved
and subtle fool—and we always suspect depth in a case like that. A man
mutters because his tongue is too large and we think: oh, he has so many
ideas that he cannot express them all!" But in the early 'forties, when
Turgenev had not yet reached his golden mean and turned into the *bien
pensant* he became later on, he never questioned what he called Bakunin's
"spiritual power", whatever doubts he may have entertained about his
character. "I arrived in Berlin", he wrote to Bakunin in September 1840,
"I devoted myself to science—the first stars were kindled on my sky,
and at last I knew you, Bakunin. Stankevich brought us together—and
death will not part us. I can scarcely put into words what I owe to you."[14]

The tremendous magnetism of Bakunin's mind was matched by that
of his appearance. He never stayed unnoticed. His voice, his demeanour,

his views, all conspired to make him the centre of attention. When he was young, he was handsome in a demonic way, and made a fascinating figure with his long black hair, with a fanatical gleam in his eyes and an ascetic face (although there was nothing particularly ascetic about his way of life and especially his eating habits). "Cold dissoluteness as a rule of behaviour and satiety as a kind of aristocratism of genius"—Ruge wrote about the young Bakunin.[15] Later, as a result of his terrible ordeals, as well as of sheer physical laziness, he became excessively obese and turned into a huge and clumsy carcass. His face became abnormally large and fleshy. It was overgrown with hair, and its features had dissolved in fat. Moving with a heavy, yet resolute tread, he seemed to seek to impress his weight upon the earth. But there remained in his eyes the old flash and brilliance.

The final impression one retains from Bakunin's appetite for exercising authority is not so much one of conceit, of a desire *se faire valoir*: it had a deeper origin and was not so different from the revolutionary destructiveness he later on extolled. He provides a remarkable example of how both these become methods by which man can set himself over against the limits and limitations of his finite state and successfully assert his freedom. His ability to persuade people to devote their lives to him and to his causes, and the apparent ease with which he almost deliberately induced opposition to himself were alike a way of release, a sign of fulfilment in all his powers, and yet of infinite dissatisfaction.

The first in time to revolt against Bakunin was Belinsky. At the end of 1838 begin dissensions with Botkin. From later correspondence, we learn that by 1837 there was already friction in Bakunin's relations with Konstantin Aksakov. The letters of Belinsky and Bakunin between 1838 and 1840 reflect all the painful details of their growing estrangement and final breach, as well as Bakunin's characteristic attitude towards his friends.[16] "I always acknowledged in you and acknowledge now", Belinsky wrote, "a noble, leonine nature, a power and depth of spirit, a remarkable mobility of mind, extraordinary gifts, an infinite capacity for understanding . . . ; but at the same time I knew and know now your monstrous pride, your baseness in relations with friends, childishness, sloth, lack of human warmth and tenderness, a high opinion of yourself at the expense of others, a desire to subjugate others, to dominate, an eagerness to tell the truth about others and a horror of hearing it told about yourself." "I will not conceal from you that more than once you have fallen greatly in my esteem, but even then you never appeared to me a petty and shallow being, or a heartless, soulless, ineffective cad: I saw you as a demon in human shape, a fallen angel. . . . I cannot express my feelings towards you otherwise than love which is like hatred and hatred which is like love." Sometimes Bakunin accepted such and similar charges, though as a rule he did not know what remorse is, for he was endowed with the enviable feminine faculty of forgetting, especially of forgetting the past, which would seem to belong not to him but to someone long since dead, whom once he had known. At other times he retorted with anger. As often as not he simply assumed an attitude of cold indifference: "If you don't like it, you can lump it!" Belinsky's sense of loyalty, on the other hand, and the persistent fascination which Bakunin exercised on him made it difficult to reconcile himself with the inevitable and final breach.

Relations with Herzen proved equally fatal, but the circumstances were different. There is no evidence that in Russia they were anything but friendly, although (partly on account of Herzen's long exile from Moscow) never as close as between Bakunin and Belinsky or Turgenev. They had a sincere respect for each other. Bakunin did not attempt to inflict his authority on Herzen, who, in any case, was fastidiously impervious to any pressure from outside, but who, despite their difference in temperament, admired Bakunin's daring thought and "enormous dialectical abilities". In fact, Herzen was the only friend to see Bakunin off on that pilgrimage to Germany, and even to subsidize it in part: all, or nearly all, his other friends had by then quarrelled with him. When the news of Bakunin's escape from Siberia reached Herzen in 1861, at the height of his political and publicistic activities abroad, he announced the imminent arrival of Bakunin in London as a great event. "We joyfully bring this to the knowledge of all our friends", he wrote in *Kolokol*. It is true that Natalie Tuchkova, Herzen's second wife, attributes to him considerable misgivings in view of Bakunin's appearance. "I must own, I am frightened of Bakunin's coming," Herzen is supposed to have said, "he will ruin our work. You remember what Caussidière—or was it Lamartine?—said of him in 1848: '*Notre ami Bakounine est un homme impayable le jour de la révolution, mais le lendemain il faut absolument le faire fusiller, car il sera impossible d'établir un ordre quelquonque avec un pareil anarchiste.*' Ogarev agreed."[17] Natalie Tuchkova's Reminiscences, however, are very biassed and in many respects palpably inaccurate. Ogarev's agreement with Herzen's alleged apprehensions are, perhaps, doubtful in the light of his subsequent relations with Bakunin. Herzen himself had previously explicitly identified himself with Bakunin's cause.[1] She also failed to add what Herzen originally remarked *à propos* of Caussidière's (not Lamartine's) verdict: "Tell Caussidière", he said to his friends, "that the difference between Bakunin and him is that Caussidière, too, is a splendid fellow, but it would be better to shoot him the day before the revolution." Later on, in London, Herzen reminded Caussidière of this. The French revolutionary Prefect in exile "merely smote with his huge fist upon his mighty chest with the force with which shafts are driven into the earth and said: '*Je porte l'image de Bakounine ici, ici!*'"

Nevertheless, Bakunin's intrusion into the "league of two" (Herzen and Ogarev) in London was bound to bring disaster. "People like you", wrote Adolf Reichel, Bakunin's faithful musical friend from his Dresden days, "grow in a hurricane and ripen better in stormy weather than in sunshine." Bakunin "fretted against prolonged study, the weighing of pros and contras, and, as confident and theoretical as ever, longed for any action, if only it were in the midst of the turmoil of revolution, in the midst of upheavals and menacing danger. Now, too, as in the articles signed Jules Elizard, he repeated: '*Die Lust der Zerstörung ist eine schaffende Lust.*' . . . The spirit of the parties of that period, their exclusiveness, their personal sympathies and antipathies, above all their faith in the Second Coming of the Revolution—it was all there."[19] Herzen admits that, however much he may have been aware that Bakunin "looked only towards the ultimate goal" and "mistook the second month of pregnancy for the ninth", he was carried away by Bakunin's revolutionary passion and even "let [himself] be led *volens nolens*"—not only from "false shame" or "the better influences of love, friendship and indulgence", but because it was "too strong for [his] reflective attitude". So it came about that the "league" in London, which, to the outside world at any rate, turned the Herzen-Ogarev partnership into a Herzen-Ogarev-Bakunin triumvirate, was plunged into the Polish adventure and became involved in the tragic and ruthless rising of the Poles on the night of January 22, 1863. The facts and their ensuing reactions on Herzen and the *Kolokol* will be discussed later. The Tsarist government, supported by liberals and conservatives alike, suppressed the rebellion with equal or greater ruthlessness. Herzen found himself deserted by public opinion in Russia and from this time began to lose his influence.

Although Bakunin cannot be held responsible for the undoing of Herzen's work, his impatience, indiscretions, thoughtlessness and "revolutionary itch" undoubtedly contributed to it, as they contributed unwittingly to the troubles of so many other of Bakunin's friends and associates. The subsequent renunciation of Bakunin and other attempts by Herzen to escape the legacy of this association could no longer redress the situation. He wrote with bitterness to Bakunin after the events in Poland: "Cut off from life, thrown from youth into German idealism, which became by force of time, *dem Schema nach*, a realistic outlook, unacquainted with Russia before prison as well as after Siberia, but full of expansive and passionate urges to noble actions, you have lived to be fifty in a world of phantoms, in full swing like a student, with great aspirations and small vices. After ten years of prison confinement you turned out the same theorizer with all the perspicacity *du vague*, a chatter-box . . . with a measure of quiet but obstinate Epicureanism and an itch for revolutionary action, which revolution does not have." However, it was no use reproaching Bakunin, for, characteristically enough, having conducted himself as he did, and seeing that Herzen was hurt and angry, nobody was more sorry or surprised than Bakunin himself, although he deplored Herzen's "inveterate scepticism" and the lack in him of the "stuff of which revolutionary leaders are made". But he did not dwell on this, and soon turned his attention with renewed determination to other revolutionary matters in Italy. Their next and last meeting, this time almost as between strangers, occurred in 1869, after which Herzen had nothing to report but that Bakunin "had much improved in health, had lost fifty pounds of fat by dieting, but was consuming enormous quantities of meat and wine", and that he worked "like a locomotive, but a locomotive which has got too much steam up and has run off the rails". Thereafter all communications ceased, save indirectly through Ogarev, with occasional requests for news by Herzen, but not by Bakunin. "There is no news of Bakunin", Herzen noted in one of his last epistolary references to his old friend, "except that his trousers have lost their last buttons and keep up only by force of habit and sympathetic attraction."[20]

Some can go, as Bakunin had gone, not only through unpleasantnesses and disappointments, but through terrible battles, the fear of imminent death and unimaginable horrors, and preserve their soul unscathed. Is it due to strength or weakness, to want or abundance of imagination, to instability of character or sequacity? What, in fact, chiefly strikes one about Bakunin is the absence of consistency in his character. It is, for this reason, impossible to explain the inner workings of his mind on the basis of their recorded manifestations. Herzen tried to do it, but, with all its brilliance and apparent conviction, his characterization removes the friction from what, for lack of a better term, can be called the dialectic of Bakunin's personality. The same applies to an even greater extent to Turgenev, who gave a full-length portrait of Bakunin in the hero of his novel *Rudin* (written in 1855). It is a picture from the outside, as so much in Turgenev. It is not sufficient to say that a man is this or that, or conducts himself in this or that fashion, and Bakunin was certainly much more complicated than this.

It is true that in one sense Bakunin's extraordinary eventful life and disordered personality present a picture of regularity, almost of monotony. It can be and has been reduced to one denominator—to his consistent, and apparently aimless impulse to domination and later to rebellion, or, as others have unkindly put it, to uncontrolled and uncontrollable aggression. In this he was a "hedgehog", an extravagant and monstrous "hedgehog", a complete character, a total man. And yet the most incongruous traits co-existed in him, or rather, two and more hardly reconciled, or indeed reconcilable, personalities. There was the unprincipled, blustering mountebank who spent his life seemingly pretending something the only value of which was that it was not pretence: always inflating himself, always declaiming, too proud to be cautious, too reckless to think of consequences, and almost choked by his own violence—"a great ship", in the words of a contemporary, "without rudder, drifting before the wind and not knowing why or whither". There was the combination of thoughtlessness and procrastination with a passionate love of ideas and a genius for sustained mental speculation. There was the conspirator and gossip who "deceived others, but seldom until he had first deceived himself" (Carr), with an overwhelming desire to talk and an absence of reticence which no rebuff could check, never fearing to bore and, surprisingly enough, never boring anyone. "He would fall", in Panaev's description, "with a sort of brutality on every new-comer and at once initiate him into the mysteries of philosophy" and later into the mysteries of his numerous political plots. There was the charming companion giving himself to every caller and giving away money which he did not have, devoid of envy and incapable of unkindness, falsehood, or hypocrisy. Even his abject *Confession* to the Tsar, which in the eyes of some critics discredits Bakunin's sincerity as a man as well as a revolutionary but about which he himself frankly wrote to Herzen from Siberia and which he later described as a "big blunder", is by no means devoid of candour, and even of dignity and courage, for he resolutely refused to implicate or name any of his friends and associates, thereby largely invalidating the confession and failing to secure any relief from his predicament. There was the seeker after freedom, beside whose pursuit all other exercises, whether of artistic service of beauty, or harmonious civilized existence, or devotion to good works were as chaff before the wind. There was the mystic and the atheist, the man who, as Belinsky said after Bakunin had repudiated all metaphysical allegiances, "was born and will die a mystic". There was, above all, the Promethean *révolté*, the prophet of total revolution, who, with all his advocacy of indiscriminate destruction of everything that stood in the way of freedom, paradoxically detected the moment of damnation when noble ends are destroyed by ignoble means.

It is curious, furthermore, that this "noisy object" was in his way a tragic figure, that his life had in it those moments of pity and terror which are said to be necessary to achieve the effect of tragedy. It is at such moments that Bakunin, as the world knew him, the grotesque, outrageous figure of the outward seeming, gave place to a very different person, melancholy, lonely in the midst of company, tortured by his own inadequacy. His letters reveal these moments more fully than any other documents. They give us intermittent glimpses into the dark of Bakunin's world, with spectres that never ceased to haunt him, and dispose of the notion of Bakunin as just a bulky piece of Neanderthal humanity and Caliban primitiveness with an admixture of charm and shrewd intelligence. He seems to have been half aware of being in some alarming void, suspended in personal loneliness. He felt alone, not only in the dungeons of the Petersburg Fortresses, but perhaps even more amidst the plots and slogans of his collective revolutionary business. His farewell letter to Pryamukhino, after his decision in 1842 never to return to Russia, is very revealing in this connection. So, in a different way, is his correspondence from Berlin: it is a strange memorial in Hegelian guise of a deliberate mental (or mystical) pursuit of self-annihilation and of death, to be found within life and within happiness, and in a sense overriding them, and to give rise to what he regarded as the only adequate understanding of reality. Even while still in Moscow, he spoke of his life as an "empty desert". "Solitude lay on my path", he wrote to his brother Nicolas in October 1842, "and sooner or later I had to enter this desert"; and, four months later (to Varvara): "I am alone, without complaint, without despair, without bitterness within; I stand before all the beliefs to which I had devoted my life. . . ."[21]

Such sentiments recurred with greater frequency in later years. Sometimes he welcomed them as a way "to turn into oneself" and hailed "withdrawal from external circumstance". At other times (in prolonged and enforced solitary confinement) they drove him mad. "The world by which his mind, feelings and sensations were formed", his brother Paul wrote to Tatyana on seeing him in the Fortress, "is alien to me. . . . He was moved by iron passions. He was the fire in the flame, suddenly torn out of all circumstance and movement, estranged from the world, plunged into sepulchral solitude and silence within and without. Oh, this, too, is a fire. Three years already it seethes in his soul. Before it was a flame of life; now it is a flame of death." A constant theme in his early intellectual development was the tension between what he called "inner" and "external" life. Later it issued in a philosophy of revolt. "I am not made for external life or external happiness", he wrote with solemn self-consciousness to Tatyana, "and I do not want it. . . . I live a purely inner life: I remain within myself, I am buried in it, and only this self unites me to God." Elsewhere Bakunin speaks of "intolerable anguish", of the "absurdity of all hopes and undertakings". "Gloom lies heavily on the mind again: I have begun feeling the same solitude in Prague as I did in Paris and in Germany." The company of innumerable revolutionaries in exile, whom he seemed to resemble in so many ways, their squabbles, vanity, malice, their "nauseating repetition of the word *bourgeois*" and their own "ingrained *bourgeois* spirit" suffocated him. He complained of not being able "to breathe freely among them". Yet he continued throughout life to hover between solitude and an irresistible hankering after people who wasted his time and whose time he wasted.

One could scarcely have thought Bakunin capable of betraying tragic depth. One even wonders whether there was a "real man" in him, an inner self, who had not yet properly revealed himself. Perhaps his restlessness, his caprice, are an indication that he also felt this doubt. "My whole life", he wrote to Stankevich in 1840, "my whole virtue has consisted in a kind of abstract spiritual force, and that force has been shipwrecked on the sordid trivialities of life, on empty family quarrels and quarrels between friends, and on my own . . . disablement." But was there anything at the centre? I have no doubt that Bakunin's confession of darkening solitude, if nothing else, bears the suggestion of something in the last resort aloof, something never entirely communicated. He was of course no introspective, no self-regarder, revelling in private pains or pleasures. Where another would go round and round, Bakunin went on and on. "Whether I shall split on the rock or, worse still, run on a sandbank, I do not know", he wrote to Turgenev in 1842, during one of his gloomiest periods, "I only know that I shall not unbend so long as there is a drop of blood left in me." But he was a solitary outsider—a being of a different order from the generality of men, not higher, not lower, but merely strange.

This element of strangeness has struck many of his contemporaries. No one perhaps was more conscious of it than Belinsky, who spoke of the "riddle" of Bakunin and whose attitude to him expressed itself in alternate love and hatred, in bewilderment, awe, revulsion and fascination. To Granovsky he was an "inscrutable monster . . . who on closer acquaintance makes one feel somehow *unheimlich*". The gentle and tolerant Ogarev refers to him as a "long reptile" and an "ogre". "My impressions of him", recalls Richard Wagner, "continuously oscillated between involuntary horror and irresistible attraction." Such estimates could be multiplied. And Bakunin himself was aware, as he wrote to Tatyana in 1842, of "carrying constantly some dark burden in the soul, something unresolved which strangles its freedom", or (in another letter of the same period) "of a host of insidious enemies creeping into [his] soul which [he] must expel", and of "being out of [his] mind and possessed by a demon" (*Confession*).

There are two factors in particular that combine to enhance the effect of Bakunin's "*Unheimlichkeit*": his merciless, cold mental energy and his total inability to love. We know already from the temper of the period of the 'thirties and early 'forties the urge among its representatives to transform every issue into high metaphysics. Bakunin displayed this tendency more than any of his contemporaries, using language that was even more unashamedly exalted, although it was on the whole more lucid, and given to even more prolonged sublunar explorations, and to speculative profundities which were still less productive of humour.[22] What was peculiar to him, however, was not idealism, but a kind of disembodied gnosticism, an ideomania, a curious cerebral passion, which had in it something of mingled iron and fire. His ideas were neither philosophical concepts, nor intellectual propositions, nor intuitions: they were neither guides nor—at any rate, until he embarked upon his revolutionary career—materials for action, but mental states. He seemed to acquire them, not by thought or insight, but by breathing the haunted air. They thronged his mind with all the vividness of sensation. For ordinary man an idea, an image is less alive than sensation. Day-dreams satisfy emotional needs and fulfil frustrated desires; but they are pale shadows of real life, and at the back of man's mind is the awareness that the demands of the world of sense have another validity. With Bakunin it was not so. His ideas and day-dreams were so significant to him that it is the world of sense that was shadowy and he had to reach out to it by an effort of the will. "Abstract minds like ours", Bakunin wrote in his *Confession*, "are so much absorbed in their own thoughts that, like chess-players, who see only their game, we pay no attention to what passes in the real world, or to the thoughts, feelings and impressions of those around us." It is, therefore, not surprising perhaps that he was so impossible to live with, that his egotism was so outrageous and his sense of loneliness so acute. He was by nature a solipsist, despite all his superficial gregarious-ness and his later advocacy of anti-individualist anarchism, and the world existed for him for the exercise of personal freedom and creative action. His thinking, as Chizhevsky observes, was directed "not *to-wards* the world but *against* it". It was completely devoid of the element of contemplation, of philosophic wonder. His cold and abstract mind was like a monstrous Baal intent on devouring the object-world; it crushed itself into life as it was present to him, like fuel to stoke a fur-nace. "All reality, all 'life'," to quote Chizhevsky again, "disappeared in his mental element: they were not absorbed by it, illumined by it, but dissolved without leaving a trace."[23] In an early attempt to give an account of his own intellectual life (in a series of letters to the Beyer sisters) he wrote: "I feel deep within me some truth which will never delude me, something which does not depend on anything extraneous." "There is but one truth—the one which I understand, the one of which I am so vividly aware; and that truth is jealous, it desires to reign, alone and indivisibly." "It is imperative to smash all that is false, without pity and without exception, for the sake of truth's triumph." Speaking of Bakunin's Hegelian phase, when he was, together with others, "accept-ing reality", Annenkov aptly remarks that, though Bakunin proposed to "legitimize too many things in the existing order", he "legitimized them in such a way that they ceased to be what they were: they became an ideal by comparison with what they were in actual fact". For Belinsky Hegel was ultimately a way of re-discovering reality, but for Bakunin he was an instrument for asserting his own independence of it, and indeed, when it came to "accepting reality" in earnest he refused to follow Belinsky, Hegel notwithstanding. Bakunin's "revolutionary tact", as Herzen said, "drove him in another direction". He partook of life only with part of him, but was never reduced to it. That is, perhaps, why all "finished" things were a source of weariness for him, and why he lacked all ability to sustain the tedium of long enterprises. Many of his writings stop midway, and some in the middle of a sentence. He derived satisfac-tion from the irreducible and the tentative. "This portrait is unfinished, as I am myself unfinished", he wrote on his portrait, a present to the

Beyer sisters. "I am an impossible person", he announced to Ogarev, "and I shall continue to be impossible so long as those who are now possible remain possible." Because things were incomplete, they gave scope for his unlimited imagination, a sense of power and of liberation from external ties, from the permanence in things, events and judgments. It is significant that he was devoid of aesthetic feeling, a fact which much offended Belinsky's acute sense of artistic beauty.[24] That which was given, realized, and finally embodied in a work of art, when he could give nothing and where his restless mind was obliged to contemplate, finished by boring him. Perfection for Bakunin was dull, and his whole attitude provides a striking example of the romantic irony that this universal aim is better not achieved.

There is a connection between Bakunin's abstract, ideomaniacal quality and his inability to love—a connection which, once more, Belinsky was the first to observe. "A marvellous man," he wrote to Stankevich, "a deep, elemental, leonine nature—this cannot be denied him. But . . . he loves ideas, not men. He wants to dominate . . . not to love." And, again, in his long epistolary confrontation with Bakunin, he charges him with "ruthless idealism and lack of simplicity", with "deliberate rejection of living reality in favour of abstract thought", with being a "dead logical skeleton", and concludes his indictment: "You have not lived at all!" "Look at this Cassius", Belinsky said to Annenkov, "no one has ever heard a song from his lips; . . . he never uttered, not even casually, so much as a single note. He is devoid of inward music, of any unison of mind and heart, of the need to give expression to the tender, feminine part of human nature. . . . He was trying surreptitiously to get at my soul in order to steal it and carry it away on the sly." Elsewhere he speaks of Bakunin's "castrated style", ridicules his chastity and calls him "a ghost groping for promiscuity". There were special grounds for this latter imputation, for Bakunin had unmistakable if secret tendencies to obscene perversity, which is strongly reminiscent of Dostoevskian backwaters.[25]

Bakunin, the "abstract hero" (Belinsky), the "monk of revolution" and "revolutionary ascetic" (Herzen), perverse, despotic and rebellious though he was, "tried" to love and even to fall in love, as he pathetically confessed to his brother Alexey. But where he loved he was urged to grasp the secret of the other's being—not in order to share that secret, but to possess and to destroy it. It is at such moments that the darkest recesses of his soul were uncovered. His turbulent, unquenchable and unavailing search to assert his abstract freedom, leaving nothing but undiluted, fanatical passion of the mind, to go beyond what is, his unwillingness to share and to submit robbed him of the consequences of the intimations of his own love. Love became a lowering curse on his horizon, a precursor of disaster, a threat to his cold and solitary independence. And though he knew its pain, anguish, ecstasy and shame, he could not or would not love, just as he could not and would not build, beget, preserve.[26] Indeed, love itself turned, by some devilish logic of his tangled nature, into hatred—a hatred "in imagination and in thought", but not in the heart, as he wrote in his *Confession*—or into rebellion, as is evident from Bakunin's relation with Johanina Pescantini, the Russian-born wife of an Italian singer whom Bakunin met in Dresden. He recoiled at it with horror, and uttered this horror by owning to a desire to smash their faces when he saw people in love with each other. "Do not call me cold-hearted", he wrote to his brother Paul, "it is time we should leave fancies and sentiment behind, it is time we should become human and be as constant and inexorable in hatred as in love:

> Wir haben lang genug geliebt,
> Wir wollen endlich hassen."

Nothing is more likely to iron out Bakunin's individuality than to reduce him to a case of "maladjustment", of deviation from healthy acceptance of existing standards and values, and write off his inclination to rebel as a neurotic symptom. There is, however, another, a more concrete and satisfying way of interpreting Bakunin's personality: it is the way of the artist and imaginative writer. Turgenev, as we have seen, meant to draw a portrait of Bakunin in *Rudin*, although Rudin barely suggests some of his features. Herzen has created a Bakunin in his own image and likeness or, rather, in the light of his painful proximity with him. Aksakov devoted a high-minded Ode and Merezhkovsky one of his more than usually portentous and sophisticated works to him. Even Wagner's Siegfried is supposed to have Bakunin as his prototype. But there is one book which may prove particularly illuminating for the understanding of Bakunin or, more accurately, of certain important aspects of his personality, *The Possessed* by Dostoevsky, "the book of the great wrath", and especially the hero of that novel, Stavrogin. I should like, therefore, before proceeding to discuss Bakunin's ideas, to take up this theme, fully conscious though I am of the precarious and controversial character of all such comparisons, and of this comparison in particular. In doing so, I shall confine myself to the psychological problem which the parallel suggests and shall not dwell on all the biographical, chronological and textual evidence which may be adduced in its favour, but which would lead me far beyond the scope of the present work.[27]

One of Dostoevsky's most effective methods in *The Possessed* is to create at the outset an atmosphere of intense expectation, uncertainty, even of incredulity. "The tone", he wrote on the margin of a draft page, "is that Nechaev (Pyotr Verkhovensky) and the prince (Stavrogin) should not be *explained*. . . . To conceal, and to reveal [them] only gradually. . . ." The principal heroes of the novel are characterized as "enigmatic and romantic", almost shadowy figures in the midst of the other clearly delineated and perfectly transparent characters. This imbues the "possessed" with a peculiarly uncanny significance, as if some gaping void is showing through their fantastic features. The figure of the "charmer demon", as Dostoevsky calls Stavrogin, appears at first in a distance: the chronicler recalls some obscure rumours about his childhood and adolescence, and then offers a few biographical details, some of which are strongly reminiscent of Bakunin's early career (in the army). When Stavrogin appeared for the first time in the provincial town where the action of the novel takes place, the narrator was struck by his appearance. "The most polished gentleman I have ever come across, exceedingly well dressed, and conducting himself in a way appropriate only for those who are most exquisitely favoured." "He is extraordinarily handsome, but his beauty is somehow repulsive." "It was said that his face reminded one of a mask." All of a sudden, the silent and apparently retiring gentleman commits, in a succession of the trite and the unexpected, a number of preposterous acts, which go to show that, with all his secretiveness, he was not as taciturn and uncommunicative as he seemed at first sight. When he subsequently reappears in the town he gives the impression that "some new thought gleams in his eyes". He displays charm, amiability and even artless exuberance, but also "impatience and irritation". After an account of Shatov's slap in Stavrogin's face (cf. the incident with Katkov) the narrator remembered that Stavrogin "remained silent, looked at Shatov and grew white as a sheet. But, strangely enough, his gaze seemed to burn itself out. In a few seconds his eyes assumed their cold and . . . calm look." In a series of such and similar fragments Dostoevsky achieves the effect of Stavrogin's bewildering and unaccountable personality.

He then proceeds to use his favourite device of bifurcation, of splitting his hero into two or more voices or characters who talk to and conflict with one another—characters that are not wholly individualized, because they each remain parts of the inner world of the hero, although they are no less real or human for that. This creates a highly charged atmosphere, conjuring up a world of systematic terror and systematic dissimulation in which Stavrogin is seen to contain and dominate at once, to attract and repel his own mental projections. The passionate love for, and the fascination exercised by, Stavrogin is succeeded in his adepts by feelings of wild hostility, disgust and unheard of insults, which, however, seem to leave him completely unmoved. He is humourless, intense, refractory—a solemn and lonely figure, embodying a subterranean force, a destructive energy, unconquered pride and independence. But his mind has a coldness and ruthlessness about it that grow into impotent monstrosity and gives the reader the sensation of shivers down the spine. We see him engaged, as Bakunin was engaged, in a terrifying struggle to reach ever greater intensity and fullness of life, yet it remains an unavailing struggle, and there is no rest for him anywhere.

It is the tragic fate of a man who has never loved and is incapable of loving anybody or anything, who wastes his prodigious spiritual endowment in a striving that does not proceed from any choice made, and has no limits and no purpose. Stavrogin reveals his secret in the letter he wrote before his death: "I have tried my strength everywhere. In trials within myself, and in trials for the sake of attracting the attention of others, as before and throughout my whole life [this strength] showed no bounds. . . . What I could not see, and do not see now, however, is where to apply it. As always and as before, I desire the good and feel satisfaction in that desire: at the same time I desire evil and also feel satisfaction in this. . . . I went in for great dissipation, and have wasted my strength in it; but I have not loved dissipation, and do not wish for it. . . . I can never lose my reason. . . . Nothing but negation issues from me, without nobility and without force."

This, I suggest, is an unmistakable echo of Bakunin's voice, and it attests the impression of Stavrogin as a mirror reflecting certain essential features of Bakunin. But Stavrogin is seen in the novel when his life's energy is already almost spent. No longer can anything move him, and he goes from depravity to depravity in the search for something, anything, by which to prove himself still capable of feeling. Senseless murders and pointless conspiracies and abductions fail to mean anything to him. In short, it would be satanic to the point of the ludicrous, if it were not for the profoundly human image which Dostoevsky succeeded in imparting to this character. Bakunin's dynamic and overcrowded nature, mind and imagination, on the other hand, endured the cold horrors of Stavrogin's life as momentary experiences. Moreover, Stavrogin seeks to be forgiven, to be able to atone, to accept responsibility for his destructive thoughts and deeds. And this, in his confrontation with Tikhon, is what he learns to do, or almost learns to do. Bakunin, prepared though he sometimes was, to admit his errors, was remorseless, seldom or never casting his eyes back, jumping from dejection to the supreme transfigurations of freedom, oblivious of the past and mindful of the future, and impelled, as Belinsky said, by the "eternal principle of movement". "My egotism", he wrote to the Tsar, "consisted in an urge to movement and action. I felt oppressed and nauseated in ordinary tranquil surroundings. People strive habitually for rest and quiet, and look upon them as the highest good. As for me, they led me to despair; my heart was in a constant turmoil. . . . This urge to movement . . . remained for ever unsatisfied. . . . [It] proved my only stimulus . . . which drove me on like one possessed into manifest perils." The mask of melancholy of temperament soon gave place to the ebullient, self-exposing, high-spirited appearance which he assumed in the eyes of many contemporaries, but which should not conceal from us, as it did not conceal from them (or some of them) his real self.

In creating Stavrogin Dostoevsky wished to hold up to ignominy and to pillory Russian "nihilism". But, like Shakespeare, who seems to have aimed in Shylock at a devastating parody, he ended by producing a mighty and tragic figure. "*Bakunin*", says Grossman, "has withstood the test of Dostoevsky's satiric indignation as neither Turgenev, nor Nechaev, nor even Granovsky have withstood it." He has preserved his primordial human substance and tragic countenance under the impact of Dostoevsky's inspired wrath. "Nicolai Stavrogin is a sombre figure . . . a monster", Dostoevsky commented on his novel to Katkov, "but it seems to me that he is a tragic figure. . . . In my opinion it is a Russian, a typical figure. I wrung him out of my heart."

2. REVOLT

With all the astonishing outward changes of his life, Bakunin's intellectual development is marked by a unity which distinguishes it from the analogous development in Belinsky, whatever thread of continuity may be detected in the latter. Belinsky's life was not rich or troubled in outward incident, but his universe of discourse was full of upheavals and dramatic moments: it was linked with his moral and emotional commitment to life, whose intimations produced immediate and momentous personal responses in him. Bakunin was wilful, self-indulgent and given to excesses, and he did not conceal the violence of his convictions and the contradictions of his temperament. But his attitude to life lacked Belinsky's dramatic quality, poetic elation and moral feeling. He was frequently driven from his normal course, but it was one urge and one passion that drove him, with, as it were, one single if almost impersonal agent of intensification.

Nevertheless Bakunin, too, underwent an intellectual crisis, which corresponds roughly to the more dramatic transition from "idealism" to "realism" of Belinsky, and coincides with his involvement in the Left Hegelian movement in Germany in 1841. It resulted for Bakunin in a repudiation of the consolations of philosophy, and carried him eventually through all imaginable and unimaginable nihilisms in regard to society, culture, morality and religion. But even before this crisis, his savage drive through the labyrinths of philosophical idealism revealed his inability to submit himself to intellectual schemata or to fix the extent and boundaries of freedom. Idealism led into another world, different from the world of the commonplace, in which man is at home, and provided a weapon with which to deny it. "The commonplace", Bakunin wrote at the height of his Hegelianism in Russia, "is the most terrible phantom binding us with vain but strong, invisible chains." In this respect he was no more than a partner in the "remarkable decade". Its idealism was neither a pursuit of tautological shadows offering the comfort of the discovery that things take the shape which they do take; nor the worship of success which seeks and finds the fount of values in the existing state of affairs; nor indeed a serious belief in the possibility of even ideal escapes from real situations. Rather, it was a refusal to admit the limits of the given, of the past and the present, as the boundary of human existence: it took nothing for granted, neither the ultimate nor the proximate ends of human thought and action. It was, in short, an attempt to account for man's free and creative attitude to life.

Already in 1836, Bakunin was combatting truths that had become irrefutable errors "forged by means of belittling man", "relative ideas", poetically and rhetorically magnified, adorned and after long usage fixed into binding canons. He wants "truth as it is, and not as adjusted to specific circumstances". Soon after, and indeed side by side with Hegelian eulogies to holy mother Necessity and pantheistic delight in the non-existence of evil, he shows signs of recognition of a world built on duality and gives vent to his need for opposition. "Harmony must be destroyed", he wrote at the beginning of the Hegelian phase, ". . . it must be subjected to the contrariety of storms, it must undergo . . . disruption, provide occasion for destruction, make man suffer and compel [him] to re-create it [harmony] by means of thought." This, however, could still be fitted into the Hegelian frame.

But dualistic tendencies became increasingly prominent throughout the Hegelian period, and Bakunin's own account of himself under the influence of Hegel, particularly in letters from Berlin, is a striking demonstration of the explosive mixture that German idealism can be when brought into contact with a rebellious mind. "God preserve us from every mournful love of peace", he wrote at the beginning of 1841; "to pursue abstraction must soon lead to a realization of its bigotry and thence to real liberation. Love of peace leads nowhere, for it only feigns to contain everything: it is incapable of re-creating anything from within; it merely receives all things into itself. . . . Yet for man only that is true and real which he creates from the inmost source of his unique personality"; and four years later from Paris: "I shall not bow before the so-called necessities of the real world and am at war with them as before . . .; my faith, an unconditional faith in the lofty dignity of man, in his sacred calling, in freedom as the only source and only purpose of life, has remained unshaken." Hegelian "contrasts" turn from being mere "empty shadows" into "real and full-blooded contradictions". True harmony "is as far removed from passive acceptance of truth as heaven is from earth: it is an act . . . and only he *is* who has created himself by himself. The dignity and enduring value of man resides in this." "Away with logical and theoretical fantasies about the finite and infinite", he wrote towards the end of 1842; "such matters can only be grasped by living action. . . . We must act, act perpetually in order to be human . . . in order to possess real awareness of ourselves."[28] One might say that the Cartesian *cogito ergo sum* (a proposition, by the way, which no

Russian could conceivably have made of his own accord) turns in Bakunin's hands into a *creo ergo sum*, and knowledge becomes to him, like the artist's activity, a way of transforming, refashioning the world from within man's freedom and creativity.

It should be noted, however, that Bakunin's affirmation of the unique personality of man, of human freedom and creative vocation had, unlike Belinsky's similar "personalism", a somewhat sombre, cold and un-smiling quality. His discovery of man had none of Belinsky's feeling for humanity. He seemed distracted from what was happening to the human person whose value he was advocating with increasing fervour, and this, no doubt, accorded with the summary attitude displayed in his personal relations. Background, ordinary life, the concreteness and the vagaries of human character, the "trappings" of personality did not interest him: they dissolved in an obsession by the thing itself, naked, raw and without the outer skin of individual traits. This obsession was itself a kind of abstraction. Man seemed to be consumed by the cold fire of Bakunin's revolt on his behalf. Similarly, the defence of action and practice against contemplation and theory did not lose its "theoretical" and cerebral character: it did not proceed from any assimilation of historical problems or historical situations, but was on the contrary conceived in terms of a radical critique, and opposition to, historical processes.

In 1842, on moving to Dresden, Bakunin published his "manifesto of negation", *Reaction in Germany*, which is a piece of brilliant philo-sophical thinking and, in style, probably the best and most cogent work he ever wrote. Belinsky's reaction was that they had "at last met in the same temple", and Herzen noted in his Diary that "the article is wonderful from the beginning to end" and that he was "completely at one with (Bakunin)". It should be regarded as Bakunin's philosophical declaration of faith, equivalent to that of the famous letter Belinsky wrote to Botkin on parting with Hegelianism. Those who are not pre-pared to conduct the obsequies of metaphysics and believe the report of its death to be greatly exaggerated will not fail to note that it is a most original and daring work, more daring, perhaps, than anything produced by the Coryphaei of Russsian revolutionary thought and of the "remarkable decade" in particular. It also marked the crowning point in the career of the otherwise dull and insignificant *Deutsche Jahrbücher*, which became the organ of the Hegelian Left under its intelligent but colourless editor Arnold Ruge. Bakunin used the journal and the editor (whose rationalism and anti-mysticism he thoroughly disliked) as instru-ments to combat what he called the "rotton, golden and unchanging mean in which they [the Germans] have rested for so long". But the importance of the essay, in which Bakunin still employed the Hegelian idiom and jargon, lay in the extreme revolutionary conclusions he drew from Hegel's dialectic, and in that it provided a persuasive philosophical basis for his own revolutionary maximalism. Bakunin pronounces Hegelian philosophy to be the summit of speculative thought and, at the same time, its dead-end and undoing. Hegel's highest attainment is seen in the principle of contradiction, and his plight in the claim to have reconciled the contradictions, in the "white sepulchre" of synthesis. Truth resides in "absolute negation . . . which has nothing outside itself", and in the "absolute disquiet" of such negation. A primacy of negation is established over every positive affirmation, for the latter is said to be sustained only by the impetus coming from the former. "The negative, which provides the source of life for the positive, contains within itself the totality of contradiction", and every attempt to supercede negation (the Hegelian *Aufhebung*) results in the "philistine quietude" upheld by "positivists". "I know thy works", Bakunin quotes from the Apocalypse, "that thou art neither cold nor hot: I would thou wert cold or hot. So then because thou art lukewarm, and neither cold nor hot, I will spue thee out of my mouth." "Contradiction survives to the end, and the power of its all-pervading vitality consists in the ceaseless self-incineration of the positive in the pure flame of the negative", "in the relentless destruction of all existing things". It is a case of "eternal conflict between freedom and unfreedom now reaching its last and highest peak". The essay ends in a hymn to the spirit of destruction. That spirit "has already, like some primeval mole, accomplished its subterranean deed, and soon he will appear as the judge of reality. Let us surrender to the eternal spirit who destroys simply because he is the inexhaustible and for ever creative fount of all life! The passion for destruction is also a creative passion."

Bakunin was little concerned with problems of political organization, despite his inordinate expenditure of energy on political plottings and the prominent rôle he played in the League of Peace and Freedom and the First International. One would look in vain for any precise formulation of social phenomena in his writings. While clearly seeing political revolution in relation to economic interest, to conflicts between the oppressed and the oppressors, and to the clash between social groups and classes, he yet regarded it as of secondary and derivative importance. "I do not believe in constitutions and laws", he wrote in a letter to Herwegh; "the best constitution in the world would not be able to satisfy me. We need something different: passion, life, a new lawless and therefore free world." Neither political theorizing nor economic discontent, class-feeling or good taste, snobbery or fear can explain Bakunin's exaltation of destruction and revolt, however intense his hatred of privilege and of the tyranny of wealth and economic law may have been. Revolt for him was that which constitutes the distinctive quality of man, and it is important to elucidate more fully the inner springs of Bakunin's rebellious attitude, and his own account of it.

Bakunin's outlook may be described as a form of anthropodicy, an apologia on behalf of man and of man's "sacred title to humanity". In his estimate of the nature of man Bakunin hotly rejects what he calls the "jejune abstraction of enlightened rationalists" and the idea of men as "equal partners of humanity"; he rejects, too, the romantic hero, "prig and self-lover", claiming some unique historic mission as well as the idea of man as the "elect of God", receiving his warrant within a social and moral order sustained by divine authority. With a schematism, to which at times Bakunin was prone, he establishes "three principles, which constitute the essential conditions of human development, collective and individual alike: (1) human animality, (2) thought, and (3) revolt". The fact that he should have singled out these three elements as constitutive of man—to the exclusion of all moral, emotional and aesthetic experiences—is interesting both in itself and as an expression of Bakunin's own personality and characteristic attitudes. He was, in fact, a profoundly amoral, unemotional and unaesthetic being, and the impelling forces in his own life were: animality, thought and revolt. "Only man endowed with spirit and thought", Bakunin continues, "is familiar with the instinct of discord and revolt, whereby life is made and the objective order is overthrown, and without which life itself would turn into a stagnant swamp." History begins, and history will end, with an "act of disobedience and of knowledge, with rebellion and thought". "God admitted to Satan and recognized the fact that he (Satan) had not deceived Adam and Eve when he promised knowledge and freedom as a reward for disobedience, for God said to himself afterwards: 'see there, man has become like one of us, he knows good and evil'." Man, admittedly, cannot undo his animality, but he can and must deny and humanize it through freedom. Freedom is the "initial principle of man's separation" from his own animal nature, which involves him in the "objective course of things", "enmeshes [him] into the causal flux of the world" and "reduces him to dependence on the laws of nature".[29] Here revolt and freedom stand for what in Moscow Bakunin called God, as when he wrote that "man becomes man by virtue of immersion in God, without whom he is a mere animal". Bakunin formulates the problem of freedom in avowed opposition to what might be called the forensic notion of freedom as blameworthiness, as a kind of instrument of torture invented for the confusion of moral consciousness. Freedom which entitles the allocation of praise and blame was to him valid only so long as it created guilt, "like the Jehovah of the Old Testament": it was an egregious trick for making man accountable in a court of law, the expression of a desire, hypocritically camouflaged, to create for oneself a right to administer punishment, or the right for God to do so. Such a freedom does not originate, or move, or create anything; it only provides the hangman with a moral alibi. He saw the looming threat of religious and secular inquisitors snatching at this freedom as though it were the devil's tail by which they hoped to bind man hand and foot; and he was even prepared to advocate man's complete dependence on society, in order to counter a notion which is, in the last analysis, a betrayal of freedom and a way of rendering the mistrust of freedom man's second nature.

The irony of the objective course of things, Bakunin argued, is that it turns out to be suicidal, for by giving rise to man it prepares the ground for its own denial. Man's life is founded on "reality" (sometimes called "rational reality", or "natural law", or "coarse matter"), yet his impetus is provided by a free act of his own, defying all reality, all natural laws, all legitimate succession and established order. He is viewed by Bakunin as in some sense, self-creating, as choosing to be what he is, as inventing or designing himself as he goes along. The creative act of man "attempts the impossible"; it is a gesture of subjective asseveration of infinite freedom, in which the human spirit declares and establishes its transcendence over the "material" and "rational" world. The search to find oneself beyond, and in revolt against, the given constitutes the human condition, and revolt, therefore, is essential to the re-creation and renewal of man. The search is infinite and unceasing and, since man is irrevocably bound to time and history and torn by finality, he is for ever driven towards an end that is at least as thoroughgoing and as absolute as the freedom from which the search received its orientation. As he scales his mountains, peak beyond peak, the insufficiency of each partial achievement and the ensuing instinctive desire to surmount the unsurmountable travel with man. He discovers new energies which serve equally for creation and destruction, for the creation of the missing superiority and the destruction of what has already been attained. Hell for Bakunin was to succeed so well that nothing remained to be done, and that is why he never did succeed. He ridiculed the heyday of idealism, when people discovered all sorts of bad reasons for satisfying themselves that "the sought for absolute has been found, and that it can be bought wholesale and retail in the capital of Prussia". "I cleave to no system", he wrote, "I am only a seeker." It was not man, however, against whom Bakunin revolted, but, as he says in his *Confession*, "above all against things", against the crushing weight of the external objective world which endangers freedom. With every embodiment he perceived, to use his earlier Hegelian idiom, the looming threat of "externality", an idol coming in sight, an anti-climax, a perversion, a falsification against whose power of resistance man measures his freedom. And having destroyed one idol, Bakunin proceeded to destroy new ones, unable ever to give himself up, and ready to abolish all courts of law and the sole court of law which had the power to release or to condemn him.

In this creative and destructive quest Bakunin's greatness began, and in it also his doom was sealed. He appears like a Russian Faust, deprived of all the conventional and vapid Goethian symbols, who in his whole life, temperament and outlook embodied the tension which holds together and divides boundless, transcendent spirit and immanent, confined nature, and which creates and perpetuates revolt. He was at bottom driven by a desire, in a world of men, to be more than man, to be a God, defying both the hostile universe which men are unable to resist and the thousand watching deities the hem of whose garments they kiss. "I suffer, because I am a man and want to be a God."[30] Something eternal abides in man: it is his ability to revolt, to put the universe in question, to go beyond the given, the irrevocable, the final, to presume nothing but the absolute, for which every triumph and every triumphant one is derision and illusion. So it was that revolt itself acquired for Bakunin an almost mystical significance.

It is significant that Bakunin retained throughout, in his atheist no less than in his theist (or pantheist) phase, a strong religious and mystical tendency. "We must act not only politically", he wrote at a crucial point in his intellectual development (in *Reaction in Germany*), "but act religiously in politics itself—religiously in the sense of freedom"; and in a letter during the same period: "faith, more faith!—in faith there is truth and depth. Only our thoughts, feelings and intentions which issue from the depth of our heart give us insight into that which is our own highest (reality), into that which gives us the right to know ourselves by the sacred name of man." Five years later he wrote to Annenkov of his revolutionary creed: "In all this, you will say, there is a great deal of mysticism: but who is not a mystic? Can there be a drop of life without mysticism? Life is only where there is an open, unbounded and therefore . . . indeterminate mystical horizon . . ."; and again, in an undated letter (probably in 1848) to a Polish friend (Eliodor Storzhowsky): "I seek God in men, in their love, in their freedom; and now I seek God in revolution." We have it on Turgenev's evidence that the last time he saw him in London (in 1861) Bakunin "still believed in a personal God, and, in a conversation with [Turgenev], in the old romantic fashion, walking in the street by moonlight, censured you [Herzen] for your unbelief". The religious note, however, had by no means disappeared even after 1869, the year in which he unsuccessfully challenged the Congress of the League of Peace and Freedom in Berne to adopt a resolution to the effect that "the existence of God was irreconcilable with the happiness, dignity, morality and freedom of man". He repudiated "God and the principle of power both human and divine" in order to vindicate man, but in that vindication he continued to undergo all the stimulation and ardours of religious experience. It was, in fact, a quest for the "absolute" liberation of the "absolute" personality of man, which is evidently inexplicable in any "relative", positivistic terms. Admittedly, he styled his intellectual position at that time "scientific rationalism" or "rational philosophy", as "positivism" (in the Comtian sense), or simply as "materialism".[31] But belief in science, which he shared with Belinsky and Herzen, led him to no deterministic conclusions and did not prevent him from declaring an unsparing war on the claim of science to dominate life, and on the myth of scientific progress that has deluded mankind into thinking that science and the systems of knowledge it has built exist and advance without man. While scientists were still groaning and travailing for the certainty of laws, Bakunin was deriding the "secure, impersonal, generalized, abstracted, insensitive quality of scientific principle and method"; and he contrasted them with "life that is all impermanence and flux, all palpitating with individuality, sensibility, sufferings, joys, strivings, needs and passions". They aim at a unity, at generalizing the particular cases into the abstract formula which includes them all, at including separate phenomena in one law. In doing so, Bakunin contends, they fail to reflect or describe things as they are and as they are related to each other and to man, and remain at a remove from concrete, living reality. "All the sources of life would dry up under the impact of their abstract and learned breath." "What I preach", concludes Bakunin, "is *the revolt of life against science*", which is "a ceaseless victimization of fleeting but real life on the altar of eternal abstractions".[32]

Similarly the "matter" of Bakunin's materialism is defined by him in conscious opposition to the mechanistic notion of a "blunt and lifeless mass"—a "residue after all that constituted the strength, movement, intelligence (what the idealists call the 'spirit') of real beings has been abstracted from them", a *caput mortuum* "infinitely more stupefying and inert than any idealistic God". In point of fact matter is "impetuous, for ever moving, active and creative"; and the way in which Bakunin describes it foreshadows certain modern physical theories which discard the concept of motion as something external and accidental, and reject the separation of what matter is from what it does.[33] But he failed to work out these, as so many other ideas, and to relate them to his anthropological trichotomy.

Since he sought "God in freedom", Bakunin could not but view the notion of man as a means to the accomplishment of divine ends, or an instrument for the execution of providential purposes, as a betrayal of man. He would not perhaps have uttered Belinsky's or Dostoevsky's conviction that God is in the child that sheds tears, rather than in the world order by which those tears are said to be justified, for he had little of their infinite compassion for the individual human being; yet for him, too, truth lay in the "particular" that rebels against the "whole", and in freedom that defies necessity. "There is no room in the world for pre-determined plans or pre-established and foreseeing laws."[34] God to Bakunin's mind was, in the last analysis, but man who in the awareness of his limitations transcends them in his divine imagining: "Heaven", he wrote, echoing Feuerbach, "is enriched by the offals of the earth"; it stands for the transvaluation of lost or unowned goods into securities of an imperishable order, and the Church is "a heavenly dram shop". Nevertheless, though religious beliefs are not what the "illusions of theology" make them, they retained for him a creative significance as symptoms of "man's inwrought passionate protest against the conditions of earthly existence". But the "heavenly signs and symbols", springing though they do from within human consciousness, have a habit of turning into hypostatized agents and of submitting man to their power. The notion arises that all life is the consequence of a compulsory force exercised over the subject. It is at this point that Bakunin's denial of religion becomes a religion of denial, and his atheism a militant antitheism, with all the religious undertones which such an attitude entails. The sentiment that if God did not exist it would be necessary to invent him turns into the less communicable and less frivolous experience of some final confrontation with God, expressed in the idea that if God does exist, then, in spite of his ubiquity and his power over life, it is necessary to destroy him or to sink to crawling, fearful worship. "If perchance God exists", Bakunin said, "there is only one way in which he might serve the cause of freedom: by ceasing to exist." "If God really exists, one must dispose of him."[35]

One can detect here a new parallel with *The Possessed* of Dostoevsky, and, in particular, with that counterpart of Stavrogin which is personified with agonizing intensity in the figure of Kirilov. Kirilov chose to kill himself so as to free man from obsession by God, who is the "pain of the fear of death". To die is passive, to kill oneself is to turn a passive condition into an exalted deed, into an act of complete, total, absolute possession of oneself. There is to be no more searching, no groping after ideals and thoughts, no qualms, no conflicts which normally unbalance man's mind. Man is to be his own master. "One, the one who is first", says Kirilov in the muffled, inarticulate fashion Dostoevsky assigns to him, "must at all costs kill himself; who else will otherwise begin and prove. But I declare my self-will and am bound to believe that I don't believe. This alone will save men, change them physically in the very next generation; because, as I see it, in his present physical shape, it is quite impossible for man to be without the bygone God. . . . I kill myself, in order to show my contumacy and my new and terrible freedom." "If God is not, then I am God. . . . If God is, then his will is all, and without his will I cannot be. If not, then my will is all, and I am bound to declare my own will. . . . I alone in world-history have declined to concoct God." A poignant, laconic dialogue ensues between Kirilov and Stavrogin, summing up with the utmost simplicity a tremendous problem:

Kirilov: "Whosoever teaches that all men are good will end the world." *Stavrogin:* "He who taught this was crucified." *Kirilov:* "He will come and his name will be man-God." *Stavrogin:* "God-man?" *Kirilov:* "Man-God, that's the difference."

136

This fantastic, wanton philosophy has its exact prototype in Bakunin's atheism, which he himself called "anti-theologism", although he stopped short of drawing Kirilov's final conclusion in suicide. To remain in relation with God, Bakunin argued in *The Knouto-German Empire*, is to abdicate each and every part of one's self, for it is upon the power of an irreducible egotism that man draws for the reality and liberty of his existence. How can man be free in any but a rhetorical sense as against the principle to which as man he ought to be subject, and how is man to exercise his free determination of himself if an almighty and omniscient Deity determines the first and final causes of his existence? "If God is all", Bakunin says, "the real world and man are nothing. If God is truth, justice, goodness, beauty, power and life, then man is falsehood, iniquity, evil, ugliness, impotence and death. If God is master, man is a slave." "With all respect to the metaphysicians and religious idealists, philosophers, politicians or poets: the idea of God is the supreme and final negation of human liberty, and necessarily ends in the enslavement of mankind both in theory and practice." "He who desires to worship God must harbour no childish illusions about the matter, but bravely renounce his freedom and humanity." The "fiction of the heavenly overlord" has condemned man to "irretrievable animality", and has, as a matter of historical fact, made God the "ally of tyrants, torturers and the exploiters of humanity". "God cannot be justified by the world, he can only be denied that way." "If God is", Bakunin concludes, "man is a slave. But man can and must be free, and therefore God cannot exist. I defy anyone to escape this circle: now therefore let us choose!"[36]

Bakunin's atheism, which Masaryk aptly described as an ontological proof of the non-existence of God, has in fact a strongly dualistic bias of a Marcionite or Manichean character, to which Belinsky had already given voice: his horror of the enslavement of man, of historical and social necessity, conjures up a view of the world as the realm of the Prince of Darkness, of an unexplained evil presence, an evil God, the creator and ruler of the world. It was an attitude bound up with a sense of evil more potent, perhaps, because imprecise, although it was sufficiently precise for Bakunin, who saw its pre-eminent embodiment in the phenomenon of power and of the will to power. In the heat of his rejection of power as the source of evil, Bakunin was burning himself in his own flames, for his judgment on power is nothing if not a Nemesis of his own intellectual hubris, and of the unquenchable instinct for domination by which he tried to sway, and succeeded in swaying, his contemporaries' minds and hearts. But this made the rejection all the more intense. "If there is a devil operating in human history, then he must be the principle of power. It alone, together with the stupidity and darkness of the masses, by which it is sustained and without which it could not operate, it alone has given rise to all the misfortunes, crimes

137

and infamous facts of history."[37] He was familiar with but one idea and one experience of God, whereby man stands in relation to God as a slave to his master, and God appeared to him solely as the pantocrator, who in the plenitude of his power sets in motion, manipulates, and makes use of, the world and each individual to his own glory and for the establishment of a common order. And it is this idea and this experience that urged him to rightful rebellion. The whole logic of *de haut en bas* and *de bas en haut*—whether in divine-human relations or in society—was to him a piece of repugnant exteriorization and objectification, leading to slavery: "Love of the highest for the lowest", he said, "is despotism, and love of the lowest for the highest is slavery."[38]

Bakunin's dualistic tendency, his refusal to see history as motivated by superior forces or a divine will, and his belief that only the devil could have inspired man to endow power with divine attributes is particularly illuminating for an estimate of the optimism, romanticism and utopianism which are customarily ascribed to him. It has been suggested that by temperament and conviction Bakunin was pre-eminently a romantic; that he was moved as passionately as Rousseau and the progressives and perfectionists of the Victorian age by a belief in the innocence of untrammelled and unperverted human nature, which requires nothing but "the enjoyment of its native freedom to achieve perfection".[39] I believe this picture to be misleading. There is, admittedly, a sense in which romanticism can be attributed to Bakunin, no less than to Belinsky and to other Russian revolutionary thinkers: it would be superfluous to dwell on what has previously been said in this connection. In some ways Bakunin was more romantic than the rest, for no one seems to have experienced the hostility of the external world more than he did, both in his early idealistic days and in his later revolutionism and anarchism. He himself said (in the *Confession*) that his "radical defect [was] a love for the fantastic, for unusual, unheard-of adventures, which open up vast horizons, and the end of which cannot be foreseen"; and Stankevich remarked that "every time Bakunin returned home he expected to find something unusual". But his attitude in this respect presents an extreme example of the conclusion of all human dramas: that there is no making out anything within the confines of this world, that the search is perpetual, that revolt must persist, since it is constantly broken on what takes shape by and congeals in human minds and hands. Such an attitude, involving, as it did for Bakunin, nothing less than to become a God, had in it something of the tragic and the absurd: it signified an endless unavailing toil with Sisyphus on the mountain-side, or, more precisely, an endeavour to reach the summit when the world is so infinitely flat, to build a tower of Babel when there is no heaven, and to reach the divine while there is no God. Can this tragedy be countered and overcome unless there is a hope at least as deeply-grounded and as ultimate as that tragedy and that absurdity themselves: that is to say, a hope in the return of God? Can it, without him, prove anything but the phantasmagoria of a Stavrogin, or, at most, of the projected figure of a posturing Zarathustra, and, behind that, of a dizzy and insane Nietzsche? But Bakunin had none of Nietzsche's torment at the death of God, none of his "*Komme zurück mein unbekann-ter Gott, mein Schmerz, mein letztes Glück!*" Although never able to eliminate in himself the religious sense that he eventually condemned in others, he was committed to one thing alone: to a perpetual crossing of all frontiers and, on the way, to laying the dynamite at their founda-tions; but also to a manipulation and dissipation of the dynamite—sometimes in the interest of political conspiracies, sometimes in order to magnify or to minimize the rôle of the established order.

It is purposeless to ask whether Bakunin's attitude pertains to romantics, idealists or materialists: it goes beyond the tidy framework of abstractions, and its ideological achievement was perhaps to have exploded all ideological systems, to have reached an extreme situation and re-kindled the soul-purging and mind-purging fire of negation. To enable a sanctuary to be built up a sanctuary has to be destroyed: indeed, it has to be destroyed in the very act of building it, because that is the price of safeguarding the truth about man and his freedom.

Whatever "romantic" folly may be attributed to Bakunin, he cannot from any point of view be considered an escapist, consolatory romantic. He had none of the introspective, head-in-the-air unreality of traditional romanticism, none of its fatigue and weary sentimentality, even while his restless mind drove him on and ultimately separated him from the ex-ternal world. Nor had the problem with which he was concerned any-thing in common with Rousseau's or Tolstoy's appeal to Nature as a way of salvation from the falsehood of civilization. His problem was not one of passing from civilized to untrammelled natural existence, but from civilized and natural existence alike to freedom. Man, to Bakunin's mind, was crushed and enslaved by the world of Nature no less than by that of civilization. In a realm where human beings, things, and events are ruled by the dark evil of power there is no foothold and no resting-place anywhere. It is a world the bottom of which had fallen out and in which nothing remained but to go on rebelling. In avowed opposition to Rousseau, Bakunin derided the notion of some pristine idyllic exist-ence in which everything tells of bucolic simplicity, innocence, love and concord. The "absolute necessity of warre" was to him, no less than to Hobbes, the mark of the state of Nature, with all the attribution of radical evil to the "natural" human condition that this view implies. The "legend of a prehistoric golden age", ignorant of good and evil, he contends, has been done away with, and he claims in support of this all kinds of evidence from anthropological, ethnological and sociological sources, probably made available to him by Réclus.[40] No harmony, whether in the past or present, can be detected in the world, and no kind of eternal, unchangeable, objective, or "natural" principles can be said to decide, or even to have decided, its course. To suppose that they do, is an illusion of enslaved minds arising from social and spiritual conformity with the existing order. Harmony may be sought for, but to achieve it is an act of creative destruction or destructive creativity, i.e. it signifies the unconditional end of this compulsory and subservient world of ours.

If it is difficult to accept the picture of Bakunin as an optimistic "advocate of a return to Nature" (Carr), it is similarly erroneous to represent him as a lucky iconoclast, like some Victorians who were faced with an expanding English universe and its boundless opportunities. He lacked the Victorian belief in reason, according to which if man reasons well, patiently and clearly enough he will discover truth; he lacked the faith in the natural balance and harmony of movement inherent in history and society, which, after all, carries all the symptoms of religious providentialism *in statu saeculari*; above all he lacked the sense of morality, useful and otherwise, and of the greatest happiness of the greatest number of Englishmen. He could not adhere, as the Victorians did, to that sense of moral propriety and obligation which made Leslie Stephen exclaim that he believed "in nothing, but not the less believed in morality" and meant "to live and die like a gentleman"; or prompted Mill, possibly after having become convinced that Noah's Flood was a fiction, to announce that "there is no God, but this is a family secret"; or moved George Eliot to translate Strauss, Feuerbach and Spinoza and write novels which became Sunday reading for Victorian parents. He knew none of their crises in which strenuous faith struggled with strenuous doubt, with an agony that almost matched the agony of the proletarian humanity outside; nor of the genuine feeling which they at times betrayed—but, had he had any, he would, unlike them, have undoubtedly known what to do with it. Above all he did not, like the Victorians, merely pretend to be unrespectable and rebellious, while in fact they were conservative, prim and touchy.

Bakunin denied completely and ceaselessly, not just by way of dropping a brick or two from the edifice of prejudice and waiting smilingly for the result: it was a genuine denial for which, in a sense, only those facts had any meaning which offered opportunities for destruction, although he did not exactly pray God, as Belinsky may have done, that he might have enemies to keep him alive. Religion, art, literature, philosophy, all social and spiritual hierarchies and values, and all settled beliefs and convictions had to be continually rejected, lest the bounds of human freedom and creativity should draw tight and man should fall prey to the illusion that perfection is attained or attainable in the here and now, in the given, and the finite. "Je ne désirais qu'une seule chose", Bakunin wrote to Herwegh in 1848; "ne pas me réconcilier, me résigner, me transformer, ne pas m'abaisser à chercher de réconfort dans une quelconque illusion—conserver jusqu'à la fin, tout entier, l'esprit sacré de la révolte." What he did deny in the end was the possibility of a kingdom of God on earth—that last eschatological resort of the idolaters of religion, society, science and civilization, and he forfeited his right to join them by omitting to worship even that other idol—the fetish of the void, of mere waste and vacant space. "Kingdoms will burst, I have no doubts about that. I only wish they would burst before my eyes." He was capable of hoisting the Sistine Madonna on the walls of beleaguered Dresden, and of raising a sacrilegious hand against the "resplendent screens of despotism"—"the Tuileries, the Cathedral of Notre Dame and even the Louvre"; but to him such projects of destruction were no art for art's sake, no divine play of arbitrary devastation. He knew, of course, the extent of his encroachments. Nonetheless, all aims and objects gained in human life could be but insecure and fleeting symbols; and even these he did not fear to lose.

3. THE REVOLUTION AND THE PEOPLE

Speaking of the latter period of Bakunin's life, Annenkov wrote that "Bakunin cast himself as the perfect type of a cosmopolitan—so perfect, as himself to assume the semblance of an 'abstraction', and become almost unaccountable in terms of the real conditions of life: a type admitting of no power of habit, or of historical and geographical circumstance, in the shaping of the fate and activity of nations, in order that on their ruins a common basis might be built for the life of toiling men". And Bakunin himself said, long before his anarchistic phase, in a letter from Siberia, that "nationality, just like the process of life, has no right to be concerned with itself until that right has been denied". In the light of this "cosmopolitanism", borne out as it is by a revolutionary career that knew no barriers and limits of any kind, it is curious that Marx, Engels and their followers should have laid at Bakunin's door the charge of turgid and chauvinistic panslavism. They, in fact, mistook for nationalism Bakunin's strong belief in the revolutionary possibilities of the Russian people, and for jingoism his concern with the liberation of the Slavs from autocracy, both Austrian and Russian. Marx disliked the Slavs and Russians (until, at any rate, he realized what a wonderful career he was making among the latter), and altogether distrusted the association of national feeling and revolution.[41] His Russophobia may even have been animated, as Masaryk suggests, by the ingrained anti-Slav sentiment of the German. Moreover, Marx was an astute and rationalistic megalopolitan who saw revolution as a product of the organized industrial proletariat in the conditions of advanced and highly differentiated capitalist society. He thought in terms of strictly determined and infallible economic laws rather than of any ill-defined creative revolutionary tendencies that may or may not be discovered among the people of an economically backward country, and he regarded the peasants ("troglodytes" as he called them) as an essentially reactionary force.[42] Bakunin, on the contrary, whilst he was removed from any national historical and geographical ties and refused to dissociate the interests of town and country, saw the real source of regeneration in man's will to freedom, to be found among the Russian peasantry or among the *Lumpenproletariat* of Italy and Spain no less, if not more than, in the advanced proletariat of western and central Europe. This revolutionary will, to his mind, could not be reduced to the mere economic relations that exist between the workers and the means of industrial production. And yet, Bakunin's attitude naturally evokes now, as it appears to have evoked then, specifically Russian historical and cultural tendencies in which "Slavophil" and the allied "populist" elements were an important force.

Slavophilism and populism are rather bewildering phenomena. They acquired, in the course of the few decades of their operation on the stage of nineteenth-century Russia, a variety of discordant characteristics: they have been successively or simultaneously conservative and revolutionary, authoritarian and anarchistic, monarchical and democratic, religious and materialist, westernizing and self-consciously Russian. What united them, however, in their origin was the conception of the people as a community which precedes logically as well as historically the political concept of the nation, and contrasted the "organic", communal quality of the people with the organized body politic of the nation. The nation, according to this view, represented an abstraction, a ruling idea, a myth which, by means of ever-increasing methods of organization, finished by dominating life irrespective of the concrete human beings who constitute it, and which, though it has done away with division from the need of keeping them organized, has rendered the separation between them the more acute. The people, on the contrary, denotes the shared, inter-personal life of concrete men and women: it is free from the pretences of egotism, and yet finds its motive power in the quest for freedom; it rests not on the principles of authority and legal obligation, but on direct human relationships. It expresses itself in the concrete setting of social and cultural patterns, in modes of thinking and feeling, in characteristic customs and habits, whereas the nation builds up the vehicles and agencies of power which enable it to rationalize and organize such expressions of the people's life in the interests of national sovereignty. The people are human and have a human face; the nation is a faceless abstraction. According to the Slavophils and populists alike, that "human" aspect of the people's life expressed itself pre-eminently in the Russian *mir* or village commune, which they regarded (not quite correctly) as a spontaneous popular co-operative association that owed nothing or little to State action and other pressures from above. For the Slavophils it represented an original Russian form of life which rendered the Russian people safe against the disintegrating influences of western European individualism; for the populists it was a means of achieving a just and free society by avoiding the stage of industrial capitalism and saving Russia from proletarianization after the pattern of western Europe.

It is in the people, then, that Bakunin sought and discovered the urge to revolution; indeed, his attachment to Russia may be reduced to that search and discovery. The first signs can be seen in a long open letter to the editor of the Parisian paper *La Réforme* (January 27, 1845) which also tells of his interest in the Polish cause, as a kind of prologue to revolution in Russia, and in the cause of the other Slavs, victims of "the monstrous Austrian empire". It provides the tone for his powerful and widely acclaimed speech in the same year on the occasion of the anniversary of the Polish Rebellion of 1831; for his part in the Slav Congress in Prague, where he felt, as he subsequently confessed to the Tsar, his "Slav heart stirring"; and for all the other attempts to induce the Slavs to rise against their Russian, Austrian and German oppressors. It received its full expression in an *Appeal to the Slavs* ("by a Russian patriot, Mikhail Bakunin"), where he tells of his belief in the Russian peasantry as the decisive factor in the coming revolution.[43] "The slavery of all the Slav peoples united under the Russian sceptre", he wrote with uncannily prophetic irony, "will be smashed in Moscow, and with it every European slavery . . .; the star of revolution will rise high and independent above Moscow from a sea of blood and fire, and will turn into the lodestar to lead a liberated humanity." It is known that, while in London, Bakunin collected signatures for a petition to Alexander II to convene a Land Assembly (*Zemsky Sobor*) in Moscow. He also wrote an article ("The People's Cause. Romanov, Pugachev or Pestel") for *Kolokol* which Herzen refused to publish, dismissing it as "a medley of Bakuninist demagogy", where he asked: "With whom, where, and in whose footsteps shall we go: with Romanov, with Pugachev, or, if a new Pestel should arise, with him? Let us be frank: we would much rather follow Romanov, if Romanov could and would change from a Petersburg Emperor into a *zemsky* Tsar."[44] At bottom, however, he would rather have had Pugachev. One is, by the way, not surprised to learn that the Polish exiles, themselves inveterate messianists of a tetchy, politico-mystical kind, regarded such prophecies and aspirations with a mixture of horror and disgust. Finally, Bakunin's *Confession* is largely a testimony of his faith in the vocation of the Russian and Slav peoples "to renew the decadent Western world". And though he repudiates his own revolutionary past in regard to Russia, he pays tribute (in the circumstances, a suicidal tribute) to the revolutionaries, and stigmatizes oppression in Russia. "I am supposed", Nicolas I noted on the margin of a page of Bakunin's text, "to take the helm of the revolution, like a Slavonic Massaniello. Thank you very much!"

Throughout all these utterances there runs a hatred of the Germans more explicit and passionate than any aversion Marx may have entertained against the Russians and the Slavs. "I preach, ardently and systematically, hatred of the Germans," Bakunin wrote to his sister-in-law: "I say about them what Voltaire said about God: 'if there were no Germans it would be necessary to invent them'." Not much credence, on the other hand, should be attached to the charge of an equally strong hatred of the Jews. Where his alleged anti-Semitism is not mere rhetoric (of which there are signs even in Herzen, although there are none in Belinsky), it was prompted entirely by uncontrolled resentment born of personal feuds with the Marxists, with Marx himself, with Lasalle, Liebknecht, Wertheim, Hess' and a minor revolutionary exile called Nicolas Utin, who was for a time a collaborator of Bakunin's but then withdrew and tried to incite Marx against him, and eventually went back to Russia, where he ended his days as a rich business man. They were all directly and indirectly responsible for a systematic campaign of slander against Bakunin as "a cunning Russian spy". The campaign went on intermittently for many years, both before and after Siberia, and Bakunin was never able to extricate himself entirely from this plainly undeserved odium. There is not a shred of evidence of any anti-Jewish feelings or utterances before these calumnies began to spread. When he denounced the "crowd of Jewish pygmies", he added: "Not Jesus Christ, St. Paul, Spinoza and other great Jewish figures"— not even Marx, for whom he had a great respect, despite his disagreements with him and Marx's own part in spreading the slanderous rumour. He was also fond of calling himself an "eternal Jew".[45] Admittedly, Bakunin had a tremendous talent for hatred (of a general and abstract kind). His hatred for the Germans, however, was *sui generis*. It was partly "tactical", for, as he said with some justification in the same letter to his sister-in-law, "nothing is more capable of uniting the Slavs than a deep hatred of the Germans". But in the main it was a case of profound incompatibility which Herzen shared with him to the full. He could not tolerate certain types of obsession which with the Germans is greater, in degree and in kind, than with common humanity: the obsession with power, authority, obedience, order and duty. One of his most incisive indictments of Germany is contained in *The Knouto-German Empire and Social Revolution*, written after the abortive Lyons rising in which Bakunin took a leading part. There he states that the difference between a German and a Slav consists in that the former "has freely swallowed a stick", while the latter "must be kept under a stick". "Have not the Germans always used [the principle of authority] as an excuse for their attempts upon freedom and upon the independence of the Slav peoples? . . . It is, so they say, the triumph of civilization over barbarism." "In all the respectable classes which represent German culture, servility is not only a natural state of affairs, resulting from natural causes: it has become a system, a science, a kind of religious cult; and for this reason it assumes the character of an incurable disease. Can you imagine a German bureaucrat, or an officer of the German army, or a German professor conspiring and rebelling on behalf of freedom . . .? Undoubtedly not."[46] A German defers instinctively to *Obrigkeit*, not because he is afraid of those who rule over him, but because he is afraid of finding himself without rulers. "The Germans are too servile and stupid for revolution." Their social and political upheavals have as a rule proceeded in perfect peace and order, and only subsequently has it occurred to historians to attach the name of revolution to what had happened. It is typical of the Germans to hold their government officials, their *Beamtentum* in high esteem: it is the bulwark of order. In Russia the word "government official" (*chinovnik*) is a word of abuse; in Germany it is a commendation. The methodical pedantry and pedantic methodology of the Germans has turned them into a people more susceptible of being organized and more capable of organizing everybody and everything than any other people in the world: it has narrowed their outlook and imbued them with the spirit of "small circumstances". They can command and obey, but they are unable to improvise or decide and act spontaneously; they instinctively say and do things calculated to quench any spark of inspiration or appetite for change, and yearn for the security of the big battalions. They always quote authorities but are themselves unquotable. They are soldiers in mind and soul, rather than from necessity or even from patriotism. Even in Russia it is Germany that Bakunin hated most: "I am firmly convinced", he wrote to Herzen in 1863, "that our principal enemy is Petersburg, more than the French and the English . . .— Petersburg which is in reality a camouflaged German. Consequently nothing will stop my continuing the life and death struggle against Petersburg." This is pure Herzen (or perhaps even a calculated imitation of him), but it is also pure Aksakov, whose early influence on Bakunin is unmistakable.[47]

Sometimes Bakunin inclined, again like Herzen and even Belinsky, to extend his diatribes against the Germans to western Europeans at large, especially where, as in his *Confession*, he gave vent to his disillusion in western Europe, which was, despite the special character of the *Confession*, perfectly sincere and squared with his attitude at other times and in other circumstances. He upbraided them for what he considered to be their reverence for power, resulting in a perpetual, frustrating desire to reduce every freedom and chaos to law and order; for their desperate urge to keep their material chattels intact, their smoothness, insipidity, liberalism and emptiness of all that is passionate or fanatic, and at the same time for the narrowness which makes them penetrating but stiff, diligent but distrustful, exacting but inflexible and presumptuous.

L

These German and western European qualities Bakunin contrasts with a familiar set of what are considered to be characteristically Russian attitudes: a large and generous humanity; a directness of apprehension, unspoiled by the standards and prejudices of cultivated and civilized existence; a readiness to take all the risks of freedom and to infringe the rules of social and spiritual segregations and exclusions; and above all a striving after infinity and a horror of erecting relative and limited forms and patterns of living into absolute norms and values.[48] Russians are known to be devoted practitioners of the art of allocating national characteristics and charting national psyches; Herzen and the Slavophils were past masters in this, although Bakunin did not lag far behind: and he was, temperamentally at least, nearer to the Russian people than Herzen, who criticized him for lack of acquaintance with the real Russia. They could never resist the temptation of generalizing and moralizing about national types—a tendency which probably springs from the painful urge to produce an explanation for the contradictions between theory and practice in the life of their own people. But their charts and allocations are no less vivid, revealing and at times even true for all that.

And yet it is essential to insist that the "revolutionary panslavism" of Bakunin, to use once more that misleading designation, was a far cry from nationalist ideas and sentiments. Even before he became a determined internationalist and his anarchist views were established, during his pro-Slav activities in the late 'forties, he learned to distrust nationalism, its leaders and its "patriotic *bourgeois* rhetoric". Later, all his writings and utterances were to be concerned with and addressed to a humanity as expatriate, and therefore as ripe for revolution and anarchy as his own. When he moved to Italy he realized the unreality of even a revolution dominated by nationalist feelings, and he took the lead among the Italian left-wing revolutionaries in the emancipation of the Italian movement from the influence of Mazzini's nationalism. There were, admittedly, many things in common between Bakunin's conspiratorial ideas and practices and those of Mazzini, the cloak-and-dagger man, but he found himself in violent opposition precisely to Mazzini's nationalism, based as it was on metaphysical sanctions and duties, and made particularly unreal against the background of the stark and sordid realities of mid-nineteenth century Italy. Bakunin was, no doubt, unfair to Mazzini, and, unlike Herzen, he failed to see his liberating significance in the Italian *risorgimento*. He perceived only ominous symptoms of nationalistic authoritarianism. But they were certainly there, and were perhaps even a pre-figuration of modern fascism.

Bakunin, "the most disobedient subject of the Russian Empire", as he described himself, and "the prototype of a free Russian", as Herzen described him, acknowledged that the name "Russian" had become a synonym for brutal oppression and slavery. Repudiation of "so-called patriotism and rivalry between nations" became a basic tenet of the Alliance of Social Democracy which Bakunin and his associates established after having broken away from the League of Peace and Freedom. In the earlier London article quoted above he says that those who rule Russia "see salvation in nipping . . . the awakened life of the people in the bud. . . . Where there are heights there are precipices too; and that same life, uncomprehended, wounded, trampled upon by the ludicrous attempts of pygmies to arrest its inexorably logical course, will throw them [the rulers] off, together with all their German counsellors, home-bred doctrinaires, with all their bureaucratic police scum, into the bottomless abyss." They are trying to turn Russia into a machine, into a sub-human organism, into the projection of an insane lust for power, of obsession with meaningless words, and of devotion to inhuman ideals. Even "the people" (in the Slavophil and populist sense), even the *mir* or communal social system—hitherto the prototypes of just and free relations—failed to satisfy him any more as a safeguard of human freedom. "You are all ready to forgive", he wrote in 1866 from Ischia to Herzen who still held on to his populist ideal, "perhaps to support everything, directly or indirectly, if only you can keep inviolate your mystical holy of holies—the Great-Russian commune, from which . . . you expect salvation not only for the Russian people, but for all Slav lands, for Europe, for the whole world. . . . Why is it that you refuse to meet clearly and in earnest a serious charge against you: you have stumbled on the Russian *izba*, which has itself stumbled and for centuries rests, with all its right to the land, in Chinese immobility? Why has this commune, from which you expect such wonders in the future, failed to bring about, in the course of ten centuries of its existence, anything but heinous slavery?[49] The odious putridity and the complete injustice of patriarchal habits, the absence of freedom for the individual in face of the *mir*, the stifling pressure which that *mir* exercises, killing every possibility of personal initiative, depriving its members not only of juridical rights but of simple justice in its decision . . . , the ruthless severity of its attitude towards every weak and poor member, its systematic oppression of those members who display the slightest independence, and its readiness to sell out truth and justice for a pail of vodka—such is the real nature of the Great-Russian peasant commune."

Still the true Russian, *vir iustus ac propositi tenax*, whom no imposition and no threatening tyrant can shake, has retained as no other the destructive and creative power of rebelliousness. It was, in fact, not the Mazzinist Italian "sacred altar on which God will descend", but the liability of the Russians to violent outbursts of revolutionary feeling, on which Bakunin's faith in Russia took its stand, and in which he saw a pledge of victory over the exaltation of social, political, cultural and religious hierarchies and disciplines above freedom, truth, justice and humanity. For this reason he proceeded to make capital out of every revolt recorded in Russian history. And the more he realized that it represented the triumph of chaos over law and order, and all the other values and sanctities that his century most revered, the more he felt it would have been cowardly and dishonourable, as well as opposed to his convictions, to refrain from the holocaust. Nobody, indeed, has ever dared to immerse himself more completely in the total experience of revolution than Bakunin. In a series of revolutionary proclamations, for which he, together with the gentle Ogarev, was at least indirectly responsible, and especially in the notorious *Catechism of a Revolutionary*, in the composition of which he definitely had a share, Bakunin conceived a passionate apologia for brigandage—the "traditional protest" of the Russian peasant.[50] "The time of Stenka Razin is at hand. Brigandage is one of the most honourable forms of Russian national life. The brigand in Russia is the authentic, the only revolutionary, a revolutionary without phrases, without bookish rhetoric, an irreconcilable, unflinching, unbound revolutionary of the whole people, not of a class. In difficult times of transition when the toiling peasants, bowed down by the weight of the State, seal their eyes in what seems an eternal sleep, the brigands continue the desperate struggle in the forests, and struggle until such time as the Russian village awakens once more. And whenever the two unite, the revolt of the brigands and of the peasants, there ensues the Russian revolution. Such were the movements of Stepan Razin, Pugachev ...."[51] "Our business", we read in what sounds an unmistakably Bakuninist outburst in the *Catechism of a Revolutionary*, "is a terrible, wholesale, world-wide and ruthless destruction. Let us unite with the wild world of brigands—this true and only revolutionary world of Russia."

Bakunin's brigands have of course nothing whatever in common with the romantic *Räuber* of the young Schiller, gloating with posturing wickedness in glamour and power. Rather they stand for the traditional Russian *volnitsa*, for the *homo viator*, cast adrift, unclaimable and unassailable in his homelessness and continual wandering. This homelessness encourages the basic passion for destruction in human nature, which revolutions use, but which revolutionaries less candid than Bakunin try hypocritically to argue away. Few men have contributed more to the elucidation of this destructive and irrational quality of revolution than Bakunin—by his whole attitude as well as by his views and actions. It may be impossible to understand revolutions without considering the ideas and rationalizations of their ideologues; but neither can one believe that such ideas and rationalizations are the real motive of revolutionary action: they are as often as not the Procrustean bed on which irrational instincts are measured, the mythology which conceals, as well as reveals, the determining factors. "In revolution", Bakunin once observed, "there are three quarters fantasy and only one

148

quarter rational reality." And it is these three quarters with which he was primarily concerned. Despite his avowed but rather uncertain rationalism, Bakunin stood opposed to the ancient and respectable rationalistic maxim that truth can be attained with the help of our four-cornered reason, and that life and the course of history should be, or can be, made subject to it. He was interested to discover what it is that reason attempts, or is alleged, to command, and discovered that the gentle and tolerant empiricism of the rationalist is quite powerless in face of the ambiguity and irrationality of human existence, and of what might be called the misuse of reason. Like Belinsky and Herzen, and more than they, he was unable to assume the existence of a rational, more or less permanent order, which may from time to time be disturbed by crises, but, fundamentally, works on the principles of moderation and of salvation through the spread of reasonableness, light and civilized living. To his mind, revolutions, unprompted, widespread, incessant and at bottom desirable, themselves testified that in point of fact there never has been a permanent rational order. However harmonious some societies may appear from a historical distance, he believed that harmony is unattainable, and that peaceful growth and endless happiness and well-being are illusions, especially when and where they rest, as they invariably do, on injustice and oppression. Revolutions are not just exceptional states, interruptions between periods of peace and order, whose ends and beginnings join across the gap. Order can no longer make both ends meet by ignoring the interruption and reverting to an alleged normal condition, because revolution is just as normal as order. Revolutions render history itself an unreasonable, explosive process in which elemental forces and instincts operate and which cannot, therefore, be contained in any social, intellectual, or moral norm. They tell of vengeance and hatred against history itself, against a sinful, idolatrous and inhuman past and present. Those who object to revolution on the grounds of its threat to the stable patterns of moral and social life are victims of self-delusion, for the measure of the destructiveness of revolution is these patterns themselves, the rotten feebleness of the order which revolution endangers. "Every society", Bakunin wrote, "gets the revolution it deserves." As often as not revolution forms part of the old sick world which it destroys, a part in which the old poison continues to work and on which it depends for its very impetus. But at the same time it is an act of deliverance, laying open the unreality of that which gave itself out as reality, and putting an end to falsehoods that had paraded as truths, even if, one should add, it creates in its turn new unrealities and new falsehoods. Revolution cannot, admittedly, change human nature and human relations, but it gives an intoxicating, almost obsessive sense of liberation from pretences, pretexts and fictions which set up their courts for the intimidation and subjugation of man. "See ye not all these things? Verily I say

149

unto you, there shall not be left here one stone upon another that shall
not be thrown down." This prophecy was no invitation to the righteous
to watch the torments of the damned or to purify themselves of a dangerous passion by discharging it with vehemence, but a witness to the
perennial antagonism between the nucleus of God's devouring fire and
the circumference of his creation, a summons to rise against the servitude to all historical creations, to all the towers, palaces, temples and
dwelling-places—once relics of human faith and generosity, but now
turned idols—which provide man, in exchange for obedience, with a
clean and sleeping conscience: a summons to share in the eternal passion
of Becoming which is also a passion for destruction.

But revolution and its advocates cannot escape the fate of all obsessions: their maniacal thirst for extermination, their elemental violence
and hatred resolve the instinct of freedom into an instinct of terror and
show revolutions as periodic outbreaks of madness when, to exorcise
the devil in its nature, mankind itself becomes possessed. They become
instances of demonic possession to which Dostoevsky provided such
shattering testimony in his "book of the great wrath". "They [the
Jacobins, whom Bakunin disliked but to whom he transferred his
apologia for brigandage and his passion for destruction] were possessed
and had attained a state in which they rendered the whole nation
possessed." "Save France", Bakunin wrote in the famous *Letter to a
Frenchman*, "by means of anarchy. Unbridle that popular anarchy . . .
let it loose in all its breadth, so that it may flow like a furious lava,
scorching and destroying everything on its way. . . . I know this is a
daring and barbarous way . . . But without it there is no salvation.
. . . It is essential that they [the peasants] should be *possessed by a
demon* [italics in the original], and nothing but the anarchy of revolution can fill their bodies with this demon. . . ."[52] It is significant that
Dostoevsky's Possessed have also a brigand in their midst—Fedka the
Convict, whom Stavrogin incites to "go on slaughtering and thieving".
In the same way, Pyotr Verkhovensky, that other offshoot of Stavrogin's
dizzy mind, the clown, gossip and traducer of revolutionary nihilism,
who, as Stavrogin observes, could reach "a point at which he ceased to
be a clown and turned into a madman", has sinuously repeated the
Bakuninist hymn of praise to destruction: "Listen to me", he says to
Stavrogin: "we shall first unloose sedition. . . . I told you so before:
we shall infiltrate into the people. We shall throw open the doors of
drunkenness, scurrilousness, denunciation: we shall bring in unheard
of debauchery; we shall smother every genius in his infancy. . . . We
shall proclaim destruction. . . . It is necessary, absolutely necessary to
crush the little bones. . . . We shall kindle fires. . . . We shall disseminate legends. . . . And then, you see, the riot will begin! There
will be such a swing (*razkachka*) as the world has never seen before. A
dark fog will descend upon Russia, and the earth will weep over its

ancient gods. . . . And then, just then, we shall let out . . . guess whom?"
Stavrogin: "Whom?" . . . *Verkhovensky:* "Prince-Harry: you, you!"
Among the blurred and shifting identities of Dostoevsky's seemingly
inappropriate and plainly demonic, grotesque and hideous kingdom of
the Possessed Stavrogin-Kirilov proves that God is not, and that
man is free by proposing to kill himself, while Stavrogin-Verkhovensky
proves the same proposition by offering to kill others and translating
his destructive vision into the language of political deeds, of political
murder.

Bakunin, too, had his evil genius, his sinister *alter ego*, in the person
of the ex-seminarist Sergey Nechaev (1847–82) who, after some minor
revolutionary incidents in which he was implicated, left Russia and in
1869 presented himself to Bakunin in Geneva with a fantastic story of
escape from the Peter-and-Paul Fortress, where he was supposed to
have been imprisoned as a leader of the students' revolutionary movement. The story was a tissue of lies and half-truths. Contrary to the
current opinion, however, Nechaev did not invent the existence of
a considerable revolutionary movement in Petersburg and Moscow,
which became increasingly involved in terroristic activities, and of which
Pyotr Tkachev, as well as Nechaev, were active members, although
Nechaev did not play the important rôle he ascribed to himself on
arriving in Geneva. Encouraged by the confidence and credulity of
Bakunin and Ogarev, Nechaev, now known by the affectionate if quite
inappropriate English nickname "Boy", grew bolder and finished by
holding the two veterans of revolution in leading-strings. It is difficult
to say with any certainty what it was that made Bakunin for a time a
devotee of this dubious character: there was simple kindness towards
an alleged victim of revolution; there was above all sheer pleasure at the
attention shown to him by someone whom he regarded as a representative of young revolutionary Russia, which indeed Nechaev was in his
ill-made way; but there must also have been a measure of congeniality
between them for Bakunin to commit himself, wittingly and unwittingly, to such far-reaching complicity in Nechaev's ingenious and
sombre machinations. The story of these machinations has been told
many times. They comprise in the first place the murder of the student
Ivanov, a member of one of Nechaev's revolutionary Groups of Five
("*pyaterki*") inside Russia, who became too inquisitive about the largely
fictitious "Revolutionary Committee" on whose behalf Nachaev
claimed to act. In committing the murder he not only removed a potential enemy, but involved a few other men and thus, by blackmail, ensured compliance with his own authority. Bakunin cannot, of course,
be held responsible for this ugly deed, but a few months before it took
place he did supply Nechaev with an identity paper issued ostensibly
by the above-mentioned imaginary Committee, and serving as creden-
tials for Nechaev's clandestine mission in Russia. Among the other deeds

must be mentioned the series of distasteful incidents in connection with Herzen's money. "It is impossible", Dragomanov observes in his Introduction to the letters of Bakunin about one of these incidents, "to read some of Bakunin's letters of that period without revulsion, especially those which betray his efforts, now insolent, now cunning, to draw Herzen's eldest daughter into the Nechaev affair." Both Nechaev and Bakunin, and at times Bakunin alone at the instigation of Nechaev, did their best or worst to extract money from any source available in order to fill the empty and bottomless treasury of their real or hypothetical revolutionary organizations. Nechaev's rôle was also a contributing factor in the Bakunin-Marx conflict and in the final expulsion of Bakunin from the International.

Nevertheless the unqualified charges, customarily made against him, of bad faith, duplicity and perfidiousness are too serried to be altogether true.[53] His personality represents a curious blend of the *fanfaron*, in the manner of Gogol's Khlestakov, of the blackguard who believed in the legitimacy of crime in the interests of revolution, and above all, perhaps, of the disinterested and dedicated fanatic. He was a thin, undersized nervous creature, with burning little eyes and brusque gestures, continuously gnawing at and around his nails, so that his fingers were covered with sores. Dostoevsky's Pyotr Verkhovensky (with some features of Shigalev added) provides, in fact, a fairly accurate picture of Nechaev. But it may be of some interest to quote the verdict of a few independent scholars and witnesses. Boris Kozmin, in one of the most valuable works on the revolutionary movement in the 'sixties,[54] says that "all who knew Nechaev are unanimous in acknowledging him as a man for whom, always and in all circumstances, the cause of revolution stood first. He had no private life of his own and no private attachments of any kind." It is known, for instance, that while in possession of a considerable sum of money which he extracted from Herzen or, rather, which Bakunin contrived to extract from Herzen for Nechaev (part of the so-called Bakhmetiev Fund left to Herzen by a rich Russian land-owner for revolutionary purposes), he did not spend a penny on himself, even though he was starving at the time. Mikhail Sazhin, Nechaev's contemporary and a friend of the leading populist Lavrov, says in his Memoirs that Nechaev "was endowed with tremendous energy, a fanatical loyalty to the revolution, an iron strength of character, and an indefatigable capacity for work". The Tsarist government spent more money and exertion on the pursuit and detection of Nechaev than on any other nineteenth-century revolutionary, not excluding Bakunin and Herzen. A number of facts concerning his imprisonment, trial and liquidation, described by eye-witnesses,[55] and from the archives of the Third Section (by then under the direct control of the Ministry of the Interior), published by Pavel Shchegolev in 1926, cast new light on Nechaev's personality. "Of all the inmates kept in the

Fortress since 1825", Shchegolev records, "Nechaev alone displayed such an indomitable opposition to, and contempt for, the Tsarist order as to be considered by the authorities in a category of his own." His hands and feet were put in heavy irons, and the chain connecting the shackles was made specially short, so that the prisoner was compelled to remain continually in a crouching position, unable ever to get up. Open wounds which never healed covered his hands and legs. For two years he sat like this chained to the wall and to himself. From time to time (during the trial, at which he behaved with dignity and defiance) instructions were issued to flog him. Yet even then and throughout his imprisonment he continued to preach revolution to the soldiers who guarded him. They called him "our eagle", "our own intercessor", a "man not of this world". It is not a legend, but an attested fact that Zhelyabov, with whom he succeeded in communicating, helped by one of these soldiers (as he did with other populist revolutionaries, with Perovsky, Aronchik, and others), told him to choose between his (Nechaev's) liberation and the assassination of Alexander II: Nechaev (together with his political fellow-prisoner Sergey Shyryaev) urged his would-be liberators to ignore his fate and to pursue their terrorist business. He died of scurvy and exhaustion about a year after the assassination had been accomplished.

All this does not seem to be in keeping with the traditional picture of Nechaev as just a cad and a buffoon; but it is in line with the attitude and spirit of all those Karakozovs, Zhelyabovs, Savinkovs, Kalyaevs and Perovskys who, in their revolutionary terrorism, were accustomed to sacrificing themselves for a cause of which they knew little more than that it was necessary to kill and to die for it, and who, because they were prepared to give their own lives in exchange for that of their victims, were not alarmed at the loss of any values, whether of morality, propriety, society, or civility. It sufficed for these values to exist in order to be endangered and destroyed. Nechaev's *Catechism of a Revolutionary*, in the composition of which Bakunin collaborated,[56] represents a kind of manual of instruction in the ascetic and spiritual life of a revolutionary which far surpasses in rigour the most extreme forms of Syrian asceticism. The true revolutionary is required to abdicate all personal possessions, interests, attachments and feelings; he must not even have a name. "Every tender, enfeebling sentiment of kinship, friendship, love, gratitude, even honour, must be stifled by the cold passion for the revolutionary cause." He is bound to obedience *ac cadaver*, in the manner of the Society of Jesus. He "despises and abhors present-day social morality in all its forms and motivations. He regards as moral everything that promotes the triumph of the revolution." There is perhaps not so much of Bakunin in this, although a certain measure of immoralism or amoralism (as far as it was not just vilification by his enemies) was typical of him, especially during his brief association with Nechaev. But there is a great deal more Bakuninist inspiration in Nechaev's nihilistic revolutionism and exaltation of revolt of the Russian piratical kind, of which there is ample evidence in his numerous proclamations.

Yet there was one important point of discord between Nechaev and Bakunin, which appears to have provided the ideological basis for their eventual break. Nechaev was at bottom an authoritarian, however much he may have identified himself with Bakunin in relying on the inborn rebelliousness of the Russian people and in wishing to destroy all existing values and institutions. The authoritarian elements in the *Catechism of a Revolutionary* are clearly his own rather than Bakunin's. His real mentor was Tkachev, an exponent of Jacobinism, an advocate of political dictatorship, an avowed enemy of anarchism, and the nearest to being a direct precursor of Lenin.[57] Inasmuch as Nechaev had any defined political views that were not directly inherited from Bakunin, they were, like Tkachev's and unlike Bakunin's, in favour of strong and widespread organization and discipline, of the seizing of power by a revolutionary minority, and of exploiting the machinery of government, as well as the readiness of the Russian people to rebel, for revolutionary ends. It is not surprising, therefore, to read in Bakunin's letters of 1870, when their friendship was on the wane, constant disparaging references to Nechaev's "Machiavellianism", "Jacobinism" and "dirty Jesuitism", and other apposite and hard words, to which Stavrogin's contemptuous attitude towards *his* double, Pyotr Verkhovensky, provides an illuminating commentary. Whether Bakunin, in shaking himself free of Nechaev, was also guided by purely moral considerations, to which the latter was quite impervious, is a controversial point. Some of Bakunin's detractors maintain that the outcome of their collaboration was just a case of "thieves falling out". But there is no reason to suspect the sincerity of Bakunin's own moral protestation: as has been noted, he was capable of going far in his amoralism, especially when the infatuation with the "Boy" was working and prevailing upon him: yet not so far as to endorse proceedings which imperilled his inmost aspirations, above all his belief in freedom, or conjured up the phantom of "Knouto-Germanism". If he persisted in speaking warmly and affectionately of Nechaev and his devotion to the revolutionary cause, even after Nechaev had been exposed and they had finally parted company, it was because Bakunin felt that Nechaev had been his link with revolutionary Russia. The Nechaev episode was, indeed, a bridge, however slippery and precarious, between one of the greatest rebels of the "remarkable decade" and the eighteen 'sixties, between the "fathers" and the "sons"—a bridge which Herzen failed to build, and for the lack of which his own work failed.

4. ANARCHY

About a century ago Konstantin Leontiev stated what he considered to be one of the fundamental paradoxes of Russian history, that while Russia had seen the rise of one of the most striking instances of powerful State authority within its borders, the Russians were, in fact, unable to produce anything but anarchy. Leontiev deeply deplored this anarchic tendency, and suggested that Russian thought should "develop on reactionary lines", and promote strong authority and "readiness to yield to any kind of coercion". This, he hoped, would advance the "freezing" of Russia and "prevent her from rotting". He believed, at the same time, that the process of refrigeration had already been greatly helped by Byzantine, Tartar and Prussian influences on Russia's political development, and by the ensuing increase in the strength of the Russian State. This is not the place to discuss Leontiev's predilection for strong authority, or the historical questions he raises. But I believe he was right in drawing attention to the widespread tendency to anarchism in Russia, which, ironically enough, in some instances may even have served to strengthen rather than to weaken the authority of the State, although Leontiev failed to notice this. It is true that the Russians have shown little liking for the State, that they tended to regard it as an extraneous and alien element, and that, frequently, they either revolted against it, or meekly submitted to its pressure. It is no doubt significant that the theory as well as the practice of anarchism is a mainly Russian creation. Moreover, their hostility was not directed merely against the modern absolutist, omnicompetent State, but against the State as it has been known by urban man from the beginning of civilization.

Long before Russian anarchism had acquired an articulate form (in Aksakov, Bakunin, Tolstoy, Kropotkin, and others), the unguided, elemental sentiment of anarchy among ordinary Russian people made them conscious of the State as unrighteous and sinful in its very nature: they surrendered to it, but not before furiously opposing it; they fought it with fire and axe, with humble petitions (*chelobitnye*), with mass exodus into uninhabited steppes and forests, carrying with them their dream of ideal social and spiritual life and of the communal *mir*. Such is the tale of the Great City of Novgorod, of the people's rebellion in Tushino, of Stenka Razin, of Pugachev, of the Cossacks and the Raskolniks or Old Believers with their numerous sectarian offshoots. At times these movements were fired with intense religious and apocalyptic expectations, and they bred inspired prophets who called upon their countrymen to renounce all mundane power: such were the monk Savva, from the Senny Island, who preached the imminent end of the world; Evfimy, the teacher and founder of the "Wayfaring Concord" (*Strannicheskoe Soglasie*); the cossack Gavrila Zimen, who returned his Military Cross and went in search of "the City where no kings exercise authority";

Egor Rozhkov, who through terrible persecution and tortures at the hands of the Government, upheld his faith in "God as freedom", to mention only a few of the more radical and heterodox representatives.[58] But analogous currents are to be found within ecclesiastical Orthodoxy —in Nil Sorsky, in the innumerable pilgrims who traversed the Russian land in search of the true City, in the popular "walkers" (*khodoki*), "fugitives" (*beglye*), "trampers" (*nogi*), who had taken the "vow of wandering and incessant prayer", in short the whole of "vagrant Russia" (*perekhozhaya Rus*), of which there are signs even in the old Russian *byliny*.

One may feel sympathy with the Russian authorities in their reaction to the sombre fanaticism displayed by some of these prophets of anarchy, whose truth would no doubt have been better served if they had been able to refute a thing by laying it respectfully on ice, rather than by spreading apocalyptic fires and, in some cases, by advocating actual self-incineration. But no mild conscientious objection was possible in the face of a system which stood for the wholesale identification of God and Caesar, and thereby impelled the conscientious man to deny the authority of the very order of which he was a part. The invidious two-headed Russian eagle, the joint concern of Church and State, was in its turn scarcely imbued with any spirit of social grace and forbearance; it was, on the contrary, intent on arresting each and every dissenting movement against its kingdom, often using, in the process, devices of unimaginable cruelty. Yet, while official Orthodoxy excelled in providing religious sanctions and support to the State, a deeply religious feeling continued to grow among the people, that there was no abiding city. Even the somewhat idyllic and disingenuous attempt of the early Slavophils to bring about a synthesis of monarchical paternalism and libertarianism did not prevent them, and especially their most outspoken and obstinate representative Konstantin Aksakov, from voicing extreme anarchistic views.[59] There is a document—a few undated notes on two sheets of paper found after Aksakov's death among his unpublished writings—which may be regarded as the first manifesto of Russian nineteenth-century anarchism. In view of Aksakov's incontestable influence on Bakunin, preceding that of Wilhelm Weitling and Proudhon, who are currently said to have sown the seeds of anarchism in Bakunin, it may be of some interest to quote from this document at length.

"Man, as a member of society and of a people", Aksakov writes, "is faced with a choice of two ways: the way of inward truth, of conscience, and the way of outward truth, of law, of compulsion. The first is the way of community . . . and the way of the truth which is compatible with the dignity of man; the second is the way of the State. [This latter] is more alluring, more convenient and downright: the inward order is projected outwards; freedom, the source of which lies within man, is understood as mere norm, as form, system, institution. The fundamental principles of life are viewed as rules, and conscience as law. . . . However widely and liberally the State may develop, were it even to reach the extreme form of democracy, it will nonetheless remain a principle of constraint, of external pressure—a given, binding form, an institution. The more the State evolves the more forcefully it turns into a substitute for the inward world of man, and the deeper, the more closely man is confined by society, even if society should seem to satisfy all his needs. If the liberal State were to reach the extreme forms of democracy, and every man to become an officer of the State, a policeman over himself, the State would have finally destroyed the living soul in man. [People] . . . begin to realize that the falsehood resides not in this or that form of the State, but in the State itself, as an idea, as a principle; that we must concern ourselves not with the good or evil of a particular form of the State, but with the State as false in itself."[60]

The Slavophil Tsardom, like the Slavophil "people", was not meant to be a State, but a community of men and women who have repudiated power and transferred it to one man alone, to the freely chosen, elected Tsar, who carried its burden, not in the strength of divine right, but, so to speak, as a curse, and thereby ensured the people freedom from the snares of exercising authority. We know that in actual fact the Russian monarchy was far removed from the Slavophil utopia, and that it employed all the means at its disposal to assert its absolutist claims. The Slavophil's love of freedom and rejection of power proved, therefore, a cloak concealing all the things from which he shrunk with horror, and he found himself dressing up his own truth to accord with the black inclemency of real history. In contrast to this, Bakunin, once his anarchist creed was established, concealed nothing, for he did not delude himself by trying to reconcile the irreconcilable.

Modern political science concerns itself in the main with the study of the techniques of politics, with the methods by which public power is used, and with the institutions which are best adapted to the realization of particular ends. It ignores or neglects the primary moral questions of the relation of individuals to each other, of the sources of authority and State power, which are often assumed to bear little relation to the substance of the political matter, save perhaps as myths to fortify particular States. Though Bakunin was in no way anxious to fortify any State whatever, he had little that was original to say about the methods by which power is exercised, but a great deal about power itself, and especially about the iniquity of power. But before discussing Bakunin's anarchism, it is convenient to say a few words about his positive political views. These are summed up in the idea of "federalism", which has been developed with far greater cogency by western European political thinkers, notably at the various Congresses of the First International which preceded the final break between Marx and the anarchists.

"Federal" society was to be based on the co-operation of small natural groups which would "functionally" combine into larger unities, and in the end form a vast universal community, a community of communities. In so building up society from the bottom upwards, rather than by means of independent organs of authority, such as the sovereign States, Bakunin and the other federalists hoped to ensure political freedom as well as to impede the centralization and the growing authoritarian tendencies of the modern State, which lead to division into opposing power groups and hence to war. Every increase in the strength of government involved to them an increased dependence on force, and therefore a diminution of freedom. Bakunin, as we have seen, was not blind to the possibility of tyranny, even in small communities (in the Russian *mir*, for example), but on the whole he believed that freedom diminishes as the community increases in size, and he was strengthened in this belief by instinctively thinking in terms of the more spontaneous patterns of life among the Russian peasants, or in the small, industrially and economically backward communities of southern Europe. As a consequence of this he had very little that was constructive or practical to offer towards a solution of the difficulties that are involved in applying federalist principles to widely developed, industrialized societies. These and other difficulties Bakunin tended to refer to the sense of cohesion natural to human "animality" and, above all, to the overriding imperative of freedom.[61]

Bakunin would never have been content to describe the plan of his ideal society, for he had that within him which would always revolt against any plan whatever. To this extent he remained throughout a romantic and an idealist in the true sense of these words: he saw, that is to say, the measure of man's striving neither in the success and excellence of social structures, nor in moral perfection, but in an ever-renewed awareness of the reality beyond attaining. Like Péguy after him, he refused to identify the institution with the mystique. No plan could circumscribe the freedom of man, who can only know himself in revolt, in perpetual infidelity. All political obligations were intolerable, and only absolute freedom could command man's loyalty. It is significant that Bakunin, the unequalled political plotter and organizer, successively broke with every political movement and organization with which he was associated or for which he was himself responsible: his search for freedom and his unruliness inevitably burst out of the confines of all party and denomination. What he wrote before Siberia (in the already quoted passage from a letter to Herwegh) was even more valid now: "Je ne crois ni en des constitutions, ni en des lois. La meilleure constitution ne pourrait pas me satisfaire. Il nous faut autre chose: des passions et de la vie et un monde nouveau, sans lois et par conséquant libre"; and, to the same correspondent soon after: "Je ne crains pas l'anarchie mais je la désire de toute mon âme. Elle seule peut par la force nous arracher à cette mediocrité maudite dans laquelle nous avons végété depuis si longtemps." Without freedom there is no good: it is "the source and condition of every good". The good itself is no other than freedom. Inasmuch as history has a purpose, its purpose is to be sought in freedom, in man's continual liberation of himself and of others. It is "the way, the truth and the life". It is "indivisible: one cannot curtail a part of it without destroying the whole." Eve was forbidden to touch the fruit of one tree alone, yet this prohibition was tantamount to a complete negation of liberty; her disobedience, therefore, was an act of rebellion initiating the history of human liberation.[62] Even to love, he wrote in a letter to his brother Paul in 1845, is "to desire freedom, complete independence from one another: the initial act of true love is liberation from the object loved. This is my profession of faith—political, social and religious . . . and the inner meaning of all my actions and . . . convictions, and also, so far as is possible for me, of my private life. To liberate man is the only real and beneficial activity for me." The varied formulae in which Bakunin expressed what he called his "fanatical partisanship of freedom" could be quoted *ad infinitum.*

And yet Bakunin was no individualist. He questioned, in the first place, the *bourgeois* idea of liberty, which assumes a happy outcome of the natural play of human interests. Indeed, to judge from his uncompromising rejection of private property, he took a highly pessimistic view of the consequences of freedom in economic life, and regarded it as a source of slavery both for those who enjoy such freedom, and for those who serve as a means for this enjoyment: for the former, because they cease to be what they *are* and become what they *have,* and for the latter, because they are at the mercy of those who have turned into what they have, that is, of those who have exclusive possession of the fruits of their fictitious freedom. The freedom conferred on man by *bourgeois* society was to Bakunin an extreme form of dependence, a bondage to goods and money, to the gains and instruments of industrial and economic processes. And in renouncing this kind of freedom he differed not only from the advocates of *laissez faire* liberalism, but also from Proudhon, whom he admired greatly and who had influenced him; for Proudhon and the Proudhonists, too, pleaded for private property, albeit of a limited kind, against collective ownership. Bakunin's rejection of private property was fully vindicated in his personal life, since, unlike Proudhon, he had never himself attached any importance to it, had spent, borrowed and given away money generously, and, when living in penury, disdained to notice it. It is not unnatural, therefore, that money should have become for him a symbol of all that is anonymous, impersonal and unfree—used simply as a means for giving anything in exchange for anything else. A sarcastic Swedish journalist of the name of Mengel, who wrote a scurrilous obituary notice on Bakunin, recalled that for his Swedish friends Bakunin "soon became rather expensive . . . and, though he had lived for an idea, he soon proved to be equally capable of living on an idea: he had too literally applied the theory of common ownership to his friends". Bakunin was scarcely aware that he himself made his ideas open to just this kind of trivial assessment, and begged his reproving friends not to pester him "with farthings and pedantry".

But Bakunin was no individualist in a more fundamental sense. He believed in a communion transcending and, in a sense, invalidating all the categories which make national, political, military, confessional or familial collectives and which are responsible for the domination of society over man. Man is "the most individual", "the freest of all animal beings", but he is also "the most communal being". There are passages in some of his letters to Herzen, in *God and the State* and elsewhere, in which Bakunin appears to advocate the primacy of society over the individual, but he never professed the belief in an illusory, hypostatized collective consciousness, and, with all his reliance on the rebellious instincts of the people, the significance of life in society lay for him in the communicability of the individual, which man may never achieve entirely, and which Bakunin was, in fact, prevented from achieving by his perpetual dissatisfaction, but which, nevertheless, marks the extent and intensity of man's personal life. All the operations in the life of an individual had for Bakunin a social meaning, and any separation of individual and social acts was for him a way of objectifying society into a separate entity, and hence a way of subjecting man to the tyranny of abstractions. He differed fundamentally in this respect from the most radical, solipsistic anarchist, Max Stirner, who regarded man as a dissociated body, and society as a collection of dissociated, extraneous bodies. But Stirner was defeating his own aim of ensuring the freedom of the individual: for if, as he imagined, there is nothing beyond the Ego, then all relations between men become self-defence or mutual exploitation, or both at once, and man is reduced to paralysis which grips him in face of a devouring objectified world. It is not surprising, therefore, that Stirner should have arrived (in his well-known book *Der Einzige und sein Eigentum*) at the conclusion that "might is right, and there is no right without might".

For Bakunin, with all his temperamental solipsism, men are not, or ought not to be, joined into an alliance of equal, extraneously related partners left prisoners of their own lives, and entering into relations with one another at the price of limiting and diminishing personal liberty; and a community is, or ought to be, more than a set of separate entities to which the same class-name applies: that is to say, it involves more than an atomistic conception of an indifferent and inhuman "order". It is in the nature of man that he should transcend himself by reason of the immanence in him of the "other", rather than from any need of

adjusting himself to his environment. And it is in the nature of community that those who enter it are communicable. Thus Bakunin wanted
revolution to be brought about not, like the Jacobins, through the State,
but by the people (in the Slavophil or populist sense of the word),
for he believed the human relations prevailing among the people to be
least affected by the forces of estrangement and, therefore, of compulsion. In isolation "man would for ever remain an animal or a saint,
which amounts to almost the same thing. . . . Freedom cannot be a
factor making for isolation: it is, on the contrary, a way of co-operation,
a way of unification rather than of exclusion. . . . I am human and free
insofar as I acknowledge the freedom and humanity of all others. . . .
Only by respecting human nature do I respect my own humanity."[63]
Earlier (in his *Confession*) he set forth his aim in life as a search for
"one's own happiness in the happiness of others, of one's own dignity
in the dignity of those with whom one lives, [as being] free in the freedom of others".

If Bakunin's idea of freedom aimed at surmounting the shortcomings
and estrangement of self-communing and self-centred solitariness, he
yet consistently spurned any notion of attachment to something outside man. Even love, as has been seen, involved for him an element of
protest, a declaration of independence from the bondage to the object
of love. He thus continued to return, even at his most collectivist, to
the sources of revolt, to "the revolt of human personality against every
power, divine and human, collective and individual [which] is an in-
alienable part of freedom".[64]

Power, i.e. every action or attitude which compels certain actions or
attitudes in others, is the negation of freedom. Power is evil in itself:
it corrupts those who wield it as well as those who yield to it. And
since one is weary of being told that all power corrupts, it is refreshing
to hear from Bakunin that, conversely, only the more or less corrupt
reach out for power and submit to it.[65] Before attacking the State
Bakunin joins issue with the very phenomenon of power and of sovereignty, whether they be invested in moral laws or divine dispensations,
in customs or traditions, in the family or in the nation, in minorities or
majorities, in theocracy or aristocracy, in democracy or communism.
To command or to enslave is all the same, and the very quest for power
is a slavish quest, "a dream of slaves". To be in authority and to be in
obedience are conditions of reciprocal dependence and slavery. He who
leads is no less a slave than he who is led, and his very authority depends
on the subservience of those who are dragged at his wheels.

What Bakunin opposed by his anarchism were the intimations of
both an all-pervasive, coercive order and of any force which impinges
on man from without: it marked for him the climax of the liberation of
the human person from the extraneous agencies and exigencies which
operate in the individual and social life of man, and of the ensuing

delusions and follies which are justified in the name of religion and politics and muffled in the pompous garments of philosophy. His anarchism differed in this respect both from that of Prince Pyotr Kropotkin (1842–1921) and of Tolstoy. Kropotkin, who was fundamentally a liberal in the classical meaning of the term, believed in the automatic harmony of interests, in the natural human impulses to solidarity and "mutual aid". He was, however, little concerned with the freedom of the human person, save in the sense of limiting political action and creating a territory where private affairs could be peacefully pursued; and, for all his sincere and moving search for truth, justice and equity, his good-humoured, somewhat idyllic optimism, untouched by the fact that it is always susceptible of invasion by alien forces, saved him from being a *révolté* in anything but name.[66]

Tolstoy's anarchism suffered, likewise, from the limitations of rationalism and impersonalism. He rejected the exercise of force as the greatest evil in the world and the chief sign of the lack of faith in the reality of the spirit. He believed anarchy to be the mark of true and perfect life, a way of establishing the kingdom of God, whose likeness is not to be sought in the kingdom of Caesar, and whose laws are not to be derived from the compulsive requirements of worldly affairs. But, with all the disparities and conflicts which his life and character revealed, he almost succeeded in putting on himself the straight-jacket of an authoritarian moralism. He not only took for granted the over-riding divine authority of the moral law, but believed that goodness and reason would operate naturally if men were convinced of their goodness and reasonableness. He not only took for granted the evil and deluding quality of power, but also believed in the illusory nature of human life itself—that very life which he made so real and so tangible in his novels. The love which he preached with wearisome repetitiveness was an impersonal love, where not only selfishness but the very self was obliterated. In one respect, however, he was a far more consistent anarchist than Bakunin: in his uncompromising demand for the absolute identity of means and ends, in his refusal to use power and compulsion for any end whatever, and in his denunciation of even revolutionary violence as a way out. He clearly saw the self-deception and the vicious circle of hatred and misery that are involved in the blind attempt to achieve noble ends at the expense of ignoble means. Bakunin, as we shall see, was not unaware of these contradictions, despite his readiness to choose the most radically destructive course, as alone commensurate with the most real revolution; whereas Tolstoy failed, in his ideas if not in his life, to show any awareness that the good he was so passionately and inflexibly seeking was fated to operate in a dark, tortuous and recalcitrant world.

Three other contemporaries of Bakunin's who have explored the ways of anarchy must be mentioned in this connection. One of them, the English anarchist William Godwin (1755–1836), has not sufficient bearing on the study of Bakunin to require any close examination. Apart from his belief that the world could be very much better than it is, apart from his distrust of the State and of the paralysis which grips human beings in their powerlessness in the face of this huge apparatus, and, possibly, his resistance to majority worship, to "deciding", as he put it, "truth by the counting of numbers", his anarchism had almost nothing in common with Bakunin's. Godwin was a Sandemanian, an heir of the Cromwellian Elect, of the chosen few who moved with an assurance that has rarely been vouchsafed to mortals. Bakunin was an uprooted *révolté*. He was completely lacking in the equanimity and aloofness which pushed Godwin to such extremes of disregard of the power of irrational elements. Godwin's utopia of "unadulterated justice", reason and morality in virtue of unlimited perfectibility and benevolence would, had Bakunin known it, have bored him to death.

Another contemporary, Proudhon, "the one free Frenchman" (Herzen), was much more congenial to Bakunin, who often spoke of his debt to him. While in Paris Bakunin became very intimate with Proudhon. He was then living with Reichel, and Proudhon used to visit them almost daily, "listening", as Herzen says, "to Reichel's Beethoven and Bakunin's Hegel: the philosophical discussions lasted longer than the symphonies". Karl Vogt, one of Herzen's closest friends, who also lived in Paris at the time, told Herzen how one evening at the Reichels he felt tired of listening to phenomenology and went home to bed. Next morning he came round for Reichel and, on opening the door of the study, saw Proudhon and Bakunin still sitting in the same place before a burnt-out fire concluding the argument of the night before. Proudhon, at this time, was for Bakunin, as he was for Herzen, the French Hegel, "the dialectician of social problems". He, too, was imbued with a "passion for destruction": indeed, the passion came largely from Bakunin, whilst it was Proudhon who helped Bakunin to distil it into the creed of political anarchism. To discuss Proudhon in relation to Bakunin, however, would need a special enquiry. I can do no more than indicate a few fundamental points of difference.

Herzen was undoubtedly right in observing that Proudhon, the "great iconoclast", was, in the end, frightened by the freedom he originally conceded to man, for he finished by sacrificing it on the altar of the "cold, inhuman God of Justice—the God of equilibrium, quiet and peace", in whose name man was to be put back into the fetters of absolute paternal power. Proudhon's motto for his *Contradictions of Political Economy*—"*destruo et aedificabo*"—must be interpreted in the light of his subsequent work, where, as Herzen says, he put on the Phrygian cap in the place of a mitre and became the "bishop of socialism". Indeed, there is, in his *Justice in the Church and Revolution*, for instance, little of the old challenge to power and authority, but, instead, a stern, inflexible, centralized order, with regulated family relations and inherited wealth, and with all this "the Roman sins, peering out of every chink with the dead eyes of statues". Proudhon rebelled against the naked steel, against capitalism, against feudal and ecclesiastical traditions, but he stopped short of rebelling against one of the deepest sources of human slavery—the family. His ideal of the family as the basis of society, his homage to patriarchal principles, his hostility to women's rights reflected all the instincts of an obdurate, stubborn French peasant and *paterfamilias*. His "freedom" turned into a form of domestic serfdom and of bondage to the soil. This may have fitted the Slavophil hope of organic, *soborny* paternalism, or the Tolstoyan experience of life which renders man immune from corruption by consciousness and will, and subjects him to the laws and mysteries of Nature, but it was utterly repugnant to Bakunin and showed the limits of his unanimity with Proudhon and dependence on him. The fact that Proudhon came to substitute the awe-inspiring monster of Justice for the Moloch of the absolute, all-consuming Hegelian Mind, and to look upon the human individual as an instrument in the service of the family, could not but invalidate what, for Bakunin, was the *raison d'être* of anarchy, the freedom of the human person. Bakunin's anarchism, no less than his rebellion, went deeper precisely because it issued from his experience of personal freedom: it was suffused with and relied on elemental passion, but its purpose was to liberate man, not to dissolve him in any collective. Similarly, his atheism was more significant, because to his mind it was not, as with Proudhon, a case of "If there were no God, there would be no property owners", but rather "If there were no God, there would be no man, and no freedom".[67]

It is to Dostoevsky, the other contemporary of Bakunin, that one ought to look for true light on his anarchism. Dostoevsky, who was not himself immune from theocratic illusions, has yet, in his "Legend of the Grand Inquisitor", delivered the most extreme and effective challenge to all power and authority. His anarchism has not received the attention it deserves, and even the "Legend" has misled his commentators.[68] It is known, for example, that Pobedonstsev, who called himself and was a determined believer in the "sacred power and right of autocracy", expressed his pleasure on reading it, because he believed it to be merely an attack on the Roman Catholic Church. Although, as with Tolstoy, Dostoevsky's anarchism is born of a religious conviction, it is concerned, unlike Tolstoy's but very much like Bakunin's, with the question of freedom. Christ rejected the three-fold temptation of power, bread and miracle because they meant the final disfranchisement of man. He is accused by the Grand Inquisitor of pitilessness towards men, of laying upon them the intolerable burden of freedom, whereas in fact they seek nothing but the happiness of innocent childhood, nothing but submission, satiety and assurance; and the Grand Inquisitor reverses Christ's deed by sinking their freedom in the obedience of assured and contented children. The substitution of obedience and power for freedom proves to be the Inquisitor's mark of Antichrist, the Prince of this world, whose laws compel man to cringe to necessity or to dominate those who surrender to it. But his success, as the success of all those who exercise dominion and triumph in the triumphs of history, is evidence of weakness, not of strength; while Christ's defeat without thought of victory, like the silent failure of Calvary, is the true and only possible victory—the victory of him who desired men to be free.

It is a far cry from anarchist revolution and Christ's refusal to assume power and turn stones into bread, and yet even Bakunin's revolt against the enslavement of man is an unwitting witness to the *deus absconditus* who has willed to be defeated so that man should choose in freedom. Bakunin had no thought of liberty without bread or of bread without liberty: he was prepared to use and sometimes to misuse this two-edged sword. Having gone to the utmost in his revolt, perched, as it were, precariously on the height of his own independence, he has turned about, perhaps in virtue of the very freedom so gained, to spend himself in political revolution. But the conflict he embodied is a token of the enduring conflict between the kingdom of God and the kingdom of Caesar, that is, the conflict between Christ and the State, which continues for ever to crucify him, between freedom and necessity, between the human subject and the "objective course of things", between man and society.

"The State . . . the coldest of all monsters!" says Nietzsche's Zarathustra. "Coldly it lieth . . .; and the lie creepeth from its mouth: 'I, the State, am the people'! It lieth with all the tongues of good and evil; and whatever it saith it lieth; and whatever it hath it hath stolen." But not even Nietzsche's denunciation of the State reaches the vehemence of Bakunin's invective. He believes that nowhere has freedom been so frankly and cynically abrogated, and nowhere has man lost so completely his birthright as in and by the State, in which ecclesiastical and secular religion, traditions, laws, customs, moral standards, scientific and philosophical procedures, and the private self-interests of individuals as well as the commonplace instincts and servility of the herd have aligned themselves to justify, with all the means at their disposal, the fetish of power. The State is the only effective, "absolute limitation of the freedom of each one in the name of the generalized freedom of all. . . . Where the State begins, there individual freedom ends, and *vice versa*." The State is the "altar of political religion for the sacrifice of authentic society; it is, like the Church . . . , its twin-brother, the devouring god who lives by human sacrifices".[69] The divine right of kings, the divine right of majorities, the divine right of freeholders and profit motives are all excretions of power fetishism, and they are all one in destroying the human person and true human relationships. Bakunin refuses to admit even the validity of the argument in favour of the partial limitation of freedom (what he meant here was precisely limitation of freedom rather than incidental rules of convenience), and in so doing, he refers to his favourite principle of the indivisibility of freedom, which he opposes to Rousseau's indivisibility of sovereignty. He is sufficiently consistent to apply this principle against the ruthless individualistic world, in which the impersonal mechanism of economic processes, in terms of the private ownership of the means of production, is protected by the massive authority of State power and is driven increasingly to maintain its legal relations and vested interests by force, as well as against what he prophesied would be the tyranny and "unbearable compulsion" of a communist "conglomerated herd of animals", similarly equipped with a relentless State machine that forces all men to be prosperous and happy, "knowing nothing of the spiritual side of man" and providing security at the price of liberty. He detested the slavery of Ancient Greece and Rome, the social mastery which the landowner exercised in the feudal period or in Russia, and the power which belongs to the capitalist in *bourgeois* society, where human relations are adjusted to the needs and privileges of the dominant group. But he equally detested communism, because, as he declared at the Berne Congress of the League of Peace and Freedom, it is "the negation of freedom, and I can conceive nothing human without freedom". He allows ultimately of no distinction between various forms of State power. The democratic State, claiming to represent the general will of the people and based on popular sovereignty and universal suffrage, which he regarded, together with the majority of Russian revolutionary thinkers, as the half-stupid, half-hypocritical farce of governing a country by the counting of millions of empty heads, can be as despotic as, or more despotic than, the "monarchical State". He admits, however, that democracy, the "Gambettist rational and positivist democracy", as he derisively calls it, can offer "partial liberty", by fashioning a breed of bureaucrats and parliamentarians who attain power and defeat their opponents by argument instead of by physical force. Slavery of the acquiescent majority to the ruthless few is the hereditary state of mankind, but the idea of popular sovereignty is no less a legitimation of slavery, of slavery to the ruthless many: it is sovereignty itself which is the great delusion, whatever myths it may employ to enforce its alleged indefectibility and its claim over the life of men.[70]

In dissociating himself from Rousseau, one of his greatest bugbears, Bakunin attacks the concept of the Social Contract for its implied optimistic falsification of history and for serving to promote a new form of tyranny. The theoreticians of the Social Contract, he argues, assert that prior to the supposedly free and deliberate creation of the State man knew no distinction between good and evil, but lived in that "fantastic golden age" when "natural egotism" issued in happy and harmonious relations: "the good was decided by success, the evil by failure, and justice was nothing other than recognition of the accomplished fact". But the impulses to good and evil, as well as the urge to social living are part of human nature, and the only thing the Social Contract theory can claim to have invented is the concept of the "common good", which, however, is no more than a piece of mythological verbalism deluding man into believing that a water-tight egalitarian system is his true self, and which tyrants use to bolster up their ascendancy.[71] Thus came into being the modern "secular and atheist State". It has scrapped Christian morality and replaced it, not with a human, but an inhuman morality of its own, even while continuing to use Christianity as a "pretext and a phrase". The real moral basis of the modern State is "State interest"—"the new idol" which is burying all other idols and making room for power politics. To defend its interests and its "collective egotism", the State not only offers human freedom as a sacrifice, but employs every means in order to "inflict its egotism on other collective egotisms". Imperialism and will to power are built into the very foundations of the State. The sovereign State, that is to say, is not a neutral phenomenon: it is aggressive and ready to take the offensive. Whether theocratic or democratic, it always holds up and foists upon others its alleged sanctities and absolutes. Whether it considers its title holy, as with theocratic empires, or based on Montesquieuan "virtue", on Rousseau's "general will", or on the rule of law, as with democracy, it always claims universal validity. "It must devour in order not to be devoured, conquer in order not to be conquered, subjugate in order not to be subjugated." In Bakunin's famous, and for those who listened to him apparently quite unforgettable speech in Geneva in 1867—that same speech which Dostoevsky, too, is said to have heard—he predicted, with remarkable insight, the mutual national, political and cultural annihilation as a result of a coming world war. "Woe to the nations", he concluded with customary oratorical ardour, "woe to the nations whose leaders will return victorious from the battlefields! Their laurels and lustre will turn into chains and shackles for the peoples who will rejoice in their victory." While condemning vice in individuals, "there is no horror under the sun, no cruelty, sacrilege, perjury, deception, base dealings, cynical theft, shameless plunder and base treason that has not been perpetrated and continues to be perpetrated every year by the representatives of the State, without any excuse save the accommodating, convenient and terrible word: State interest". But because there is no escape from them, these things are worse in a State than they are in an individual. Machiavelli was not mistaken: "Crime . . . is a necessary condition of political wisdom and true patriotism. . . . Powerful States can only support themselves by crimes."[72]

167

In view of what is known of Bakunin's own advocacy of revolutionary destruction and of his implication in the Nechaev affair, it may well seem a piece of cynicism or hypocrisy on his part to protest against the craft, duplicity and prevalence of expediency over truth and loyalty where the State was concerned. His attitude in this respect shows, in fact, a curious ambivalence, though no cynicism and certainly no hypocrisy are entailed. There is no evidence that he ever prescribed, as Nechaev did, the pursuit of lofty ends with the aid of fulsome means; and his praise of elemental revolutionary outbursts and anarchy has as little in common with Machiavelli's or Nechaev's recommendation of the art of deceiving, and of the advantage and necessity of this and other expedients, as it had with Machiavelli's political wisdom and perspicacity. Bakunin was sincerely horrified by Nechaev's success in living up to what he (Nechaev) regarded as his master's principles, and in practising them against his fellow revolutionaries. In the already quoted London article, which failed to receive Herzen's *imprimatur*, Bakunin wrote that "owing to human stupidity, bloody revolutions often become inevitable, but they are invariably an evil and a great misfortune". Nevertheless, there are a few ominous utterances which suggest that at his most "demonic" Bakunin would not have rested till he knew that he had destroyed, utterly destroyed, all that stood in the way of the irrational impetus to rebellion, by which his whole character took life and which gave rise to his revolutionary anarchism. And at such times he would have destroyed without a moment's hesitation and without a moment's regret. "I believe in nothing", he is said to have replied to a question about his aims; "I read nothing; I think of but one thing: twist the neck, twist it yet further, screw the head off, let not a trace of it remain!"

And yet it is significant that he should have repeated again and again that his revolution was aimed against *things*, against the petrified and petrifying rigidity of the world of objects, against solid "organized bodies" and "social positions" rather than against people. He condemns Louis Blanc ("*ce Robespiere en miniature*" and "*communiste d'Etat*" as Bakunin calls him), and especially the Jacobins and the Blanquists for their idea of revolutionary dictatorship, or of a conscious minority of revolutionary leaders, but also for dreaming of a bloody revolution against individual human beings—a dream which he suspected to be no less a sure way than dictatorship to substituting one kind of oppression for another. He desired to destroy, not in order to manifest power, but in order to liquidate it. He could never have identified himself with those who set out as liberators of the human mind and body and end as their iron-handed masters, despite, or because of, the fact that this is precisely what he practised in his early years; and he would never have accepted the dilemma as stated by Dostoevsky's Shigalev: "starting from unlimited freedom, I arrive at unlimited despotism".

It is true, Bakunin believed in the creative rôle of the proletariat in a stagnant *bourgeois* society; he agreed with Marx's prediction of the collapse of capitalism before the advance of the working class; he even admitted the need for some direction while proletarian revolution was in actual progress. But in his indictment of tyranny he makes no exception (after his confrontation with Marx) of the dictatorship of the proletariat, which was to be a transitional stage in the progress towards a class-less communist society. The workers, Bakunin says, on becoming statesmen, "inevitably turn into *bourgeois*, and will probably become more *bourgeois* than the *bourgeois* themselves". For revolutions to manufacture and impose a pattern of life out of the materials of physical and social necessity was, in his view, their own death warrant. All "cobweb plans for a better life" spun by a host of "honest and dishonest socialist dreamers" prove an "impediment in the cause of liberation".[73] No future can be construed out of the present. It is unpredictable and depends largely on the human innovator; and its very novelty and unpredictability threaten all things conceived in, and decided by, the present. Revolution all too easily ceases to be revolutionary; but it can retain its identity if it is anarchical, if it is perpetuated by the irreducible polarity between what ought to be and what is, if it imperils every attempt to fix or divinize an actual situation, if it sheds every new comforting illusion and returns continually to its destructive and creative sources. That may be of very little use for those who see in revolutions, and in revolutionaries, only the triumph or the defeat of statesmanship, but then Bakunin's rôle was both more modest and more important: "We must", he said himself, "overthrow the material and moral conditions of our present-day life. . . . We must first purify our atmosphere and completely transform the milieu in which we live; for it corrupts our instinct and our will, and constricts our heart and our intelligence" (*Appeal to the Slavs*).

Chapter Four

Alexander Herzen

(1812–1870)

---

1. A STRICKEN VOLTAIRE

"WHAT a prodigious writer!" Tolstoy wrote of Herzen in 1888 to the painter Nicolas Gué. "Russian life in the last twenty years would have been different if this writer had not remained concealed." And, again, in 1905 he noted in his Diary: "Our intelligentsia has sunk so low that it is no longer fit to understand him. He . . . awaits his readers in the future. He imparts his thoughts far above the heads of the present crowd to those who will be able to understand him." The "crowd", represented by the epigoni of the Russian intelligentsia and by what Belinsky called the "accursed Russian reality" alike, was indeed responsible for the conspiracy of silence which surrounded Herzen's name in Russia until the revolution of 1905—a silence all the more bewildering if one remembers that no less a man than Tolstoy regarded Herzen as one of the greatest Russian writers. But, though the year 1955 marks the eighty-fifth anniversary of Herzen's death, there still exists no really satisfactory biography of him.[1] This omission may be due, however, to another, less tangible reason: it is that Herzen exists in his memoirs (*My Past and Thoughts*), from which we know about him more than we know about most Russian writers. It has been said that everything becomes a legend with time, and this truth, at once melancholy and consoling, provides the key to most autobiographies and to their peculiar difficulty. For experience has no shape at the time of its happening: put into words it assumes a design, a fixity, and fades. Herzen's *Memoirs*—the greatest autobiographical masterpiece in Russian literature—have, on the contrary, not lost their first, original quality after nearly a century. If his life could speak now, it would speak as he spoke in them; and any attempt to say more or to say something different seems unnecessary and presumptuous. My own aim, therefore, is not to fill a gap or to give a new account of Herzen's life and work, but merely to comment on them.

Herzen was born on March 25, 1812. He was the illegitimate son of Ivan Yakovlev, who left his mark on history by being almost the only nobleman to remain in Moscow when the city became, in Tolstoy's words, "a queen-less hive" as a result of Napoleon's invasion. Subsequently, Yakovlev lived under the shadow of what in the circumstances amounted to a treasonable act: for he consented to carry a message from Napoleon to Alexander I in Petersburg, and thereby secured his own and his family's safety. Although Herzen observes that his father knew neither great passions, nor mistakes, nor losses in his life, this fact may to some extent explain his bitterness, his ill-humour and "perpetual dissatisfaction". In his youth Herzen seems to have remembered only the morose and unhappy side of his father's character and the "terrible dullness which reigned in the house". "Always on his guard", he writes, "always displeased, he saw with a pang the hostile feelings he roused in his whole household; he saw the smile pass from the face and words checked at his entrance. He spoke of this with mockery, with vexation, but made not a single concession and went his way with the utmost persistence. Mockery, irony—cold, malignant and scornful—was a weapon which he used like an artist; he employed it equally against us and against the servants. In early youth one can bear many things better than sarcasm, and until I went to prison I was really estranged from my father, and joined with the maids and menservants in leading a little war against him."[2] Yet this and Herzen's illegitimate birth did not prevent his father from bringing him up in every respect as the son of a rich nobleman and even from being fond of him in his ill-tempered, "Voltairian" fashion. It is difficult to establish precisely in what measure Herzen's "false position" affected him psychologically. He was impressionable, high-minded and pugnacious in his early youth, and he must have had a bad time of the prejudice-ridden society in which he lived. What surprises is how little it did affect him, and how immune he seems to have been from the expected frustrations, repressions and resentment. To judge from his own account he derived from his position only a sense of independence of society and a feeling of being "thrown back on [his] own resources".

Herzen's early education was entrusted to two tutors. Bouchot, an unlovely and relentless Frenchman, a revolutionary exile, began by sternly conjugating verbs, dictating copies and scolding his pupil for persistent inattention; but, on discovering Herzen's "sympathy with regicide ideas", he finished by encouraging in him these "generous feelings", and by regaling him with enthusiastic accounts of 1793 and of how he, Bouchot, left France "when the dissolute and the dishonest got the upper hand". The other tutor was Protopopov, a seminarist and early representative of the *raznochintsy*, who were to play such an important rôle in the 'sixties and 'seventies and eventually to turn their back on Herzen. He was distinguished by "that vague and generous liberalism which often passes with the first grey hair, with marriage and a settled job, but which yet ennobles a man". It was to him that Herzen confided his "political dream", which, as he says, "occupied me day and night", and his youthful political disaffection. In return, he received from his tutor clandestine copies of forbidden and unpublished verse by Pushkin. But Herzen's reading consisted mainly of western European writers from his father's library: Voltaire, Schiller and Goethe were his favourite authors.

One of the deepest and most indelible impressions of his childhood was bound up with the events of the Decembrist rising. He was present, as a boy of fourteen, at the *Te Deum* sung in Moscow in honour of Tsar Nicolas's "victory over the Five" (the executed Decembrists Pestel, Ryleev, Bestuzhev, Muraviev and Kakhovsky). In 1855 Herzen still vividly remembered the occasion. "In the midst of the Kremlin", he wrote in the *Polar Star*, "the Metropolitan Philaret thanked God for the murders. The entire Royal Family took part in the service, near them the Senate and the Ministers, and in the immense space around packed masses of the Guards knelt bare-headed; they also joined in the prayers. Cannon thundered from the heights of the Kremlin. Never have the gallows been celebrated with such pomp. Nicolas clearly understood the importance of the victory! . . . On this spot and before that altar defiled by bloody rites, I swore to avenge the murdered, and dedicated myself to the struggle with that throne, with that altar, with those cannons. I have not avenged them: the Guards and the throne, the altar and the cannon all remain, but for thirty years I have stood under that flag and have never once deserted it."

Another and equally important event in Herzen's life was his meeting with Nicolas Ogarev (1813–77), who became his greatest and life-long friend—sometimes an irksome but more often an inspiring friend—and, in particular, the vow they took on the Sparrow Hills near Moscow "to sacrifice [their] lives to the struggle for freedom". The interest of the incident, familiar to the reader of Herzen's *Memoirs*, is not belied by its apparent melodramatic character and setting, and Ogarev did not exaggerate when he wrote to Herzen that "on that spot (that is, on the Sparrow Hills) the history of our lives, yours and mine, was made". Indeed, their whole life went to show the significance and sincerity of the vow and the friendship.

Ogarev's fame has, of course, suffered a great deal from the proximity to Herzen, by whom he is completely overshadowed; and yet he deserves more than a passing reference.[3] Apart from his place in Herzen's private and public life, Ogarev has a name in the history of Russian literature, for he was a minor poet with a considerable gift for describing the "great", "ennobling" feelings of the romantic tradition.

Despite the surfeit of poetic elation, impassioned sentiments, revelations of universal love, and a tendency to live in the nirvana of the *mystique manqué*, he was a man of sincere nobility of soul, with a great capacity for kindness and sympathy, and a kind of feminine quality of attraction. "Herzen", observed a contemporary, "is the ever active European, living an expansive life and assimilating ideas . . . in order to clarify, develop and disseminate them. Ogarev is quietistic Asia, in whose soul slumber deep thoughts unclear to himself." If this is true it yet did not prevent Herzen from speaking, not only of their common faith, but, even more, of their "selective affinity". He was attracted by Ogarev's noble, passionate if umbrageous and erratic character, by his hatred of his environment—the environment of paternal intolerance and tyranny, under which he grew up, and of social and political oppression —by his candour, disinterestedness and even, in a protective kind of way, by his vulnerability, spiritual as well as physical. For Ogarev was born and remained a profoundly pathetic man, whose personal life presents an almost unrelieved chain of failures and disappointments borne with humility. The fact that he was committed to life by feeling, to the exclusion of almost every other faculty, and that this played a large part in his political doctrine as well as being the essence of his romantic poetry and vaguely idealistic outlook, does not seem to have greatly disturbed Herzen, at any rate not until much later, when Ogarev came to be involved with Bakunin and Nechaev. For Herzen never ran away, not even from *Weltschmerz*, or romanticism, or mysticism. They were both in their different ways attaining maturity by willing surrender to the imagination, with day-dreams which inevitably "ended in Siberia or the scaffold, and hardly ever in triumph". "Can this be characteristic of the Russian imagination", Herzen asks, "or is it the effect of Petersburg with its five gallows and its penal servitude reflected on the younger generation?"

On overcoming the opposition of his father, who had planned for his son a career in the civil service, Herzen became a student at the University of Moscow. To Herzen, who for no particular reasons entered the Faculty of Physics and Mathematics, it was a time of intense intellectual activity, but also of tempestuous gaiety.[4] Though not a hedonist, he was endowed with an enormous capacity for enjoyment: he enjoyed the new friendships, the clamour of conversation, the spontaneous play of ideas, the eccentricities of Bohemian student life and the rowdy champagne parties. His gay vitality made him known as the most prominent figure of merriment among his fellow-students and enabled him to get, on the whole, a great deal of fun out of life in face of all the surrounding sorry sight. But his laughter was no mere diversion: it was his alternative to doctrinal or pedagogical fervour, and few men have succeeded in using it more effectively for moral ends than Herzen. Speaking of contemporary bohemian life abroad, he observed that in France it had passed under the guidance of "some worn-out sinner, some faded celebrity, *d'un vieux prostitué*, living at some one else's expense, an actor who has lost his voice, or a painter whose hands tremble; and he is the model who is imitated in accent, in dress, and, above all, in a haughty view of human affairs and a profound understanding of good fare". In England it has given place to "a paroxysm of charming originalities and amiable oddities", with "senseless tricks, absurd squandering of money, ponderous practical jokes, heavy, but carefully concealed vice, pointless trips to Calabria or Quito, to the North and to the South", with "horses, dogs, races, and stuffy dinners by the way, then a wife and an enormous number of fat and rosy babies; business transactions, *The Times*, Parliament, and old Port which weighs them down to the earth".[5]

Russian bohemia, as it was practised in Moscow in the 'thirties, was by comparison a much more romantic affair. It was, in Herzen's words, immune against "vulgar vice and vulgar virtue". "We played pranks too, and we caroused", but "our main stimulus was faith in our vocation". "Twenty-three", Ogarev exclaimed one night, bringing his open hand down on a wine glass and cutting it badly, "and nothing done for eternity!" It was a life that never lost its purpose, or at any rate its questioning quality, its high seriousness, and its awareness of and hospitality to ideas. They resolutely repudiated past and present solemnities in bearing, word, tone and pursuit, but, at the same time, they were full of the "anxious searchings of a soul in travail." For Herzen and his Circle, moreover, the searchings did not involve a withdrawal from social and political problems to the remote regions of historical memories or of abstract speculation, as was the case, to some extent, with the other philosophical and literary Circles in Moscow.

The group around Herzen included, among a few others, Ogarev, Vadim Passek, the proud and reckless son of a well-known political exile in Siberia, Nicolas Sazonov, a rather typical "repentent nobleman", who became later a prominent figure among Russian *émigrés* in Paris, and Nicolas Ketcher, "an eternal student in the rôle of a Schileresque youth", who translated Shakespeare into moderately good Russian, all of whom have been vividly and sensitively portrayed by Herzen in his *Memoirs*. They were the first in Russia to study the doctrines of the French precursors of socialism, and of Saint-Simonianism in particular. The political orientation of the Herzen Circle evoked little sympathy in the other Moscow groups. "They considered us *frondeurs* and French", Herzen recalls; "we thought them sentimentalists and German." But the gulf appeared perhaps greater to the protagonists than it does now across the span of a century; and, in any case, there was also much contact and reciprocation, and there were some, Granovsky, for example, who belonged to both camps. Moreover, for a time, until the split between the Westerners and the Slavophils became explicit, it was, Bakunin notwithstanding, still possible to exclude anything resembling aggression from personal relations.

So ended the first part of Herzen's youth; the second began in prison. The small Moscow circle attracted the attention of the authorities and, in 1834, the twenty-two-year-old Herzen was arrested. The pretext for the arrest was flimsy in the extreme: a student song, a few sentences from intercepted letters, and even Thiers's *History of the French Revolution* and Cuvier's *Discours sur les révolutions du Globe Terrestre*, which the police found on the bookshelf and confiscated as evidence of revolutionary activities.[6] The general indictment ran: "Opposition to the spirit of the Government, and revolutionary opinions imbued with the pernicious doctrines of Saint-Simon." But both prison, where he had to pay for his own keep, and the subsequent exile were comparatively mild. Despite the frequent and interminable interrogations, Herzen was throughout treated with the greatest civility—which was, indeed, a general practice (except towards Fortress prisoners and those condemned to penal servitude in Siberia), since political prisoners belonged for the most part to the gentry. "To know what the Russian prisons, the Russian law-courts and the Russian police are like", Herzen observes, "one must be a peasant, a house-serf, a workman, or an artisan." His own sufferings were due more to the sound of thrashings or beatings of the less fortunate victims belonging to the lower classes, mostly peasants caught in or suspected of arson and rebellion against their masters, than to his own position; to their wailings, screams and entreaties, together with the shouting of the police officers and the monotonous reading of the clerks. "At night I dreamed of those sounds and woke in a frenzy at the thought that the victims were lying on straw only a few paces from me, in chains, with lacerated wounds on their backs, and in all probability quite innocent." "Peter III abolished torture and the Secret Chamber", Herzen comments in conclusion; "Catherine II abolished torture; Alexander I abolished it once more."[7]

Unlike some of his fellow-prisoners, three of whom were sent to the Schlüsselburg Fortress, Herzen was merely declared "a daring free-thinker, extremely dangerous to society", and sent to "civilian duty for an indefinite period to remote provinces", to Perm and then to Vyatka and Vladimir, where he was to live under the supervision of the local police authorities. The punishment amounted, in effect, to nothing more than condemnation to great boredom and separation from his friends, but provided him with an opportunity for learning a great deal about provincial life and provincial government administration, of which he has left a most illuminating account in the last six chapters of the Second Part of his *Memoirs*.

Two events stand out among the scenes and figures, affairs and incidents, which Herzen witnessed, or in which he took part during his exile, in the setting of dreary provincial existence, of official routine

Herzen at the age of 36

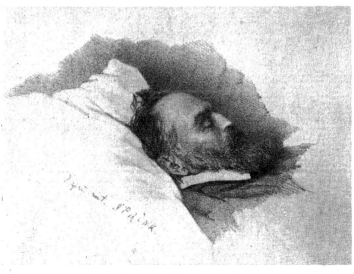

Herzen on his death-bed

[face page 176

and red-tape. One was his meeting with Alexander Vitberg (1787–1855) and the other his secret visit to Moscow and secret marriage to Natalie Zakhar'ina.

Vitberg was an architect commissioned by Alexander I to draw the plans for a Cathedral on the Sparrow Hills near Moscow in commemoration of the Russian victory over Napoleon. As a result of several intrigues, however, he was charged with embezzlement of funds and removed to Vyatka. Besides being a gifted artist with an eager and highly imaginative mind, he was also a mystic, and he produced a great impression on Herzen. Herzen's two and a half year long association with Vitberg is an important landmark in his spiritual development: it was his most religious and mystical phase, which, later in life, he preferred to play down, and to describe it as a mere hesitation, a "wavering", as he says, on the threshold of a "realistic outlook". The evidence shows that he immersed himself with considerable fervour and even exaltation in the study of mysticism (Böhme, Swedenborg, Paracelsus, Eckartshausen, the Polish messianic and mystical philosopher Cieszkowski, and others), and tried to acquire its idiom. The idiom was not his own, but the interest expressed, no doubt, something fundamental in his nature.[8]

A similar and simultaneous religious or mystical influence was exercised on Herzen by his future wife Natalie Zakhar'ina. The circumstances of their relations, which culminated in elopement, have all the marks of ultra-romantic fiction. Natalie was an illegitimate cousin of Herzen's (the Yakovlevs went in for casual and not-so-casual *liaisons* on a very big scale), brought up by a prosperous and charitable titled aunt whose benefactions, however, proved to be a form of cheap blackmail which the lady paid to a poor and defenceless girl in order to enjoy her own prosperity with a better conscience. Herzen had met his cousin before his exile, but in exile his feelings of brotherly affection and sympathy with her melancholy fate grew into passionate love, and their correspondence towards the end of his stay in Vyatka and then in Vladimir is one of the most remarkable records of romantic love in the annals of epistolary literature. In the spring of 1838, Herzen, to whom the charitable aunt never referred otherwise than "that miserable son of brother Ivan's", decided to save Natalie from her oppressive and bigoted benefactress, and marry her against the wishes of the whole family, including those of his father. The story of the elopement and clandestine wedding is familiar to the reader of Herzen's *Memoirs*, and more will be said about Natalie in another, less happy connection.

At the beginning of 1840 Herzen was allowed to return to Moscow. His friends, he wrote, received him "as people receive exiles and old champions, men who come out of prison or return from captivity and banishment, that is with respectful indulgence, with a readiness to let us share in their friendship, although, at the same time, refusing to yield a single point, and hinting at the fact that they live 'in the present', whereas we belong 'to the past' ". His friends demanded allegiance to Hegel and to their interpretation of him; for 1840 was the meridian of Russian Hegelianism. Very soon, nevertheless, Herzen began to occupy a leading position in the intellectual circles of Moscow. It was then, and during the six years preceding his departure abroad, that he made his brilliant contribution to the "remarkable decade". He was largely responsible for the formulation of the issues which divided the Westerners and the Slavophils. His Short Stories, *Dr. Krupov* in particular, and his novel *Who Is Guilty?* (1846), although not entitling him to a place among the greater novelists, helped to elaborate the ethos peculiar to the Russian realistic novel and to destroy the literary pseudo-romanticism against which Belinsky raised his voice. But his primary contribution was to the philosophical debate.[9] Faced with the heavy artillery of Muscovite Hegelianism he embarked on a serious study of Hegel. His well-trained and perceptive mind enabled him to do this more thoroughly and deeply than any of his philosophizing contemporaries in Russia. Preoccupation with theoretical questions, however, could not hold Herzen's attention for long. He begins to complain of being stifled by the philosophical abstractions and regimentation involved in a world created by logic, and longs, as he wrote to Ogarev in 1841, for "the development of philosophy into life".

The sojourn in Moscow was of short duration. In less than a year Herzen moved with his family to the capital, where he entered the civil service. But soon the Secret Police was once again pursuing him. He was accused of "spreading rumours injurious to the Government" and again banished, this time to Novgorod. This second exile was brief and painless, but he returned from it, not in the previous mood of vague and undefined radicalism, but in deep and bitter hatred of autocracy. From 1842 he lived in Moscow, where he was allowed to reside under police surveillance, until he succeeded in obtaining an exit permit to go abroad—not an easy matter in the conditions of Nicolaian Russia and for a past political prisoner at that.[10] He never returned to Russia, or returned to it only, and perhaps never really left it, in mind and soul.

The last six years in Russia, though full of success, of new and exciting friendships, and of intellectual and literary activities which exhibited the inexhaustible variety of his interests and accomplishments, were yet a very painful period for him. Not only did he feel less and less able to submit to the oppressiveness and frustrations of the surrounding atmosphere, which, as he noted in his Diary of 1842, "crushes all my craving for self-expression, till my search is stifled and I am ready for a life of emptiness", and which filled him with depression that seemed to penetrate his deepest and most solitary self: the period marked also the beginning of a long series of disasters in his private life. Indeed, it is astonishing with what savage indifference life snatched from him the mask of happiness, although, unlike Natalie, he does not even appear to have ever been much interested in happiness as such. It is astonishing, too, how and where he found the strength to endure the many blows. "What an endless capacity for suffering is given man", he noted in his Diary, "and what a tiny capacity for enjoyment." Death pursued him wherever he went: the death of many of his children of both first and second marriage, the drowning of his mother, the death of many of his dearest friends, the death of his wife, preceded by the greatest tragedy of his life—her betrayal of him some two years after their escape from Russia.

The escape from Russia occurred on the eve of the French revolution of 1848, on the eve of a catastrophe which buried the hopes of more than one expatriate Russian revolutionary. Herzen experienced the French revolution as a personal as well as a social and political disaster, for, with all his display of wisdom after the event, he welcomed it at first as a kind of Second Coming, in the same way as he had gone to western Europe as one entering a promised land. The failure of 1848, the swift reaction that followed it, and the descent into the *bourgeois* swamp of the Second Empire—both of which marked the effective end of French and, generally, of western European revolutionary leadership —impelled him to revise a great many things in his outlook. He foresaw the continuation of the awful victory of self-satisfied, liberal and democratic virtue and vice, and all that this implied for the spiritual and physical life of Europe; and this victory filled him with unspeakable nausea. He writes his *Letters from France and Italy* and, in a sort of fury that slew his own dreams and hopes, his angry *From the Other Shore*.[11] As previously, from the bleak north-eastern corner of Russia, he had turned his gaze to western Europe, whence he expected something like salvation for the world, so now, from his western European exile, he begins to look back and forward to Russia. It was what he called his "return to the motherland", "with faith and hope, inwardly rejoicing that I am a Russian". His hopes in Russia grew into a kind of anarcho-socialist Slavophilism which placed him at Bakunin's side but which neither drove him to a complete renunciation of western Europe nor to an excessively romanticized view of Russia, while leaving all the time a curious gaping void in his soul.

The last twenty-three years of his life were in effect no less, or more, of an exile than Perm, Vyatka, Vladimir and Novgorod taken together, with no roots of any kind and no possessions. The death, in 1846, of his father left him, admittedly, a fairly rich man. He was in a way careful with money, and yet he not only felt the guilt which the *rentier* feels in his better moments, but gave away thousands and could have parted without a pang with the rest, however much he may have valued the freedom it gave him. No possessions could penetrate his essential aloofness. Wandering through Europe, living, with his numerous household and their hangers-on, in hotels, furnished flats and semi-detached villas, and for ever suspended in some alien ambience—whether in Paris or London, in Nice or Geneva, in Rome or Venice—he became the prototype of the *gentilhomme russe citoyen du monde*. This is, in fact, the epithet Dostoevsky chose in his contempt and admiration to describe his older contemporary. Herzen's whole outlook and attitude to life relieved him from being a citizen, or from striking roots in any soil whatever.

Life abroad for Herzen was exceedingly rich in experience and incident, in encounters and active involvement in political movements and discussions which make his record of this life, the *Memoirs*, more than a mere autobiography: it is an important historical document communicating an entire Europe in turmoil, with all her discords and variety —"a reflection of history", as Herzen said himself, "in a man who has perchance found himself at its cross-roads". Historical events are woven here into the life of characters, and introspection and reflections give way to the bustle of keen, direct observation, thus enabling Herzen to ask vital questions about human behaviour and the significance of his time. In the midst of, and intertwined with this, there are two events of particular importance for the understanding of Herzen as a private and public individual. The first is his family drama; the other is his active entry on the stage of social and political life in Russia from his far-away London base.

The introductory chapter of the section of the *Memoirs* dealing with the family drama contains these lines: "We know events as a whole, but have no record of the lives of the persons who were directly involved in them, though it was through those events that lives unchronicled were broken and ruined in conflict, blood gave way to tears, devastated towns to desolate families, the field of battle to forgotten tombs." However remote and fanciful it may appear to the mere detached observer, Herzen viewed his personal drama in intimate relation with the events outside: he saw his life "devastated, crushed at the meeting of two historic worlds". The two worlds were Russia and western Europe: the one, as he says in the same connection, "savage like a wild beast of the forest, but full of slumbering forces", and the other "cankered, time-worn", full of the "hereditary, intangible subtleties of corruption". And the latter abomination assumed for him a personal character in the chief author of his tragedy, the German poet Georg Herwegh (1817–74).[12]

The *Memoirs* offer, of course, Herzen's own, personal record of the tragedy, with the inevitable rationalizations which a testamentary assessment of such matters involves. It was, after all, a crude and common drama, in which it is customary to blame all and none. And yet Herzen was right in seeing it in the setting that was so well designed to enhance its tragic element. His story, except perhaps where he evidently tries to shield and to exonerate his wife, rings true in all essentials; and this is not denied even by such a severe and sceptical critic as Professor Carr. He speaks with bitterness but quite without the hysteria so characteristic of his ex-friend Herwegh, without dramatization, and without "literary" handling. "There was a time", Herzen wrote, "when I judged the man who shattered my life harshly and passionately. There was a time when I earnestly desired to kill him. Seven years have passed since then; a true son of the age, I have worn out all desire of vengeance, and have cooled my passionate view by prolonged, persistent analysis. In those seven years I have learnt both my own limit and the limits of many others, and, instead of a knife, I have a scalpel in my hand; instead of curses and abuse, I set to work to tell my story of psychological pathology." Turgenev, on reading this section of the *Memoirs* wrote: "It is written in tears and blood. It burns and sears. . . . He alone among Russians could write like this." It is that section also for which, as Herzen himself said more than once, he wrote all the rest of his memoirs. What he wrote here is blotted throughout with signs of great pain and great sorrow. To assess it truly is to weigh it not against some romantic canon derived from George Sand, who, as Professor Carr insists, loomed so large on the horizon of this family tragedy, nor against Herwegh's protestations and Natalie's self-delusions, but against the incomparable grief and loss of Herzen.

The circumstances of Herzen's marriage show, admittedly, the mystico-romantic atmosphere in which he lived and thought at the time of his marriage (largely under the influence of Natalie as well as of Vitberg), and the correspondence between him and his future wife provide striking evidence of this atmosphere. And yet, whatever romantic libel might be attached to their relationship, it leaves the impression of just a young love, idealistic, deeply felt, vehemently sexual, at least on Herzen's part, and no more or less romantic than any other young love. But Natalie, sensitive, intelligent and sincere though she was, seemed unable to know, then or later, the difference between the pretence and the real. She not only remained loyal to the idea of "sublime love", but showed all the symptoms of strenuous and ingenious sentimentality, and the exalted and tumid language of her letters makes her subconscious and her immaturity as a woman visible miles away. She believed in love or, rather, in the essence of love, in love's loveliness, quite unaware of its largely illusory and wilted nature. Herzen shared in this up to a point, but there came a moment when these sentimental mystical emotions began to cause him such discomfort that he was prepared to bury himself alive in order to escape this overbrimming of the heart, this strenuous cultivation of the soul and thrusting of erotic religion in each other's face. "Chronic enthusiasm", he observed, "is exhausting and irritating." Perhaps he was, in the end, too jealous of his independence or incapable of conveying complete intimacy, of completely surrendering himself. That he never ceased to love Natalie with all the love and surrender of which he was capable is evident from his own avowals, even though he, too, had a flutter, which however, as his Diary testifies, had no emotional significance for him, except in as much as it made him realize more deeply his love for Natalie. Above all it is evident from his attitude at the crucial moments: he experienced, as few others have done, that the great tragedy of life is not that men and women perish, but that they cease to love.

Still, as Herzen wrote later, he refused to "admit the sovereign place given to love in life", its "autocratic power", its "chains", which man may hug, but, knowing they are chains, cannot but hate them too. Unlike Natalie, he had a fascinated interest in all people. He had a delight in watching and participating in the movement of life around him. He responded generously to every manifestation of this life. Natalie was shy and feared the throng. In the feminine exclusiveness and intensity of her love she resented at bottom interests and passions other than anything she could evoke: they were a threat to her Narcissistic disposition and portended a moment when the myth she had created with Herzen's help of sublime, idyllic marriage was to be blown sky-high, and she felt restless and dissatisfied.[13]

It was then—in Paris, their first residence abroad, where Herzen, together with Bakunin, became the object of admiration by a great number of Russian and foreign friends and acquaintances—at a time when Herzen's hopes and convictions were shattered under the "ghastly reality of the June days", that Herwegh, already a friend of Bakunin, Ogarev and Sazonov, came into his circle "bringing more ruin into our private life than did the black days of June into our public life". Herwegh was a revolutionary poet, an extremely handsome man, whose literary reputation rested mainly on a collection of political verse under the title *Gedichte eines Lebendigen*, designed as a counterblast to the then popular reflections, *Briefe eines Verstorbenen*, by the misanthropic Fürst Hermann Pückler-Muskau. The *Gedichte* are distinguished mainly by their excessively bombastic tone and, unlike the *Briefe* that stimulated them, are almost unreadable today. They can be cited as striking evidence for the unsuitability of the rebellious attitude to the German temperament, and Herwegh succeeds as few other Germans in invalidating, or rendering such an attitude banal, by a capacity for dramatizing it. However, on the strength of these poems Herwegh became a celebrity, especially among young Germans, whose democratic fervour they reflected. Although his native heroic virtues were few, the rôle of political as of any other hero was very much to Herwegh's taste, and especially to the taste of his unlovely but adoring wife Emma, who later was to play the part of aider and abetter as well as of victim in Herzen's family drama. When the revolution of 1848 broke out, he placed himself, or was placed by Emma, at the head of a legion of French and German revolutionaries who invaded Baden with the intention of converting the State into a republic. Herwegh died as late as 1874, but this episode spelt the end of his career as a politician and, incidentally, as a poet too; for when the legion began to crack he lost his head at the sight of danger and fled from the battlefield, or, as a more sympathetic critic put it, "sought concealment in a ditch". "Our hero", Heine observed, "could no more bear the smell of powder than Goethe that of tobacco"; to which Turgenev added somewhat less maliciously: "Poor devil! He should either not have started the affair or got himself killed." He returned to Paris "with his laurels faded and his temper impaired" (Carr).

Herzen, disarmed by Herwegh's miserable condition and constant if suspiciously emphatic self-accusations, appears to have become his *confidant* and guardian, defending him from others and giving him money and advice, to which he listened with a mixture of genuine humility, self-pity and envy of his friend's superiority. In any case Herwegh found himself at Herzen's feet and, in due course, at the feet of Herzen's wife. So began a catastrophe, which, at the instigation of Herwegh, came to involve almost the entire community of revolutionary exiles and to assume the proportions of a European scandal.[14] For Natalie it was no ordinary affair: it was a case of woman going the way of all flesh once the flesh has gone all the way. She showered on Herwegh all the love and passion of her frustrated nature, without counting the cost to herself or to Herzen, convinced that honour was well sacrificed and shame a cheap price to pay. Known though she was to her Moscow friends as "*une froide anglaise*", apparently detached, prim and insensitive, Natalie became a victim of the kind of passion which whirls one to destruction, which dies itself if it does not destroy. And she was destroyed by it, in spirit and in body, dying a few months after the *dénouement*, released from her spell and in great physical and mental suffering, which she bore with equally great and simple nobility, but with all her life's energy burnt out.

"At ordinary times I am quick to become acquainted and slow to become intimate, but that was no ordinary time. All our nerves were laid bare and smarting; trivial meetings, insignificant reminders of the past, made one quiver in every fibre." This is how Herzen tries to explain what he called, with more persuasion than conviction, the "rapid approach of a person who forced himself on us without giving us time for consideration". Herzen's letters to Herwegh before the crisis, however, show that he was by no means passive in this relationship, the story of which is, in fact, a pitiful tale of the tyranny of the weak over the strong, of friendship, generosity, trust, hospitality thrown away on an utterly selfish and inferior being. It was a great error of judgment on Herzen's part. He was completely taken in by Herwegh's declarations of lofty idealism and loyalty: he was deceived even while the latter was actually betraying his friendship. It may be a matter of debate whether or not Herwegh was a political hero. If an emendation was due to him in this or in other respects, Professor Carr has made the best of it. But the fact remains that at the critical moments in this whole affair he showed himself a great coward, cheating his way out of difficulties, hypocritical towards his friend and odious towards Natalie—in all, a vain and spineless creature, an egotistical *poseur*, devoid of good faith and chivalry. No one, on the other hand, can deny Herzen the virtue of courage and magnanimity, however contemptuously he may have expressed himself on occasion, or attribute to him a single insincere action. The tragedy of their encounter was to that extent essentially a tragedy of character. And it is not surprising perhaps that Herzen should have seen in the man who all but destroyed his life a symbol of "that effete civilization . . . , rotten through and through with self-seeking, sick with envy and *amour propre*, with insatiable self-indulgence and petty egotism to which every feeling is subordinated . . .", a civilization in which men are "intent on playing a part, on posing on the stage, on keeping [their] place at all costs"; and that he should have seen himself as one of the "sons of the Steppe who are long before [they] come to their senses, receiving one blow after another, often not seeing whence they come; who are stupefied by them and then fling [themselves] like wounded bears, tearing up trees and howling and flinging up the earth—but too late, and our adversary points a finger of scorn at us. Much hatred will yet be engendered", Herzen concludes, "and much blood will yet flow through this difference in the two stages of growth and education."[15]

Herzen's tragedy was crowned by yet another "sudden, brutal and irrelevant calamity": the drowning, shortly before Natalie's death, of his mother and his little deaf-mute son Kolya, who were returning from Paris to Nice, where the Herzens had lived since 1850.[16]

For some time to come Herzen lived in a state of complete prostration, hardly conscious of the world around him, not knowing where to go and what to do. He felt that his entire hold on life was loosened, that there was no escape from the dreadful reality of disaster, staring at him from every corner, taking the joy out of joyful things and, in the end, leaving nothing but the consciousness that everything happened as if he could for ever, vainly and emptily, play his strokes again. In this mood he came to England—for no particular reason and with no particular plans for the future. "I had absolutely nowhere to go and no reason to go anywhere." Of his remaining family two daughters (Natalie and Olga) stayed for the time being in France, and his oldest son Alexander went with him.

"There is no town in the world", Herzen wrote, recalling the first years in London, "which is more adapted for training one away from people and training one into solitude than London. The manner of life, the distances, the climate, the very multitude of the population in which the individual is lost, all this, together with the absence of Continental diversions, conduces to the same effect. He who knows how to live alone has nothing to fear from the dullness of London. Life here, like the atmosphere here, is bad for the weak, for the frail, for him who seeks a prop outside himself, for him who seeks cordiality, sympathy, attention: the moral lungs here must be as strong as the physical lungs, whose task it is to get rid of the sulphuric acid in the smoky fog. The masses are saved by struggle for daily bread, the commercial classes by their absorption in heaping up wealth, and all by the fuss and hurry of business. But nervous and romantic temperaments, fond of living among their fellow-men, of intellectual sloth and emotional idleness, are bored to death and fall into despair."

The visit to England which was to be no more than a short period of "hermit-like seclusion" turned into twelve years of almost continuous residence (with no less than fifteen changes of lodgings in London alone), and marked the second most important event in Herzen's life abroad—his incursion into Russian politics.

Herzen does not say what it was that made him find new strength to live beyond his unhappiness, griefs, humiliations and hopes abandoned. His whole life seems to be a remarkable example of advances in what appeared like complete dead-ends, of regeneration, of the inexhaustible potentialities of life. But he was not among the lucky ones who find an answer in wreaths and prayers: he found it in humanity, in a passionate solidarity with man. His despair had cleaned and revived his eyes with the rediscovery of his own and other men's identity. In any case, it was not in his nature to stay still, in brooding introspection or passive surrender to an aching void. And he remained at bottom surprisingly free even in his misfortune, which itself became an element, out of which he constructed his own freedom and his message of freedom to others, and to Russia in particular. Above all, he never made a creed of necessity—and this is characteristic of his whole outlook, no less than of his behaviour and feeling for life.

He found release, at first, in communication. "I had", he says, "at all costs to get into communication with my own people, with Russia", "to win their judgment; . . . and little by little I set to work upon *My Past and Thoughts*, and upon founding a Russian printing-press". His immediate surroundings, on the other hand, do not seem to have evoked any response whatever in him. Indeed, it is surprising that, with all his characteristic susceptibility, he should have remained unaffected by England, and his contacts there were, with a few exceptions, confined to foreign political exiles. His memoirs and letters contain a number of brilliant, amusing and not very flattering accounts and descriptions of English life and people—it was, one should remember, the height of mid-Victorian England—but they are on the whole the impressions of a mere observer. He approved of England in a somewhat distant fashion; he valued English political freedom; he admitted that England, "with all the absurdities of feudalism and toryism peculiar to it, is the only country to live in"; and he regretted that the English had lost their love and reputation of frivolous regicides, to become, as he says *"un grand peuple bête,* bored to the glory of God", a nation of shop-keepers and John Bulls. But he scarcely admired them, realizing perhaps that it is impossible and unnecessary to do so, since they did that themselves.

This did not prevent Herzen from becoming in due course a well-known and respected public figure even in the eyes of Englishmen, who were yet most suspicious of all refugees and outlandish political busy-bodies, regarding them as guilty of poverty and unreliability but, at the same time, never tolerating any interference with their right to political asylum in England. "There [in Leicester Square and the adjoining back-streets]", as *The Times* informed its readers in 1856, "lives a wretched population of foreigners wearing hats as no one wears, and hair where none should be, a miserable, poverty-stricken, harassed population who set all the powerful monarchs of Europe trembling except the Queen of England." But Herzen was not poor and, despite the peculiarities of his domestic arrangements, he showed all the signs of respectable and civilized living. The right of asylum, indeed, was re-sponsible for a regular flood of refugees streaming into England from a politically oppressed western, central and eastern Europe. Of many of them Herzen has drawn in his memoirs and letters vivid portraits, sometimes extraordinarily penetrating, sometimes burlesque, coldly respectful or ironical, sometimes enthusiastic, and in a few cases one-sided and prejudiced. More will be said of his estimate of the attitudes and activities of political *émigrés* in another connection.[17]

Herzen's rôle among the exiles, however, was a minor factor when compared with his importance and achievement as the first independent Russian political publicist. In 1855, at a time when, subsequent to the Crimean War and the death of Nicolas I, Russia seemed to be able to breathe again and his own interest had turned from western European to Russian revolution, Herzen founded *Polyarnaya Zvezda* ("Polar Star"), reviving the short-lived Decembrist journal of the same name. This solid and ambitious review, appearing at infrequent intervals throughout the following years, was soon joined by the more popular Weekly *Kolokol* ("The Bell"), which was issued regularly between 1857 and 1867 at Herzen's expense by his Free Russian Printing-Press in London. *The Bell* at once acquired great influence, pouring clandes-tinely into Russia in numerous copies. The political, though not the financial, success of the journal was enormous. It was read by everyone and became the mainspring of inspiration for the younger intelligentsia;

it found its way even into Ministerial Cabinets and the Winter Palace, and, more surprisingly still, it has now been established that it reached the peasants, or at any rate some of the leaders of peasant revolts. In fact, for the space of about five years *The Bell* exercised the function of a dominant political force and served as the originator and promoter of public opinion in Russia—a case unique in modern history, considering the political and geographical circumstances of the whole venture. Within Russia Herzen, known by his *nom de plume* of Iscander, was referred to as her "new terror", her "new conscience", her "new idol". Most of the 245 issues of *The Bell* are accusatory documents, based in the main on secret information on the spot and providing an infinite variety of data for the study of conditions in mid-nineteenth-century Russia. The impression is one of unrelieved political, cultural and moral darkness, with shocking revelations of systematic injustice, cruelty, oppression, and continuous abuses and misgovernment, some of which were actually remedied as a result of these revelations. It was scarcely possible to say anything more devastatingly discreditable to official Russia. Many of the ideological articles, both in *The Bell* and the *Polar Star*, written by diverse hands but mainly by Herzen himself, were ultra-revolutionary, anarchistic and Bakuninist in character.[18] All this, however, did not debar Herzen, both for tactical reasons and in virtue of his acute historical sense, from giving his support to a monarchy which was prepared to constitute itself the spokesman and guarantor of true socialist traditions, and of the principles of justice and freedom, which he saw betrayed by the *bourgeois*-ridden, capitalist western Europe, but which he believed to be still operative in the life of the Russian people, and of the peasantry in particular. Relying as he did for a time on the sincerity and good intentions of the monarchy, he welcomed, therefore, the reign of Alexander II as a new era of great changes in Russia. And his fervent hope, his encouragement, his advice, his fulminations and his threats were an important contributory factor in the emancipation of the serfs in 1861. When Alexander II said that he was faced with emancipation from above or revolution from below he was merely repeating an important political message of "the great London exile".

Before concluding this biographical account, it is necessary to say again a few words about Herzen's closest friend Ogarev. During the darkest years of Nicolaian reaction in Russia and the darkest years of Herzen's voluntary exile abroad Ogarev lived in Simbirsk, managing a paper-mill and writing poetry. Pressing invitations from Herzen, however, finally persuaded him to join his friend, and in the spring of 1856 Ogarev arrived in London. From that time he became Herzen's constant companion and collaborator in all his publicistic undertakings. But Ogarev was not alone. He came to England with Natalie Tuchkova, his second, though unofficial, wife, and this proved to be a new source of misfortunes, in which not only Herzen, but also his children came to be involved. Natalie became Herzen's mistress, and the situation, with rôles inverted so far as Herzen was concerned, had all the appearance of repeating the drama with the first Natalie. But there was an important difference: the arrangement turned into a *mariage à trois*, to be more precise, a *mariage à trois à la russe*, involving none of the twists, mystifications, sublimations and betrayals of which the Herwegh affair provides such abundant evidence. Besides, Herzen undoubtedly loved Ogarev more than his mistress, and Ogarev, in turn, loved Herzen more than his wife. The real misfortune lay in the character of the second Natalie, who displayed all the symptoms of suffering from an extreme and hysterical form of *Bovarysme*—the faculty, that is to say, of seeing herself as other than she was, and from the concomitant refusal to face facts. This may have made her feel up to a point and time that life was worth living, but it made life hell for those around her, and especially for Herzen and his children. Indeed, the facts of the case, which Natalie so persistently refused to face, became the more unpleasant the less she was prepared to face them, and ended by making the last twelve years of Herzen's life a burden beyond bearing. His own attitude grew into one of perpetual self-reproach, exasperation and acerbity.[19] Meanwhile Ogarev, by way of consolation or from sheer indolence, began to drink and attached himself to an English prostitute, Mary Sutherland, to whom he remained touchingly faithful until the end of his life. He died in Greenwich seven years after Herzen, cut off and abandoned, but tended by his uncouth, homely and affectionate mistress.

To conclude, then, the story of Herzen's life, it may be fitting to refer to an incident, which Natalie Tuchkova describes in her homespun reminiscences: it was an augury of the decline of *The Bell* and eventually of the undoing of Herzen's public career. When the aim to which Herzen had largely devoted his work had been achieved, and he learned that the emancipation of the serfs was an accomplished fact, he decided to hold a "monster fête", to which every Russian and foreigner in London who sympathized with the cause was invited. While the festivities were in progress, the news was brought of a riot and of shooting by Russian troops in the streets of Warsaw. Herzen's toast at the dinner to the health of the "Tsar-Liberator" died on his lips. "An atmosphere of doom descended on the festival." Instead of proclaiming, as he wished, "Thou hast conquered, Galilean", Herzen wrote shortly afterwards his famous article *"Mater Dolorosa"*, denouncing the Tsar and the Warsaw massacres. "You have buried *The Bell* today, Alexander Ivanovich", Martyanov exclaimed on reading the article; "no, you can't revive it now, you have laid it in its grave."[20]

Bakunin, as we have already seen, was instrumental in dealing the final blow in connection with the Polish insurrection of 1863. The events in Poland and the peasant risings, due to the disappointing conditions

and ways of implementing the Reforms, produced a rift in the ranks of
the radical intelligentsia whose spokesman Herzen had been. Herzen
began to waver. His revolutionary instinct moved him to support those
radicals within Russia who, driven underground, advocated extreme
revolutionary doctrines and measures. But they were people of a new
generation and, above all, of a new build of character, which could not
but alienate Herzen from them; and they, in turn, lost confidence in
him. On the other hand, he was equally unable to identify himself with
the optimistic, progressive, westernizing liberals of his own generation,
who by definition had no opponents and who were largely satisfied with
the Reforms, as well as determined to uphold Russian interests in
Poland.[21] Herzen's oscillation between these two main forces lead to
his eventual disappearance from the political horizon of Russia. In 1865
the dying *Bell* was transferred to Geneva, and in the same year Herzen
left English soil for ever. For two years he tried to revive the journal and
build a bridge across the widening political and moral gulfs in post-
Nicolaian Russia, but the effort, for all its importance, just as his effort
to bring peace to his disunited family, proved a failure. "We have gone
astray", he wrote to Ogarev in 1868; and, somewhat earlier, he noted in
his Diary: "I see no hope of any bright point either in my personal or in
my public affairs." The last two years of his life were a time of aimless
and restless wandering during which he seemed to have finally adopted
the tired scepticism of a mind that had plumbed the secret of existence
and discovered nothing to which he could attach enduring value. He
died in Paris, after a short illness, on the 21st of January 1870. In
February his body was removed to the ill-fated Nice, where his first
wife and children lay in a family vault.

Although the fact that Herzen died in Paris could not possibly have
had the slightest political significance for France, the French police,
fearful of disturbances, gave instructions to forestall the previously
advertised interment. Only a few friends, therefore, were able to be
present at the funeral. Among them happened to be Malardier, a
member of the French Constituent Assembly of 1848; and it was he
who on this occasion spoke of Herzen as *"un Voltaire russe"*. The
remark has become a by-word and offers a suitable vantage point for
estimating Herzen's character.

Like Voltaire—and this seems to be the only parallel that occurred
to Malardier—Herzen disliked kings, priests, teachers, policemen, civil
servants and all who hold positions of authority, which encourages love
of power and indolence of mind. Like Voltaire he was a sceptic by
habit and cast of mind and by temperament. Like Voltaire he refused to
take life at its face value, and mistrusted great professions, knowing all
the secret hiding places where idols and ideals are to be found and
where they find their dungeons. Like Voltaire he knew how to lay error

quickly on ice, how to smile like a satirist and apply his irreverent, lucid and trenchant mind. Like Voltaire he attached value to precision—a trait which acts like the sudden, delicious shock of a cold shower after the opaque, intractable atmosphere of so much Russian thought. Like Voltaire he had the manner of a *grand seigneur*, which some of his compatriots could never forgive him, and was remarkable for his ease among men and ideas, for his tolerance, irony and wit. The similarities could be enlarged and multiplied. And yet Malardier's comparison, when met with in the views of others who knew Herzen better than he did, must be counted as misleading: and this not merely for the reason stated by another Frenchman, who said that "*Voltaire ne pouvait en effet guère reigner qu'au XVIIIe siècle et en France*" (Tocqueville).

What strikes one in the first place in this connection is Herzen's passion for the world of sense, for seeing men as they are. Voltaire, too, was interested in men, but he tended to watch them misanthropically. Herzen loved human beings, and his human beings, unlike Voltaire's, were no wraiths lacking flesh and bone. Because he hated stupidity, he was prone to believe, as Voltaire believed to a much greater extent, that evil came from stupidity. He could afford perhaps to think so, because by all evidence he was the most intelligent Russian of the nineteenth century, as Voltaire had been the most intelligent Frenchman of the eighteenth century. And yet he did not suffer from that defect of human understanding which led Voltaire to suppose that the battle was never between good and evil, but always between intelligence and stupidity. Voltaire had dedicated his life to two ends: the cause of liberty and progress and the reputation of M. de Voltaire. It was, admittedly, easy for him to keep in sight both, because they tended to coincide. Herzen, on the contrary, felt no inclination to applaud even the former end, since it amounted to no more than the ideal of harmlessness and well-being, with "well-cultivated gardens" and an assured Catholic funeral. An elegant representative of the spirit of his time, Voltaire was in reality turned towards the past and had nothing new to offer except a trenchant criticism of tradition which was complete by the death of Louis XIV. This may explain why even Voltaire's irony rings sterile: it seems to reflect an age of foregone conclusions, of spent or impoverished emotion, insensitive to the unknown and unpredictable, and provoking a laughter in which he took no part. Herzen's irony had nothing cloistered, supercilious or thin-lipped about it: it was a form of controlled intensity, a way of concealing the passion and violence of his own nature which yet came out from time to time (as, for instance, in *From the Other Shore*), albeit without war-like postures and contorted limbs. Whilst concealing that passion and violence, the irony never supplanted them, and therefore never turned into deprecating and complacent flippancy. It was, as Herzen himself observed in another connection, "our native Russian irony, the irony that is a comforter and an avenger".

His heart and mind were open to the dimension of truth which the *philosophes* had blandly ignored, to forces that lie beyond or beneath our consciousness; and the period of his greatest fascination by their thought also marked his most deeply felt need to respond to the irrational qualities of life.[22] Indeed, he saw life itself in the midst of the whirling unseen, unknown, creative and destructive forces and knew the dread in which man stands of the mystery of his own existence.

Voltaire, caught as he was in the most inconvenient dilemma between *ancien régime* and revolution, preferred to live, both literally and figuratively, in a kind of fox-hole with two exits, one on French and one on Swiss soil. He even offered to make peace with the clergy, whom he ridiculed throughout his life, because he was afraid that his old bones would find no suitable resting place. He would never have questioned the values and benefits of civilization. Herzen's feeling of the world's burden as his own, his resolute involvement in history and society, on the other hand, were a measure of the extraordinary courage of his denials. His mind, unlike Voltaire's, was profoundly historical, interested in history not just as an ammunition dump for firing at prejudice, but as man's destiny, although reflection on that destiny brought him to the painful realization of its enslaving power over man. For him to question the values of civilization, together with the necessity for perpetual revolt against them which such questioning entailed, was almost a matter of personal integrity, of being true to himself. In this, as in many other respects, he was capable of allowing moral and other passions to prompt his reason which, naturally enough, did not always make for temperate views or for a support of accepted notions and patterns of life. It made him a mystic and a romantic one moment, and an empiricist the next. To philosophy he brought the tastes of a scientist and to science a sense of humanity. He was a humanist who remained in love with the dark powers; a materialist who was enraged by materialism; an atheist with a humble devotion to the Gospels, which, he says, he could never open and "remain unmoved"; a rationalist, without any "irritable reaching after fact and reason", and moving uncertainly in an alien and hostile world.

There is one final and most important point which should put Herzen's "Voltairian" nature in the right perspective: it is that he was endowed with the faculty, which Voltaire conspicuously lacked, of being saddened by what he knew. Truth itself appeared to him as sad and bitter truth—"the sickness of truth", he used to say—and knowledge as the *Unglück des Bewusstseins*, of which Hegel spoke at his most perceptive. He desired knowledge and pursued it as one who had fallen in love with truth: yet everything he came to know added to the force of his conviction that life has no meaning, and that to know it is but to wrench from chaos the secret of its nothingness. This fundamental sadness at the end and within all knowledge, in addition to, though not apart from, all the unhappiness that has befallen him, invested his life with the bitterness of ironic tragedy. He was, it is true, capable, as few other Russians were capable, of transposing tragedy into a clear key, of making us feel that even pain can be lucid, sun-lit; but this only served to deepen it, and he could have escaped it only by ceasing to know, to think, and to feel. It was with him almost from the start, even while he was most prone to display his capacity for enjoyment: his Diary, began in the early 'forties, is instinct with it.[23] "*Mir gab der Gott zu sagen was ich leide*", he used to quote Goethe's Tasso. It seems as if there were two halves to his nature: one strong, vivacious, gay, magnificently turbulent and prolific, imbued with delight in physical things and a sense of the body that would have made him at home in the Renaissance—a rather unusual quality, for there was very little of such positive, masculine love of life in Russia after the Pushkin period. The other was melancholy, painfully remote, seldom surrendering without reservation, keeping him a stranger in the world of actuality and bringing him face to face with the most hidden, terrifying truth of man's precarious and isolated existence. He never really succeeded in bridging the gulf between the two halves, except momentarily, through humour, which provided him with relief, and sometimes no more than with a cloak to cover his real self.

A similar dichotomy can be detected in regard to the rebellious and revolutionary element in Herzen's character and outlook. His whole life and public career provided tangible evidence of dedication to the cause of revolution, in the widest sense of the word, that is to say, as an attitude of mind and as a political creed. He rebelled in virtue of his humanity and his infinite capacity for interrogation. Acceptance of any permanent order, natural or supernatural, of any objective teleology, was for him a form of slavery, a way of divinizing inhumanity, a threat to the freedom and personality of man. He had little sense of reverence, or, rather, he knew that there is a great deal too much of it in the world, and that it is claimed for many objects that do not deserve it. "*Bürger Herzen*", a German revolutionary announced, "*hat kein, aber auch kein Organ der Venerazion.*" We shall see that it made no difference to him whether the gods which endanger man and to which he reserves sacrifice and devotion belong to theism or atheism, to capitalism or socialism, to the left or to the right: he rebelled on behalf of freedom on all flanks and against all comers, and professed an anarchism that did not fall short of Bakunin's. He did not even shrink with distaste from extreme revolutionary destruction. And yet it is just here that he appears to have been struggling with a baffling division of purpose. Bakunin and even Ogarev, as well as some of those young radicals within Russia who turned against him in the 'sixties believed that he lacked the courage, the integrity and the imagination to be consistent in carrying his rebellion to the end. But in fact, for all his destructiveness, which

Natalie Herzen shortly before her death at the age of 30

Nicolas Ogarev at the age of 47 ("To my dear Tata
[Herzen's eldest daughter] from the original")

sometimes broke out like lava from a volcano, he felt, as he tried to impress on Bakunin, that man is unable to destroy without constructing something other than what he is destroying, and, indeed, reconstructing what he is destroying. No amount of bombast could make this untrue for him. And, at a still deeper level, he could not eliminate in himself the moral and aesthetic sense. Despite his acute political insight, despite, or because of his *engagement* and disinclination to take refuge in any superiority whatever, he was at bottom a spiritual aristocrat, with an almost physical distaste for the organized cruelty and organized stupidity of *Realpolitik*. This unfitted him for the commonplace business of revolution. He seemed himself to suffer hurt from the very devastation he advocated. To that extent he remained true to himself even in his dividedness and inhibition. And his successors in Russia, who came into conflict with him, repudiated Herzen as the man he was, with all his reticences and disenchantment, rather than with Herzen as a teacher.

During the "remarkable decade", however, and throughout the 'fifties, Herzen's contemporaries were unanimous in their estimate of him as one who, in both these capacities, was to exercise "the most powerful influence on his time" (Belinsky). Turgenev, Granovsky, Nekrasov, and even the Slavophils spoke at first in a similar vein. The most vivid record of their impression of Herzen is contained in Annenkov's well-informed reminiscences. "From his first appearance in the public eye", Annenkov writes, "it was apparent that Herzen's talent placed him in the ranks of great Russian writers and thinkers. . . . There are but few people who, like Herzen, are able to keep the respect, regard and interest of others at a time when they are carried away by emotion. . . . In this he resembles Belinsky, although Belinsky, wrapt as he was in the world of ideas, had no gift of character reading, no sharp wit, or talent for psychological observation. Herzen, on the contrary, was born with a critical mind, added to which he was given to unmasking the darker sides of life and coming to grips with them. . . . Already in Moscow he was showing himself to be of a very independent and unaccommodating temperament, with an innate abhorrence of everything resembling an established, tacitly assumed rule concerning some unverified truth. All the predatory instincts of Herzen's mind were aroused by such phenomena, and his caustic and inventive tongue filled his hearers with astonishment." "As though to redress the balance of his moral make-up, nature had endowed Herzen with an unshakable belief in the moral instincts of the heart of man. His inclination to analyse was checked by his respect for the moral impulses of the human heart, which to him were the only unquestionable truth of life. Any noble, passionate enthusiasm, however misplaced, was held in great esteem by him and was never the object of his sarcasm. . . . And in all that he did and thought himself there was no grain of falsehood, not the slightest

o   193

sign of calculation or buried resentment; on the contrary, his whole being was reflected in his every word and action." Despite his "grim scepticism and unrestrained, stinging wit", Annenkov continues, "his heart was that of a child. He knew how to be tactful and tender, albeit in a rather clumsy way, and sometimes, when he had dealt a particularly cruel blow to his antagonist, he knew how to ask forgiveness instantly."[24]

On the whole, however, there was little to forgive, for Herzen was never unfair, or malevolent, or envious. He did not accuse anybody, except the accusers. He had no revulsions, except against the insincere and the inhuman, and no horrors, except of minds made up in advance. He could not grant the slightest concession to a lie, even if by doing so he might have promoted the triumph of truth. Yet he never suffered from pedantry, never moralized and never preached, and when he drew a moral, he did so usually with a shrug of the shoulders. His natural warmth in personal relationships, and the vein of tenderness in him, to which Annenkov draws attention and on which many, Herwegh above all, knew how to play, was impeded by reflectiveness, and hence by an uneasiness which he never mastered. He reproached himself both for the tenderness and the reflectiveness, and, as a rule, followed the promptings of the former. Above all, he was gifted with a sense of cleanliness, moral, intellectual and emotional, the keenness of which was quite phenomenal; so much so that he could ascertain physiologically (a term, by the way, he was very fond of using in a variety of quite un-physiological contexts) the core of human ideas and actions. It did not always save him from errors, particularly from errors in judging people; but he could smell falsehood from afar, and his genius resided largely in his nostrils. He was able to judge philosophies, ideas, valuations and attitudes by their smell, more even than by their subtlety and coherence. The defect of this natural sensitivity was that he tended to be too discriminating, too fastidious, too much, as it were, concerned with the process of creation to be creative, if indeed one could evolve a standard for measuring creativity. Bakunin's daring, and manner of living and seeing in a gigantic way are possibly more indicative of creative energy than the astonishing virtuosity and brilliance of Herzen's mind.

But this virtuosity gave his life and work a peculiar fragrance and generosity, which are absent in Bakunin or even in Belinsky. It is sufficient to peruse the casual entries in Herzen's Diary to be convinced of the infinite variety of experience and the innumerable facets of human life and thought to which he responded. There appears to be no subject with which he had not been concerned at one time or another, as can be gauged from the table of contents in the twenty-two volumes of his collected works. He could never adopt an attitude which would have meant foregoing the intoxication of knowing everything and feeling everything. If his whole work remained fragmentary, it was not because, like Bakunin, he was incapable of completing any undertaking, or because, like Belinsky, outside and inside pressures drove him to and fro but just because he was universal in his scope. Indeed, one has a sense of powers so widely distributed that the central force is only evident as a distant echo. This universal, ubiquitous quality, especially in the period preceding his career as a publicist in London, damages the organic wholeness of his work, leaving a feeling that he failed to exercise a choice of, or preference for, a subject, or even that his sole gift was a miraculous intellectual and verbal skill. And yet, as will be seen in the next chapter, his outlook constitutes a complete philosophy, in the sense in which a philosophy entails a *Weltanschauung*, a characteristic attitude to human experience and behaviour. The universality and ubiquity, on the other hand, were no more and no less than the index of an infinitely rich imagination. He could not think, except in the open air, and felt something oppressive and oppressed in the meticulous, restrictive ways of scholars who mirror the cramped conditions of a nook, an ink-bottle, a study filled with rattling bones and categories. "Neither the learned fathers, nor the spiritual fathers", he wrote to Turgenev, "can bring us any relief: the monks of knowledge, like the monks of ignorance, know nothing outside the walls of their monasteries, . . . and while men are perishing from the eruption of the volcano, they are blissfully beating time, listening to the music of their narrow spheres and marvelling at its harmony." Herzen's own erudition was immense, but it was at most his handmaiden, and never his muse.

When Herzen first appeared in the Moscow salons he immediately acquired the reputation of a great conversationalist, stimulating, dynamic, ironical and subversive. His terseness—and Moscow at the time could do a little with this—acted like a wind in whose breath inflated speculations shrivelled and the springs of pontifical utterance dried up. He had but one equal and rival—Alexey Khomyakov, whose dialectical and polemical abilities may even have surpassed his own. But Khomyakov was the bull: he came charging forth, bellowing conviction and determined either to chase his opponents into the arms of Mother Church, or to hold them up to intellectual ignominy. Whenever Herzen confronted him, he felt the fascination of his opponent's strength. Like an accomplished picador, he usually managed to plant an elegant dart or two, and finally side-stepped out of the arena. Neither can be said to have ever won, for there was hardly any real contact between them.[25]

Herzen's verbal skill is fully reflected in his writings. His braced and vivid style is elaborate and ornamental rather than simple; but there is nothing massive, solemn, or affected about it. The sentences follow each other like a succession of fireworks, and there is hardly a dull moment. He never said the same thing twice, as Bakunin continually did, or, at any rate, he never said it in the same way. No one in Russia, with the exception of Vladimir Soloviev, has written philosophy with more clarity and vividness; but even his memoranda composed on official duty in Vyatka and Vladimir are still enjoyable reading. Herzen's ideological enemies (Shevyrev, Bulgarin, and others), it is true, made a special point of attacking his language, which they nicknamed "Iscanderism"; and Turgenev also described it as "monstrously incorrect", although he hastened to add that it enraptured him: "a living body", he said in a letter to Annenkov.[26] It was spiced with extravagant vocabulary, with violations of Russian syntax, and a maze of Gallicisms, Anglicisms and Germanisms, which became the more pronounced the longer he lived abroad. But even this served to enhance the individuality of his writing, and seemed to be a most suitable medium for expressing his interest in the vagaries, incongruities and oddities of experience. What he lacked completely was a well-organized system, political, moral or philosophical; and whilst he never avoided intellectual analysis, his real gift lay in the crystallization of condensed thought, in summary utterance and aphorism, which makes him also one of the most easily quoted Russian writers. "I have no system", he wrote in *From the Other Shore*, "and no interest, except in truth; and I speak of it as it occurs to me." The lack of a generalized view of life made for patternlessness, for odd and improbable mixtures, and destroyed the symmetry of his thought, but it also betrayed his awareness of the elusive and baffling quality of truth, and stamped his thought as the direct fruit of an individual mind and individual experience.

2. A PHILOSOPHY OF EXISTENCE

The title "A Philosophy of Existence", under which I propose to discuss the philosophical views of Herzen, needs some preliminary explanation.[27] The word "existence" has unfortunately been allowed to exercise the function of a magic formula, at least in Continental philosophical idiom, with associations which are, if not irrelevant, anachronistic when speaking of Herzen. Yet there is a real vision or experience which this word denotes in its contemporary context, even for those who have no particular interest in the gratifying apocalyptic visions of an atomized "existential" world, and which is clearly recognizable in Herzen's own account of his philosophical position. The vision or experience expresses itself above all in the attempt to establish an absolute end of man's existence on the ground of his consciously and voluntarily affirmed finiteness, to realize his own, individual and never definable image. It entails an attitude of refusal to direct one's life according to extraneous, objective standards. And it is felt that unless man refuses assent to such standards he does not really "exist", which means that he is not really himself, but a puppet at the mercy of ruthless fate, or of vast impersonal physical processes, or of an equally impersonal universal mind, or of some other impersonal mass, by whose standards he thinks, wills, acts, and feels wretched or at ease. "Existence" is the living, changing, concrete fact in a world seen as a sphere of radical contingency, with man engaged in contingent discoveries and a contingent choice, and with life unmotivated except by the will of individual man. It is not something to be taken naïvely for granted, but is to be called in question, to be understood, without freezing its living texture into fixities which one may manipulate like counters or group into a conclusive logical system. "Existence" reflects the vanishing certainties of concept, of all attempts to make life intelligible by relating it to anything that empties it of its moving quality; and it is more easily understood in terms that attach primary importance to will rather than to intellect, and set life in relief in its most personal character.

From the beginning philosophers have noted the prominence of movement and conflict—in the Heraclitan cosmic strife of material contraries, in the Platonic antagonism between the ideal and sensible worlds, in the Hegelian discovery in history of a fresh manifestation of that universal warfare which is "the father of all things". But this philosophical movement has been attended by a persistent tendency to eliminate the contrasts by applying rational criteria to life and attributing meaning to it only or primarily on account of its part in the totality of all things, or in a complete rational system. A philosopher of existence claims no competence for the human mind to resolve the contrasts: he only claims for him a capacity for assuming them by an effort of the will, which does not create rationality, although it can humanize the irrational by making man face it and seek his own, individual path through it. No Greek ever dreamed of considering problems of individual behaviour and individual eccentricity as such worthy of philosophical interest; and he would have regarded a philosopher who concerned himself with biographical incidents, or with the drama of conflicting personalities as not to be taken seriously. But then the philosopher of existence is a product of avowed disillusion in conceptual and contemplative thought, a product of reaction against the hypertrophies of the rational side of the European mind which has reached its culmination in Hegel's absolute or "objective" idealism. He has taken a new step, by placing man, with all his unique, irreducible character and unpredictable liberty at the very centre of philosophy itself. The strength or weakness of such a step lay in that he was bound to speak in the first person, and that his philosophy was not a philosophy concerning existence, but a philosophy of *his* existence. It could not, therefore, be communicated and it carried no conviction, except to another person who had shared it in some degree. Yet the philosopher of existence is able to turn this limitation to advantage. He affirms that the contrary attempt to eliminate the subjective factor from philosophical discussion and so to arrive at an allegedly true picture of the world is a mistake and a delusion fathered upon

philosophy by science, whose prestige some philosophers have tried
to win for their own studies. For while the statement that a whole is
greater than a part, that $2 \times 2 = 4$, or that the Volga flows into the
Caspian Sea is not necessarily infected with subjectivity, no such objectivity can be assigned to the less ascertainable but more important fact of
man's search for truth, to his acts of will and choice, or to the question of
his place in the universe. Whatever sobriety one may endeavour to
achieve in dealing with such matters one will still find oneself drunk with
the memories of one's own history as god, man, and beast. The objectivity of one's philosophical procedure, then, stands in direct proportion
to one's alienation from the matrix of human existence.

What is completely individual, however, can in the last resort be a
subject only of biography and autobiography. And Herzen's thought at
its most intense is an autobiography: his memoirs, his Diary, his novel
and short stories, and his letters (to real and imaginary correspondents)
convey in manner and matter a personal attitude to the many problems
to which he turned his mind; and this is Herzen's real claim to greatness
as a thinker.

The philosophical, as distinct from the social and political, views of
Herzen are mature and independent by the time he wrote his essays on
Dilettantism in Science, Letters on the Study of Nature, Who is Guilty?
and the Diary. His earlier work and development (before his return to
Moscow from exile) is marked by the influence of a splendidly incongruous intellectual mixture: the French *encyclopédistes*, Saint-Simon's
utopian socialism, Laurenz Oken's philosophico-scientific ideas, Schelling's *Naturphilosophie*, Victor Cousins's idealism, Schillers's aestheticism, and French and German mysticism. It needed Herzen's great
imagination to permit all these and other less ascertainable ingredients
to co-exist without cancelling each other out or removing the tension
between them. This was, no doubt, facilitated by his ability to treat
ideas not as finished product but, so to speak, as acts of creation forming
in the human mind, and by his interest in the state of mind of a thinker
rather than in mere ratiocination.

Two themes, however, become increasingly prominent against the
background of these early eclectic philosophical preoccupations, and
they contain the nucleus of ideas which went to the making of Herzen's
"philosophy of existence". One pertains to the dispute between materialism and idealism; the other concerns the question of freedom and human
personality. His attitudes to the former issue were shifting all the time,
each apparently reversing the value of the last, and materialism immediately following on the resolute affirmation of the independence of the
human spirit. Although this inability to adhere genuinely to either of the
contesting doctrines showed that the whole contest in its traditional form
was in the end unreal to him, the opposites rung within his nature irre-

spective of their connection with technical philosophy. When he took a stand in favour of materialism he did not wish to equate the real and the ideal which idealists and materialists alike tend to do, thereby making it comparatively easy for themselves to appropriate each other's methods. Nor did he wish to advocate the epistemological view that the human mind is a *tabula rasa*, wherein the impressions gathered in by the senses are elaborated according to certain determined rules—a view which, in fact, Herzen explicitly repudiated. Rather, he welcomed in materialism the "redemption of the flesh". "*Tout accepter et rien exclure*", he quotes at the end of his first and most idealistic philosophical essay (*O meste cheloveka v prirode* ["On the Place of Man in Nature"]). Humanity grew sick after "the holy vampires of the Middle Ages" have sucked out so much life-blood. "*Humanitas, humaniora!* resounded on all sides, and man knew that in these words, taken from the earth, there rings a *vivere memento* which was succeeding the *memento mori*; that thereby he will be re-united with Nature. *Humanitas* reminded men, not that they will turn to earth, but that they proceed from it, and they rejoiced at having found it under their feet." It was necessary to offer grand expiatory sacrifices to matter, in order to atone for old offences against it. The senses have been forced to become hypocritical, loosing self-respect and eventually avenging themselves on the spirit. To "rehabilitate matter" was a way of reconciling it with the spirit and hence of restoring the integral image of man. To be a materialist in this connection meant for Herzen to exhibit the predicament of mortality, as opposed to the empty and shapeless eternity of the philosophers and theologians, who, as he says in the same essay, "have turned living man into a corpse". It is to re-create the pulse of life and restore savour to things. But both then and later, when he expressed (e.g. in his essay *Opyt besed s molodymi lyudmi* ["Essay in Conversations with Young People"] Moleschottian ideas of the "circular motion of life" which sucks into its vortex all that is understood as mental or spiritual; or when he quoted, half seriously and half in jest, Feuerbach's dictum "*der Mensch ist was er isst*"—he was far removed from that "pale metaphysical materialism of blessed memory" which leaves men prisoners of their own world, or slowly suffocates them in an imaginary world of corporeity. The materialist, Herzen wrote, "by knowing nothing but matter and corporeity, knows, for that very reason, neither the one nor the other". Matter itself he defines, curiously echoing Bakunin, as "moved by an inherent repugnance against its obtuse, senseless and heavy inertia: it is self-corroding, it ferments, so to speak", and this fermenting process, this "perpetual transformation in the dark region of life", "denies material extension, strives to free itself from it, and at last is freed in the spirit of man . . ." Matter *per se*, just as mind *per se*, remained unintelligible abstractions to Herzen: he knew only of events, of mind and matter in union.[28]

In seeking to restore the wholeness of human nature and its link with the natural world, Herzen did not envisage man as a blind slave of cosmic striving which drives him this way and that and dwindles until it goes out like a candle. Within the cycle of Nature, to which he belongs, man is, indeed, a creature of inexorable necessity. He evolves from it and is to that extent conditioned by it; yet such evolution is not the mechanical result of the action of extraneous forces: rather, it is true e-volution, a development from within, with man as the centre of self-renewing vitality, which cannot be explained as a mere psychical counterpart of external circumstance. Man is conditioned and conditionable, and yet an ever unique and ever unpredictable self. He is, in Herzen's words, the "wholly new in Nature". He possesses the power to mould his intentions, to direct his actions, to create and to destroy. Man is free, not because he presumes to do or does what no animal could have done, but because he refuses to do what the animal within him wished to do, and he thus becomes man without aid from the gods of Nature or of society. Nature tells us that life follows the line of least resistance or the strongest motive, but the mind prompts us to protest for the dignity of man against the crushing power of Nature and society. Thus, starting from an attempt to recover the wholeness of the image of man, Herzen proceeded, as an anti-idealist gesture, to abolish "the spirit", but carried his search for the truth about man through to the point where it served as an affirmation of human freedom and independence, and an elucidation of man as the maker of his own world, determined, not by the necessity of external influences, but by that of his own character. He thought, by the very foundation of his philosophy, that rebirth could only come about from sources within the world, which by those same foundations proves to be radically insufficient. This provides a recurring pattern throughout Herzen's intellectual development, whether at moments of marked leanings towards idealism, as in the essay *On the Place of Man in Nature*, or at his most materialistic, as in *Conversations with Young People*, or in the more important philosophical essays of the middle 'forties and in the later letters to his son Alexander.[29]

We have seen already that, on his return from exile, Herzen undertook a serious study of Hegel, and of German philosophy in general, but, despite Bakunin's efforts, he never became a Hegelian. It appears from his Diary that he immediately detected the secret of German philosophical thought, namely, theological pantheism. While Belinsky and even Bakunin had for a time succumbed to the lure of this open secret, at least in as much as it had a bearing on the problems of history, and helped them, in a measure, to wrap up in metaphysical abstractions their sense of the oppression which reigned in their environment, Herzen remained throughout unsusceptible of the lure, partly because of his deep-seated irony, ready at any moment to destroy illusions and show them for what they are, partly because of his growing anti-religious conviction, and mainly because of his single-minded loyalty to the human person. But before dealing with these latter aspects of Herzen's outlook it is important to consider his excursions into Hegelianism.

There was more to his interest in Hegel than merely the need to learn to use the instruments of the contemporary philosophical discussion. It is true that he disliked intensely the thick idealistic fog which descended on him on his return to Moscow—all those Hegelian necessities and relations with no possibilities and no subjects; but, capable as he was of being drawn below the surface and seldom tempted to adopt an attitude that ties ideas to words and appearances, he did more than generate precision in a discussion which sorely needed it. Once he had become used to Hegel's language and mastered his method he came to believe that, as he put it, "a man who has not *lived through* Hegel", "who has not passed through that furnace and been tempered by it, is not complete, not contemporaneous". Besides, he was the first Russian to realize the primary importance of Hegel in his younger "phenomenological" phase, of Hegel, that is to say, at his least scholastic, at his morally and intellectually most refreshing, when he was yet removed from what Herzen called "Buddhistic quietism" and "Prussian Christianity". This Hegel alone was acceptable to him: Hegel whose dialectical philosophy is, in Herzen's celebrated phrase, "the algebra of revolution", who "emancipates man in an extraordinary way and leaves not a stone of the old world standing".[30]

Hegel helped Herzen to formulate the nihilistic, destructive side of his outlook, as the disillusionment of 1848 did with his social and political views. It is of some interest that Herzen was one of the first to point out the origin of Hegel's thought in the strange, obscure and highly original doctrines, or rather visions, of the German mystic Jacob Böhme, whom Herzen admired greatly. In expounding Böhme's ideas (in *Letters on the Study of Nature*), Herzen stresses Böhme's mystical voluntarism and nihilism, which marked a break with the intellectualism of Greek and Scholastic philosophy and provided Hegel with some of his most important ideas. Böhme's vision of life as embraced by fire and pervaded by the conflict between light and darkness, and his notion of *Ungrund*, of "*blosse begehrende Sucht des Nichts*", with its rich imagery, expressing the irrational, groundless, indeterminate nature of being, are important ingredients in the Hegelian dialectic, although Hegel has rationalized them out of recognition and deprived them of their fascinating poetic quality. They are particularly evident in Hegel's system of the world of forms, permeated through and through by movement and constantly issuing in "dynamic process", in "becoming", in which every concept leads beyond itself. But, more particularly still, they have influenced Hegel's doctrine of Nature, with which Herzen was mainly concerned in his *Letters*. For Hegel, as for Plato and Aristotle, all things are essentially engaged in a process of becoming, because they are always trying to be adequate embodiments of their own forms and never wholly succeeding: hence the element of indeterminacy, of irrationality and potentiality in Nature. But, whereas Greek thought tended to blame matter for the inadequacy, Hegel maintained that it is due to the peculiarity of the forms themselves, and conceived irrational elements as essential to them. They demand to be embodied and yet, by their own changing, dialectical nature, break the bounds of every instance or expression of themselves, constituting, as it were, the immense notes of interrogation over each and every embodiment, a No, a protest, a purification. They preclude the possibility of isolating any single factor in Nature or history and of making it an absolute standard. They subvert the search for any static point from which timeless judgments may be delivered. Indeed, they make the individual apprehension of the ever-changing reality itself necessarily partial and relative, and subject all views to the process of continuous change. Hegel, as has been seen in the chapter on Belinsky, was not at all consistent in applying these ideas in his philosophy of history; but for Herzen they were the only ones worthy of application, and he saw in them the most destructive weapon in Hegel's armoury, which Hegel has failed to use or which he has betrayed.

The emphasis on negation in Herzen's interpretation of Hegel owes a great deal to the influence of Bakunin, whose *Reaction in Germany* Herzen welcomed with enthusiasm. But the nihilistic theme pervades all Herzen's philosophical writings after his return from provincial exile. It is clearly apparent in *Dilettantism in Science*, in *Letters on the Study of Nature* and in *From the Other Shore* which I shall have mainly in view in this discussion and from which the quotations that follow are taken. Since all revolutions have their philosophy but not all philosophies have their revolution, it is necessary to devise, in Herzen's words, "a philosophy of revolution". Philosophy, like every rational activity, is defined as a "perpetual revolutionary tribunal", as "the guillotine within man". It performs the function of a "Last Judgment". It is "ruthless, stopping at nothing, and bringing to the bar supreme being itself. . . . There is a curious likeness between the phenomenology of terror and logic." "It abhors canonized truths" and "turns all that is religious and political into that which is simple and human, and subject to negation". Heraclitus is commended for his "demonic principle of negation, . . . which for ever destroys all that serves to congeal life or to immobilize it". The Sophists are acclaimed for "the free expanse of negation (*razdolie negatsii*), . . . shattering the obdurate and doing away with the spurious", for their "terrible frankness". Hume and particularly Kant are extolled for having submitted the faculty of knowing to a merciless investigation, for having sounded the depth of this faculty and ascertained its limits, and for their mortifying discovery that about many things of which we were certain we know nothing. Even in Christianity Herzen welcomes an original impetus to negation "forceful, candid, inexorable and unabashed", in face of the time-worn ancient world.

"Knowledge arises in a passion of denial", in a conflict between the knower and the known, between freedom and necessity: it breaks out from the slavery to the objective, the given, the ready-made, the once-for-all; it is a source of perpetual transcendence; it is an act of the mind which lifts itself above the data which the world provides in an attempt to discover their meaning and to master them. Irreconcilable enemy of the dichotomy of mind and body, of thought and the world, of matter and spirit though he was, Herzen stresses everywhere the experience of a dualism which underlies the process of knowledge and reveals the "dramatic quality" of man's efforts to know. "The split between man and Nature, which acts like a wedge tearing everything apart and producing conflict is the *divide et impera* of knowledge." He sees the un-doing of Greek philosophy and of medieval Scholasticism in a kind of epistemological optimism, in its failure to take into account the profound cleavage between man and the world which true knowledge entails, "to experience the sweetness and bitterness of denial, and to understand all the power of the human spirit thrown back upon itself, upon itself alone". It is this experience of a divided universe which impels the philosopher to span the awful distance, to fight not only for his conclusions but for his data too: it makes truth attainable for him, not by way of a naïve and self-confident discovery of or submission to finished objects, or by virtue of an assumed conformity of thought and fact, but because he wins it by a creative act, in which meaning outruns verifiability and turns upon imaginability, enabling him to acknowledge new possibilities beyond his reach and making him prefer on all occasions the possible to the actual.

It is not surprising, perhaps, that, with this attitude, Herzen felt no sympathy for those who extract epistemological principles from the devotional injunction to contemplate and marvel at the world. Knowledge for him—and he was more Kantian than Hegelian in this—was essentially the result of human activity. The conviction of the Greek and Scholastic philosopher, or for that matter, in a different context, of the Cartesians and empiricists, that the highest knowledge is attained while we are passive and receptive, in contemplation, or while we are empty "subjects" to be filled with "objectivity", was to his mind a betrayal of the creative nature of man and the creative unfolding of reality.[31] Merely to wonder at things, rather than to explain and to change them, struck Herzen as tantamount to inhabiting an ivory tower. He attached special importance to the rise of science in this connection, which has tainted all post-Renaissance philosophy and which signified to him the emergence of man's creative attitude to the world. The fact that it has led to the views of knowledge as exclusively utilitarian and pragmatic, which Herzen did not share, should not nevertheless, in his view, make man desire to return to a pre-scientific wisdom and humility.

There was, indeed, no retreat for Herzen from his own dualist position into naïve belief, or into some lost harmony maintained by a sublime conviction of being in the Almighty's confidence. He regarded it as an exaggeration of the native dogmatism of human nature or a piece of lucky rather than virtuous innocence that man continued to rely on truths that are unambiguous and find certainty that used to discharge itself in metaphysics, and in his century discharged itself in scientific, positivist fashion, but in every case expressed a longing for something stable, the longing for a hold, a support. To Herzen, philosophy appeared as an attitude of questioning rather than of answering, and *epoché* as the primary condition of wisdom. He doubted and questioned with a persistence that might have well surprised Descartes himself. Real, unflinching doubt, pursuing its unserene way and marking everything with a query, liberated Herzen's mind not only from the certainties of marketplace, academy and conventicle, but from the "methods" of doubt itself, from the fixity and limitation of thought-processes. He practised it in love as well as in retribution, and that is why his eyes were opened at once to the meaning of the things he doubted and to his own responsibility. It was this combination of doubt and responsiveness which gave all his ideas, quests and aims a peculiar character of spontaneity, freedom and awareness.

It may appear that Herzen's doubts wavered on the threshold of science. In some respects, it is true, he was very much a representative of the nineteenth century, for he acknowledged the enormous prestige of science, in the general sense of the pursuit of knowledge with the sole aim of ascertaining truth, of diligently searching for all relevant facts, and of exercising one's critical judgment from which all fixed ideas have been eliminated. His work *Dilettantism in Science* is largely devoted to this problem. He shared to some extent the whole modern scientific trend of extending the realm of natural knowledge more and more and repressing the claims of the supernatural, of regarding sense experience as the main source of knowledge and accounting for life without recourse to whatever is merely magical, or mysterious, or mythological. He seemed to need, as it were, a solid block of reality as part of his extraordinary openness to life in all its concreteness and variety, and he needed a scientific account of that reality as part of his search for truth and of his profound revolt against the unassailable traditional system of life and thought.

It required, therefore, an unusual blend of vision and courage, and perhaps a touch of mischief, for a believer in science such as Herzen was, to do what is now one of the most hackneyed of undertakings, but which acted then like a breath of fresh air, namely, to apply his doubt to science too, and to expose the limitations and presumptions of science. He invited the readers of his *Dilettantism in Science* to watch the spectacle of science with less of the reverence appropriate to a church and with more of the freedom appropriate to the seeker after truth, and he regretted that iconoclasm is no less deficient in the priests of science than in those of religion. He expressed a horror of what he called the Buddhism of science, which turns into the hiding place of every kind of stintedness, bad conscience and cowardice, and issues from lack of vision and love. The object of knowledge, to Herzen's mind, was neither a corpse to be dissected nor even a living body to be vivisected: knowledge, if it succeeds, must be a spark which strikes the tinder of the knower's imagination. Even in scientific laws he refused to see mere statements describing regularities and uniformities, but saw them—not perhaps without some influence from Goethe, whose scientific studies he found deeply illuminating—as pictures or models, imaginatively conceived and serving to relate and make intelligible different living aspects of Nature.

People who believe in the omnipotence of science do so on the Laplacian assumption that every event is determined by earlier causes, to which ideally it might be traced without ambiguity. We are uncertain of a further event, it is argued, because we do not happen to know these causes fully. For Herzen, no method, scientific or not, is fit in any important sense to determine the future, and he found no Laplacian angels at his disposal. Events for him did not necessarily follow from their antecedents and were not determined either by them or by any ends whatever. Even Nature must in the end elude man. "We see", Herzen writes, "in all the domains of natural science signs of perplexity: something is lacking, something which no abundance of facts and theories can substitute; the truths which it reveals contain a fundamental insufficiency. Every domain . . . leads continuously to a painful realization that there is something elusive, irrational in Nature, . . . and this brings to man an awareness of Nature's irresistible strangeness." "All that is in time has a latent element of the fortuitous and arbitrary, which overrides necessary development and cannot be deduced from the determinate nature of things." Herzen felt bound to reject a deterministic world, whether of metaphysical or scientific making, because its causes and ends mutilate life, because it is so notoriously indifferent to its means and its effects. This theme provides the context for his preoccupation with the problem of human freedom and personality.

"Believe me", Herzen says to his questioner in the last dialogue of *From the Other Shore*, "men are not predestined to anything at all."

"—Why then do they live?"

"—For no other reason than that they are born to live. . . . Life is both end and means, cause and effect: it is the perpetual disquiet of intense and active living in search of equilibrium, which it loses again whenever it has found it. It is ceaseless movement—the *ultima ratio*. There is no way beyond that. . . . Life does not reach out to a goal, but realizes all the possibilities and pursues all the actualities; it is always ready to step further, in order to live more intensely and, if possible, more fully. There is no other aim. . . . And if we look to the limit, we find no other end save death."

This theme, recurring in many of Herzen's writings, appears to show him as an advocate of surrender to the irresponsible vitality of the moment without consequence, with the Rousseauesque implication, made by some students of Herzen, that since Nature is good it only requires to be set free so that it may develop and be perfect. What, indeed, could be more agreeable than to be born, to grow, to live, and at last for ever to fall asleep in the belief that no purpose has to be served in life. There was undoubtedly an element of sheer *élan vital* in Herzen's consistent rejection of purpose beyond life itself—a sense that life is nothing but passion that burns, gets weary, gets lost, burns again and changes. There was an element of simple self-assertion which is in every living thing and which keeps it alive.[32] His plea for the spontaneous, undetermined, incalculable evolution of life suggests a comparison with Bergson's idea of *élan vital* as an immanent principle, which pervades, which indeed is, whatever is life. It is significant that Bergson and Herzen alike adopt and elaborate the Heraclitan doctrine of continuous change, and that they both devote considerable attention to biology and tend to speak in biological terms. In addition, Bergson's critique of the mechanistic theory of evolution in which the universe appears like the works of a gigantic clock wound up once for all and proceeding by the mere interaction of parts, is very similar to Herzen's. But the Bergsonian universe of continuous flow, and Bergsonian evolution as the mere movement of that flow, preclude in the last analysis anything *that* flows and changes; for, according to Bergson, in asserting the existence of that which changes, we are asserting something which, from the mere fact that it undergoes change, is not itself change. There is simply change. Bergson, in fact, presents us with a reality which is a continuous stream, abstract and without feature or individuation of any kind, the distinctions and shapes that we discern in it being due merely to the dissecting and discriminating operations of the mind.

Herzen, on the contrary, was keenly sensitive to the diversity and solidity of the universe, as well as to what he called "the creative agency of the mind". He would never be satisfied with pure, unindividuated reality, and he would never surrender human personality to the monistic claims even of the life force. Life was to be lived in transforming and refashioning it in terms of the human person—life unmotivated by anything but the will of individual man. The emphasis throughout is not on the mere spontaneity of the living being, not on a mere search for life's reward in the satisfaction of living, nor, indeed, on what is sought, or even on the seeking, but on the seeker. He saw life in terms of a historical rather than a biological process, and his critique of purpose originates in an idea of history the meaning of which is to be sought in each particular instant of the historical process, to be more precise, in the life of individual man who is at once end and means, cause and effect, whole and part of a whole. He welcomed the importation by Hegel of rationality into a field where formerly inscrutable providence held sway, yet he regarded Hegel's historical logic, and indeed all teleologies, as the great metaphysical spider which traps and strangles man in its dialectical or causal web, as an attempt to persuade man that slavery to history is freedom. Metaphysical, scientific or social teleologies were for him all alike forms of determinism endangering man; but he tended to regard metaphysical and religious teleology as the most merciless of all, because it assigns to itself an exalted character.

Man himself is the *logos* of history, a *logos* which, as Herzen was fond of saying, is itself "a-logical", for man is the a-logical, free, undetermined "improvisor". "History improvises; it seldom repeats itself; it takes advantage of every contingency, knocks at a thousand doors at once, which may open . . . who knows?" "There is no libretto. . . . In history all is improvization, all is will, all *ex tempore*: no limits ahead and no itinerary. There are conditions, holy disquietude, the fire of life, and the perennial challenge to try one's strength, to transcend the limits wherever one chooses, wherever there is a way; and where there is none a passage is forced by genius", who is "not a necessity of history . . . but its luxury, its poetry, its *coup d'état*, its leap and creative triumph." History is "an epopee of ascent and descent, full of passion and drama, in which the given becomes the chosen, and in which eternal thought is thrown into time. Its bearers are not universal categories or abstract norms, as in logic, nor speechless slaves, like the productions of Nature, but personalities . . . struggling against fate which hovers indifferently over Nature."[33]

In the end the only reality to which Herzen was prepared to ascribe enduring value was man—not, it is true, to the substance man, not to "humanity" or the human race, which he was too fastidious and too well-informed to like, but to individual man or men, to concrete characters. He owed it to Hegel as well as to his own philosophical insight to have discarded altogether the naïve concept of being, meaningless as it is in its application to the things of the spirit no less than to those with which science deals. He did not, therefore, regard the human person as a substance, an entity which undergoes change, while remaining one and the same. Its very being was to him its process of experiencing, so that it is at once the subject and the outcome of its experiences. "Action itself is personality", Herzen observed. And yet there is something which or rather someone who experiences, and who is more than the experience: a self which endures through the life of a person, although it cannot be conceived apart from experience. It is both that which experiences and experience itself: they are different aspects of the one concrete being which is man himself. Herzen insists that it is a fallacy to think of man's personality as a kind of private room, as something behind his face, or as a manikin behind the eyes. But he also refused to regard the human body as an impersonal, faceless physiological phenomenon: if it were no more than that, why, Herzen asks, should it occasion so vehement an attraction to one person rather than another, or make us perceive in human eyes the unseen, inward world of man? He saw man from the core outwards, never deferring to that confident behaviouristic ostentation which speaks of the lack of inner life; and he felt, as few others did, the threat to the inner man by the hardening and hollowing tradition of success, of "getting on", which characterizes the *"bourgeois"* ways and habits of life, and makes modern man dumbfounded at the thought of being anything at all.[34]

Even at his apparently most hedonistic, when Herzen spoke of "catching at the present moment, actualizing in oneself all the possibilities of life . . . and after that come what may"; when he brought down his fire on morality which proceeds from an instinct for "sinister, vulgar, malignant disparagement of life", and on "moral eunuchs and niggards", old maids of both sexes who get nothing from life but their own innocence: even then he did not envisage man as a plaything of elemental forces, enslaved and stupefied by a surfeit of self-gratification. He recorded his aversion from "the pathological, physiological dogma of the absolute infallibility of the passions and the incapacity of man to struggle against them", because he denied, not the freedom of human passions, but their slavery. Man, "invested with the fullness of his concrete nature" and "revealed in the splendour of temporal existence" ought no more to be surrendered to the alluring forces of Nature and to the "all-devouring Moloch of love" than to the laws of morality and the collective elements of society or nation, which all alike serve to emancipate man from the pain and passion of personal existence. And the ideology which imperils, or even leaves out of account, man as a "free, thinking, feeling, willing character" was, in his view, not worth the paper it is written on.[35]

"Outside everything is changing, everything is shifting", Herzen wrote: "we stand on the edge of a precipice and see it crumble. Twilight approaches, and there is not a loadstar anywhere on the sky. We shall find no haven except in ourselves, in the consciousness of our limitless freedom and our sovereign independence." Freedom is the "decisive truth and reality of human existence". "Man", he told his son, "is for ever in search of his autonomy, of his freedom, and, driven though he is by necessity, wants to do nothing except that which he wants to do: he refuses to be either the passive grave-digger of the past or the unconscious midwife of the future; he looks at history as his free and necessary task. He believes in his freedom as he believes in the existence of the external world. . . . He has deified free will as he has deified the soul. . . . Physiology throws the idol from its pedestal and denies freedom altogether. But there still remains the problem of freedom as a pressing demand of the human mind, as a spiritual reality." Elsewhere he speaks in even stronger terms of the "unique and ungoverned life of man which could discover within itself the sources of salvation even if the whole world around us were to perish". Freedom was, to Herzen's mind, not a mere attribute man possesses, for man is nothing without it: he is what he is by freedom, or, rather, he is what he is in his specific, individual character by freedom. It was neither mere independence from the fixed and inviolable laws of physiology, nor just absence of physical coercion exerted by human beings over one another; neither a means of inculcating a sense of responsibility, of tracing guilt to someone in order to judge or punish him, nor a mere individual reaction which necessarily follows upon external stimuli. As with Bakunin, freedom served Herzen as an affirmation of human creativity, which enables man to really affect, move and change life in this indifferent, necessitarian universe, of "will as the creative agency of the spirit". But it also served him as an affirmation of the kind of independence which is the retort that humour makes to the tragic absurdity of fate.[36]

If freedom is an illusion which we have of the way our mind works because we are not conscious of the forces causing it to work that way, it was yet an illusion which had its own efficacy for Herzen. In any case he could not believe that living in the condition of not knowing the various causes of the events in one's life is the same as living in a world where chance and freedom operate. But Herzen was not concerned with the metaphysics of freedom, and the only spheres where he consistently applied his idea of freedom were the moral and social spheres.

Herzen's ethics may be summarized as variation on an anti-Kantian theme, although he did not specifically discuss it in connection with Kant. His philosophical writings are full of praise for Kant's "titanic critical achievement"; but the spirit of studied moralistic uniformity and moderation, and the peculiar ethical problems which perplexed Kant's mind and made him adopt the rule of acting "according to maxims and principles", instead of being "dependent on impulse", were too exiguous and uncongenial a foundation to make Kant's formidable moral system attractive to Herzen. Nothing, indeed, is further removed from Herzen's moral ideas than the concept of a categorical imperative as a basis of a generally acknowledged morality, whereby Kant succeeded in proving to the whole world that the whole world is right. Any moral principle which degrades the concrete individual, the irreducible to an abstract universal, and the individual law to a norm for all, was for Herzen a betrayal of man, and so was the disquieting suggestion of the idealist that the transcendental self is the same in us all.

The moral life of man, in Herzen's view, is a dynamic process, an activity, a new inserting creation, which stands opposed to any subsumption of the individual concrete case in a universal law. It is the pressing call from within, an imperative which makes man completely dependent on himself; it is destructive of every norm, habit and custom; it is revolutionary in its nature. Moral value, therefore, attains for Herzen a totally different significance than is the case with Kant, for whom it is fixed and finished in "the starry firmament above". With Herzen everything remains unfinished and incomplete, confined within the finite and yet bursting its limits and urged beyond the given. But the standpoint of utility or that of common sense is equally inapplicable, for, dealing as it does with so volcanic a reality as human freedom, moral value cannot be turned into a crystallization, a reservoir of the already existing, universally validated or useful norms. A virtue, according to Herzen, must be man's invention, his most personal need and calling. "Free man", Herzen observes, "creates his own morality". "Duty", "goodness", "justice" in themselves, stamped with the character of impersonality and universal validity, are abstractions, by means of which man is imperilled. In as much as moral activity is based on an "outside oneself", requiring as a condition of its existence objective stimuli, in as much as its action is a reaction, rather than a creation, Herzen tended to reject it altogether. He saw nothing but stupidity in constant appeals to an outside standard of normal behaviour, which does not exist. And he saw the moralist always faced by a dilemma, which is his surprise at the complexity of human nature and the variety of human experience.[37]

Herzen never discussed explicitly the familiar question which arises in any such rejection of objective moral standards: why make value judgments at all? Why invent ethical significance with which to invest certain concepts and activities unless some ethical standard was there to begin with? Why, it may be asked furthermore, is the unique sacred? Why is it more valuable than the common and the general? In his more mischievous moments Herzen would have probably retorted, as he did, in a somewhat different context, to Blanqui, that his attitude was no more than a private whim, and no other person has a right to it. It was part of the attractiveness of Herzen's attitude that ideas could on occasion take his breath away, that, with all his regard for scientific truth, he was not tied down by guarantees and tangible evidence, and that he knew of truths that are attainable not so much as objective discovery, equally possible for all, as in proportion to man's own insights and properties. That may have been a survival of idealism, or, perhaps, just the inherent conviction to which Proust had given expression when he said that "*la seule perception grossière et erronnée place tout dans l'objet, quand tout est dans l'esprit*". In any case Herzen never displayed the bad taste of wishing to agree with everybody, or of wishing everybody to agree with him. "Is it possible", he asked, "that man should be wrong merely because others disagree with him?" The expression "common good" was to him, in fact, something like a contradiction in terms. "That which can be common is always of small value." "There are discredited words and notions that dare not appear in respectable society, just as a hangman does not dare to appear in society, which rejects him for having carried out its wishes. What, for instance, would it think if a man were to advocate *prejudice*, and say that prejudice is so much superior to justice as love is to indifference?"[38]

It is interesting to note in this connection once again that Herzen never kept his discussion within the boundaries of common sense, although some students of Herzen have, according to their respective tastes, commended or reproached him precisely for this. He never appealed to common-sense, except by way of expressing something that was self-evident to him; he never invoked the lowest common denominator of understanding and action; he did not regard, as Hume did for instance, a right action as one for which all or most men feel approval, and he did not show the slightest respect to truths arrived at statistically, by means of counting heads. "And why", he asked, "do you wish that everything in the human mind should be only just enough? What a prosaic reduction of everything to the extremely necessary, to the unavoidably useful, to the valid for all?"[39]

But Herzen's real ethical contention was to deny the very question of objective, external criteria, statistical or otherwise: even ultimate moral standards and truths were to be considered subjective, created by man. Their general validity was seen by him to be an acquired characteristic, a means of communicating them to other people, whereby they turn into a socialized morality, with its dehumanizing, impersonal norms and obligations. Herzen's moral man may appear at times as merely the embodiment of a mixture of conscience and enlightened egotism which survive after man has lost, whether by his own fault or not, faith, love and hope. What he really demanded of man, however, was a heroic attitude that prevents man from attaching himself to something outside, instead of continuing the effort of being himself—an attitude as far removed as possible from that of the *homme moyen sensuel*, embodying the generally accepted views about what is or ought to be, an attitude, in fact, not of common but of uncommon sense.

For Herzen there were as many moralities as there were men, just as there were as many worlds as there were beholders of the world. There was no normal human behaviour, but incommensurable, individual moral acts. There is nothing to guide man, except personal choice and freedom, with all the terrifying risks that such choice and freedom entail, and with all the awareness that every one of the acts of man stakes the meaning of the world and the place of his fellow-creatures in it. To make a choice is not so much a matter of pursuing exalted ends, as of employing truthful means, for of what manner of spirit man is is known by the means he uses; it is not so much a matter of choosing the right, as of the candour, the earnestness, the "pathos" with which one chooses, for the value of the norm according to which one chooses is given by the choice itself. Thereby personality announces its inner infinity, and thereby, in turn, the personality is deepened.[40]

Since, then, every moral action is performed in an entirely unique and inimitable manner, all precepts of conduct, however subtle and esoteric, can apply only to the coarse exterior, and attain only a semblance of equality. Once subsumed in the external world and translated into the social sphere, truths and values turn into the fixities, failures and falsifications of history. They became shallow, stupid and common, and man becomes "all the poorer for that part of his ideal which has passed into reality".[41] Their impact, no longer kept alive by the unpredictable power of creativeness, takes on the desolating flatness of the "*bourgeois*" world, which holds sway and exercises its compulsory authority over the lives of men. It is this *bourgeois* world, with its inflated claims and perversions, that turned Herzen into a rebel.

Herzen tended often to appeal to reason, while refusing to treat men as reasonable beings. Early on, during his association with Vitberg, he could still speak of irrationality, of accident and chance as "an absurdity invented by unbelief". But a consciousness of the inimical working of some thwarting element in life, as well as his deep-rooted indeterminism, brought him more and more to a recognition of what he called the "outrageous power of chance" in human existence, and the symbolic use of chance became eventually a corner-stone of his whole outlook. "Is it possible that all life must be a torture and agony, followed by a short respite, to ward off the inevitable annihilation of man. . . . Man stores up, bit by bit, by unhappy toil, by sweat and blood, but chance carries off everything, and with one stupid blow destroys all that has been won by suffering." "In what an awful mire of hazards is human life entangled! I feel powerless to struggle with the dull but savage power which reigns over the human person and all that is individual in life." "I have become convinced of the absence of rationality in the individual life of man." These casual entries in Herzen's Diary between 1842 and 1844 are amplified in his memoirs and letters of a later period, when he began to see, not only individual life, but Nature and history too as involved in the "vortex of chance".[42]

Historians, Herzen contended, who have discovered in their study of history some magic law, to which the course of history was alleged to be subject and by which the future could be foretold, differ from one another only in the length of their run before they are proved false prophets. There is no reason why there should be any law according to which history developed. "Irony", he wrote, "gives expression to the uneasiness aroused by the fact that logical truth is not the same as the truth of history, that apart from dialectical development it has its own development through chance and passion, that apart from reason it has its romance."[43]

If there is freedom, the future is unpredictable, and history represents nothing but "dishevelled improvizations"; if there is no freedom, or in as much as there is no freedom, the future is not shaped by any law whatever, but by pure chance, which no one can escape, "not even the philosopher," but which awakens in man "the need to retrieve something of his own from the vortex . . . , to preserve the moral identity of his personality".[44] Chance brings to man the sense that life is overpowering, full of darkness, which he can but seldom illumine by his own devices; it brings a sense of evil, of the unaccountable, the irrational, the brutal, which are forcing their way like some black river into men's homes and choking them, a sense of evil that covers a far wider area and is possessed of far greater intensity than a sense of morality, however acute.

Few, if any, students of Herzen have paid due attention to this aspect of Herzen's thought, and his own ease, his lightness of touch and distaste for mystification have been apt to distract them from these darker meanings. The ease proves to be largely on the surface: at any rate, it never detracted from his "negative capability"; nor could it ever dispel the sorrow and melancholy which pervade Herzen's outlook and attitude to life. Evil was there, omnipresent: pain and disease, the death of those he loved, and the death of love itself, injustice, cruelty, frustrated hope—the list was interminable, supplied by the experiences of his personal life and by impressions gained from the world outside. The explanations of the philosophers and theologians failed to satisfy him. To speak of logical, or ontological, or dialectical necessities, of harmony between the imperfections of the relative and the perfections of the absolute, of punishment for sin and improvement by pain was as offensive to him as attempts to erect in contrast with the follies and absurdities of life barren edifices of perfection, based on a clear-cut view of history, or on the blessings of civilization conferred on the whole world, or on man's efficient mastery over fate which in fact he manifestly does not possess in this world. There was no experience which would bind existence into a coherent whole. He continued to see life as coming from nowhere and being on the way to nowhere. It was as if it and the world were given to him parenthetically between two nothings, between "two mute and blank abysses", as he put it himself in his *Memoirs*. And this nothingness was revealed to Herzen more than anywhere else in the experience of death—"the standing proof of the fortuitousness of life", as he says, "the *ultima ratio*, the irrevocable and therefore the most intolerable event" in human existence. But whereas the sentimental romantic would not have perceived it, and the mystic would have escaped from time to eternity, Herzen could only endure, conscious of the futility of trying to outrun the human lot.

As has been shown previously, a similar experience was familiar to Belinsky, but Herzen gained by it a greater depth and awareness, and, in his view, no attitude to life could be very deep which did not advert to its mortality. "Accept this skull—it belongs to you by right", he quoted from Pushkin in dedicating to his friends the work (*Zapadnye arabeski. II* ["Western European Arabesques. II"]), which contain some of his most heart-stricken reflexions on human life. There was no other end in life for Herzen except that it exists so as to come to an end. He was too sure of the interconnection of body and mind to think that any survival apart from the survival of the whole man would be in any sense the survival of the same. Survival in some general consciousness, survival in the immortality of the human race, survival in mankind's future happiness, or in the establishment of a perfect civilization and society to come were no comfort to him, for death called in question all such comforts: they are tragically incommensurable with the unique destiny of each human individual, and, worse still, they are a mockery of man's mortal predicament. In fact, man continues to be haunted by the consciousness of the essential *hiatus* in his existence, of the void which pervades, and continues itself downwards to, the very foundations of life.

It was this also that made Herzen reflect on the strange precariousness of human existence. The universe did not seem to him to have been designed for human life, which appeared to him, as it appeared to Pascal, like a tiny glow flickering uncertainly and doomed to extinction in the immensities of time and space. He saw man standing, as it were, on a stone of terror in this vast and indifferent world, free and alone, unprotected by anything against the power of nothingness: man, the tiny mortal amidst the whirling destructive forces, yet revealing, in the very precariousness of his predicament, his true value. "Man", Herzen wrote to Ogarev in 1845, "can least of all be reconciled to the strange ambiguity and precariousness of all the best he possesses. The matter seems quite simple: the more durable, the more resisting a thing is the greater its value. But it is in the flickering *des Schwebenden*, in the frail and contingent that life reveals its true aspect and fragrance, because the durable is immobile, apathetic, whilst the frail bespeaks process, movement, *das Werden*." "The more developed life is, and the higher the sphere to which it is transposed, the deeper is the conflict and the greater the nearness between being and non-being. A stone is more resisting than a human being: in it being predominates over non-being. . . . Passive, inert being crushes life by its coarse conspicuity. The life of a stone is a permanent paralysis. Life is freer wherever it approaches non-being; it is weak in its highest manifestations; it loses, as it were, in substantiality when reaching the height, where being and non-being are in balance. . . . Every beautiful thing is frail, scarcely existing: it is the flower that dies from the icy wind, but the rigid stem is strengthened by it . . . ; instants of joy flicker and fade, but they contain a whole eternity."[45]

Herzen professed, in fact, a kind of inverted, Nietzschean Darwin-ism, which he extended to the whole of human history and in which the struggle for existence appears always to the disadvantage of the great, the noble, the lofty, the exceptional. The insignificant, the feeble, the trivial ones always prevail over the best and the great, because it is the feeble who wield power, who are more crafty, who are the majority. Indeed, failure is, in some sense, higher than success—a fact of which Herzen perceived the greatest symbol in Calvary. The higher values in the world appear to be weaker than the lower; the higher are crucified, whilst the lower triumph: hence the curious Manichean tendency in Herzen, which we have already encountered in a different form in Belinsky and Bakunin. "It mortifies us to find", he wrote in the same *Western European Arabesques*, "that the idea is impotent, that truth has no compelling force over the world of actuality. A new kind of Manicheanism takes possession of us: we are led, *par dépit*, to believe in rational, that is, purposeful evil, as we did believe in rational good. This is the last tribute we pay to idealism." And a similar attitude underlies Herzen's view of history as a terrible failure and a tragedy—a realm where everything is distorted, all great ideas belied and perverted, although there is nowhere for man to go from it.[46]

However, Herzen was not prone to revel in spiritual melodrama and had none of that perverse pleasure in or concentration on points of break-down and failure in which modern existentialists take their refuge and find their comfort; none, too, of that cynicism which is the indolent ally of privilege and maintains a frivolous belief that there is nothing worth man's search or strife. He even envied "those happy lunatics who have no lucid intervals", who "know nothing of the inner conflict", who "suffer from external causes, from evil men and evil chances, but for whom all is whole within, conscience is at rest, who are content".[47] Besides, he saw in this meaningless and cruel world of ours moments of generosity, courage, kindness and beauty that made life all the more dramatic and, at the same time, denied to him an unreal black and white world of the wholly good and the wholly bad, showing it as pitiable, distressing and pathetic as well as petty, vulgar and nauseating. His sense of evil, his pessimism was of an active kind which, while preventing him from coming to terms with the world, did not issue in mental and moral paralysis, especially at other people's expense or by proxy. His whole life, after all, provides evidence of an untiring fight for a better world, far away from what he called "the natural quietude of being incapable of hoping and of losing hope". If time and history appeared to him like an absurd comedy without meaning, in which we are involved, in which we drift, with all the meanings we try to give it going down water-logged, he saw them also as occasionally cheated by the imagination, by the momentary joy of living, above all by man's awareness of his freedom even in this stunningly indifferent world.

But there was more life for Herzen, wider and deeper life in pain, in perplexity, than there is in the ease, efficiency and confidence of bourgeois existence. The very uncertainty calls for adventure, for the unwieldiness of life is the consequence of its wealth and variety. A world where there is no mystery, or anything but commonplace prosperity was not liveable for him. Even that subsistent and irreducible void in human existence was somehow desirable—as a warrant perhaps for maintaining the ironic attitude, or as a retreat from religious, philosophical and social hedges against ambiguity. Herzen seemed to need the free air of nihilism, and in the end, he could find no other word to describe his attitude to life but "nihilism". It stood for him not for the simplifications of the "Sons" over against the indolence of the "Fathers" —in accordance with the familiar pattern of Turgenev's novel—but for what he called "humility in the face of truth": a truth which reveals the " 'darkness' that is the logical conclusion of life beginning with 'the dream' "; a truth which teaches idols what it costs to have feet of clay, and which teaches man that in proportion as idols and ideal worlds have been set up reality has been robbed of its value, that is, of its truthfulness, and mankind turned false and mendacious.

"Now I am accustomed to these thoughts," Herzen wrote in 1855, "they no longer terrify me. But at the end of 1849 I was overwhelmed by them; and in spite of the fact that every event, every meeting, every contact, every person seemed bent on tearing away the last green leaves, I still frantically and obstinately sought a *way of escape*. That is why I now prize the courageous thought of Byron so highly. I saw that there is *no escape*, and proudly said so. . . ." "Neither Cain nor Manfred, neither Don Juan nor Byron, has any deduction, any solution, any 'moral'. Perhaps, from the point of view of dramatic art, this is a defect, but it gives a stamp of sincerity and shows the depth of the gulf." "I was unhappy and perplexed when these thoughts began to haunt me; I tried by every means to run away from them . . . ; like a lost traveller, like a beggar I knocked at every door, stopped every one I met and asked my way, but every meeting and every event led to the same result—to *humility* in the face of the *truth*. . . . Three years ago I sat by Natalie's sick-bed and saw death drawing her mercilessly, step by step, to the grave; that life was all that was precious to me. About me all was darkness; I sat alone in dull despair, but did not comfort myself with hopes, did not betray my grief for one moment by the narcotic thought of meeting beyond the grave."[48]

One final question must be considered in this discussion of Herzen's philosophical views—his attitude to religion. The variety of the existing estimates of Herzen's religious position is so bewildering that in reading them one wanders into a wood which it is impossible to see for all the trees; and the estimates contradict each other so wildly that no complete reliance can be placed on any one of them.[49] There seems to be, therefore, no other way to discuss the matter but to record one's own impression. On the other hand, Herzen himself has, here as elsewhere, struggled with ideas and experiences which were not settled in his own mind, and it may, in the end, prove more illuminating to try to convey these perplexities than to dogmatize about them. He did, after all, explicitly state that he was prepared to accept intellectual contradictions, that he had no ready-made answers to anything, and that the only things he could claim were approximate symbols and intimations.[50]

There is abundant evidence, particularly in Herzen's correspondence from his first exile, and in most of his other writings between 1834 and 1839, that until the late 'thirties Herzen, as well as his friend Ogarev, showed signs of profound, or at any rate intense, religious feeling of a semi-mystical and semi-romantic kind, but with a pronounced leaning towards social preoccupations.[51] But it appears that he had doubts even then. "I was not destined to rise into the third heaven," he wrote about the impact of Vitberg's mysticism on himself, "I was born an earthly creature. No tables turn at the touch of my hands, nor do rings shake at my glance. The daylight of thought is more akin to me than the moonlight of fantasy. But I was more disposed to mysticism at the period when I was living with Vitberg than at any other time. Separation, exile, the religious exaltation of the letters I received, the love which was filling my soul more and more intensely, and at the same time the oppressive feeling of remorse, all reinforced Vitberg's influence. . . ." "My realistic temperament, nevertheless, gained the upper hand"; "I stretched the bow [of mysticism] until the string snapped and the scales dropped from my eyes."[52] In 1843 he wrote of Vadim Passek's death: "What a mystery, a threatening, terrible mystery! And how tangibly one realizes in the face of it that the *Jenseits* is a dream. . . . His [Passek's] wife repeated: 'We shall meet again, we shall soon meet again'—the warm, assuaging belief, my last belief to which I held on with all my force! But even this I sacrificed for the sake of truth."

It was this "*Jenseits*" which at the time in question brought about the rift between Herzen and Granovsky, and contributed to the breaking up of the whole circle of Herzen's Moscow friends, which in turn weighed heavily in Herzen's decision to leave Russia. The disagreement with Granovsky is illuminating because, according to Herzen's own account, it concerned "the real foundation of [their] lives".[53] It was a conflict between, on the one side, the enlightened, infinitely humane and wonderfully rounded and balanced man that Granovsky was, a man who was certain of the "*allweise Güte über der Welt*", who believed in the river of life widening towards the close till it merges into the "divine ocean", and in the "*Jenseits*" as the impregnable base for man's advocacy of a just moral order; and, on the other side, Herzen, a man in whom some old, profound confidence has turned into doubt, who has chosen or was driven, or both, to live in a void, with no mitigating factor, even in the form of a controlling deity. The greatness of Herzen as a man and a thinker rests largely on the integrity with which he had measured himself against this experience.

I was unable to find any convincing evidence for the view that Herzen was "a religious nature". On the contrary, he strikes one as far removed from anything normally associated with *homo religiosus*. He was for this reason quite unacquainted even with atheism as a spectacular event in his life: it was in a sense inborn in him, instinctive, precisely because he was too incredulous, too distrustful, too questioning, too aware to be satisfied with master-keys or, to use his own expression, "the wholesale solution of things". Only now and then, at the death-beds of his children or during the calamities of the early 'fifties did he turn, by some instinctive gesture, to God. But instead of catching a glimpse of the divine countenance he could only see a void and the silly grimaces of fate. "You think that doubt is easy", Herzen replies to his questioner in the last dialogue of *From the Other Shore*; "but you scarcely know how much man would give at times—in moments of pain, of weariness, of weakness—for one grain of faith. But where am I to find it?" He had no Nietzschean thought like Bakunin of "killing God": he found him dead in his own soul and in the soul of his time, or, perhaps, not God but his substitute, who has taken so many forms in the life of tormented and deluded men, for Herzen knew a great deal of the God of the metaphysicians, of the God of society and of the divine guarantees for social values, but scarcely anything of the God of Abraham, Isaac and Jacob.

In Russia his incredulity found its vent whenever he was brought face to face with the Slavophils, and, more particularly still, with the "Moscow Gorgias" Alexey Khomyakov. One such encounter has been vividly described by Herzen himself.[54] Herzen does not conceal either the spiritual strength of Khomyakov's religious position or, by contrast, the apparent weakness and vulnerability of his own unbelief. While Khomyakov spoke from the centre of a dominant conviction, Herzen remained sadly perplexed. He had nothing positive to answer to Khomyakov's confident, forcible, un-selfconscious faith. His generous but uncertain humanism seems almost like feebleness against the assurance of Khomyakov. He was not even able to betray any real interest in Khomyakov's Orthodoxy: he was merely fascinated by his vitality and power. And yet one retains from this account as well as from other evidence about Khomyakov the impression that the absence of any breath of doubt in him, of any hint of struggle at any time to find or hold his faith, the impregnable way in which he wore his certainty even at his most playful, were a symptom not of strength but of weakness. He was a master of assertion, but, though he was not defective in sympathy, he was deprived of something deeper: of intellectual compassion that makes one even at the most sublime and awe-inspiring conscious of weaknesses shared with the less assured. While contending against Herzen that it is impossible to attain truth by reason, he did, nevertheless, adopt the attitude of a rationalist, for whom all differences are composed, all objections argued away, and who administers dialectical drubbing to unbelievers ("immanentists", as he called them), so as to bring them nearer to Christianity. His God seems as large and no larger than his own extraordinary capacity for disposing arguments against God's existence.[55] "He dealt blows and thrusts, attacked and pursued, pelted with witticisms and quotations, terrified and drove into a maze from which there was no escape without prayer."

Herzen, on the other hand, could not help being reminded, whenever he came up against the religious attitude, of all those annoying "exceptions", "distinctions", queries and objections which easy habits of thought conveniently forget. He was inclined to look for the evidence and question assumptions rather than rely on reflexions that seem to come straight from heaven but may just as well be due to glandular disturbances. He had none of the old assurance as to the design of the universe and the intentions of the Creator. He was, as we have seen, altogether unable to think in teleological terms, or to postulate a cosmic order, which was to him a piece of vicious abstraction, unthinkable in anyone who has the slightest awareness of the concrete. The definite assurance that there is a providence that wisely rules the fate of man, when translated into reality, amounted for him, as it did for Belinsky, to nothing more than that man was in the worst possible hands and that he is trying to extenuate the circumstance by assigning a divine quality to it. Here, as elsewhere, Herzen found himself perpetually anticipating the whirligig of time in its revenges, perpetually scraping whitewash off sepulchres. He was a saint of interrogation: "the great incendiary in search of truth", as Strakhov, the eminent critic and friend of Tolstoy, called him. "There is a peculiar demon in me", Herzen once observed to a friend: "doubt. I have not got that fanatic faith; there is conviction, but there is no faith."

Still, Herzen was not entirely devoid of a sense of reverence, but he believed that this quality, rather than promote the building up of sanctuaries, should induce a realization of the shamefacedness with which truth has concealed itself behind enigmas and motley uncertainties. He wished to discover, as he wrote to the Slavophil Yury Samarin, *"whether truth is true"*. In fact, he had more distrust than was good for him, and the unrewarding conviction that "truth" does not remain true when the veil is withdrawn from it, that things are not worth what men believe them to be worth, was about the surest thing his distrust was capable of grasping. It is natural, therefore, that he should have responded so eagerly to Feuerbach, whose optimistic belief in humanity he rejected, but whose widely acclaimed book *The Essence of Christianity* served to confirm him in his own view that, although religious propositions are not nothing, they are not what the illusions of the religious mind make them out to be.[56] He was not able to embrace even that kind of infidelity which consists in putting away religion while keeping unimpaired the morality which was part and parcel of it.

All this, it is true, did not prevent Herzen from realizing that religion had a logic of its own, and that it was such a risk that only passion made it worth while. He admired the ability to choose between everything and nothing, once one has been able, as religious people have been able, to distinguish within themselves that which can be everything and that which is nothing. With all his tendency to side with the questioning, destructive power of reason, he showed himself fully aware that neither belief nor unbelief are rationally grounded, that the one and the other are attitudes to life, ways of committing one's feelings and will, which are governed by other than mere rational considerations.

It seemed, nevertheless, as though Herzen was conscious all the time of a never wholly surmountable barrier with religious people, as though they would have been more human in his eyes if they could have left God out of it now and then. It was not reason but his taste that, in the long run, decided against them, or, rather, against the peculiar atmosphere they exude—"the rococo of the soul", as he called it, the twisting angles and fancy touches, the conventicle air and occasional bucolic sweetness, the chronic "hobnobbing with God", the cant, the "deep slumber of decided opinion", the instinct of "everlasting funeral", of turning upon life with a subterranean lust for vengeance, and, above all, the combination of servility and arrogance of them that know the truth, the hell at the back of the religious minds.[57] He was repelled by the pious, because they find in devotion reasons for doing evil which a simple honest man would be incapable of finding, because they take delight in picturing the agonies of hell to be endured by those whom for one reason or another they repudiate. He could not forget that the vilest crimes and the worst atrocities in history were committed in the service of God and with a good conscience. There was, he thought, a progressive character about the self-elevation of the religious man, who from disapproving of the unbeliever comes to despise, to hate, to fear, and to seek to destroy him on the pretext that in doing so he is ensuring the unbeliever's eternal salvation.

"I am not so religious", Herzen wrote in his first letter to Samarin, who rebuked him for his unbelief and attacked the condemned Russian revolutionaries, "as to step over corpses with a cold smile and see off martyrs of their idea and loyalty to forced labour or the gallows with an edifying look of reproach." "To divide men into sheep and goats is not a difficult or a very new occupation: to place all religious people, and particularly the Orthodox, into one category, and all the rest, and particularly the materialists, into another is an easy matter. Unfortunately none of these classifications are relevant in life. For you, as for all the idealists and theologians, this does not matter in the least: you build your world *a priori*, you know what it ought to be . . .—and all the worse for it if it is not as it ought to be! . . . Assured of your infallibility you press on." "You find it inconsistent that a man who does not believe in future life should intercede for the life of his fellow-men. But in my view he is the only one who can value this transitory life, his own as well as that of others, because he knows that there is none other. From the theological point of view death does not appear to be such a disaster . . . : indeed, it obliges man by bringing him nearer to eternity. . . . The sin of murder, from this point of view, consists not so much in the destruction of life as in the untimely, arbitrary elevation of the patient to a higher rank. Our hanging generals have easy and ample justification in this attitude: they send the accused to a court of the highest instance; there he may justify himself, and the more innocent he is the better his fortune. You are surprised that we should value human life, because we are 'materialists' (I repeat the term for your benefit—it does not, of course, express the heart of the matter and is merely a scholastic label). In other words, you claim the sole right of compassion, but then why is it that you do not avail yourself of this right? Why is it that you fail to display in your letter the slightest sympathy and compassion . . . ? Why is it proper to assume that all these men are guilty, as though there could be no one devoted to his cause among the thousands of victims? And even if they were guilty, why should they be punished for their guilt with indifference towards their fate? Why are you altogether so much concerned with allotting blame and punishment, rather than with acquitting the accused?" [58]

Khomyakov appeared to think that belief in God was easy, indeed almost self-evident; that if one acted as if one believed belief would be granted; that if one prayed doubt would be dispelled, and if one surrendered to the beauties and satisfactions of religion peace would descend. For Herzen this was a piece of dishonesty, as well as repugnant in its implied idea of the relation of God and man which makes of God a despot to be appeased by a creature reduced to a puppet and, as he said, "deceived by the flattery that religion pays the human heart". He felt bound, out of intellectual honesty, to reject such self-delusions. Yet he was honest enough to acknowledge also man's confrontation with experiences which transcend time. And whether or not he could make anything satisfactory for the theist of that, he realized that there are certain more or less permanent human problems which no materialistic or scientific philosophy could explore. He realized, whether on theoretical grounds or by virtue of his remarkable sensitivity, that the attempt to build a world of sense data to bear the spiritual and emotional weight, which for others is borne by some intellectual attitude which takes into account man's experience of communion with God and of mystery, never succeeds. What he wrote in the late 'thirties was valid throughout: "some inner voice, instinctive rather than conscious, fought against the coarse sensualism of this school [the Encyclopaedists]. My spirit claimed its rights and eschewed narrow explanations. . . ."[59]

I have already discussed the extent and significance of Herzen's materialistic tendencies, and have mentioned his disagreement with his son who professed Karl Vogt's extreme version of eighteenth-century materialism. Vogt was distinguished by the same intellectual narrowness, self-confidence and imperturbability which Herzen observed in religious minds. "His researches", Herzen wrote, "were not exactly superficial, but he felt no impulse to pass beyond a certain depth below which everything clear ends, and this was in truth, after a fashion, an escape from reality." Herzen adds that he himself "had not and could not have the harmony and unity that Vogt had": he did not, after all, reject untenable religious and metaphysical orthodoxies in order to seek new ones and lie down in scientific and positivist pastures. "The absurdity of dualism was so clear to his [Vogt's] simple outlook that he could not enter into serious controversy with it, just as . . . the theologians of chemistry and the holy fathers of physiology cannot seriously discuss magic and astrology. Vogt brushed aside the attacks with a jest —and, unluckily, that is not enough."[60] Vogt saw no reason why principles and methods suitable for dealing with physical facts and relations should not be equally suitable when transferred to human life as a whole. For Herzen this was not merely an illegitimate extension of certain scientific procedures: it was a degrading confusion of thought, an attempt to deduce representations, or rather misrepresentations, of one kind of phenomenon from the conception of another kind which does not contain it, to account for a higher experience in terms of a lower one and thereby to reduce the irreducible variety of human existence. To analyse away creative inspiration, freedom, spiritual insight and illumination by identifying these with that which they are not—in accordance with the principle of "no sulphur—no thought", or any other subtler enormity of a similar kind—was to him a typical instance of *speculation à la baisse*, which his good taste, if nothing else, forbade him to adopt. He admitted that a materialist may say a great deal about the mechanism by which man thinks and acts, but this did not explain the nature of thinking or the reason for thinking, which were as mysterious to Herzen as the experience of freedom, of love and death, of creativity and chance. He was no longer able to believe in God, but this is not to say that he did not believe in mystery, or that he could side with the "pundits of rationalism" who, as he said, "enjoy explaining away the mysteries of religion".

What we are faced with in Herzen is not disguise, mythological or religious, the unmasking of which was, indeed, his constant and melancholy business, but something much more genuine and much more complex, namely, transformation. He was a master of symbolic transformation, of the power to transpose knowledge from one mode into another, rendering unto each its own reality and its function in the pattern of living. He had experienced the liberation from the illusions of human consciousness, from orthodoxies, superstitions, traditions, and received ideas of all kinds; he had tasted the new accretion of humanity brought by post-Renaissance man, by the Enlightenment, by the critical thought of the nineteenth century, and he neither could, nor would he have wished to, repudiate it. But he had also experienced a reaction against this, and saw very clearly the limitations, presumptions and rigidities of the "realistic philosophy". Religious belief, though suspended through man's persistent questioning endeavour, and unrelated to any theistic conviction with its comforts and conveniences, still retained a profound meaning for the symbolizing activity of man and irradiated Herzen's own groping amidst the immortal intimations, quests, desires and affections of man. The early mystical experience of the "un-self-sufficiency of the world" persisted to that extent even in his irreligious or anti-religious mood, and corresponded to something fundamental in his attitude to life. It was, in particular, related to his very scepticism, to his consistent refusal to divest existence of its ambiguous character, and he seemed to reveal thereby the strange agreement between the mystic and the sceptic—which is that at the end of all our intellectual endeavours there remains a great mystery. It is not surprising, therefore, that he should have been horror-struck at the flight from mystery reflected in the countenance of the "*bourgeois*" world; that he saw the monstrous disfigurement of the contemporary human face, which has lost its secret look; and that he failed to rejoice in the emergence of a universe from whose sky the angelic hosts had fallen at the withering trumpet of the progressive, liberal, scientific and positivist trumpet. "Will you explain to me why it is ridiculous to believe in God, and not ridiculous to believe in mankind? Why it is stupid to believe in the kingdom of heaven and not stupid to believe in earthly utopias? Having cast away positive religion, we are left with all our religious habits, and having lost the heavenly paradise, we believe in the advent of an earthly one, and make a boast of it."[61]

3. THE BOURGEOIS WORLD

In a penetrating essay entitled *The Bourgeois Mind* Berdyaev has insisted that the term "*bourgeois*" ought to be applied in the first place in the spiritual and psychological, rather than the social and political sphere.[62] Others (Flaubert, Ruskin, Léon Bloy, for instance) have done so before him, but Berdyaev's interpretation is characteristic of many Russian thinkers of the nineteenth and early twentieth century. It has prompted one Russian scholar (Ivanov-Razumnik) to present the whole history of Russian thought as a variation on the anti-*bourgeois* theme—

an attempt which suffered from this scholar's overstatements and scholastic method. But in Herzen the anti-*bourgeois* theme is so prominent that it provides a key to some important aspects of his outlook. Three of his works—*Letters from France and Italy* (1847), *From the Other Shore* (1848-9) and the later series of letters to Turgenev entitled *Ends and Beginnings* (1862-3)—are largely devoted to an analysis and critique of the *bourgeois* world, using the term in its wider and deeper context, of which Berdyaev speaks, as well as in the restricted social and political sense.

Who were they, the *bourgeois*, who made the world, and the western European world in particular, almost uninhabitable for Herzen? The "third estate"? The new, or not-so-new, middle-class, struggling for freedom against feudal privileges and challenging the system established in the combined land-owning and commercial interests in the eighteenth-century aristocracy? But this provided no more than the then already distant background, and only helped to bring into play the peculiar virtues and vices of the *bourgeois* that affronted Herzen. What Herzen found on arriving in the Paris of 1847 was "a carnivorous crowd, mad for money, tearing each other to pieces and starving each other to death, and leaving heaps of their dung and ponds of their spittle on every palace door and altar stone". The words are Ruskin's, not Herzen's, but they convey with accuracy the impression which Herzen received when he watched the ascendancy of the French *bourgeoisie* in a France governed, as he reported to his friends in Moscow, by a "*grénouille à paraplui*", and by "the cross-eyed *crétin* Louis Bonaparte", by "the syphilitic Cavaignac" and "the walking corpse Guizot". The *bourgeoisie* epitomized for him the evils of nineteenth-century civilization, the enslavement of man by illusions and myths and phrases, the squalor of the Industrial Revolution, and the lie in the soul of *laissez-faire* democracy, threatening to extinguish culture and degrade the virtues of vision, courage and vitality. He learned of the victory of synthetic beliefs and simulated emotions, and of the triumphant substitution of the benevolent operations of the free market and the sovereign State for the medieval operations of the Holy Spirit. He witnessed the unheard of increase in the power of money as a weapon of slavery and in the service of humiliating men to the semblance of broken puppets. He watched the *bourgeois* containing life within a rigid framework of morality as firm as it was hypocritical, camouflaging dishonesty with moral whitewash and defending "spiritual values" and "principles", which have turned into commodities, but the spiritual value and principle of which it was hard to discover. He watched him proclaiming these values and principles as a substitute for faith, and describing himself as having principles just as he described himself as having a private income. He looked, sickened, at the infinite cosiness of the *bourgeois'* rounded up thoughts, feelings and actions, of his hermetically bottled art and learning, of his culture for its own sake, of self-sufficient little decencies and indecencies, of artful dilemmas and moral questions felicitously answered. He saw the turbid pleasures and secret vices of the *bourgeois*, who enjoyed no freedom even in evil, who never wasted a thing but kept a budget of his pleasures, who enjoyed "display in beauty but not beauty in display", who was senile of heart and mind, hedged round by the constricted virtues of egotism, thrift and the family instinct, and crawling with principles like a corpse with maggots.

"The *bourgeoisie* appeared on the stage after the most dazzling fashion in the person of the cunning, shifty, sparkling barber and court attendant Figaro; now it occupies the stage in the shape of a sentimental manufacturer, the patron of the poor and champion of the oppressed. In Beaumarchais' time Figaro was an outlaw; in our time Figaro is the law-giver. Then he was poor and humiliated, snatching bits from the master's table and therefore feeling with the hungry; his laughter was full of fury. Now God has blessed him with all the gifts of the earth; he has grown flabby and sluggish; he detests the hungry and does not believe in poverty—he calls it idleness and dawdling. The two Figaros have one thing in common—they are both flunkeys. But you can see a human being under the livery of the old Figaro, whilst nothing but a livery appears under the tail-coat of the new one; and, worse still, unlike his predecessor, he cannot throw it off: it has grown to him, and you cannot remove it without the skin. With us this class is scarcely in sight; in Germany nothing else exists, with an admixture of philosophy and learning, but it is rather meek, petty and exceedingly comical; here [in France] it is impudent and overweening, warping aristocrats, philanthropists and statesmen alike." "Figaro has not abandoned his exacting principles: when he felt offended he incited the mob to stick up for him and waited round the corner to see how it would end. The mob was victorious, and Figaro sent it packing from the market-place. He installed a National Guard [by comparison with whom, as Herzen pointed out elsewhere, 'the Cossacks and Croats are meek as lambs'], with police at every gate to keep out the riff-raff. The spoil was his and Figaro became an aristocrat—Count Figaro-Almaviva, Chancellor Figaro, Duke Figaro, *Père* Figaro."[63]

"The *bourgeoisie*, the last word of civilization, founded on the absolute despotism of property, is the 'democratization' of aristocracy and the 'aristocratization' of democracy. In this order Almaviva is the equal of Figaro—everything below is straining up into the *bourgeoisie*, everything above sinking down into it, unable to preserve its own identity. . . . The German peasant is the petty *bourgeois* of agriculture; the workman of every country is the petty *bourgeois* of the future. Italy, Europe's most poetic land, was not able to hold out, but at once forsook her fanatical lover, Mazzini, and betrayed her husband, the Hercules Garibaldi, as soon as Cavour, the petty *bourgeois* of genius, the little fat man in spectacles, offered to keep her as a mistress." For a time Herzen studied America in the hope of finding there some symptoms of freedom from the perversions of European *bourgeois* society, but could discover nothing but trends towards an even greater spread, more hasty, more self-deafening and self-important, of the *bourgeois* spirit. The *bourgeois* is everywhere, or rather, as Herzen put it, *"überall und nirgends"*, for he has no other presence than in his ubiquitous "material triumphs and material interests that have become the obsession of every class and have stifled all other interests"; and no ideals other than " 'the chicken in the soup', of which Henry IV dreamt", and by means of which the *bourgeois* "substitutes the bright image of the shop-keeper for that of the medieval knight and priest". His highest common denominator is desire for power, the lowest is vulgarity. He can even be an artist: he "makes kitchen-gardens instead of parks" and "in place of palaces hotels open to all, that is to all who have money"; "he dresses up Robert Peel in a Roman toga" and "strips the banker of his clothes . . . , so that if he could see his own bust after death he would be covered with blushes before his wife"; he conjures up a new Vandyke and a new Rembrandt in the shape of *Punch* and *Charivari*—"the *bourgeois*' portrait gallery and pillory, his family record and his whipping-post". Meanwhile, the proletarian contemplates the desirable but un-obtainable ideal "until his tired and bony hands drop on his sunken chest, or until he looks at life with that Irish tranquillity of despair that precludes every hope, every expectation, except the hope of a whole bottle of whisky next Sunday".[64]

The trouble with the *bourgeois*, however, is, as Herzen discovered, not even in his vices and virtues, nor in his collective, historical and cultural excretions, offensive though they are, but in what he is. What horrified Herzen most was, as he wrote to Turgenev, the emergence of a type of man whose "individual character is effaced", whose features are stamped on him, whose conscience is not dimmed but hardened, who has become a galvanized puppet, not being anything at all, but "only having". It seemed as though, on arriving in western Europe, Herzen found himself surrounded, not by men, but by faces that have turned into human grimaces—men grown ugly and disfigured by the strain of their own business and falsehood, men for whom society became that by which they lost their identity as men, who belonged to it but to whom it did not belong, and whose subjection to it, and to the visible world, was only matched by the vigour and passion with which they strained to establish their position in it. The *bourgeois* has no basically existing person: there are no subjects but only objects in his world, no selfs but only "bundles of perception". The *bourgeois* may and does claim freedom from the State and from the encroachment of society. But this is an illusion, since there is nothing for which freedom is claimed. His individualism turns out to be the cheap individualism of competition between compulsively busy people, between standardized individualities making man the perfect market. He imagines that he lives on the level of freedom. In fact he does not. He lives on the mechanical level, where events happen in accordance with the laws of great numbers. He is a collectivist, whose mind, conscience, judgments and attitudes are socialized; and the only freedom he knows is the freedom of private interest. He does not tolerate being deprived of his private property, in which he sees a guarantee of his independence, but he wants property only for himself, the kind and the amount of property that becomes at once a means for the oppression of those who have none, and a source of his own enslavement to a material world where even ownership loses its individual character, where it is unknown who is the owner and what is owned. He is the average man, even at his most individualistic, the "conglomerated mediocrity", the practitioner of the "felicific calculus" of the greatest good of the greatest number.

This *"bourgeois"* may be no more than a democratic fiction, an abstraction or ghost figure of nineteenth and twentieth-century civilized mythology which do not exist except in the mind of idealists who like universals. However fastidious and even captious Herzen's reactions may at times have been, he could scarcely forget that the *bourgeoisie*, too, consists of loving, hating, suffering, dying men. But he also saw that fictions and myths have here turned into hypostatized agents, exercising compulsory force over human thought and behaviour, and invading the minds of men like an obsession, until they have no alternative but to dance to their tune. The *bourgeois* triumph appeared to Herzen, therefore, as the result not so much of the evil of certain people as of the intensification of certain obsessive ideas. It turns into a kind of self-propelling machinery of deeper and deeper degradation, which affects all great ideas, the idea of revolution, the idea of perfect society, the idea of culture, learning and science. Indeed Herzen went so far as to regard the triumph of an ideal as always a *bourgeois* triumph, a retrograde movement; for the moment an ideal is given shape it becomes corrupt, every embodiment is invariably combined with a generalization, a vulgarization, a falsification. It may be said that the only idea which survived incarnation was the idea of God, but when the Incarnation (Herzen does not, of course, employ this term, but speaks of Christianity) had itself, so to speak, become incarnate in persisting and visible social and cultural forms, then the falsification was at work again. The hope is incessantly contradicted by the degeneration of the world, which will not come to an end so long as the *bourgeois* exists, and which must come to an end because the *bourgeois* exists. Until then man has no choice but to be a perpetual renegade, and his life perpetual infidelity.[65]

"I was in haste", Herzen wrote in 1853, about the mood in which he left Russia, "to tear myself away from the little group of men who had been so closely knit together and had come so close to each other, bound by a deep love and a common grief. I was lured by distance, space, open conflict, and free speech. I was seeking an independent arena, I longed to try my powers in freedom." He was lured, too, by the revolutionary fame of the French capital, whose name "was closely associated with the noblest feelings of contemporary humanity", and he entered it "as men used to enter Jerusalem and Rome". But the spectacle of the victorious *bourgeoisie* "outraged everything within". Herzen found himself "again pulling everything to pieces, and again there was nothing. The principles of moral existence, worked out long ago, were turned again into questions, facts had risen up sullenly on all sides and refuted them. Doubt trampled under foot that little we had gained: it was now tearing to shreds, not the vestments of the Church, not the robes of learned doctors, but the flags of revolution."[66] This may have been, as Professor Carr insists, a case of "romantic hopes giving place to romantic disillusionment", but then Herzen himself had voiced his bewilderment at the fact that "after passing through so many trials, after being schooled by contemporary criticism, [he] had so much left in [his] soul to be destroyed". [67] At any rate this does not detract anything from the hideousness of the *bourgeois* fallacy or from the importance of Herzen's analysis and critique of it.

"Weary of fruitless discussions", Herzen wrote, "I snatched up my pen and, with a kind of inner fury, slew my own old dreams and hopes. The energy that was breaking and fretting me spent itself in these pages of cursing and resentment, in which even now, when I read them over, I am conscious of the fevered blood and indignation that passed beyond all bounds."[68] The fruit of this account with himself and with the new world around him was *From the Other Shore*, which made Herzen known in western Europe and which is, next to the *Memoirs*, his most remarkable work and greatest claim to immortality. Although dated in some of its details, it shows Herzen's historical insight and understanding of contemporary Europe at its deepest. It is also the most rebellious and revolutionary of his works, more rebellious and revolutionary than many of his later political writings, for it proclaimed revolution not, in the first place, for the sake of inciting others to political action, but for the sake of truth—a revolution against the *bourgeois*-ridden revolutionaries as well as against the *bourgeois*-ridden world which they claimed to revolutionize, against the "privileged liberators of humanity" as well as against the humanity which they were intent on liberating.[69] He wished to speak on behalf of "the struggle of free men against the liberators of mankind" and expose "the inescapable undoing of old Europe". "I do not regret anything in the existing order, neither its educational achievement nor its institutions. . . . I love nothing in the world except that which it persecutes, and respect nothing except that which it castigates." "Proclaim the tidings of death, show men every new wound on the breast of the old world, every success of destruction! Show them the infirmity of all its undertakings, the pettiness of all its strivings! Show them that it cannot recover, that it has neither foundations nor faith in itself, that in reality nobody loves it, that it rests on misunderstandings! Show that every one of its victories is a self-inflicted blow! Proclaim death as the good tidings of coming redemption!" "What", Herzen asks, "will come of this blood [in revolution]? Who knows? But, whatever the issue, it is sufficient that in this unleashing of madness, vengeance, discord, retribution the old world . . . will perish. It is excellent that it should perish, and therefore: long live chaos and destruction! *Vive la mort!*"

This dramatic note of destructive, Bakuninist nihilism beneath the surface of Herzen's ordinarily restrained and cultivated manner was in no way a false note. There was nothing self-conscious, inflated or declamatory about it. It conveyed his true intention no less than the more apparent acid irony and laughter, or the occasional grim and bitter lyricism which pervade the pages of *From the Other Shore*. Indeed, laughter itself appeared to Herzen as a weapon of revolutionary destruction, and man as the only animal that laughs and rebels. "There is no doubt", he said, "that laughter is one of the mightiest instruments of destruction. The laughter of Voltaire struck and burnt like lightning. Laughter destroys idols, wreaths and moulds, and a miracle-working ikon turns into a blackened, badly drawn picture. This revolutionary power of laughter is terribly contagious. Once begun in the quiet of a study, it grows in ever widening circles to the end of the world."[70]

Herzen's revolutionary attitude, however, introduces a new element, which is absent both in Belinsky and Bakunin: it is the idea of aristocracy, or of the aristocratic nature of human freedom and revolt which Herzen contrasts with the characteristic deportment of the *bourgeois* and the *parvenu*, whose desire to be foremost, whose self-importance, snobbery and scramble serve only to bring out his fundamental servility and complete dependence on the world in which he strains to occupy a privileged position. In the essay, which has already been mentioned, on the development of the idea of honour, Herzen gives a psychologically most illuminating, if somewhat romanticized, version of the history of the aristocracy (curiously reminiscent of the historical views of the pagan, aristocratic aesthete Konstantin Leontiev) as owing its origin not to an increase in wealth and power, or to services rendered to society and the State, but to its struggle *against* society, to its defence of freedom as a privilege of the rebel. The feudal lord's pledge of freedom lay originally in his valour, in the fact that he was his own master, the true revolutionary who takes the law into his own hands, rather than in his social position, or in the power he exercised within society. This enabled him to be the first in European society to acquire a sense of personal dignity and honour, and evolve the idea of chivalry which Herzen regarded as a symptom of awakened personal consciousness. The true aristocrat is not concerned with defending a society or a social order and its collective achievements, but with nurturing a distinctive personal character and personal greatness. He is determined by what he is, not by what he has, by his personal endeavour, by his qualities as a human being. His characteristic virtues are nobility, disinterestedness, magnanimity—virtues which the *bourgeois* does not know in his perpetual struggle to climb upwards. Whilst the *bourgeois* is imbued with envy and resentment in regard to his fellow-men, the aristocrat tends to feel guilt and compassion towards them. He is far more revolted by the stupidity of men than by their wickedness, by the ugliness of everyday life than by the decline in social morals. He begs no one for kind attention or reward and is indifferent to the result of his actions: he does not avoid an action which might have harmful effects for himself or for society, for that would be tantamount to avoiding all noble and truthful actions. He is always in the minority, mostly in a minority of one, for, as Herzen observed, "falsehood is for all, but truth is in the minority". The mass of men do not seek either truth or freedom, and they do not know what to do with freedom when they have got it. Their pleasure is to serve: this they attain by security, which is their deepest need. That is why they have decided long ago that the only freedom worth having is the freedom to do right, and right is decided by might.

"For the second time", Herzen replies to his critic in the last dialogue of *From the Other Shore*, "you have called me an aristocrat, which reminds me of Robespierre's dictum: *l'athéisme est aristocrate*. If all Robespierre wished to say was that atheism is possible for the few, just as the differential calculus or physics are for the few, he might have been right. But in saying that atheism is aristocratic he implied that atheism is false. To my mind this is a piece of intolerable demagogy, of submission to the voice of the majority. The inexorable logician of revolution missed his mark and proclaimed a democratic untruth. . . . I said that truth belongs to the minority. Didn't you know this? Why do you think this so strange? Because I failed to provide it with some suitable rhetorical phrase? Believe me, I am not responsible for the utility or harmfulness of this fact; I am merely stating it. I see, in the present and in the past, knowledge, truth, moral vigour, striving for independence, love of beauty vested in a small group of people, who are lost in an unsympathetic, hostile environment. On the other hand, I see the dullness of the other sections of society, their hide-bound notions based on customs, their narrow needs, their small aspirations to do good and their small inclinations to do evil."

"There you have them," Herzen takes up the argument later on in the same book, "the crusading knights of freedom, the privileged liberators of mankind! They are afraid of freedom; they need a master that they should not become spoiled; they need power, because they cannot depend on themselves. . . . And yet *they* are more up to date, more useful, and, being more practical, they will find greater response among the masses. They are in greater demand. The masses are intent on restraining the hand that dares to snatch away the piece of bread they earn—for it is their greatest need. They do not care for personal liberty, for freedom to speak. The masses love authority; they are dazzled by the offensive splendour of power; they are shocked by the man who stands apart. They understand equality as equal oppression; they fear every exclusiveness and privilege, they look askance at talent and do not tolerate any man who does not do what they are doing. The masses want a social government that would govern them—for them but not against them as at present. They do not dream of governing themselves. That is why the liberators are much nearer to the upheavals of today than any free man. A free man may be a wholly useless man; but this does not mean that he ought to act against his convictions."

In point of historical fact, however, the aristocratic few have also betrayed freedom, for they have substituted the nobility of race and family for the nobility of the spirit of man. They have fallen into a slavery to the past, to ancestry, to tradition and custom. They have readily seized the opportunity of giving social status to their aristocratic quality and proceeded to defend the vested interests and privileges of their social group, caste, family or clan, which bear all the marks of *bourgeois* self-satisfaction and snobbery. "The knight, the freeman *vis-à-vis* the State has become a slave within. . . . He has elaborated a petty casuistry of affronted honour instead of pursuing the living universal idea of human dignity."[71] Herzen revolted against the vulgar uniformities and pretensions of the historical aristocracy and of the *bourgeoisie* alike. And he revolted, too, against the revolutionaries, who turn revolution into tyranny or who, after having sown their wild oats, become respectable citizens, full of aches and prejudices, stubborn, conservative, despising everyone who does not respect the venerable traditions of their ancestors. In fact, Herzen saw everywhere the familiar story of the betrayal of the freedom of man.

"Personality, the true and real monad of society had always been sacrificed for some kind of general idea, of some kind of collective name or banner. Nobody considered asking for whom one worked, why sacrifices were made, who was taken advantage of, who was liberated, whose personal freedom was surrendered?" "It is but a small matter", Herzen wrote in a famous passage of *From the Other Shore*, "to hate the crown: what is necessary is to give up revering the Phrygian cap. It is a small matter to see a crime in an insult to majesty: what is necessary is to recognize *salus populi* as a crime. It is high time to bring to the bar republic, legislation, representations, all notions of citizenship and of the citizen's relation to others and to the State. There will be many executions; it will be necessary to sacrifice many familiar and cherished things. There is no virtue in sacrificing what one hates. The fact is that we must surrender the things we hold dear, whenever we have become convinced of their untruth. Therein lies our real task. We are not called upon to gather the fruit, but to be the executioners of the past—to discern it in all its guises, to pursue and to destroy it . . . in the name of the human spirit."

Herzen acknowledged the true aristocratic and revolutionary spirit solely in those who affirm the dignity of all men. In this respect he attributed a unique importance to Christianity, because in professing the divine image of every man and man's sonship of God it has destroyed the confined and exclusive aristocracy of classical civilization and has given origin to a spiritual aristocracy, which is universal and unbounded in character and which yet belies the standardized world of a nameless and faceless humanity. For Herzen, the idea of true aristocracy was, in fact, inseparable from his socialism, about which more will be said presently: it contained a challenge to the attitude of the privileged social groups, struggling to protect themselves against the violent hands of those whom they have deprived of their humanity. The "few" are nothing without reference to their responsibility towards the "many". The few ought not to justify themselves by means of the many, by turning other men into the objects of their own power and self-interest. Their very existence ought to be their justification, which in fact, it is not, since in any case they consciously set themselves over against the many and are to that extent dependent and obsessed by them, and by the fear they inspire. Unlike Leontiev, who saw in Herzen "one of the few kindred Russian souls", Herzen could not adopt the attitude of a detached and indifferent aesthete, taking refuge in his superiority, or of a priggishly amused outsider and *rêveur*, trying to be different from every one else. He was identified with others, as few were, mixed with his age and immersed in its interests. He was too much of a humanist to turn his own aristocraticism and aestheticism into a moral and social safeguard against life, for that life, with all its hallucinations, horror, squalor and greed, was not, in the last resort, about beauty, culture or even about politics and society, but about the appalling, amorphous human tragi-comedy.

Herzen's strength as a figure on the political stage, even at the time when his influence was at its greatest, lay primarily in his denials. He was an accuser first and foremost, a scrutator, a quickener of human conscience, and a rebel. *From the Other Shore, The Bell, Polar Star*, the pamphlets *Voices from Russia*, all alike exposed and confuted evils and falsehoods, and they contain little evidence of systematic social and political thinking. The impression is enhanced by the strong anarchistic elements which pervade his revolutionary ideas and his quasi-Slavophil, populist socialism. Like all his contemporaries of the "remarkable decade" he did, indeed, no more than seek after truth. It

232

would not be relevant to say that this carried the tacit qualification "provided truth shall never be found", but he did believe that, in the conditions of this stricken world of ours truth is unattainable, except where it is unimportant. Since practical men and dogmatists have no use for such a belief, it is not surprising that they sent Herzen, together with his associates, to the hell of romanticism for seeking after truth.

Nevertheless, an attempt must be made to elucidate Herzen's basic social and political attitude. We have seen that his early political ideas derived their inspiration from French utopian socialism. The acquaintance with Saint-Simonianism seemed then, as Herzen recalled in his memoirs, "like a revelation". But the excitement and sense of discovery came not from the characteristic industrial, technocratic, "totalitarian" aspects of Saint-Simon's social doctrine, or even from his attempt to establish a secular science of society, but from the less characteristic, unpragmatic side: from what Herzen called its "aim to bring about a world of new relations between men", from its "total judgment on the old order of things", and its critique of power as an absolute of government and an oppressive force exercised by men over men. The true heirs of these ideas were Proudhon and the French Syndicalists rather than Marx and Lenin. This early political influence has to a great extent affected Herzen's later political leanings and associations, especially with Proudhon and with that section of the European socialist movement which included the Blanquists and the followers of Babeuf and Buonarroti, of whom Stanislav Worcell—one of the very few Polish exiles whom Herzen respected—was one.[72]

Herzen's revolutionary ideas were primarily connected with "Russian socialism", which will be considered in the next chapter. But, in as much as they had a bearing on western European political movements, they were full of explicit references to and undertones of the pre-Napoleonic revolutionary era and of that radical tradition for which the Empire meant the destruction of Revolution, and revolution the overthrow of all centralized power, as a constant threat to human freedom. When the First International came into being Herzen's sympathies were in the main on the side of the Proudhonist (and hence anti-Marxist) elements, which continued to have a strong hold on many, especially French, members of the International. Communism, or rather the communism of the *Manifesto* of 1848, appeared to him as "Russian autocracy turned upside down", although he admitted its originality and importance. It is well known that, for his part, Marx was very critical of all socialists who harked back to the great days of the French Revolution: he questioned their ability to understand the social revolution in its historical perspective and accused them of ignoring the class-struggle. As for Marx's attitude to Herzen this was openly hostile: he called him a "Cossack"—an epithet Marx tended at the time to apply to all Russians—and refused even to appear with Herzen on the same platform, let alone to enter into any personal contact with him, for which there were many opportunities during their simultaneous residence in London. "I will nowhere and at no time appear on the same platform as Herzen", he wrote to Engels, "since I am not of the opinion that 'old Europe' can be rejuvenated by Russian blood."

However, all this did not prevent Herzen from acknowledging the industrial proletariat as an essential revolutionary force in western Europe, even if he was pessimistic about its early victory over the all-pervading and all-powerful *bourgeoisie*. Towards the end of his life he came to assess anew its rôle in the social revolution in the light of the First International. The most important evidence for this later development is contained in a series of letters which Herzen wrote to Bakunin in 1869 under the title *Pisma k staromu tovarishchu* ("Letters to an Old Comrade") and which have given rise to an acute controversy between the various commentators of Herzen's political views.[73] They have served as a kind of *pièce de résistance* for the "liberal" exponents of Herzen, such as Vetrinsky, Struve and, more recently, Nikolaevsky, on the one hand, and for Lenin and the majority of Soviet Russian scholars (of whom Chesnokov is the most recent and extreme representative), on the other. Lenin, in a much-quoted article published in 1912 on the occasion of the centenary of Herzen's birth, contended that the *Letters* prove Herzen's conversion "from the illusions of 'super-class' *bourgeois* ideology to the stern, inflexible, invincible class-war of the proletariat. ... Herzen breaks away from the anarchist Bakunin. Admittedly, Herzen still views this break as a tactical disagreement, and not as a gulf dividing the outlook of the proletariat, sure of the victory of its class, from the petty *bourgeois* who has despaired of his salvation. Admittedly, Herzen repeats, even here, the old *bourgeois* democratic phrases to the effect that socialism must come out with 'a message addressed to the worker and the proprietor, to the farmer and the *bourgeois* alike'. Still, in breaking with Bakunin, Herzen turned his eyes not to liberalism but to the International, to that International which was led by Marx, to that International which has begun 'to gather the ranks' of the proletariat, to unite the 'labouring world' that has 'quitted the world of those who profit by not working'!" In any case, Lenin claims, Herzen has preserved his "wholehearted loyalty to revolution".[74] This is completely denied by the "liberal" exponents, one of whom maintains that "in these letters Herzen breaks away decisively from the idea of revolution and comes out, more consistently than ever before, as a partisan of evolution"; that, although Herzen "did express sympathy with the International, one need have no more than a slight acquaintance with the controversies of the time to realize that he was wholeheartedly on the side of Marx's opponents ..."[75] The contention about Herzen's attitude to the International cannot be disputed, and Lenin does not seem to have done so explicitly; but the same cannot be said of the other statement about Herzen's alleged repudiation of revolution. In this respect all the evidence seems to bear out Lenin's assertion.[76]

Only a misunderstanding could have suggested to the champions or detractors of Herzen that he was a liberal. The epithet "liberal" is, admittedly, surrounded by a great number of vague associations. If it is taken to signify what it signified originally, namely, that revolt against political and religious authority which started in the French Revolution, then Herzen might be looked upon as a liberal. But even this would require qualification, since the preoccupation with the idea of order, with rational harmony and system in human affairs turned this liberal doctrine in due course into a dogmatic creed, uncompromising and universal in its demands. The transition came when it was found that the late eighteenth-century belief that liberty favours order was untrue. Then liberalism entered on the phase of democratic authoritarianism, which was one of the chief targets of Herzen's criticism.

But Herzen was equally hostile to certain basic tenets of liberalism in the more specific sense—the liberalism which is based on the belief, miraculously surviving to this day, that universal suffrage and parliamentary democracy are the only instruments of perfect political organization, that the gradual extension of the principles of *laissez faire* and free trade would ensure the spreading through the world of the blessings of prosperity, and that no insoluble problems or insuperable barriers could arise to bar the triumphant march of mankind towards a better and fuller life. Herzen listened no more to the sirens of the future than to the market-place of his day. He was repelled by earthly utopias, because to his mind they were bound to be under any circumstance utopias of the most abysmal mediocrity and "Chinese fidelity". What he saw through more clearly than most of his contemporaries, and what he exposed with devastating force and humour was the whole liberal doctrine of progress that had, in the nineteenth century and later, such compelling social and political force. He frankly disbelieved in progress, except of course in the technical sense, as applied to science, machinery and invention, and disliked its naïve and credulous claims. For him men did not inevitably grow better as their political and economic liberties were enlarged. Indeed, he thought, at his most pessimistic, that since men are congenitally stupid and nasty animals, any attempt to improve them must be foredoomed and therefore unreasonable. In his more considered judgment progress appeared as a colossal secular illusion that had come to replace religious teleologies, to permit men to rise to higher and more perfect things on the stepping stones of their dead selfs. It was, he said, "the soulless city of a faceless future", "the Moloch of brutal depersonalization", whereby man's life is reduced to a kind of coral, building with its own débris a reef of which it never sees the completion, to a frightful and hideous cemetery for the victims of the secular church of progressive evolution. For Herzen there was no bliss for a future life or even in a future life: there was but present joy with its present laughter, and present pain with its present tears, and man with his life on earth.

The pessimistic conclusion about progress did not, however, really imply for Herzen the suggestion to abandon the effort to improve society by changing the environment, by improving the material lot of our fellow-men, and to concentrate on individual salvation, which was, in fact, a feature of the very liberalism which he criticized. He was a socialist, an avowed enemy of capitalism, but he was that precisely because he did not believe that mere reliance on the beneficent operations of society would improve men, because, unlike the champions of liberalism, he took a pessimistic view of the consequences of economic freedom and refused to pin his faith to the free play of economic interest. He did not repudiate all liberal institutions: he was a fervent advocate of free speech, of a free Press, of civil liberty. But he did not share the liberal belief that the free competition of ideas—the "constitutional twilight of neither this nor that", as he called it—is the best way of discovering truth; he disliked intensely what he described as "liberal smoothness and insipidity", and never made any concessions to perfectionist and reformist theories. He became convinced, too, that no more grievous and thorough enemies of freedom exist than liberal institutions once they are soundly established: they bring about the levelling of mountain and valley exalted to morality; they make people small, cowardly and common, and usher in the triumph of the gregarious animal, who is nothing until somebody else has been something else first. In fact, Herzen saw little evidence of any real freedom in the theory and practice of nineteenth-century liberal acquisitive society, in which gregariousness went hand in hand with excessive self-assertion, in which man was crushed and crushed others by means of "tooth-and-claw" ethics and economics. To equalize men by depriving them of this freedom seemed to Herzen not to endanger their individual character, but, on the contrary, to expose their relevant inequalities, their true individual distinctions, if there are any left to be exposed, concealed or suppressed as they are by the dehumanizing differences of class, wealth and social position—to expose if not to create, for whether human personality would triumph or be trodden underfoot was still a question which depended on the human will. That some should oppose such equalization is not surprising, since it is of the essence of the paradox of freedom that man should view their own slavery and the slavery of those whom they enslave as freedom, and remonstrate against any threat to their familiar world as violation of freedom, as an exercise of brute force. To fight for freedom presupposes and provokes resistance. In this sense, at any rate, Herzen remained a social and political revolutionary to the end of his days, and to this extent his *Letters to an Old*

Comrade do not belie his most destructive utterances in *From the Other Shore*.

"The workers", Herzen wrote in these *Letters*, "by uniting among themselves, by standing out like a 'State within a State', which attains its organization and its rights independently of the capitalists and proprietors, independently of political and ecclesiastical frontiers, constitute the first recipients and the germ of the future economic order. The International Association may grow into an Aventine Hill *à l'intérieur*: in retiring to it, the workers, hand in hand, will abandon the world of those who profit by not working to its profitable unproductivity. . . . And this world, cut off, will *nolens volens* come to terms. If, however, it fails to do so, it will put itself outside the law—and then its undoing will be delayed only so long as the new world proves itself powerless." Herzen's disagreement with Bakunin, as he stated at the outset, lay not in that he repudiated the revolutionary principles which Bakunin advocated, but that he questioned his "methods and practical measures", and his sense of the historical moment. He objected, not to revolution, but to playing with revolution, to loosing that tact which consists in knowing where and when to go too far, to "prophets and nostradamuses, to heresiarchs, fanatics and professional revolutionaries". He believed such prophets to defeat their aim by evoking revolutionary cataclysms at any time and out of time. He insisted that destruction not only "makes space"—which he welcomed—but also spreads "religion and politics, establishes autocratic empires and indivisible republics"— which he abhorred; that it may mean liberation, but also brute force in the ascendant, "Petrograndism" (from *Pierre le Grand*) as he called it, which ends by ousting the rebel himself from any place where his voice might be raised or his influence felt. "Terror destroys as few prejudices as nationalism. Fear serves to drive customs and forms inwards; it hinders their functioning, but does not touch the heart of the matter. The Jews were persecuted for centuries; some perished, others went into hiding and reappeared after the storm, richer, more powerful and stauncher in their faith." The mass of men are not revolutionary at all, Herzen told Bakunin, who himself expressed similar views in his more lucid moments: they are "conservative by instinct, and since they know nothing else, they have no ideals outside the existing order. Their ideal is *bourgeois* contentment, just as the ideal of Heine's Atta Troll was . . . an absolutely white bear. They hold fast to oppressive habits, to narrow moulds into which they are driven: they believe in the stability and security of such habits and moulds, unaware that it is they who invest them with stability. The further people are away from the movement of history, the more obstinately they hold on to the acquired and the familiar." "You cannot liberate men in their outward life more than they are liberated *within*." "We cannot fight any more against false doctrines, against beliefs, however mad, by negation alone. . . . To say 'don't believe!' is as authoritarian and at bottom as absurd as to say 'believe!' " "We must once and for all abandon the forensic point of view." "The new order to come must appear not only as a hewing axe, but also as a preserving agent. In delivering its blow to the old world, it must not only save everything in it that is worth saving, but leave alone all that is not a bulwark, every variety and peculiarity. Woe to the upheaval which is poor in spirit and weak in creative meaning, which will turn all things past and acquired into a dull workshop, and the sole achievement of which will consist in subsistence, and nothing but subsistence!" "I feel sorry not only for people, but for things too, and for some things more than for some people."

The attitude Herzen appears to have adopted was that of a revolutionary who could no longer believe in revolution, but what he desired at bottom was not less revolution, but more and better revolution—a revolution that goes beyond mere ideologies, beyond the nameless confections of the future, beyond mere hatred and knock-down blows, all of which seemed to him to be profoundly reactionary, trivial and commonplace, a revolution that is capable of effecting a change in the very structure of human existence. The revolutions which Herzen had witnessed were not achieving any of these objects: on the contrary, he saw them subjected to the familiar instincts of fear, power, cruelty and inhumanity, and to the familiar disputants flinging old slogans and catch-phrases at each other, spreading the same spirit of allegiance and mental prostitution. There was, too, that other practice of revolutionaries which Herzen resisted—the practice of oblivion and ingratitude towards all things and all men, even those that had inspired revolution itself. His whole life was dedicated to the destruction of the idols of history and civilization; and yet he could not altogether betray the past by forgetting it, because it was to him not merely a world of repugnant or precious facts, but *erlebtes Leben*, life born of human creativity, action, discovery, sacrifice, emotion, and his heart seemed to bleed in the face of a revolution that struck at that life with its weapon of ingratitude. "To men of action, to agitators who move the masses", Herzen wrote in his *Memoirs*, at a time when he was far less critical of Bakunin's revolutionism than in the late 'sixties, "these bitter hesitations, these heart-rending doubts are incomprehensible. They see in them nothing but useless lamentation, nothing but feeble despondency. . . . [They are moved by] the revolting desire to restrict the freedom of personality, to force men into categories and ranks, as though political activity were like slave-labour to which the bailiffs drive weak and strong, willing and unwilling alike, without consulting their wishes." Like Belinsky, Herzen was advocating a revolution on behalf of the human person—in its memories of the past, commitments to the present and aspirations towards the future, as well as in its independence of past, present and future—a revolution transcending the myths and certitudes of liberalism and communism, whose

238

fate in history was to revolutionize very little in respect of the human person, despite the changes they may have effected in other respects.

4. RUSSIA: DREAM OR REALITY?

Russia occupied a central place in Herzen's life: it was an object of his faith, hope and love, a source of anxious expectation and sad disappointment. There was a great deal of unconcealed passionate attachment in him to his native land, enhanced by separation, a deeply-felt self-identification with its fortunes and misfortunes. "I belong to the Russian people with every fibre of my soul", he wrote towards the end of his life; "I work for it and it works in me: and this is by no means mere historical reminiscence, nor just a blind instinct or blood-bond. It is a consequence of the fact that through the crust and mist, through blood and the glow of fires, through popular ignorance and Tsarist civilization, I perceive a great force, an important element which enters the historical stage, together with the social revolution, and which must capture, *volens nolens*, the old world if that world is not to petrify and perish."[77] Even his attitude to western Europe was of a peculiarly Russian kind. He often spoke, as so many Russians before and after him, of the loss by western Europe of creative vigour and resources, and yet he loved, or at any rate understood it, as Dostoevsky said of all Russians, *because* he was a Russian. One need only read what Herzen wrote about Italy and the Italians, about France and the French workers, or even about England at which he discharged some of the most penetrating arrows of his irony, to convince oneself of his extraordinary insight and capacity to feel himself into, to bring to life and evoke the atmosphere of the western European world.

Herzen's love for and hope in Russia had much in common with the characteristic attitude of the Slavophils, for whom, to the great annoyance of many Westerners, he had a warm feeling. Himself a Westerner, disbelieving in "a separate Russian culture" and doubting whether "the inner strength for the development of the Russian people would have been found without the Petersburg period, without the period of European culture", he spoke, none the less, of the Slavophils as *nos amis, les ennemis*, as "our strange opponents": "we had the same love", he wrote in *The Bell* on the death of Konstantin Aksakov, "but not the same way of loving; and like Janus or the two-headed eagle we looked in opposite directions, although the heart that beat within us was but one". Many of Herzen's essays and articles read like professions of the Slavophil creed. The most outspoken of these is the small essay *The Russian People and Socialism*, in the form of a letter to the French historian Jules Michelet. It was Herzen's declaration of *ex Oriente lux!*, and the first voice in western Europe which spoke of Russia, not as the only hitherto familiar geographical, diplomatic and military factor, but as a spiritual, cultural and social force.[78] I quote at length from this essay:

"Some tell us", Herzen wrote, "only of the unlimited power of the Tsar, of the capricious tyranny of his government, of the slavish spirit of his subjects. Others assert, on the contrary, that the imperialism of Petersburg has nothing in common with the people who, crushed under the twofold despotism of the Government and the landowners, bears the yoke, but is not resigned to it; that it is not crushed but only unfortunate; and, at the same time, they declare that it is this very people which gives unity and power to the colossal Tsardom that crushes it. Some add that the Russian people is a contemptible rabble of drunkards and knaves; others maintain that Russia is inhabited by an able and highly gifted race. It seems to me that there is something tragic in the senile heedlessness with which the old world mixes up the different accounts it hears of its antagonists. In this confusion of contradictory opinions there is apparent so much senseless repetition, such distressing superficiality, such petrified prejudice, that we are involuntarily moved to a comparison with the days of the fall of Rome.

"Then, too, on the eve of catastrophe, on the eve of the victory of the barbarians, men loudly proclaimed the eternity of Rome, the impotent madness of the Nazarenes, and the insignificance of the movement that was arising in the barbarian world. . . .

" 'They (the Russians, you say) are without any true sign of humanity, of moral sensibility, of the sense of good and evil. Truth and justice have no meaning for them; if you speak of these things—they are mute, they smile and know not what the words signify.' Who may those Russians be to whom you have spoken? What conceptions of 'truth and justice' appeared beyond their comprehension? This is not a superfluous question. In our profoundly revolutionary epoch the words 'truth and justice' have lost all absolute meaning identical for all men.

"The 'truth and justice' of old Europe are falsehood and injustice to the Europe which is being born. . . . The past of the western European peoples serves us as a lesson and nothing more; we do not regard ourselves as the executors of their historic testaments. We share your doubts, but your faith does not cheer us. We share your hatred, but we do not understand your devotion to what your forefathers have bequeathed you. We are too downtrodden, too unhappy, to be satisfied with half-freedom. You are restrained by scruples, you are held back by second thoughts. We have neither second thoughts nor scruples; all we lack is strength. This is where we get the irony, the anguish that gnaws us, that rouses us to frenzy, that drives us on till we reach Siberia, torture, exile, premature death. We sacrifice ourselves with no hope, from spite, from boredom. . . . There is indeed something irrational in our lives, but there is nothing vulgar, nothing stagnant, nothing *bourgeois*.

"Do not accuse us of immorality because we do not respect what you respect. Can you reproach a foundling for not respecting his parents? We are independent because we are starting life from the beginning. We have no law but our nature, our national character; it is our being, our flesh and blood, but by no means a binding authority. We are independent because we possess nothing. We have hardly anything to love. All our memories are filled with bitterness and anger. Education, learning, were given us with the whip.

"What have we to do with your sacred duties . . .? And can we be honestly contented with your threadbare morality, unchristian and inhuman, existing only in rhetorical exercises and speeches for the prosecution? What respect can be inspired in us by your Romano-barbaric system of law, that hollow, clumsy edifice, without light or air, repaired in the Middle Ages, whitewashed by the newly enfranchised petty *bourgeois*? . . .

". . . We are held in too many chains already to fasten fresh ones about us of our own free will. In this respect we stand precisely on a level with our peasants. We submit to brute force. We are slaves because we have no possibility of being free; but we accept nothing from our foes. . . . Russia will never be Protestant; Russia will never be *juste milieu*."

What Herzen did, in the first place, was to question—in terms that have a curiously modern ring and relevance—the supremacy of western Europe as an immutable law of Nature; to enquire if the "values of civilization", which western Europeans claimed to bring to mankind and which made them so confident at home, were really an unmixed blessing, if these values had not, in fact, largely lost their human quality and were sustained by the obscene trinity of Mammon, Mars and the Pharisee; to ask, furthermore, if people in western Europe were entitled to be angry and astonished that the Russians were not behaving with the propriety expected of them, or that the spiritual and material benefits of "western civilization" were not taken at their face value. Again and again Herzen used the analogy of the ancient world, which also regarded itself as unprecedented and beneficial, but succumbed to the barbarians leaving behind what was in the last resort but a thin deposit. Nothing could be more superficial and foolish to his mind than to view the relation between western Europe and Russia as a relation of freedom and tyranny. He was, of course, too candid and too realistic to suppress or in any way whatever to camouflage, as the Slavophils tended to do, the tyranny and inhumanity of "Russian reality". But he believed that the body politic of Russia is, to quote again the letter to Michelet, an "unfinished building in which everything smells of fresh plaster, in which everything is at work and being worked out, in which nothing has as yet attained its object, in which everything is changing, sometimes for the worse, but anyway changing". Above all, he insisted that the difference between western Europe and Russia is that here, apart from the actual political and economic oppression prevalent in the mid-nineteenth century, man has been effectively tempted, while there, in Russia, he was ineffectively compelled, to be inhuman, and the temptation appeared to Herzen as more ominous and more corrupting than the compulsion, because more humanity survives under ineffective compulsion than under effective temptation, even though Herzen himself chose temptation, with all the dangers and responsibilities which it entailed.

The pattern of the age was set for Herzen by the decaying *bourgeois* culture and capitalism, on the one hand, and the social revolution, on the other. The Russian equivalent of the latter was peasant communism, which has been stifled in the social and political marasmus of the Tsarist order, but which survived, at least vestigially, as a pattern of life, as a form of internal social organization, and as a means of dealing with the power of the landlords. It remained alive in the *mir* or village commune, which combined a common tenure of land, periodically re-distributed among its members, with individual cultivation and enjoyment of the produce, and exercised a local self-government of its own. It survived also in the *artel* or union of workmen, entering into a free agreement to work jointly in various trades for a definite period, while preserving their rights as individuals. The sociological importance of communal village life in Russia was similarly stressed by the Decembrists and, especially, by the Slavophils, for whom it had, in addition, religious associations, for they regarded the *mir* as the social refraction of the idea of *sobornost* or catholicity, of the congregation of the faithful as the repository of truth. To Herzen the free development of the village commune appeared as Russia's challenge to western European society, and an answer to its impasses and aberrations, and, at the same time, as a bridge between Russia and "Europe *in extremis*", that is, Europe in the extreme situation of revolution. For Russia such a development of communal ownership and co-operative labour would be an antidote to capitalism and the rule of the *bourgeoisie* even as a transitory state of social and political evolution, although Herzen was quite prepared to see her adopting western European techniques for the improvement of agriculture and small-scale industry.[79]

"The commune", he wrote in the same letter to Michelet, "has saved the Russian people from Mongol barbarism and Imperial civilization, from the Europeanized landlords and from the German bureaucracy. The communal system, though it has suffered violent shocks, has stood firm against the interference of the authorities; it has successfully survived *up to the development of socialism in Europe*. . . . How fortunate it is for the Russian people that it has remained outside all political movements, outside European civilization, which would undoubtedly have undermined the commune, and which has to-day reached in socialism the negation of itself. . . . At the first step towards the social revolution Europe is confronted with a people which presents it with a system, half-savage and un-organized . . .—that of constant re-distribution of land among its cultivators. And observe that this great example is given us not by educated Russia, but by the people itself, by its actual life. We Russians who have passed through European civilization are no more than a means, a leaven, mediators between the Russian people and revolutionary Europe. The man of the future in Russia is the peasant, just as in France it is the workman."

Herzen's discovery of "the same love" with the Slavophils, his belief in the beneficent potentialities of the Russian people and in social and political revival through Russian peasant communism was a gradual process, which began almost immediately after he set foot on western European soil. Its culminating point is marked by his conflict with Turgenev, one of the few consistent Westerners in the whole of nineteenth century Russian history, who combined a life-long admiration of western European civilization, and of Germany in particular, with an amazing gift of conformity with official Russia, of not giving offence, and with anxious appeals for recognition by it. A long correspondence ensued between Herzen and Turgenev, and they broke off relations altogether after the latter had visited London in 1863 to discuss these problems with Herzen, Ogarev and Bakunin. Turgenev's case was the familiar argument of the Westerners that Russia's salvation depended on the cultural *élite*, which was to imbue the Russian people with the principles of western European civilization. Russia, he contended, was not a Venus of Milo and did not differ much from her western European sisters "except, perhaps, that her behind is a little larger". He advised Herzen to read Schopenhauer (whom Herzen called a "seedy termagant") and discontinue the worship of "the Russian Sheepskin", "the Absolute Sheepskin, the Sheepskin of the Future, the Sheepskin of Communism and Socialism". It has been noted before that Bakunin, who also read Schopenhauer, was similarly to accuse Herzen of such worship. "All your ideals", Turgenev told Herzen, "have been smashed and, as you can't live without an ideal, you are now erecting an altar to the new god, about whom, fortunately, nothing is so far known. It is true this god does not behave as you expect him to behave, but that, you say, is only a temporary aberration, an accident, something that has been forcibly grafted on him by the authorities. Your god loves the things you hate and hates the things you love; he accepts what you repudiate in his name: but you turn away your eyes, you shut your ears, and with the ecstasy that is so typical of all sceptics who are sick of scepticism, with this ultra-fanatical ecstasy, you go on talking of fresh spring breezes, beneficial storms, and so on. History, philology, statistics—you care nothing for them, you care nothing for anything in the world; you care nothing for facts, for the incontrovertible fact, for example, that we Russians belong by language and racial origin to the

243

European family of nations, *genus europaensis*, and therefore must go along the same road; yet you attack everything that ought to be dear to every European, and therefore also to us; you attack civilization, you attack the European conception of law, you even attack the revolution."[80]

Turgenev was scarcely entitled to make personal charges against Herzen, for, although he did not prostrate himself before the Russian sheepskin, he eagerly prostrated himself before the Russian Tsar when his own political reputation was at stake, assuring him of his devotion and the unfailing moderation of his political opinions.[81] Nevertheless his obloquy was not entirely beside the point, for there is a curious, almost jarring discrepancy between the quality of Herzen's search and that of his discovery, between the importance of his question and the apparent triviality of his answer. It may be possible to appreciate the sentiment which moved Herzen to say, after he had reached the nadir of depression as a result of the tragic events in the late 'forties and early 'fifties, that "having begun with a cry of joy on crossing the frontier, I finished by a spiritual return to my motherland. Faith in Russia saved me on the brink of moral catastrophe. . . . I am grateful to my motherland for this faith in her, for this recovery through her."[82] There may even be some justice in Professor Carr's suggestion that in pronouncing the damnation of western Europe Herzen settled accounts with Herwegh (although the damnation preceded, in fact, the Herwegh affair), and in his cult of Russia venerated the memory of the ill-used Natalie. Herzen himself, after all, saw his personal tragedy in the general historic setting, or saw the historic setting against the background of his tragedy—it does not matter which, for Herzen was conscious, like many another, of a reciprocal relation between the hours of man's individual life and the centuries of time, of hours enlightened by the ages and of ages explained by the hours.

It is different, however, when we learn that "moral catastrophe" issues in a belief in the beneficial power of the cultivation of the arable in separate lots. The anti-climax is such as to bewilder the most sympathetic critic who is prepared to indulge in the ultimate romantic follies. Or was it just another instance of that characteristic tendency of the Russian intelligentsia, to which reference was made in another connection, to place too much of its moral capital in social and political preoccupations? In adopting the Russian agrarian scheme Herzen, it is true, was guided by weighty social and political considerations, the importance of which is not invalidated even by this astonishing descent from the sublime to the ridiculous. Nevertheless, it may be asked if Herzen, whose keen intellect and sense of discrimination never betrayed him, who saw, as few others did, through false illusions, who deliberately chose to live without the aid of faith: if Herzen was not driven, pathetically, to fill the void with something, anything to offset the loss, and thus found a last desperate hope in a mystique of the eternal peasant? Has he not, in the end, become the victim of exile, which creates dreams and fixations, which, in its uprootedness and insecurity, made him feel secure in exaggeration?

However plausible such or similar explanations may have appeared to Turgenev and Herzen's later detractors, they do not entirely reveal his true motive, although it must be borne in mind that here at least his intuitions were more important than what he deduced from them. What Herzen sought in the uncertain, quasi-mystical notion of "the people", overcharged though it was for him at times with poetry, character and significance, was neither divine substitutes, not dreams, nor illusions, nor oblivion, but humanity. It marked his coming down "into the valley", as he once said himself, where all mankind lives, an attempt to embody and to humanize, a means of love for man, and an instrument of struggle on his behalf. The hopes which were entertained in his time of universal suffrage he could not share. For the kingdom of God on earth which was being planned he felt only repugnance, and of the kingdom of God in heaven he could not catch a glimpse. With what then was he left?—with man alone. This was his only "Absolute", lurking in the background of worldly affairs. And he believed man to be, not better or nicer, but more human in the image of the Russian peasant than in that of the *bourgeois*, of whose ubiquitous triumph he became such a melancholy witness. He saw, no doubt, little difference between the western European kingdom of the *bourgeois* or the *parvenu* and its germanized counterpart and transplantation on the banks of the Neva; but beneath the pressures, frustrations and controls of this in-human structure there remained for him the free Russian, scarcely influenced by authority and therefore capable of creating on his own "free and communal premise" just and human relations. This, indeed, was the burden of Herzen's letters to Turgenev (*Ends and Beginnings*), which, as Herzen regretfully realized, Turgenev in his "moderation" was quite unable or unwilling to understand.

Herzen's unanimity with the Slavophils had its obvious limits. "I have never denied", he wrote to Turgenev shortly after the explanations in London, "that the Slavophils have a true sense of the living soul of the people, that they 'look for the world to come', but unhappily I must repeat that their instinct is clearer than their understanding, clearer, indeed, than their conscience." He was unable to share, not only their religious assumptions, but all that faintly hagiolatrous air about them, their curiously archaic tone and attitude—"the ikon painter's ideal and incense smoke", as he said, "which prevented us so long from under-standing the Russian people and its history", and which revealed its odious countenance and mounted the throne in Russia with Alexander III, attended by Katkov and Pobedonostsev. He could not but smile at the Slavophil treatment of Russian history as a vindication of Provi-dence, at their obstinate desire to disguise too many ill-winds to good account. He was too "uprooted" and too free to hold that man, torn from his native soil, from hearth, family and home, degenerates. As for alien influences, against which the Slavophils tried to immure themselves, he believed that it was through them that men have learned to know themselves. In addition, he was no nationalist, and, here again, what mattered to him were the universal human elements which, in his view, stimulated trends and developments in the life of the Russian people.

When Herzen wrote to Michelet of the Russian cultural and literary heritage he did not proceed in the confident Slavophil fashion from the assumption of an eternal national substance that was said to exist in a venerable harmonious past, in ancestral traditions, or in a realm altogether outside time and space, but spoke of it as "the sphere of pathological anatomy", of historic conflict and "tragic self-awareness": "in it", he wrote, "there is a constant reference to the evil consuming us— persistent, pitiless, peculiar only to us. Here you do not listen to voices from heaven, promising Faust forgiveness for sinful Gretchen: here the only voices raised are those of doubt and damnation. Yet if there is salvation for Russia she will be saved only by this profound recognition of our predicament, by the truthfulness with which she lays man's plight bare before all. . . ." ". . . The true character of Russian thought, poetical and speculative, develops in its full force on the accession of Nicolas to the throne. Its distinguishing feature is a tragic emancipation of conscience, a pitiless negation, a bitter irony, an agonizing self-analysis. At times all this breaks out into insane laughter, but there is no gaity in that laughter. Cast into oppressive surroundings, and armed with a clear eye and incorruptible logic, the Russian quickly frees himself from the faith and morals of his fathers. The thinking Russian is the most independent man in the world. What is there to curb him? Respect for the past? . . . But what serves as a starting point of the modern history of Russia, if not the denial of nationalism and tradition?"

Herzen's positive social aim was the advancement of a decentralized, pluralistic agrarian communism, of independent and spontaneous associations, capable of acting against the State as well as with it, in which the *mir*, reinstated in its ownership of the land and strengthened by the liberation of the peasants from serfdom, would play the decisive rôle. This idea is summed up in a statement made by Herzen in 1866 which has become the *locus topicus* of populist social doctrine. "We bring a new relation between man and soil", he wrote: "our people seek to develop individual freedom without letting the right to the land be lost, to limit the sovereign right of real property by the sovereign right of each man to individual possession. As colonists who have cleared our soil for ourselves and are accustomed to a certain agricultural re-distribution, with no overlay of conquerors on our shoulders, it is easier for us than for the other peoples of Europe to solve the problem in a social sense. The relation of man to soil, as we understand it, is not a new invention in Russia: it is a primordial fact, a natural fact, so to speak. We wish now, with sincere remorse, to develop it with the aid of western science and experience."[83] The problem uppermost in Herzen's mind was that of the relation between the individual and society. It seemed to him that the perennial conflict in human society which expresses itself in the oscillation between collectivized, depersonalized man and man at the mercy of his isolation, using others as an instrument of self-affirmation, has found its approximate practical solution in the Russian commune, which, without formal procedure, holds rights and responsibilities in constant balance, and in which economic slavery is impossible because individual rights are dependent on the means of exercising them. In western Europe, Herzen contended, liberalism has made the unoriginal discovery that everyone has a right to work; but in Russia, even during serfdom, every *muzhik* knew of each man's right to free land and hence of his effective right to work. Russia can and must at all costs avoid the dreaded stage of western European capitalism. The idea that only private enterprise or self-interest is socially creative, and that men in all their social actions are self-regarding, without which the collapse of society was alleged to be inevitable through desolation and lack of productivity was, in Herzen's view, belied by the existence of the Russian village commune and the *artel*. On the other hand, these institutions presented an effective challenge to the contrary tendency of the capitalist system, criticized by Marx and the anti-utilitarian social thinkers in western Europe and by some of the Decembrists in Russia: the tendency expressed in the famous "greatest happiness principle", which interprets economic life in terms of national efficiency and well-being, rather than in those of the individual, stressing the general, not the particular, product, and, in deference to the principle of *laissez faire*, "letting mischief work and evils go on". In short, the *mir* existed for Herzen as a focus of social life uncorrupted by the theory and practice of social and political monism, whether of the individualist or the collectivist variety, with its massive organization of urban industrial life, with its destruction of personal liberty by exploiting human labour or by absorbing man in the total solidarity of the organized masses and the organized State.

In his anarchism, as has been noted before, Herzen did not differ essentially from Bakunin, for which he was censored by the readers of *The Bell*. Some of his essays (for instance, the article "What is the State?" published in the *Polar Star* in 1855) were an attack on the very institution of the State. In *From the Other Shore* the State is defined as the political concretion of the *bourgeois* spirit. He saw a characteristic quality of modern politics in the attempt to divinize society on a pattern in which social activity, with Government as the leader, turns into a work of salvation and imposes a particular kind of transcendental representation, whether Catholic or Orthodox, Protestant or liberal, progressive or communist. The "truth" of such a pattern bears no relation to the human condition, for, as he wrote in *From the Other Shore*, it always means "the subjugation of the human person to society, to the nation, to humanity, to an Idea"—in short, "a continuation of human sacrifices". Anarchism is nothing more or less than an attempt "to reduce what is political and religious to what is simple and human". He commended the Russian peasant commune to Michelet as a truly human pattern of social relations, because the peasant does not believe in the immutable rights of any authority, in earthly providence, sustained by law and order, and because the peasant's own social life, his rights and duties within the village commune are independent of "contracts and written agreements". The suggestion that laws and regulations are the best guardian of freedom, and that apart from them the pursuit of social aims becomes an exercise in utopianism would have been met by Herzen with the comment that it is just this assumption which is at the basis of nearly all utopias, for most of them were concerned with devising laws and elaborate State machinery to force men to be happy and contented. To avoid the enormities and monstrosities of utopia one must live, as the Russian peasant lives, in the interstices of society, and put one's trust in disestablishment and fluidity. "The peasant", Herzen told Michelet, "finds himself in the literal sense of the word an outlaw. . . . His share in the existing order of things is entirely confined to the two-fold tribute that lies heavily upon him and is paid in his toil and his blood. Rejected by all, he instinctively understands that the whole system is ordered not for his benefit, but to his detriment, and that the aim of the Government and the landowners is to wring out of him as much labour, as much money, as many recruits as possible. As he understands this and is gifted with a supple and resourceful intelligence, he deceives them on all sides and in everything. It could not be otherwise; if he spoke the truth he would by so doing be acknowledging their authority over him; if he did not rob them (observe that to conceal part of the produce of his own labour is considered a theft in a peasant) he would thereby be recognizing the lawfulness of their demands, the rights of the landowners and the justice of the law-courts."[84]

It would be wrong to assume, however, that Herzen was unaware of ambivalence in the relations obtaining between the peasant and the State in Russia. He never joined with the Slavophils in their attempt to rationalize these relations, to claim, as a matter of fact as well as of principle, collective innocence for the Russian people in regard to the State, and to idealize the non-acceptance of responsibility for the acts of the Government. Indeed, he saw in this attitude a cause of the characteristic tendency in the conservative sections of Russian society to obliterate facts, both past and present, which should have been discerned and rejected, with dangerous social and moral consequences for the future. And all his activity as a publicist throughout the 'fifties and 'sixties was concerned with making his public in Russia face the predicament of Russian society. Similarly, he was not blind to signs of corruption within the peasant commune itself, when inequality began to creep in, when, with the inadequate and ill-conditioned emancipation of the serfs, a monetary economy began to affect the life of the Russian village; and when, despite the restraining influence of the *mir*, the peasantry began to be differentiated into all those Kolupaevs and Razuvaevs, *kulaks* and semi-*kulaks*, who secured themselves in the possession of more than their share of the better land, on the one hand, and the dependent peasant proletariat, on the other. Besides, however much Herzen may have been deluded in his reliance on the potentialities and actualities of the Russian people, he did not speak wistfully and devoutly of "the people" as if from the fringe of the crowd, like some of his minor populist successors. There are even signs, in *Letters to an Old Comrade*, for instance, that he was uneasily conscious of the imbecilities of "the people".

And yet he believed that nowhere in Europe has freedom been so deeply experienced as in Russia—not, of course, among the "German Russians", in "Petersburg", but among the men of the people, in "Moscow", for, as he announced in 1853, with, one must suppose, unconscious prophetic irony, echoing Bakunin, "if Tsarism falls, the centre of liberty will be at the heart of the nation, in Moscow". In concluding his apologia for Russia, Herzen reminded Michelet of a popular Russian fable which tells how a Tsar, suspecting his wife of unfaithfulness, shut her and her son in a barrel. The barrel was sealed up and thrown into the sea. For many years it floated on the water.

Meanwhile, the Tsarevich grew with each day and each hour, and his feet and his head began to press against the ends of the barrel. Every day he became more and more cramped. At last he said to his mother: "Queen-mother, let me stretch in freedom!"

"My darling Tsarevich," answered his mother, "you must not stretch, the barrrel will burst and you will drown in the salt water."

The Tsarevich thought for a while and then said: "I will stretch, mother; better stretch for once in freedom and die."

That fable, Herzen observes, contains the whole of Russian history.

Armed with the populist creed, with a programme of extensive social and political changes in Russia, and a demand for the independence of Poland, Herzen, assisted by Ogarev, entered the Russian political stage. As can be seen from the very title of his first propagandist publication in London (the *Polar Star*), the original aim of Herzen's enterprise was to continue the revolutionary tradition of the Decembrists in the new historical setting and atmosphere which obtained in Russia after the Crimean War—an aim, which, as we know from Herzen's *Memoirs*, he and his associates had already nurtured in their student days. The story of this enterprise, with its vicissitudes, triumphs and disappointments, has been told many times, and its details need not detain us here. Summing up the "great quinquennium" (1857–62), which marked the highlight of Herzen's political activity, Professor Carr writes: "For about five years, Herzen, living in London, dreamed, in visions of unprecedented clearness and splendour, the aspirations of enlightened, liberal Russian opinion, both inside and outside Russia. In tones of fervent missionary zeal and in a pungent literary style, he proclaimed aloud the hopes which Russia scarcely dared to confess even to herself. The conjecture soon passed; and the vision faded. But the memory remained in history." Some aspects of this story, however, must be recalled for a proper estimate of the *dénouement* of Herzen's life and work.

Although Herzen believed, at any rate until the reforms of 1861, that his social aims could be carried out within the framework of the existing political order in Russia, he expressed repeatedly, even when the moral and political atmosphere had changed for the better subsequent to Nicolas I's death, a mood of disappointment and frustration. He made no secret of his "empty dream" and "wishful thinking". "Nothing can be expected from the Government", he wrote shortly before the Reform. "It is the old *régime* of Nicolas, but stewed and with treacle added." He remained characteristically hesitant in admitting the certainty of his own hopes. The famous first appeal to Alexander II which Herzen made in the *Polar Star* in March 1855 reflected his presentment of "revolution from below". "Make haste!" he appealed to the new Emperor. "Save the peasant from future cruel deeds, . . . from blood, which he will be driven to shed." In 1858 an article in *The Bell* even called upon the peasants to take the axe: "Sharpen the axe, go to it, lads—quash serfdom from below! Put your hand to it! . . . You have been waiting long enough!" It is true, Herzen hated what he called "revolutionary declamation" and abhorred blood and terror when it was a question, not of logic, but of actually practising an organized system of intimidation. "Terror", he wrote, with perhaps deliberate ambiguity, "is as necessary to us as genius is to the world to-day." "We shall not appeal", he explained to the readers of *The Bell* in 1860, "to the axe, to this *ultima ratio* of the oppressed, until there is the slightest reasonable hope for a solution without it"; but, at the same time, he felt compelled to admit the apparent unanswerability of a total revolutionary challenge, the apparent inevitability of revolutionary destruction: "in them [revolutions] the social organism gets rid of lingering diseases, of suffocating malignant tumours; they are a fateful consequence of deep-rooted aberrations, and, finally, a matter of vengeance. . . ." It seems as if he could never entirely dispense, even at his most enlightened and humane, with the theme of revolt and revolution: it retained its emotional and intellectual power for him, and he persisted in deriving his symbols, ideas and images from it.

This betrayed itself not only in the face of the western European *bourgeois*, but also in his opposition to the Russian liberals, to "our westernizing doctrinaires", as he called them, who "write with milk and honey", who have "slackened their anger", or surrender to "sedative despair". Herzen's use of the term "liberal" in this connection is misleading, for there never existed a liberal movement in Russia, nor were there any signs of liberal "ideology" that might have had any appreciable influence on Russian public opinion in the nineteenth century. The idea of freedom in Russia found its most characteristic and adequate expression in anarchism rather than in liberalism, strictly so called. But there were a few Russian liberals, advocates of moderate constitutional reforms and believers in the *bourgeois* order as the surest way to social and political progress both in Russia and in western Europe. These, together with the senior representatives of the Tsarist bureaucracy, became Herzen's pre-eminent *bêtes noirs*. Among those who occur most frequently in Herzen's polemical writings are Turgenev, Granovsky, Annenkov, Herzen's ex-friend Ketcher, and especially Boris Chicherin and his associate Konstantin Kavelin.[85]

Chicherin (1828–1904) is a prominent and interesting figure in the history of Russian thought, for he was that unique phenomenon in Russia—an exponent of classical liberalism. He was a philosophical optimist and a perfectionist; he greatly valued the principles of law and order; he believed in a kind of absolute society, in which there are no vested interests, no pressure groups, and no frictions; he had a great predilection for the *bourgeoisie* and a profound respect for the rights of property, for the profit motive, for commerce and industry. His enlightened, somewhat legalistically inclined intellect enabled him to combine successfully, in religion, philosophy and politics, a moderate rationalism of a quasi-Hegelian type with an equally moderate empiricism; and his "administrative mind", to use Soloviev's felicitous description, was repelled by the slightest odour of anything extreme or rebellious.[86] At the beginning of Herzen's activities as a publicist, Chicherin, together with Kavelin, supplied him with material for his *Golosa iz Rossii* ("Voices from Russia"). "We are ready", he wrote, however, in a letter to the editor of the *Voices*, "to gather round every even slightly liberal Government and support it with all the power at our disposal, for we are firmly convinced that one can act and attain some results only through the Government. . . . What is there in common between you and us? . . . Revolutionary theories are not only inapplicable to us but are contrary to all our convictions, and shock our moral feeling. . . . Your revolutionary theories will never find any

251

response in us, and the bloody banner flying over your tribune provokes our indignation and disgust."[87]

Later on a meeting took place between Chicherin and Herzen in London which they both described in their respective memoirs. Chicherin's aim to try, as he put it, to "guide Herzen in a direction favourable to Russia" was unavailing. Their subsequent polemic on the pages of *The Bell* only served to deepen the difference. In setting himself over against what he called Chicherin's "liberal conservatism", "civic religion" and "administrative progress", Herzen declared that he himself and his associates wanted to be "Russia's protest, her cry of liberation and of pain: we wished to be those who expose the evil-doers . . . ; we wished to be the vengeance of the Russian, and his irony too". "If all mankind could believe you", Herzen addressed himself to Chicherin, "it might become rational but would die of world-wide boredom. The late Filimonov put as an inscription on his 'fool's cap': *Si la raison dominait le monde, il ne s'y passerait rien.*" "We are afraid of the Russian Germans and the German Russians, the learned friends of our western doctrinaires, who wear out the old clothes of political economy, jurisprudence, and the rest—centralizers *à la française* and bureaucrats *à la russe*. They are more businesslike than the gentry and more honest than the officials: that is just why we are afraid of them. . . . Their opinions are liberal, they favour reasonable freedom and moderate progress; they speak against bribery and the law of the jungle; they wish to make improvements on evil and, for all we know, will compel us to respect the scrivener, the police, the provincial law-courts. . . . They will reconcile us with all that we hate and despise, and, by improving, consolidate all that should be thrown overboard." "We must smite you, you, cold doctrinaires; you, apprentices of false science; you, who reign and deaden everything; you, who must be swept away." For his part, Chicherin politely and soberly summed up their differences as "the contrast between liberalism and radicalism, or perhaps something else besides".[88] The differences grew still more when *The Bell* began to reflect the dissatisfaction which many felt with Alexander's agrarian and educational reforms, when Herzen openly admitted the fruitlessness of mere appeals and threats, and allowed his language to become more extreme and explosive than ever.

Meanwhile, Herzen turned to the younger generation, especially to the students, against whom the Tsars waged a savage and almost unremitting war throughout the nineteenth century and whose revolutionary mood on the eve of the Reform led to a number of new repressive measures by the Government. "Listen!" he wrote to the students who had been expelled from the Petersburg University as a result of measures taken by the Minister of Education, Putyatin, "listen, since the darkness does not prevent you from hearing: from all parts of our vast land, from the Don to the Urals, from the Volga and the Dnieper, you hear a groaning and grumbling of increasing volume. That is the first roar of the ocean waves, which are seething, threatening a storm after the frightful and wearying calm: Go among the people! Go to the people! That is your place, outcasts of learning. Show the Bistroms [a Tsarist General] that you will become, not Government clerks, but soldiers; not mercenaries without a country, but soldiers of the Russian people!" Herzen's call was, in fact, an incitement to revolution (and that is how it was interpreted in Government and in liberal circles) as well as an appeal to educate and enlighten the masses of the people; and the phrase "going among the people" became the motto of that radical movement which is known as populism and which absorbed a large section of the younger intelligentsia.[89]

Yet opposition to Herzen came not only from the liberals but also from the radical wing. The charge made in this quarter was that Herzen's appeals contained too much of "jejune revolutionary phraseology", too much inane romantic feeling, elation, even vanity, that his "appeals to Alexander from the banks of the Thames" were nugatory and irrelevant. A frequently quoted letter, published in *The Bell* on March 1, 1860, signed "A Russian" and dubiously attributed to Chernyshevsky, warned Herzen not "to delude himself with hopes": "Don't mislead others, don't deprive them of energy, for they might put it to good use. Hope in the matter of politics is a golden chain, which is easily turned into fetters by him who offers it. No, our position is awful, intolerable: only the axe can liberate us, and nothing but the axe will be of any use. . . . You have done everything you could to advance a peaceful solution of the matter, but now change your tone, and let your *Bell* not call for prayers, but sound the tocsin! Call upon Russia to take up the axe! Farewell, and remember that for hundreds of years Russia was ruined by faith and the good intentions of the Tsars."

Herzen scarcely needed the warning, for these apprehensions were largely his own, and, in fact, he could not describe it otherwise than "an extreme expression of our own trend". But he began to be annoyed by the increasingly truculent tone of his radical correspondents, by their reproach to him of being out of date, of displaying the restlessness of someone uneasily conscious of having run his course. It was an instance of the well-known rift between the Fathers and the Sons described in Turgenev's novel. No profound ideological divergences can be detected in Herzen's disagreement with the new generation. Even in as much as it described itself, or was described by others, as nihilistic, Herzen was able to produce evidence of a nihilism that was deeper and more thorough-going than anything conceived by the Bazarovs of his day. Herzen himself pointed out that the new generation has failed to produce any new ideas. "And if it has," he asked, "where are they?"[90]

Nevertheless, the Sons represented, typologically if not ideologically, a new phenomenon, very different from the intelligentsia of the "remarkable decade" to which Herzen belonged. They were sterner, harsher, stiffer and more prosaic. Their manner was obtuse and matter-of-fact. Their opinions were clear-cut and unambiguous. They had an element of what Herzen called Arakcheevian ruthlessness, "a passionate rigidity, and an eagerness to despatch their victims. To satisfy his grenadier ideal, Arakcheev flogged living peasants to death; they flog to death ideas, the arts, humanity, past leaders, anything you like." They were plebeian by origin and in outlook, immune from the artistic and aesthetic culture, from the subtleties and sophistications of the educated gentry, or even of the *raznochintsy* of Belinsky's generation. Many of their leading spokesmen—Nicolas Chernyshevsky (1828–89), Nicolas Dobrolyubov (1836–61), Maxim Antonovich (1835–1918), and others— were sons of priests, trained in theological seminaries, and they kept much of the confined moral and intellectual atmosphere in which they were brought up but against which they had revolted. Herzen detected in them "the oligarchic pretension of the have-nots to be the exclusive sufferers from the social system and to possess a monopoly of the feeling of social injustice". "Neither through Christian pity", he told them, "nor through democratic envy will you ever get beyond philanthropy and violent spoliation, the division of property and universal poverty. In the Church it has remained a theme for rhetoric and a sentimental exercise in compassion; in the ultra-democrats . . . it has confined itself to the feeling of envy and hatred; and in neither case has it gone on to any constructive ideas, to any practical results."[91]

A polemic ensued between Herzen and Nekrasov's *Sovremennik* ("The Contemporary"), the new radicals' literary organ, now in charge of Chernyshevsky and Dobrolyubov. Like Chicherin before him, Chernyshevsky proceeded to London in order to meet Herzen and to clarify the position. The result of the meeting can be gauged from Herzen's article in *The Bell* of October 15, 1860, entitled *Lyshnie lyudi i zhelcheviki* ("The Superfluous Men and the Bilious Ones"). The bilious ones were the Sons, whose "spreading bile" drove Herzen to the point of siding with the "superfluous men". The bilious ones had lost "the juvenility of their youth", and "have faded without ever blossoming". "They know nothing of space and freedom, nothing of frank speech. They bear on their countenances deep traces of a soul roughly handled and wounded. Every one of them had some special neurosis, and apart from that special neurosis they all had one in common, a sort of devouring, irritable and distorted vanity. The denial of every right, the humiliations they had endured developed a secret craving for admiration; these undeveloped prodigies, these unsuccessful geniuses, concealed themselves under a mask of humility and modesty. All of them were hypochondriacs and physically ill, did not drink wine, and were afraid of open windows; all looked with studied despair at the present, and reminded one of monks who from love for their neighbour came to hating all humanity, and cursed everything in the world from desire to bless something." "They mark, undoubtedly, a step forward, but it is a painful step." "The superfluous men are disappearing from the horizon; their place is taken by the bilious ones. Yet these also will disappear soon: they are too morose, they work too much on other people's nerves to keep afloat for long. Life, despite eighteen centuries of Christian contrition, remains disconcertingly faithful to its Epicurean ways, and will not be able to endure for long the gloom-inspiring Daniels by the waters of Petersburg who mournfully reproach people for dining without gnashing their teeth and for forgetting the miseries of this world while admiring a picture or listening to music." "Yes, the iron had entered deeply into their souls. The Petersburg world in which they had lived has left its imprint on them; it was thence they took their restless tone, their language—*saccadé*, yet suddenly passing into bureaucratic vapidity—their elusive meekness and haughty fault-finding, their intentional frigidity and readiness on any occasion to break out into abuse, the insulting way in which they scorned to justify themselves, and the uneasy intolerance of the director of a Government department . . . Tone is not a matter of no importance. . . . Extremely kind at heart and noble in theory, they, I mean our bilious ones, may drive an angel to fighting and a saint to cursing by their tone."

Such an estimate was not, perhaps, surprising, if one learns that Chernyshevsky, for his part, spoke of Herzen as at best "a restless old man who had lost his wits" and "still imagines himself sharpening his tongue with Khomyakov in the aristocratic salons of Moscow", at worst "a mammoth's carcass" or "an interesting fossilized bone". Herzen was mistaken in thinking that the bilious ones were a passing phenomenon: in fact they were to dominate the intellectual and cultural, if not the social and political stage in Russia for some decades to come. But then, while exposing their mental poverty and repudiating their tone and manner, Herzen did not fail to recognize the importance of the new revolutionary generation as a liberating force, and could not deny their contemporaneity, their greater closeness to the people. "You and I", he wrote to Ogarev in 1868, pathetically, humbly, but with dignity, "belong to the old pioneers, to the 'sowers', who early in the morning, about forty years ago, went out to plough the land, over which Nicolas indulged in his savage man-hunting, trampling down everything—fruit and buds. The seeds which we and our few friends inherited from our great predecessors we threw into new furrows and nothing perished. . . . The new generation is going its way. It does not need our advice. It has come of age, and is aware of that. To others we have nothing to say."

The irony was that the growing estrangement from the radical Sons coincided with the complete rift with the liberal and not-so-liberal

Fathers. At this difficult moment *The Bell* drove matters to an extremity by issuing an open challenge to rebellion. In 1861, as we know, Bakunin appeared in London: his presence and influence acted like oil on the flame of Herzen's pro-Polish sympathies. Whatever passing hesitations and misgivings Herzen may have entertained at times, the position he did adopt in the end in regard to the events in Poland in 1862–3 squared with his fundamental revolutionary conviction.[92] This served to repel from him finally all those sections of opinion in Russia which were anti-revolutionary and, on the other hand, succeeded only momentarily in winning the favour of the young radicals. By 1866 the conflict with the latter was as complete as with the liberals, and, significantly enough, it was provoked by an article of Herzen's in December of that year in which he boldly stated that there had never been any basic ideological opposition between the movement led by Chernyshevsky (now in exile in Siberia) and that represented by Ogarev and himself abroad. The reaction, however, came not from within Russia, but from revolutionary *émigré* circles in Geneva, to which Herzen had by then transferred his disunited family and his printing-press together with *The Bell*.

Herzen's relations with the Russian political exiles in western Europe during the last five years of his life is a tangled subject, and this is not the place to attempt to unravel it.[93] It will be sufficient to mention a few of the fundamental reasons for their mutual hostility, which, despite various efforts towards a *rapprochement*, persisted until Herzen's death. For Herzen, whose sensitivity was more developed than his capacity for self-adaptation, many disagreements with his exiled countrymen were due to the peculiar spirit prevalent among political *émigrés* of all times, all nationalities and all political allegiances. At one time he thought, in what he described as "a fit of irritation and bitter mirth", of writing a pamphlet "in the manner of Grandville's illustrations: *Les refugiés peints par eux-mêmes*". He never did write it, although his memoirs contain a number of brilliant sketches of the multi-national *émigré* communities in the various capitals of Europe. He watched the "frustrated development" of the refugees, their invariable progression "from the activities of life into the domain of fantasy. Leaving their native land with concealed anger, with the continual thought of going back to it on the morrow, men make no advance, but are continually thrown back upon the past; . . . irritation and trivial but exasperated disputes prevent their escaping from the familiar circle of questions, thoughts, and memories which make up an oppressive binding tradition. Men in general, and especially men in such an exceptional position, have a passion for formalism, for the coterie spirit, for looking their part, that they immediately fall into a groove and acquire a doctrinaire stamp. All exiles, cut off from the living environment to which they have belonged, shut their eyes to avoid seeing bitter truths, and grow more and more accustomed to a narrow, fantastic circle consisting of inert memories and hopes that will never be realized. Add to this, aloofness from all who are not exiles and an element of exasperation, suspicion, exclusiveness, and jealousy, and this new stiff-necked Israel becomes perfectly comprehensible."[94]

Unfortunately the new stiff-necked Israelites also believed themselves to be major political strategists, whereas in fact they were provincial busy-bodies consumed by watchfulness, paralysed by fear and suspicion, and engaged, like all political *émigrés*, in a continual search for scapegoats on to whose heads they might transfer their own frustrations. For Herzen such an attitude was the worst foundation, not only for understanding, but even for relevant political action; and when he saw it feeding, and being fed by, reckless and irrational hatreds, the results appeared to him both ludicrous and dangerous. He watched the characteristic instinct of fear plunging its victims into a world of nightmares, in which nothing operates but the pernicious mythology of dividing mankind into sheep and goats, in which facts become irrelevant, and the nightmares more and more fantastic. By fostering his fears and hatreds the *émigré* loses his capacity for freedom, for independent thought and action. Having himself suffered injustice, he soon forgets the justice whose ends he claims to serve, and turns reactionary, even though he may profess revolution. Herzen, even at his most violent and revolutionary, never lost this inward freedom, never as a human being became consumed and dulled. His clear-sighted but deeply-felt attachment to Russia, and understanding of her historical pathways, which remained no more intelligible to the young Russian Genevese politicians than to his liberal, westernizing antagonists, were yet another sign that he never let extraneous obsessions and hatreds paralyse his humanity or impede his comprehension. That is why one of the main concrete factors dividing Herzen from his exiled co-revolutionaries was his conviction that revolution can proceed, in the last resort, only from social and political movements within Russia, and not as a result of interventions, plotting and conspiracies from without, by *émigrés*, whose importance he considered to be altogether inflated or even illusory.[95]

For the Genevese Russians, on the other hand, such reactions meant merely indifference to the lowly business of revolution on the part of an outmoded, fastidious *grand seigneur*. In addition, the considerable wealth of the *grand seigneur* was evidently insufficient to support all the needy Russian *émigrés* in Geneva, although there were few whom he did not support; and, furthermore, it was withheld when it came to financing the lives and activities of the more obnoxious among them. There ensued a campaign of vilification against Herzen, who at times could scarcely show himself in the streets of Geneva without being subjected to the jeers and insults of his radical compatriots. Herzen's article, mentioned above, provided an opportunity for a decisive confrontation, and Alexander Serno-Solovievich, his one-time friend and collaborator, and the ablest of his new radical opponents, published an open letter which was privately printed in Vevey in 1867, under the title *Nashi domashnie dela* ("Our Domestic Affairs"). This is what he wrote to Herzen:

"I have long since ceased to read, or at any rate to be interested in, your news-sheet [*The Bell*]. Hackneyed, long familiar sounds; rhetorical phrases and appeals, ancient variations on an ancient theme; witticisms, sometimes fairly clever, but more often flat; commonplaces about 'Land and Liberty'—all this has become too tedious, too boring, too repulsive. . . .

"Yes, the young generation has understood you. Having understood you, it has turned away from you in disgust; and you still dream that you are its guide, that you are 'a power and a force in the Russian State', that you are a leader and representative of youth. You our leader? Ha! Ha! Ha! The young generation has long outstripped you by a whole head in its understanding of facts and events. Failing to perceive that you have been left behind, you flap your enfeebled wings with all your might; and then, when you see that people are only laughing at you, you go off in a rage and reproach the younger generation with ingratitude to their teacher, to the founder of their school, the first high-priest of Russian socialism! You are a poet, a painter, an artist, a story-teller, a novelist—anything you please, but *not* a political leader and still less a political thinker, the founder of a school and a doctrine. . . .

"So you were the complement of Chernyshevsky! You marched shoulder to shoulder with Chernyshevsky! Such an idea I never expected even from you, and I have studied you closely. . . . You the complement of Chernyshevsky! No, Mr. Herzen. It is too late now to take refuge behind Chernyshevsky! *Troppo tarde*, the opportunity has passed. Between you and Chernyshevsky there was not, and could not be, anything in common. You are two opposite elements which cannot exist side by side or near one another. You are the representatives of two hostile natures, which do not complement, but exterminate each other—so completely do you differ in everything, not only in your philosophy of life, but in your attitude to yourself and to other people, not only in general questions, but in the minutest details of your private life. . . .

"Come down to earth; forget that you are a great man; remember that the medals with your effigy were struck not by a grateful posterity, but by yourself out of your bloodstained wealth. Look more closely at what is going on around you, and you will then perhaps understand that dry leaves and paper kites interest nobody . . . that you, Mr. Herzen, are a dead man."[96]

Herzen read this vulgar execration in a mood of hopelessness, and wrote nothing in reply. No display of his incomparable superiority in polemical skill and apposite argumentation was appropriate, or would have served any purpose. If we were to look for an answer, we might find it in what Herzen said on a very different occasion some eight years before he received this squib. It is contained in his reply to a well-meaning Christian lady from Russia who called upon him to repent: "You say, then", Herzen wrote to her, "that I do nothing but bring doubt into the hearts of the younger generation and quicken its thirst. This 'nothing but', is it not itself something? The man who doubts will feel disturbed, will search for an issue from his doubt. The man whose thirst is quickened will seek to quench it. After the moral inertia of the last three decades, after the marasmus of senility that has contaminated the very heart of youth . . . every provocation to life, every human voice that hurls a question at man, destroying indifference . . . is a salutary voice. I am unable to provide the solution of which you speak. I am no teacher; I am a seeker, a fellow-traveller. You and I are seeking—that is, perhaps, why there is sympathy between us. I do not presume to tell them what is needed; the best I can hope to do is to show them fairly accurately what is *not* needed. The conflict, the dissatisfaction which you detect in me is, of course, absent in doctrinaires, as indeed in all religious people. . . . But if I have no doctrine, if I do not proclaim precepts from a mount, nor issue decrees from a chancery, why should I not shout about the slavery of man? . . . Why should I not preach the freeing of thought and conscience from all the lumber that has not passed through the purifying fire of the mind?"

Herzen was now completely alone. It was not only that he had lost the prestige which he had won in as far as he was preaching to his countrymen. They repudiated him as a man and a teacher alike. This was an extraordinary irony, for much as he may have tried to be a teacher and a propagandist, he was, in fact, remarkable not so much by what he said, as by the way in which he said it—by what he was; and this is more lasting than anything he may have been professing at any one time, even if it could not change society or save Russia. That his contemporaries should have renounced him as a man is his greatest failure, making him a very tragic and very heroic figure. Yet the failure of the great is more important than the success of lesser men, and Herzen's failure was not only tragic but also vital and fertilizing.

Notes

CHAPTER ONE, *pages* 1–45

¹ See, e.g., B. Yakovenko, *Ocherki russkoy filosofii* ("Essays in Russian Philosophy"), Prague, 1922; also G. Shpet, *Ocherk razvitya russkoy filosofii* ("Essay in the Development of Russian Philosophy"), Part I, Petrograd, 1922, one of the most important and readable, though unfinished, surveys of Russian thought; and, more outspokenly, the anonymous author of a penetrating and provocative essay in *The Times Literary Supplement*, March 27, 1953, entitled "Thinkers or Philosophers?"

² The most recent example of such claims is provided by V. Zenkovsky's *Istorya russkoy filosofii*, 2 vols., Paris, 1948–50 (English transl., *History of Russian Philosophy*, London, 1953). My references are to the Russian original. Its merit consists in a good bibliography and it may be most profitably used as a work of reference. But the obscure and tortuous arguments and a regrettable tendency to unctuous religiosity which attend Zenkovsky's exposition only serve to prove the precariousness of his claims, especially where they concern the teaching of numerous metaphysical writers whose speculative abstractions are seldom distinguished in thought and hardly ever in formulation.

³ The above mentioned Yakovenko is a case in point. His work is really a survival of Hegelian history writing, with its notion of philosophical development as a self-propelled dialectic of ideas.

⁴ *Iz istorii russkoy filosofii* ("From the History of Russian Philosophy"), edited by I. Shchipanov, Moscow, 1952, is a recent example of history writing which reduces human minds to the semblance of lifeless puppets. The works of Soviet writers on the history of philosophical, social and literary ideas in Russia, however, are very important and without them it is virtually impossible to study it.

⁵ G. Pavlovsky's contention in *Agricultural Russia on the Eve of the Revolution*, London, 1930, that throughout the history of Imperial Russia the State consistently upheld the interests of the peasants is belied, not only by the Imperial measures in the eighteenth century, but also by the avowed policy of Nicolas I after 1848. See V. Semevsky, *Krestyansky vopros v Rossii v XVIII veke i pervoy polovine XIX veka* in *Krestyansky Stroy* ("The Peasant Question in Russia in the 18th Century and First Half of the 19th Century"in "The Peasant System"), Petersburg, 1888; also E. Morokhovets, *Krestyanskaya reforma 1861 g.* ("The Peasant Reform of 1861"), Moscow, 1937.

⁶ See Ivanov-Razumnik's *Istorya russkoy obshchestvennoy mysli* ("History of Russian Social Thought"), 2 vols., Petersburg, 1911; vol. I contains a well-documented and vivid account of this aspect of nineteenth-century Russia.

⁷ See his *The Russian Peasant, and Other Studies*, London, 1942.

⁸ See the illuminating Story with this title by Gleb Uspensky (1840–1902).

⁹ The one striking exception is Patriarch Nikon (1605–81) whose claims to independent power resulted in his deposition by a Council on the charge (amongst other charges) of attempting to introduce the principle of papacy into the Orthodox Church.

[10] These claims are explicitly stated in Ivan's epistles to Prince Andrey Kurbsky and illustrated by the part he played in the "Hundred Chapters" Council (*Stoglav*) in 1551.

[11] "God has chosen Thee, my Lord, in His stead on earth and has elevated Thee to the throne, entrusting to Thee the favour and life of the whole of Orthodoxy", wrote Metropolitan Makary, member of Ivan IV's "Chosen Council", to the Tsar. See M. Dyakonov, *Vlast moskovskikh gosudarey* ("The Power of the Muscovite Sovereigns"), Petersburg, 1889. The Tsar's jurisdiction did not, however, extend to matters of belief, in the strict sense of the term. See V. Waldenberg, *Drevne-russkie uchenya o predelakh tsarskoy vlasti* ("The Ancient Russian Doctrines of the Limits of the Tsar's Power"), Petersburg, 1916.

[12] On early Christianity in Russia see G. Fedotov, *The Russian Religious Mind*, Harvard, 1946.

[13] A. Shchapov ascribes the Cossack search for freedom from the pressure of society (the case of Stenka Razin is particularly typical) to the Schism of the Old Believers. See his *Raskol* ("Schism"), Works, 2 vols., Petersburg, 1906, vol. I.

[14] See Pierre Pascal, *Avakuum et les débuts du raskol. La crise religieuse russe au XVII-e siècle en Russie*, Paris, 1938.

[15] This weapon has been extensively used and misused in the best work on the history of Russian religious and theological thought: *Puti russkovo bogoslovya* ("The Ways of Russian Theology"), Paris, 1937, by G. Florovsky, to which I shall refer at greater length in another connection.

[16] One of these historians, Zenkovsky, speaks of the theocratic order in Russia as an "expression of the mystical conception of history", and of the Tsar's power as—*horribile dictu*—"the point at which a meeting occurs of historical being with the will of God" (op. cit., vol. I, p. 50). To admit such claims requires the kind of historical and moral digestion that can swallow camels.

[17] Zenkovsky, ibid., p. 82.

[18] See, e.g., M. Iovchuk, in the already cited *Iz istorii russkoy filosofii*, pp. 16 ff.

[19] Novikov was condemned to fifteen years in the Schlüsselburg Fortress and Radishchev to ten years' exile in East Siberia, from where he returned in a state of mental derangement and committed suicide soon afterwards.

On early Russian journalism, see *Ocherki po istorii russkoy zhurnalistiki i kritiki* ("Essays in the History of Russian Journalism and Criticism"), Leningrad, 1950, I, part i.

[20] To maintain, as some historians do, that, subsequent to Peter's reforms, the Church "begins to adopt a freer attitude towards the State" and "for that very reason gives scope for free ecclesiastical thought" does not appear to have any meaning in the light of the actual historical evidence; and the detection of some mystifying "new tonality in the sounding of the Church principle" makes confusion worse confounded (see Zenkovsky, op. cit., ibid, p. 61 and elsewhere).

[21] One figure, however, stands out in this sea of eager ecclesiastical conformity: bishop Tikhon of Voronezh (1724–83). See the biographical and historical study of him by Nadezhda Gorodetsky (*Saint Tikhon Zadonsky*, London, 1951).

[22] The literature on this question is very extensive. The most useful documentary work in English is G. Fedotov's *A Treasury of Russian Spirituality*, New York, 1952. See also I. Smolich, *Leben und Lehre der Starzen*, Vienna, 1936.

[23] See, e.g., N. Berdyaev's autobiography *Dream and Reality*, London, 1950.

[24] Christopher Dawson in *Understanding Europe*, London, 1952. It is noteworthy that Charles Maurras (see *Romantisme et révolution*, Paris, 1925) and Henri Massis (see *Défence de l'occident*, Paris, 1927) speak of a similar "lopping away" with regard to practically everything east of the Rhine, although they do not confine this to the twentieth century.

[25] See his *Journey for Our Time*, London, 1953 (abridged English version of Custine's *La Russie en 1839*, 4 vols., Paris, 1843).

[26] After the publication of the first Letter, *Telescope*, the review which printed it, was suppresssed and Chaadaev declared, on special Imperial authority, a lunatic, and placed under medical and police supervision. He continued to live in Moscow and, as Herzen recalled later on in his *Memoirs*, "Chaadaev's melancholy and original figure stood out sharply like a mournful reproach against the faded and dreary background of Moscow 'high life'. . . . For ten years he stood with folded arms, by some column, by some tree on the boulevard, in drawing-rooms and theatres, at the club, and, an embodied veto, a living protest, gazed at the vortex of faces senselessly twisting and turning about him. He became whimsical and eccentric, held himself aloof from society, yet could not leave it altogether, then uttered his message, quietly concealing it, just as in his features he concealed passion under a layer of ice." Zenkovsky is probably right in stressing that Chaadaev's views on Russia, which, by the way, subsequently changed to a belief in her mission to resolve the problems of western European civilization, are by no means the most important aspect of his thought. But Zenkovsky's general tendency to system-mongering moves him to ascribe to Chaadaev a coherent philosophical system, which is not his. The best works on Chaadaev are M. Gershenzon's *P. Y. Chaadaev, Zhizn i myshlenie* ("P. Y. Chaadaev. Life and Thought"), Petersburg, 1908; and Ch. Quenet's *Tchaadaeff et ses lettres philosophiques*, Paris, 1931.

[27] The most recent example of such abstractions is to be found in *The Limits and Divisions of European History*, London, 1950, by O. Halecki, who, however, being a Pole, has a familiar Polish axe to grind. They have been convincingly refuted by D. Obolensky in "Russia's Byzantine Heritage", *Oxford Slavonic Papers*, vol. I, 1950. This essay gives the lie to a number of other misleading notions concerning "Russia and the West". See also the illuminating essays in G. Barraclough's *History in a Changing World*, Oxford, 1955.

[28] The most extreme instance is that of the Russian precursor of Spengler, Nicolas Danilevsky (1822–95), who, in his *Russia and Europe*, draws a sharp line of separation between Russia and western Europe and denies Russia any share or part in European civilization.

[29] See Shpet's (op. cit.) not very flattering account of these and other philosophical tendencies in eighteenth-century Russia.

[30] More than a hundred translations of Voltaire appeared in Russia before the end of the eighteenth century.

[31] All this has been cuttingly satirized in Fonvizin's (1744–92) comedy *The Brigadier General*. But the classical theatre in Russia, under the distinguished patronage of Alexander Sumarokov (1717–74) was itself infected with this mentality. See A. Veselovsky, *Zapadnoe vliyanie v russkoy literature* ("Western Influence in Russian Literature"), Moscow, 1896.

[32] See A. Pypin's *Russkoe masonstvo XVIII veka i pervoy chetverti XIX veka* ("Russian Masonry in the Eighteenth Century and the First Quarter of the Nineteenth Century"), Moscow, 1916; and the illuminating analysis in Florovsky's book quoted above.

[33] See V. Bogolyubov, *Novikov i evo vremya* ("Novikov and His Time"), Moscow, 1916.

[34] See the editor's essay on Radishchev's social, political and philosophical views in *From the History of Russian Philosophy* mentioned above.

[35] *Istorya molodoy Rossii* ("A History of Young Russia"), Moscow-Petrograd, 1923.

[36] A Nikitenko, *Zapiski i Dnevnik, 1804–1877. Moya povest o samom sebe i o tom chemu svidetel v zhizni byl* ("Notes and Diary, 1804–1877. My Account of Myself and of What I Have Witnessed in Life"), 2 vols., Petersburg, 1904–5, vol. I, p. 327.

[37] See his *Romantic Exiles*. A Nineteenth-Century Portrait Gallery, London, 1933.

[38] His Notes and Diary are an important source for the study of some nineteenth-century Russian thinkers. See *Literaturnoe Nasledstvo* ("Literary Heritage"), nos. 22–4, Moscow, 1935. See also P. Sakulin, *Knyaz V. F. Odoevsky. Iz istorii russkovo idealizma* ("Prince V. F. Odoevsky. From the History of Russian Idealism"), Moscow, 1913, which contains an excellent account of early Russian idealism.

[39] For a fuller discussion of "sentimentalism" among the intelligentsia of the early 'thirties see D. Ovsyaniko-Kulikovsky's *Istorya russkoy intelligentsii* ("History of the Russian Intelligentsia"), Collected Works, 9 vols., Moscow-Petrograd, 1923–4, vol. VII.

[40] The thick and damp philosophico-theological fog produced by this manner of thinking and writing survives until today. It can be seen in the pages of most modern Russian speculative religious writers.

[41] A. Herzen, *Byloe i Dumy* (English transl., *My Past and Thoughts*, 6 vols., London, 1924, vol. II, pp. 117–18), hereafter referred to as *Memoirs*. I quote throughout from the English translation, with changes whenever they seem indicated.

[42] See D. Chizhevsky, *Gegel v Rossii* ("Hegel in Russia"), Paris, 1939, p. 214, and the whole chapter. There is a preliminary German version of this important work by the author himself entitled *Hegel bei den Slaven*, Reichenberg i. B., 1934. My references are to the Russian text.

[43] *Memoirs*, ibid., p. 115.

[44] P. Annenkov, *Zamechatelnoe desyatiletie* (" The Remarkable Decade") in *Vospominanya i kriticheskie ocherki* ("Reminiscences and Critical Essays"), Part III, Petersburg, 1881, p. 126.

[45] On the rôle of the Circles in Belinsky's intellectual development see A. Pypin's *Belinsky, evo zhizn i perepiska* ("Belinsky, His Life and Correspondence"), 2 vols., Petersburg, 1876, vol. I, ch. iii. See also N. Brodsky, *Literaturnye kruzhki i salony* ("Literary Circles and Salons"), Leningrad, 1929.

[46] See the depressing account in Nikitenko's Diary quoted above. Granovsky, the eminently moderate, gentle and very popular professor of history at the University of Moscow, who played a rôle of some importance in the "remarkable decade", wrote to a friend in 1849: "I am compelled daily to endure . . . rude attacks. The authorities look disapprovingly on my relations with the students. . . . They will probably turn me out soon. . . . Desert all around." In the same year Metropolitan Philaret (Drozdov) summoned Granovsky: "He demanded my explanation", Granovsky continues, "why I do not mention in my history lectures 'the will of God' which governs the events and the destiny of the nations. 'I am informed', he said, 'that you are a harmful professor, that you darken the minds of the loyal sons of our Sovereign. . . . In your activity there is something secretive; I must know what your beliefs are.' " See *T. N. Granovsky i evo perepiska* ("T. N. Granovsky and His Correspondence"), 2 vols., Moscow, 1897 (ed. by A. Stankevich) vol. I, p. 276 f.

[47] The note was published after the first complete edition of Turgenev's works (1883) in *Vestnik Evropy* ("The Messenger of Europe"), January 1899.

[48] Herzen, op. cit., ibid.

[49] See the above quoted *Hegel in Russia*, ch. iv. Gershenzon (op. cit.) gives a much more convincing estimate of Stankevich's ideas and influence. As in the case of so many of his contemporaries Stankevich's views are contained mainly in his letters (see N. V. Stankevich, *Perepiska* ["Correspondence"], Moscow, 1914).

[50] See Annenkov, op. cit. One of the best documented accounts of the period is to be found in the standard work on the young Bakunin by A. Kornilov, *Molodye gody Bakunina. Iz istorii russkovo romantizma.* ("The Young Years of Bakunin. From the History of Russian Romanticism"), Moscow, 1915. An excel-

lent summary of Stankevich's real importance was given by Bakunin: "Il était impossible de vivre près de lui", he writes, "sans se sentir en quelque sorte amélioré et ennobli. En sa présence aucune pensée lache ou triviale, aucun instinct mauvais ne semblait possible; les hommes les plus ordinaires cessaient de l'être sous son influence. Il appartenait à cette catégorie de natures à la fois riches et exquises qui . . . [sont] douées d'un grand genie [mais] qui ne le manifestent par aucun grand acte historique, ni par aucune création, soit scientifique, soit artistique, soit industrielle; qui n'ont jamais rien entrepris, rien fait, rien écrit, et dont toute l'action s'est concentrée et s'est resumée dans leur vie personelle, et qui néanmoins ont laissé après eux dans l'histoire par l'action, exclusivement personelle, il est vrai, mais tout de même très puissante, qu'ils ont exercée sur leur entourage immédiat, des traces profondes. . . ." (Œuvres, 6 vols., Paris, 1895–1913, vol. III, pp. 389–90).

CHAPTER TWO, pages 46–107

[1] Annenkov, op. cit., p. 11. Alexander Komarov was an engineer who dabbled in literature and played the rôle of a Maecenas.

[2] Annenkov, op. cit., ibid.

[3] See particularly his article, written while still in Moscow, about Zhukovsky's poem on the anniversary of the Battle of Borodino, and published in Otechestvennye Zapiski ("Annals of the Fatherland") in 1839.

[4] All the relevant documents pertaining to this incident are to be found in Literaturnoe Nasledstvo ("Literary Heritage"), no. 56, Moscow, 1950.

[5] The most interesting evidence is contained in the already quoted reminiscences by Herzen, Turgenev and Annenkov; also in K. Kavelin's Vospominanya o V. G. Belinskom ("Reminiscences of V. G. Belinsky"), Collected Works, 3 vols., Petersburg, 1899, vol. II; in I. Panaev's Vospominanya ("Reminiscences"), Academia, Leningrad, 1928; in Vospominanya ("Reminiscences"), Academia, Leningrad, 1927, by Panaev's wife (A. Panaeva-Golovacheva); in A. Goncharov's Biographical Note to Pypin (1874) in connection with the latter's preparation for the well-known biography of Belinsky; and in Dostoevsky's Dnevnik Pisatelya ("Diary of a Writer"), Complete Works, 18 vols., Petersburg, 1906, vol. X (1873). Unless otherwise stated, all quotations from the respective authors are from these works. The most satisfactory biography of Belinsky is Letopis zhizni Belinskovo ("The Chronicle of Belinsky's Life"), edited by N. Piksanov, Moscow, 1924.

[6] It is curious that Chizhevsky (op. cit.), who regards Belinsky as one of the most over-rated figures in the history of Russian thought and letters, and who has scarcely anything to say in his favour, should be full of praise for his style and language.

[7] So far as the censorship is concerned, its treatment of Belinsky's writings appears to have been rather wayward: it was uncompromising and ruthless after his death, but tended to treat them during his lifetime as wild and mystifying nonsense which could be tolerated on account of their very unintelligibility. This did not prevent Count Orlov, who later was to play such an ugly rôle in impeding the plans for the emancipation of the serfs, from ordering the censors "to subject all Belinsky's writings to the most severe examination before publication". See M. K. Lemke, Nikolaevskie zhandarmy i literatura 1826–1855 gg ("Nicolaian Policemen and Literature between 1826 and 1855"), Petersburg, 1908. Belinsky himself wrote in this connection not long before his death: "Nature has condemned me to bark like a dog and howl like a jackal, but circumstances compel me to purr like a cat and twirl the tail like a fox."

[8] Such reactions to Belinsky persisted even after his death. Some of the most abusive later pronouncements about him belong to the sycophantic pen of the

conservative journalist Ksenofont Polevoy who called him "a man possessed by the devil", "an impudent wretch intent on discrediting everything and dragging it through the mire". Polevoy concludes that "it is better to forget him altogether". See *Severnaya Pchela* ("The Northern Bee"), no. 229, Petersburg, 1859.

⁹ *O kritike i literaturnykh mnenyakh Moskovskovo Nablyudatelya* ("On the Criticism and Literary Opinions of the 'Moscow Observer' "). Unless otherwise stated, I quote throughout from S. Vengerov's edition of Belinsky's works, 12 vols., Petersburg, 1900, hereafter referred to as *Works*. There is an English edition of Belinsky's *Select Philosophical Works*, Moscow, 1948.

¹⁰ In one of his letters he confessed that, while feeling no inclination to dislike people for personal injuries, he was "capable of hating a man for difference of conviction" (see *Pisma Belinskovo* ["The Letters of Belinsky"], edited by E. Lyatsky, 3 vols., Petersburg, 1914, vol. III, hereafter referred to as *Letters*). Such differences were frequently accompanied by dramatic scenes which have all the proverbial qualities of "Russianness", even among people who were less prone to angry convictions than Belinsky. Thus, during a very critical phase in the relations between the Westerners and the Slavophils, Konstantin Aksakov appeared in Granovsky's flat in the middle of the night, woke him up, threw himself into his arms and embraced him firmly. He then proceeded to explain that he had come to fulfil one of the most painful duties in his life, namely, to sever all relations with him and to say farewell for the last time as to a dearest friend he was about to lose, notwithstanding the deep admiration and affection he felt towards him personally. In vain did Granovsky (who was a very moderate Westerner) try to persuade Aksakov to look more detachedly at their differences. In vain did he impress upon him that, apart from the ultimate destiny of Slavdom and the messianic mission of the Russian people, there were other bonds which united them and which could in no way be endangered by these differences. Aksakov remained adamant and eventually left him (for ever) in a state of extreme agitation, tears pouring down his cheeks.

¹¹ The incident refers, significantly enough, to a period when Belinsky had left far behind his romantic phase of "art for art's sake" (see below).

¹² Herzen, op. cit., vol. II, p. 294. See also Herzen's description of his reconciliation with Belinsky, ibid., p. 127. About *Moskvityanin*, see below, p. 135.

¹³ See N. Tyutchev's Note on Belinsky in vol. III of Belinsky's *Letters*.

¹⁴ The reviews in which Belinsky collaborated are, in chronological order:

1833–6: *Telescop—Molva* ("Telescope" and its Supplement "Rumour"), edited by N. Nadezhdin.

1838–9: *Moskovsky Nablyudatel* ("The Moscow Observer"), edited by M. Bakunin and Belinsky himself.

1839–46: *Otechestvennye Zapiski* ("Annals of the Fatherland"), edited by A. Kraevsky.

1840: *Literaturnaya Gazeta* ("The Literary Gazette"), edited by A. Kraevsky.

1847–48: *Sovremennik* ("The Contemporary"), owned by Nekrasov and Panaev and officially edited by A. Nikitenko.

Belinsky's average salary for contributions to these journals (he had practically speaking no other income) was 130 roubles, i.e. about £7, a month, but Nadezhdin paid only 60 roubles.

¹⁵ The latter wrote that "for Belinsky there was nowhere to learn: our routine-ridden Universities could not satisfy his highly logical [!] mind; the banality of most of our professors evoked nothing but contempt in him. Senseless persecutions—no one knew to what purpose—gave vent to his bile, which permeated his original philosophical development and drove his fearless syllogistics [!] to the limits of the extreme." V. F. Odoevsky, *Iz bumag kn. S. F. Odoevskovo* ("From the Papers of Prince S. F. Odoevsky"); *Russky Arkhiv* ("The Russian Archive"), 1874, I, p. 341.

¹⁶ See Annenkov, op. cit., p. 5.

¹⁷ Op. cit., p. 342.

¹⁸ *Belinsky. Sbornik statey* ("Belinsky. Collection of Articles"), Moscow, 1923. Next to Ivanov-Razumnik's *Velikie iskanya*. *Literatura i obshchestvennost* ("Great Searchings. Literature and Society"), Petersburg, 1910, vol. III, and the Commentary to Belinsky's works in 3 vols. by the same author, I found Plekhanov's work the most interesting among the considerable number of books and essays on Belinsky. Ivanov-Razumnik's section on Belinsky in the *History of Russian Social Thought* (vol. I), mentioned above, is less helpful. See also the already quoted standard work by A. Pypin (*Belinsky, His Life and Correspondence*), which is thorough but dull. He stresses, with some justification if perhaps for the wrong reasons, the last period in Belinsky's development which he regards as "the natural outcome of all his activities" (vol. II, p. 343). There is a great deal of material, especially on this latter period, in P. Sakulin's *Russkaya literatura i sotsializm* ("Russian Literature and Socialism"), Moscow, 1924, ch. iii. The most important studies on Belinsky in other than the Russian language are contained in P. Milyukov's *Le mouvement intellectuel russe*, Paris, 1919; in T. Masaryk's *The Spirit of Russia*, London, 1919; in A. Koyré's *La philosophie et le problème national en Russie au début du XIXe siècle*, Paris, 1929; and in *Etudes sur l'histoire de la pensée philosophique en Russie*, Paris, 1950, by the same author. See also Richard Hare's *Pioneers of Russian Social Thought*, London, 1951. For further bibliographical details see Masaryk, Koyré, and Zenkovsky. H. E. Bowman's *Vissarion Belinsky, 1811–1878*, Harvard, 1955, came out after the present work was nearly finished.

¹⁹ See Belinsky's letters to Botkin, who furnished him from time to time with a hotch-potch of philosophical opinions held by the members of their Moscow Circle. Whatever the precipitancy and roughness of their manner, they provide evidence of his critical mind and philosophical acumen. On Belinsky's independent position among his Circle friends see Pypin, op. cit., vol. I, ch. iii. See also the evidence to that effect in Kavelin's *Reminiscences*.

²⁰ See his *System des transzendentalen Idealismus*, *Sämtliche Werke*, 10 + 5 vols., Stuttgart, 1858, Abt. 1, vol. III, chs. I, II, III. About Schelling's influence on Belinsky and other Russians see the well-documented *Schellings Einfluss in der russischen Literatur der 20-er und 30-er Jahre des 19 Jahrhunderts*, Leipzig, 1939, by V. Sechkarev.

²¹ This emphasis is recognizable in all his contributions during this early period, and especially in his *Opyt sistemy nravstvennoy filosofii* (" Essay in a System of Moral Philosophy"), written in 1838. Most of these articles are literary criticism interspersed with metaphysical speculations.

²² *Works*, vol. I, p. 318.

²³ There is a contemporary cartoon representing a Fichtean goose. The poor bird has a liver so large that it no longer knows whether it is a goose or a liver. On its belly is the caption "I = I".

²⁴ *Letters*, vol. I, p. 213.

²⁵ Fichte's works abound in utterances of unrelieved impersonalism. "Die gänzliche Vernichtung des Individuums und Verschmelzung desselben in absolut reine Vernunftform", he wrote in a book bearing the ironic title *Die Bestimmung des Menschen*, "ist letztes Ziel der endlichen Vernunft". "Nicht das Ich hat Bewusstsein, sondern das Bewusstsein hat das Ich"; "die Vernunft ist Zweck, die Personlichkeit Mittel". In the end, the word "subjective" becomes a form of abuse. See *Sämtliche Werke*, 8 vols., Berlin, 1845, vol. II, p. 608; vol. III, p. ii. It is strange that German romantic thought which, in Herder, began with an affirmation of the "*undurchdringliche Geheimnis des Characters*" should have issued in such philosophical dehumanization.

²⁶ *Select Philosophical Works* (Russian edition), Moscow, 1948, vol. I, p. 544.

²⁷ Everything was "absolute" at the time, even the expression on Schelling's face, as Pyotr Kireevsky discovered when he met him in Germany.

²⁸ So far as I know Hegel is the only modern idealist philosopher whose works have been published in Russian after the Revolution. On Hegel in Russia, see the already quoted book by Chizhevsky, the best on the subject. To suggest, as Masaryk does, that all Slavophils were Schellingians and all Westerners Hegelians is incorrect. But the Westerners were concerned mainly with the social and revolutionary implications of Hegelianism, whilst the Slavophils' interest in Hegel confirms one's suspicion that all German philosophers are disguised theologians. It should be noted also that many characteristic features of Hegel's philosophy were drawn from Schelling.

²⁹ See *The Russian Idea*, London, 1947.

³⁰ Other examples of Hegel's good fortune in Russia have already been quoted in the introductory chapter. I will add one more: the encounter of the hero of Gogol's *Dead Souls*, Chichikov, with the Hegelian spectre in the library of Colonel Kochkarev. "Six huge volumes emerged before his eyes under the title of *Preparatory Introduction into the Realm of Thought. The Theory of Generality. Conjunction and Substance as Applied to the Understanding of the Organic Principles of the Mutual Disjunction of Social Productivity.*"

³¹ *Collected Works*, Petrograd, 1919, vol. III, pp. 753–4; *Letters*, vol. I, p. 339; *Works*, vol. XI, p. 272.

³² *Letters*, vol. I, pp. 228, 204.

³³ Op. cit., vol. II, p. 5

³⁴ Plekhanov (see "Belinsky and 'Rational Reality' ", op. cit.) shows conclusively that this was, in fact, the current interpretation of Hegel's proposition in contemporary German Hegelian circles.

³⁵ See *Gore ot uma* ("Woe from Wit"); *Menzel, kritik Goethe* ("Menzel, Goethe's Critic"); *Rechi, proiznesennye v torzhestvennom sobranii moskovskovo universiteta 11 iyunya 1838 goda* ("Speeches made at the Solemn Meeting of the University of Moscow on the 11th of June 1838"), and other articles written in 1839 but published mainly in 1840 when Belinsky joined the Petersburg review *Annals of the Fatherland*. All these tell the excruciating tale of his "reconciliation". Panaev recalls how Belinsky told him with great agitation à propos of these articles: " 'I am not ashamed, I am proud of them. . . . Why should I respect the devil knows whose talk and opinions?' He came up and stopped in front of me. His pale face lit up, blood rushed to his head, his eyes aflame. 'I swear on my honour that nothing can bribe me.' . . . It would be easier for me to die of hunger—in any case I daily risk dying that way (on saying this he smiled in embarrassment)—than to trample on my human dignity, to degrade myself before anybody or to sell myself.' "

³⁶ What Herzen must have had in mind, however, was not Pushkin's poem of that name, but Zhukovsky's patriotic verse which Belinsky praised in his article.

³⁷ See *Works*, vol. I, pp. 1, 66, 67; vol. IX, pp. 66, 108.

³⁸ *Letters*, vol. I, pp. 229, 231, 235, 349.

³⁹ That Hegel was, in fact, responsible for a new form of idolatry is evident at least from his well-known theory of the State as "*die Wirklichkeit der sittlichen Idee*" and "*der Gang Gottes auf der Welt*". Fichte, who had climbed up to heaven by the ladder of thought and had groped about with daring hand in its empty chambers, fairly quickly turned into a creature bowed down with obsequious humility before the Prussian idol and wrote his *Anweisungen zum seligen Leben*. Hegel, on moving to Berlin, faired no better, for he, too, mistook the kingdom of Prussia for the kingdom of Heaven, except that, in addition, he came to believe that his own installation in the Prussian capital marked the highest and final stage of the world process. And, like all philosophers, both complained that they had never been understood.

[40] Op cit., p. 34.

[41] Chizhevsky (op. cit., p. 139) attributes Belinsky's renunciation of Hegel exclusively to what he chooses to call the "mental infection" of Bakunin, Herzen and Botkin as well as to the increasingly suffocating atmosphere of the Russia of Nicolas I. To do so is to overlook the evidence of the inner crisis through which Belinsky had passed. It is interesting that a similar and simultaneous move away from Hegel, though in a less striking and dramatic form, can be observed among the Slavophils. But Belinsky's crisis was predominantly moral in character, whereas theirs was religious.

[42] "Die Weltgeschichte", wrote Hegel in the Introduction to his *Philosophy of History*, "ist die Darstellung des göttlichen, absoluten Prozesses des Geistes in seinen höchsten Gestalten, dieses Stufenganges, wodurch er seine Wahrheit, das Selbstbewusstsein über sich erlangt." He assumes the unity of *"für sich"* and *"an sich"*, that is to say, the "determination" (*Bestimmung*) of the individual by a "permanent universal essence" (*bleibende Allgemeinheit des Wesens*). The purpose of history consists in the triumph of the general law over the individual. This law, admittedly, *"erscheint nicht als eine vor aller besonderen Wirklichkeit abgeschiedene, farblos reine Einheit"*. None the less, particularity (*"die Discretion der Einzelnheit"*) is only apparent (*"hat den Schein als ob sie als solche wäre"*). In actual fact its instances are but "moments or vanishing entities" (*Momente oder verschwindende Grössen*). The individual is justified solely as an "organ of universal Mind". See *Sämtliche Werke*, 26 vols., Stuttgart, 1935, vol. II, pp. 380 f.; vol. IV, p. 721; vol. VII, p. 75; Vol. X, pp. 76, 430; vol. XI, pp. 63, 64, 71, 118; vol. XVII, p. 385.

[43] I have not been able to account for this likeness. Belinsky's letters were published long after Dostoevsky's death, and there is no evidence that he ever saw Belinsky's letter to Botkin before its publication.

[44] *Works*, vol. VII, p. 388.

[45] These ideas found a certain confirmation in Feuerbach's *Essence of Christianity*, with which Belinsky became acquainted subsequent to his repudiation of Hegel. As in the case of other German thinkers, the news of Feuerbach reached Belinsky through his German-reading friends. Feuerbach's somewhat undeservedly neglected masterpiece enjoyed a great popularity among Russian revolutionary thinkers. His substitution of anthropology for theology was an expression of revolt against the power exercised over man by all forms of objectification and estrangement (*"Entfremdung"*) which claim to possess metaphysical reality. More particularly, Feuerbach saw man as deluded by a shadow of himself which has been pathetically worshipped as an independent being and pseudonamed God. But Feuerbach was still very much in the grip of abstract idealistic categories. His "man", unlike Belinsky's, was "man in general", the species man rather than individual man. He merely put the Hegelian impersonal Absolute upside down and attributed it to mankind instead of, as in Hegel, to Godhead. Moreover, despite the mystico-religious manner in which *The Essence of Christianity* was written, there are elements of the crudest materialism in Feuerbach's humanism which he expressed in his famous and not altogether pointless dictum: *"Der Mensch ist was er isst."*

[46] *Works*, vol. XII, p. 337; vol. V, p. 466; *Letters*, vol. II, p. 267. See also Belinsky's article dealing with the works of Gavrila Derzhavin. Nihilistic ideas, however, can be found even in the most optimistic phase of "reconciliation with reality" when he was still thinking in Hegelian terms and his mind was impelled by Hegelian dialectics. "The element of negation", he wrote at the time, "is necessary because whoever has never been at odds with truth has never been in proper peace with it. . . . Every spiritual process is realized through pain and suffering, and the encounter of subjective personality with the objective world must be, in the first place, a painful conflict. . . ." And still earlier, in *Literary*

Musings, he exposed those who "pray to and worship the gods of our crowded Olympus and do not care . . . to enquire if the objects of adoration are really of celestial origin".

[47] *Letters*, vol. II, pp. 30, 195.

[48] Ibid., p. 30.

[49] See, e.g., his views on the place of political action in history: *Works*, vol. XII, p. 465.

[50] Naturally, this does not apply to Soviet scholars. See, e.g., V. Illeritsky, *Istoricheskie vzglyady V. G. Belinskovo* ("The Historical Views of V. G. Belinsky"), Moscow, 1953, especially ch. i, which deals with the development of Belinsky's revolutionary ideas in the 'forties.

[51] *Letters*, vol. III, p. 339.

[52] See his observations on the effects of proletarianization on man: *Select Philosophical Works* (Russian edition), vol. II, p. 547; and *Works*, vol. VIII, p. 471. There is no evidence that Belinsky was familiar with the arguments of Marx in *German Ideology* and other Marxist works of the 'forties. Belinsky's reference to Marx in a letter to Herzen in January 1845 is inconclusive in this respect.

[53] Annenkov, op. cit., p. 130. During his short residence abroad Belinsky heard of a German liberal who expressed his liking for progress, but moderate progress, and for moderation even more than for progress, on which Belinsky commented that, as for him, he liked soup boiled in a saucepan, but liked the saucepan more than the soup. Belinsky's serious suspicions of liberalism and its perfectionist ideas of progress can be inferred from his references to the liberal *Journal des Débats* in *Parizhskie tayny* ("Parisian Mysteries"), and (in an undated letter to Botkin) to the "sugary and exalted phrases of the spotless and blissful Gironde". See also his article (excluded from the edition of his complete works before the Revolution) about Friedrich Lorenz's book *Rukovodstvo k vseobshchey istorii* ("A Guide to General History"), *Select Philosophical Works* (Russian edition), vol. I, p. 375.

[54] *Letters*, vol. II, pp. 191–2.

[55] This, ironically enough, is in the same letter in which Belinsky speaks of negation as his God.

[56] For Flaubert she was *"la chère grande femme"*; Balzac spoke of the "vigour and dignity of her mind", whilst for Sainte-Beuve she was, in the end, *"une Christine de Suède à l'estaminet"*; Baudelaire could not think of her *"sans un certain frémissement d'horreur"*. See André Maurois, *Lélia ou la Vie de George Sand*, Paris, 1952.

[57] See, e.g., *Works*, vol. I, p. 122; *Select Philosophical Works*, ibid., pp. 582–3; and the already quoted *Letters*, vol. II, pp. 246, 266–8.

[58] *Works*, vol. X, p. 406. Elsewhere, however, Belinsky's "materialism" does not go beyond denying the "ghost in the machine", beyond stating that "the spiritual character of man cannot be separated from his physical character" and that "mind without body, without the face as an index of the mind . . . is a logical dream, a dead abstraction". *Letters*, vol. III, p. 175; *Works*, ibid., p. 407.

[59] A first-class summary of Aksakov's ideas will be found in Chizhevsky's book on Hegel in Russia. See also Florovsky, op. cit.; A. Gratieux, *A. S. Khomiakov et le movement slavophile*, 2 vols., Paris, 1939, vol. I; and N. Brodsky, *Rannie slavyanofily* ("The Early Slavophils"), Moscow, 1909. There is no adequate edition of Aksakov's works, and the one published in Moscow in 1861–80 is incomplete. For Aksakov's historical writings see vol. I of that edition. See also Boris Chicherin's *Vospominanya, Moskva sorokovykh godov* ("Reminiscences. Moscow in the 'Forties"), Moscow, 1929.

[60] See Belinsky's references to Aksakov in a letter dated as early as August 19, 1839.

[61] It is worth noting that legal elements were fully operative both in Kievian Russia and in Muscovy. The popular assemblies (*veche*) in the Russian principalities had many characteristics of political organization. Contractual elements in the Kievian period played an important part in the relations between the prince, his armed followers (*druzhina*) and the popular assembly. Similarly, the Moscow Land Assemblies (*zemskie sobory*) were incipient representative institutions or parliaments, even if not very effective ones in view of the general monolithic structure of the Moscow Tsardom. There was nothing particularly homely or familial about the early Russian codes of law, about the eleventh century *Russkaya Pravda* (which, however, is usually regarded as milder and more humane than its Byzantine model), about the *Sudebniki* of the fifteenth and sixteenth centuries, or the seventeenth century *Ulozhenie* which made of serfdom a State institution. See V. Sergeevich *Lektsii i issledovanya po drevney istorii russkovo prava* ("Lectures and Studies on the Ancient History of Russian Law"), Moscow, 1910; also Vladimir Soloviev's skilful polemical article on a later version of Aksakov's idyll: *Samosoznanie i samodovolstvo* ("Self-consciousness and Self-satisfaction"), *Collected Works*, 9 vols., Petersburg, 1901, vol. V, pp. 323 ff.

[62] Apollon Grigoriev, himself a believer in the "organic" truth of the Russian people and a one time Hegelian, wrote a humorous apologia of Slavophilism in verse, entitled *Dva egoizma* ("The Two Egoisms"). As the name of the hero of the poem indicates (Baksakov) Grigoriev had Aksakov in mind. The other hero is called Mertvilov (probably Samarin, but the name is derived from *mertvyi*— dead or deadly) with whom he studies Hegel, as Aksakov studied Hegel with Samarin. The family turns out to be a specifically Slav phenomenon:

> How wives and husbands should agree, alone
> The Russian people rightly know;
> And they have always known . . .
> With them, the wife's no chattel, she is something important, though

> Freedom, of course, she lacks. But then
> The Law protects her. When
> Her husband beats her, he must not risk her life;
> It's only spiritually that he owns his wife.
> He must produce her body . . . And besides,
> In this tradition, this profound conception, of his right resides

> A deeper meaning than at first appears.
> If a hard crust conceals it, cries and tears,
> Formal assault and battery—what are forms? Under
> this crust I find the family a most touching sight.
> Her meek submission, his unbounded right,
> Mark the true Slav: an endless source of wonder!

Khomyakov, whose admiration for England was only matched by his intense dislike of France, was, it is true, prepared to admit that the family is also an English phenomenon, but then he was convinced that the English are Slavs. It is doubtful, however, if he meant to imply also that the Slavs are English.

[63] See Soloviev's brilliant series of articles *Natsionalnyi vopros v Rossii* ("The National Question in Russia"), *Collected Works*, vol. V. So far as I know, the only full study of Katkov is by N. Lyubimov, *Mikhail Nikiforovich Katkov i evo istoricheskaya zasluga* ("M. N. Katkov and His Historic Merit"), Petersburg, 1889, which reads like a protracted obituary panegyric and has no critical value. S. Nevedensky's study *Katkov i evo vremya* ("Katkov and His Time"), Petersburg, 1888, is equally unhelpful.

[64] *Works*, vol. X, p. 400.

[65] *Works*, ibid., p. 410. The charge of "humanistic cosmopolitanism" (which sounds familiar to modern ears) appears to be aimed particularly at the gifted but somewhat doctrinaire Valerian Maykov who succeeded Belinsky as literary critic of the *Annals of the Fatherland*, after Belinsky left the review for Nekrasov's *The Contemporary* (see note 14 above).

[66] See, e.g., *Works*, vol. VII, p. 106.

[67] See also *Works*, vol. X, p. 401.

[68] The best guide to Gogol, as to so many other of Gogol's contemporaries, is Gershenzon (see his *Istoricheskie Zapiski* ["Historical Notes"]), Moscow, 1923; and K. Mochulsky, *Dukhovnyi put Gogolya* ("The Spiritual Way of Gogol"), Paris, 1934. See also Janko Lavrin, *Nicolas Gogol* (1809–1852), London, 1952.

[69] See the letter from Salzbrunn, dated July 3, 1847, *Letters*, vol. III. "Jerusalem" refers to Gogol's intention to make a pilgrimage to Jerusalem of which he informed his public. The pilgrimage took place only later, but it failed to bring any peace to Gogol's mind.

[70] *Moya vstrecha s Belinskim* ("My Meeting With Belinsky"), published in *Moskovsky Vestnik* ("Moscow Messenger") in 1860, no. 3, p. 40. The meeting took place in 1842. It is interesting to compare this and similar evidence from other contemporary writers with Belinsky's later detractors, some of whom charged him with straightforward plagiarism—from Stankevich, from Nadezhdin, and, of course, from the Germans. Chizhevsky positively relishes such charges (his pet cow, which Belinsky is supposed to have milked, being Stankevich), completely oblivious of the fact that even when Belinsky did take from others he possessed some key, some alchemy of his own by which to transmute what he took.

[71] "It may be boldly said", wrote Goncharov in the already quoted Biographical Note, "that Gogol would not have emerged as the great figure he was were it not for the light thrown on his work by Belinsky. The same is true of Gogol's successors." See also Annenkov, op. cit., p. 104.

[72] See, e.g., *Works*, vol. XI, pp. 98–9.

[73] See *Letters*, vol. II, p. 108, and Panaev, op. cit., ch. viii. A description of the first meeting will be found in *Pochin* ("New Departure"), Moscow, 1895, pp. 237–41, by Nicolas Satin, who was exiled at the same time as Herzen and Ogarev.

[74] See, e.g., *Works*, vol. V, p. 109; vol. VI, p. 340.

CHAPTER THREE, *pages* 109–169

[1] The most important biography is E. H. Carr's *Michael Bakunin*, London, 1937, which makes the heavy and detailed Life in German by Bakunin's faithful disciple Max Nettlau (3 vols., 1896–1900, existing only in a few duplicated copies, available, amongst other big libraries, in the British Museum) largely redundant, and which is also more discerning than the massive work in Russian by Y. Steklov (*M. A. Bakunin*, 4 vols., Moscow-Leningrad, 1927). The only other biographical works of enduring value are by A. Kornilov: the already cited *Molodye gody Bakunina* ("The Young Years of Bakunin"), and *Gody stranstvya Bakunina* ("Bakunin's Years of Wandering"), Moscow, 1925. These last two works (hereafter referred to as Kornilov I and Kornilov II respectively) contain important material for the study of the whole period as well as of Bakunin himself, based on letters, memoirs, and biographical and historical essays. They also embody the invaluable documents of the Pryamukhino archives. Some additions to Kornilov's material is to be found in the best available, if unfinished, edition of Bakunin's works in 4 volumes by Y. Steklov, Moscow, 1934–6, thereafer referred to as *Works I*, and in *Materyaly dlya biografii M. Bakunina* ("Documents

for a Biography of M. Bakunin"), edited by Vyach. Polonsky, 3 vols., Moscow-Petrograd, 1923–8. For Bakunin's writings after 1861 see Michel Bakounine, *Œuvres*, 6 vols., edited by Nettlau (vol. I) and J. Guillaume (vols. II–VI), Paris, 1895–1913, hereafter referred to as *Works II*; and the least satisfactory select edition by the anarchist *Golos Truda* ("Voice of Labour"), 5 vols., Petrograd-Moscow, 1919–22, hereafter referred to as *Works III*. See also Bakunin's correspondence: *Pisma M. A. Bakunina k A. I. Gertsenu i N. P. Ogarevu* ("Letters of M. A. Bakunin to A. I. Herzen and N. P. Ogarev"), edited by M. Dragomanov, Geneva, 1896 (there is a French and German version of this work). For a fuller bibliography see, e.g., H.-E. Kaminsky, *Michel Bakounine, La Vie d'un révolutionnaire*, Paris, 1938, pp. 349–53. I give the titles of Bakunin's works throughout in English. A great many of his works abroad were originally written in French, with the help of his friends, who not only improved his language, but, as often as not, helped to put them into shape.

² The most satisfactory account of Bakunin's early philosophical views are to be found in the previously quoted book on Hegel in Russia by Chizhevsky. See also Masaryk, op. cit., Koyré, op. cit., and a symposium edited by I. Balashev, *M. A. Bakunin*, Petersburg, 1906 (especially the essay by Dragomanov); also the extremely valuable full-length study by Benoit P. Hepner, *Bakounine et le panslavisme revolutionnaire*, Paris, 1950. On Bakunin's social and political ideas see F. Venturi, *Il populismo russo*, 2 vols., Turin, 1953, vol. II; and G. D. H. Cole, *Marxism and Anarchism*, 1850–1890, London, 1954.

³ Pavel Bakunin (1820–1900), though little known and completely overshadowed by his eldest brother Mikhail, was a gifted thinker in his own right whose ideas have found eager recognition by Tolstoy. See P. Bitsilli's study of him in *Put* ("The Way"), no. XXIV, Paris, 1932.

⁴ See Kornilov I, pp. 31–9, 79; Carr, op. cit., pp. 7 ff.

⁵ According to Herzen these intellectual pursuits were interspersed with diversions into "reality". "Let us go", Bakunin is supposed to have said to Turgenev, "and plunge into the whirlpool of reality, . . . and they went to ask Varnhagen von Ense to dip them like a dexterous bath attendant into the gulf of practical life and to introduce them to a pretty actress" (*Memoirs*, vol. II, p. 405).

⁶ *Works I*, vol. III, p. 126.

⁷ *Works I*, vol. IV, p. 99.

⁸ Vol. V, "Bakunin and the Cause of Poland". Bakunin, who read this chapter, called it half in earnest and half in jest "a pasquinade".

⁹ Pyotr Martyanov was a Russian peasant serf who bought his freedom and came to London in the same year as Bakunin. He became friendly with Herzen and issued an appeal to Alexander II which was published in *The Bell*. Later, in 1863, he returned to Russia, but was immediately arrested and condemned to forced labour in Siberia, where he died two years later. Like Bakunin for a time, he believed that the Russian Emperor should and could turn into a *zemsky* Tsar (see below, ch. 3).

Liza was Herzen's daughter by Natalie Tuchkova, born in 1858.

¹⁰ Long after Bakunin had left London stories were told at his lodging house in 10, Paddington Green, of his habits which, as Herzen reports, "upset all the accepted notions and religiously observed customs . . . of English middle-class life". Yet the maid and the landlady alike were passionately devoted to Bakunin and did everything he bid them to do.

¹¹ *Works I*, vol. I, p. 209.

¹² Belinsky, as we know, fell in love with another of Bakunin's sisters (Alexandra) during his stay in Pryamukhino in the summer of 1837. On discovering that she in turn showed an interest in Belinsky, Bakunin's behaviour became offensive in the extreme. The above-quoted letter, however, was written some time after this still-born Pryamukhino romance. There were similar abortive "meta-

physical entanglements" between the other Bakunin sisters and Stankevich and later Turgenev (the latter, however, kept an eye on a convenient exit). In both cases Bakunin hastened to liberate his sisters from such entanglements turning not so metaphysical, and he was, to his great satisfaction, duly assured by one of them (Tatyana) that the man she could love "exists only in my imagination". "Perhaps I shall only meet him in heaven", she wrote. It is not possible to speculate on Tatyana's heavenly encounters, but on earth she remained a faithful and determined spinster until the end of her days.

[13] Alexandra Weber, in *Byloe* ("The Past"), July, 1907.

[14] *Pisma* ("Letters"), Turgenev's *Collected Works*, 11 vols., Moscow, 1949, vol. XI, p. 49.

[15] See Dragomanov, op. cit., pp. 32–3.

[16] See especially the revealing and longest letter in Lyatsky's edition of Belinsky's correspondence, vol. I, pp. 227 ff.

[17] See Natalie Tuchkova's *Vospominanya* ("Reminiscences"), Leningrad, 1929, reproduced in part in the Introduction to vol. VI of the English version of Herzen's memoirs.

[18] See, e.g., his speech at a Polish meeting in 1853, commemorating the twenty-third anniversary of the Polish rebellion of 1831, Herzen's *Complete Works* (Lemke), vol. VII, p. 359.

[19] Herzen's *Memoirs*, vol. V, p. 132. "Jules Elizard" was the pen-name under which Bakunin published *Reaction in Germany* in Ruge's *Deutsche Jahrbücher*. It should be noted that these and the following remarks were written by Herzen shortly after his break with Bakunin.

[20] *Works*, vol. XX, p. 274. The growing tension in the relationship between Herzen and Bakunin, and their eventual break, were considerably enhanced by purely personal reasons, in particular by a quarrel between Herzen's son Alexander and Bakunin, for which the former's narrow-mindedness and petulance are largely to blame.

[21] This is in no way invalidated by his admission in a letter to Reichel's sister Matilda Lindenberg that "there is nothing more hopeless than to be compelled to remain eternally with oneself. . . . Man can only be something in the society of others." This was written in the interval between being chained in the Saxon rock fortress of Königstein and incarceration in Austria where he was to spend six months chained to the wall.

[22] I shall refrain from describing in detail Bakunin's early philosophical development: as has already been noted, it does not greatly differ in substance from what is known about Belinsky's intellectual evolution. Chizhevsky's account of it (op. cit., ch. v, probably the best in the book) provides all the relevant data and a very able analysis of them.

[23] Op. cit., p. 85.

[24] According to Wagner, whose acquaintance with Bakunin dated from Dresden, Bakunin acknowledged only one work of art—Beethoven's Ninth Symphony, to which he could listen indefinitely: "everything, including all music, is destined to perish in the conflagration, but this Symphony must be rescued at the risk of one's life" (see Wagner's *My Life*, pp. 468 f). It is in Dresden also that Bakunin is said to have suggested during the insurrection to hang the Sistine Madonna on the barricades, because the Prussians were "too cultured to fire on Raphael".

[25] He is known, for instance, to be the author of an unpublished pornographic novelette in which the hero abuses three virgins at the instigation of their father. There are a few typical Dostoevskian situations in Bakunin's own life, of which the Katkov incident in Petersburg a few days before Bakunin left Russia has been described by Belinsky (see *Letters*, vol. II, p. 145). In the course of an altercation Katkov shouted at Bakunin: "Eunuch!" Belinsky saw Bakunin's

body "quiver as from a sudden shock". A brawl ensued, and Katkov spat in Bakunin's face. Bakunin stood silent in a curiously fiendish way. He failed to challenge his offender, or, rather, suggested that the duel should take place in Berlin, which his enemies used as evidence of his cowardice and lack of a sense of honour. In point of fact, he was neither cowardly nor lost to honour, as can be seen from his behaviour during the Dresden rising and at the military tribunal which condemned him to death.

²⁶ Bakunin's romantic attachments and infatuations were many, but all of them were cerebral and, therefore, ineffective or even unreal, with the exception of the joyless, insidious and incestuous love for his sister Tatyana, who was temperamentally more akin to him than any of the other sisters and brothers. His letters to her are undisguised love letters. He wrote that he "did not want this love" and realized with horror that he had no control over it (see Kornilov I, p. 210). Tatyana's replies are loving and if anything more fervent, but there is no evidence in them that her attitude was anything more than admiration, which she shared with the other sisters, and sisterly affection. Bakunin's marriage in Siberia to Antonia Kwiatkovska remained a *mariage blanc*, and the father of his children was a young Neapolitan, Carlo Gambuzzi, a friend of Herzen's and one of a group of Italian revolutionaries who gathered round Bakunin when he settled in Naples in 1865.

²⁷ The idea that Stavrogin represents an imaginative reincarnation of Bakunin is not new. It has been put forward by Leonid Grossman, the leading contemporary authority on Dostoevsky, and he has fully and very skilfully substantiated it in the course of a literary debate with Vyach. Polonsky, which took place in Leningrad in the middle of the 'twenties (it was published in 1926 under the title *Spor o Bakunine i Dostoevskom* ["Dispute about Bakunin and Dostoevsky"]). Grossman bases his claim on extensive literary and biographical material. He proceeds, not only from the undisputed fact that the plot of *The Possessed* was provided by the terrorist activities of Nechaev, Bakunin's associate at the end of the 'sixties, but also from the hypothesis that the novel, which appeared in 1871, was conceived in its present form during Dostoevsky's visit to Geneva in 1867, where he met Bakunin. The latter was at the time taking part in the International Peace Congress under the auspices of the League of Peace and Freedom—a body established for the purpose of bringing about a European union under republican government. Bakunin, before he became committed to the First International, was an extreme revolutionary leader within the League. The Congress in question was largely dominated by Bakunin's figure and oratory, and it is there that he produced his famous speech in which he predicted the total destruction of European civilization. Dostoevsky heard the speech and, according to Grossman, conceived his hero Stavrogin, as depicted in the finished novel, largely under the impact of Bakunin's words and personality, as well as of other facts he may have learned about Bakunin from contemporaries who knew him. Grossman's claim was supported by Sakulin, another well-known student of Dostoevsky, and by Steklov, the eminent biographer of Bakunin. Polonsky, on the other hand, defended, with considerable polemical acumen, the traditional theory, for which there is weighty but no more conclusive evidence, that Stavrogin's prototype was Nicolas Speshnev, a member of the Fourierist group of Petrashevsky, of which Dostoevsky himself was a member in the 'forties and in connection with which he was exiled to Siberia. The whole question seems to be very much a case of and . . . and rather than of either . . . or. There is no reason why these theories should be regarded as mutually exclusive: Stavrogin may well incorporate features of both Bakunin and Speshnev (none of whom are explicitly named in Dostoevsky's drafts and papers); indeed, to mention yet another hypothesis, put forward by G. Katkov in the *Slavonic Review*, London, May, 1948, he may even embody certain traits of the hero of Dickens's *David Copperfield*, Steerforth.

For an analysis of Dostoevsky's work on *The Possessed*, see K. Mochulsky, *Dostoevsky. Zhizn i tvorchestvo* ("Dostoevsky. Life and Work"), Paris, 1947, ch. 17.

[28] See *Works II*, vol. III, pp. 253, 384. Later, in his essay *The State and Anarchy*, written in 1873, Bakunin described the Hegelian universe as "a *fata Morgana*, suspended between heaven and earth, intent on converting the life of its reflexive and poetizing inhabitants into an unbroken chain of somnabulistic imaginings and experiences, and making them unfit for life or, what is worse, condemning them to doing in the real world the exact opposite of that on which they dance attendance in the poetic or metaphysical ideal". Even the materialistic heirs of the Hegelian Left, "Messrs. Büchner, Marx, and the rest, are in the grip of metaphysical abstractions". Aversion from metaphysics and, indeed, from all philosophy—partly, no doubt, because it had eaten itself so venomously into his system—prompted him to write in 1848 that he "could not now open any philosophical book without a feeling of nausea". This did not prevent him from remaining true to his "abstractness" and exclaiming on another occasion: "Great is logic; perhaps it is the only great thing!" See also *Works II*, vol. I, pp. 79–80.

[29] For fuller textual evidence of these ideas see *Works II*, vol. I, pp. 105–6, 109, 110, 112, 139, 253, 275; vol. III, pp. 19–21, 23–4, 38, 244.

[30] See *Works II*, vol. I, pp. 179–83 (cf., however, footnote on p. 351 of vol. III); vol. III, pp. 228–9.

[31] See, e.g., *Works II*, vol. III, pp. 152–5; vol. IV, p. 54; also Steklov, op. cit., vol. II, p. 285. It should be noted that Bakunin's "materialism" was derived not so much from eighteenth-century sources as from the school of naturalist anthropology which began to emerge in the 'sixties of the last century and of which Elisée Réclus (1830–1905) was a leading spokesman. Elisée Réclus and his brother Elie were Bakunin's friends and adepts of Bakuninist anarchism. The influence of Comte is evident in Bakunin's account of the origin and development of religion and of the progress of human knowledge, with its three stages— the theological, the philosophical, and the "positive" or scientific. But he was far removed from, and explicitly rejected, Comte's worship of science or of idealized humanity, although his own humanism was probably more extreme than any devotion to the abstraction *Grand Etre* could convey.

[32] See *Works II*, vol. I, p. 76 (italics in the original); vol. III, pp. 88–9, 92–4, 95, 98–9.

[33] *Works II*, vol. III, pp. 24, 80.

[34] *Works II*, vol. I, p. 131; vol. III, p. 233; *Works III*, vol. III, p. 162.

[35] *Works II*, vol. I, pp. 61–2, 133, 134; vol. II, pp. 41, 48.

[36] *Works II*, vol. I, pp. 63–4; vol. III, pp. 42–4.

[37] *Works II*, vol. V, p. 16; see also vol. I, p. 287; and *Works III*, vol. IV, p. 255; vol. V, p. 6.

[38] See *Works II*, vol. IV, pp. 61, 260.

[39] This is the view taken by Professor Carr in his biography of Bakunin and particularly in the already cited *The Romantic Exiles*. The sub-title ("From the History of Russian Romanticism") in Kornilov's *The Young Years of Bakunin*, on the other hand, has no specific connotations, and the word "romanticism" is used by him in a rather general and uncertain sense.

[40] See *Works II*, vol. I, pp. 137, 140–1, 159, 228, 254; vol. III, p. 237; also Polonsky, op. cit., vol. III, p. 422

[41] By the force of irony and the capriciousness of the Russian censorship, the first foreign version of Marx's *Das Kapital* appeared in Russia in 1872 (whereas the almost simultaneous translations of Hobbes's *Leviathan* and of Spinoza's works were forbidden). The Marxist movement in Russia was ushered in by the failure of the *narodniki* or populists to find support for their agrarian socialism among the peasantry. The failure prompted the populists, who were originally

moved by the desire to bridge the gulf between the intelligentsia and the people and to redeem the "guilt" of the former *vis-à-vis* the latter, to resort to terrorism in the towns. This resulted in the assassination of Alexander II, but also put an end to the populist form of socialism as well as initiated the reactionary period of Alexander III. Meanwhile a new movement, known at first as *Osvobozhdenie Truda* ("The Liberation of Labour") and led by Plekhanov, Axelrod and Zasulich, laid the foundations of Russian Marxism. It was anti-terrorist, and, unlike populism, expressed itself in favour of the development of capitalism in Russia which, in accordance with the Marxist pattern, was to intensify proletarian consciousness and bring about a revolutionary situation. By the beginning of the 'eighties Marx's derogatory references to Russia turned to almost unqualified approbation. "The Tsar at Gatchina," he wrote in 1882, "is the prisoner of the revolution", and "Russia constitutes the *avant-garde* of the European revolutionary movement". As is known, Marx went so far in his new estimate of Russia as to suggest that the existing form of peasant society "can become the starting point for a communist evolution", provided it is complemented by a working class revolution in western Europe.

⁴² I shall not dwell on the intricate but well-documented history of the relations between Bakunin and Marx, with which the fate of the First International was largely bound up. An objective and lucid account of the matter is to be found in *Marxism and Anarchism* by G. D. H. Cole, cited above, which contains a useful bibliography. For a more detailed discussion see *L'Internationale, documents et souvenirs*, 1864–1878, 4 vols., Paris, 1905–10, by Bakunin's Swiss disciple J. Guillaume, and K. Kanafick's *Michael Bakunin and Karl Marx*, Melbourne, 1948; and, from a Marxist point of view, Y. Steklov's *Istorya pervovo Internatsionala* (" History of The First International"), Moscow, 1918 (English transl., London, 1928).

⁴³ *Works I*, vol. III, p. 317.

⁴⁴ See *Works II*, vol. III, p. 75.

⁴⁵ Dragomonov, op. cit., pp. 230–1.

⁴⁶ See *Works II*, vol. II, pp. 345–6, 400, 415–16; also "Fragment" (1872), and elsewhere (especially vol. IV, pp. 487–8, 493).

⁴⁷ See V. Polonsky's introductory essay to his edition of Bakunin's *Confession* (Moscow, 1921). Hepner (op. cit.) describes Bakunin's "revolutionary panslavism" as a branch of the Slavophil tradition. But he tends to overrate the revolutionary origins of Slavophilism, which, as has been shown already, had a settled and prescriptive character even before it acquired its specifically conservative colour in the middle of the nineteenth century. It is true, of course, that the Slavophils looked to Moscow not only for enlightenment but also for liberation from the "German tyranny" of Petersburg, but this is far from saying that they thought of such liberation in terms of a revolution.

⁴⁸ See Kornilov II, pp. 298–9 for Bakunin's illuminating description and estimate of the Russian people.

⁴⁹ This is, of course, a debatable point, for the evidence that the Russian *mir*, with its periodical re-distribution of land held in common, existed before the middle of the sixteenth century, or that individual did not precede communal land tenure, is inconclusive.

⁵⁰ The question of the authorship of the proclamations, issued during Bakunin's association with Nechaev, has been fully discussed by E. Kusheva and B. Kozmin in vols. 39–42 of *Literaturnoe Nasledstvo* ("Literary Heritage"), Moscow, 1941.

⁵¹ That these were not the ravings of a madman is supported by evidence even from nineteenth-century Russia. The peasant rebellions were then on a relatively small but ever-growing scale. According to the facts in the possession of the Tsarist Ministry of the Interior, published after the Revolution, there were:

145 risings in 1826–34
216 ,, ,, 1835–44
348 ,, ,, 1845–54
474 ,, ,, 1855–61

The risings did not cease with the reforms of Alexander II, which were, in fact, followed by 1,200 peasant rebellions (those in the Kazan district are particularly well known) and were met with a series of punitive expeditions in the course of which 210 people were killed, 1,712 imprisoned without trial, 1,213 tried and sentenced to various terms of imprisonment, 4,777 punished with birch-rod and gauntlet, and 220 sent to forced labour in Siberia. See E. Morokhovets, op. cit.

[52] For these and similar utterances, see *Works II*, vol. II, pp. 233–4; vol. IV, pp. 125, 157–8; *Works III*, vol. II, p. 49.

[53] The most devastating recent portrait of him is that by E. H. Carr, *The Romantic Exiles*.

[54] *N. P. Tkachev i revolyutsionnoe dvizhenie 1860 godov* (" N. P. Tkachev and the Revolutionary Movement of the 1860's"), Moscow, 1922. See also *Nechaev i nechaevtsy. Sbornik materyalov* (" Nechaev and the Nechaevians. Collection of Documents"), Moscow, 1931, by the same author. For other literature see Venturi, op. cit., ch. xv.

[55] See, for instance, P. M. Kantor, *V pogone za Nechaevym* ("In Pursuit of Nechaev"), Leningrad, 1925; also *S. G. Nechaev v Alexeevskom raveline v 1873–1883 gg.* ("S. G. Nechaev in the Alexis Ravelin in 1873–83"), *Byloe* ("The Past"), July, 1906.

[56] The original, written in Bakunin's hand, was found among Nechaev's papers in Paris. The first account of it (from a ciphered copy seized by the police in December 1869) was published in the *Pravitelstvenny Vestnik* ("Government Messenger") of July 9, 1871.

[57] On Tkachev see the above quoted book by Kozmin and also Venturi, op. cit., vol. II. His writings were published in Moscow in 1933 in 4 vols.

[58] On these and other similar movements see the works of A. Shchapov, especially *Zemstvo i raskol* ("Zemstvo and the Schism"), Petersburg, 1862; and *Umstvennye napravlenya russkovo raskola* ("The Intellectual Trends of the Russian Schism"), Petersburg, 1864. See also *Materyaly k istorii i izuchenyu russkovo sektanstva i staroobryadchestva* ("Documents for a History and the Study of Russian Sectarianism and Old Belief"), edited by V. Bonch-Bruevich, Moscow, 1901; and A. Prugavin's study *Religioznye otshchepentsy* ("Religious Dissenters"), Petersburg, 1904. But there is no work dealing with the history of pre-nineteenth-century Russian anarchism as a whole.

Bakunin took an active interest in these movements and even claimed some knowledge of their doctrines. This has been regarded as just a piece of Bakuninist pretence, to win some Old Believers to his cause. In fact, it was due to a perfectly consequent and valid estimate of these movements as a revolutionary force. I am not sure, however, if that would cover the singing of Orthodox troparions which Bakunin tried to do on one occasion (he had no ear and a squeaky but loud voice) to impress a prospective Old Believing adherent.

[59] See *Teorya gosudarstva u slavyanofilov* ("The Slavophil Theory of the State"), Petersburg, 1899, a symposium comprising the relevant writings of I. Aksakov, K. Aksakov, A. Gradovsky, Y. Samarin and S. Sharepov.

[60] Aksakov, Works, vol. I, pp. 592–3, 596.

[61] Bakunin's programme after 1867, i.e., after he moved from Italy to Geneva and when he became one of the most powerful and controversial figures on the stage of revolutionary Europe, is summarized in a resolution submitted by him and his associates to the Second Congress of the League of Peace and Freedom in Berne in 1868. It reproduces some arguments of his earlier pronouncements and begins with the characteristic declaration that it is " absolutely essential not

to separate the three fundamental aspects of the social problem: the religious question, the political question and the economic question". The programme then proceeds along these three lines.

1. That religion . . . should be eliminated from political institutions and also from public education, so that the Churches may no longer be able to impede the free development of society.

2. That the United States of Europe can have no other organization than that which is based on popular institutions linked together in a federation and guided by the principle of the equality of individual rights as well as of the autonomy of the communes and provinces in the arrangement of their respective concerns.

3. That the present economic system requires a radical change, if the aim is to attain an equitable distribution of wealth, work, leisure, education: this is an essential condition of the enfranchisement of the workers and of the abolition of the proletariat.

The resolution ends with a repudiation of "any attempt at social reform made by any kind of despotic power". See Guillaume, op. cit., Vol. II, pp. 126 f.

⁶² See *Works II*, vol. I, pp. 144-5, 204, 284; vol. III, p. 79; Polonsky, op. cit., vol. III, p. 123.

⁶³ *Works II*, vol. I, pp. 237-8, 278-9, 281; vol. III, p. 11; Polonsky, op. cit., ibid., p. 125.

⁶⁴ *Works II*, vol. I, p. 282.

⁶⁵ *Works III*, vol. III, pp. 202-3.

⁶⁶ See his *The Memoirs of a Revolutionist*, London, 1899 (published originally in English). It is one of the best Russian autobiographies and the only work among Kropotkin's voluminous output that retains its permanent value.

⁶⁷ An unfinished programme by Bakunin for one of his numerous secret, not-so-secret, and overt societies, alliances and brotherhoods which sets out with the already quoted declaration against "God and the principle of power, both human and divine", contains a special section demanding the abolition of paternal power, family ties, right of inheritance, classes and ranks. The dissolution of the "tutelary, transcendental, centralized State, the twin-partner of the Church"—"sources of . . . deception and enslavement", comes second. See Steklov, op. cit., vol. II, pp. 337-42.

⁶⁸ One of the few writers to show the importance of anarchistic trends in Dostoevsky was Berdyaev. See his *Dostoevsky* (English transl.), London, 1938.

⁶⁹ See *Works II*, vol. I, pp. 224-5; *Works III*, vol. III, p. 186; vol. IV, p. 88.

⁷⁰ *Works II*, vol. I, pp. 10, 12, 169-71; vol. III, p. 235; vol. IV, p. 476.

⁷¹ *Works II*, vol. I, pp. 139-40, 146-8; vol. II, pp. 326-7; vol. III, p. 212; *Works III*, vol. III, pp. 187-8.

⁷² *Works II*, vol. I, pp. 150, 152-4; vol. IV, pp. 55-6; *Works III*, vol. I, p. 84; vol. II, p. 230; vol. III, pp. 34, 192.

⁷³ *Works II*, vol. I, pp. 12, 39, 78; vol. II, pp. 38-9.

CHAPTER FOUR, *pages* 171-259

¹ The most important biographical studies, both in Russia and abroad, have appeared only after the October Revolution. A great amount of invaluable material has been collected, introduced and commented upon by Soviet scholars (Kamenev, Mendelson, Kozmin, Elsberg, Chesnokov, Ginsburg, and others), especially in the massive volumes of *Literary Heritage* (nos. 7-8; 39-40; 41-2, and 61; two more volumes, containing additional Herzen material, are to come). To this must be added the material embodied in E. H. Carr's *The Romantic Exiles* (see also his "Herzen's Unpublished Letters" in *Oxford Slavonic Papers*, vol. III, 1952) and the less important letters published by V. Rudnev in *Sov-*

remennye Zapiski ("Contemporary Annals"), nos LXVI–LXVIII, Paris, 1938. The most complete edition of Herzen's works is by M. Lemke, with the assistance of Herzen's daughter Natalie, in 22 volumes (Leningrad–Moscow, 1919–1925), hereafter referred to as *Works I*. The first eight volumes appeared in a slightly censured form before the Revolution. This edition is supplied with extensive commentaries, but it is inconvenient and occasionally indiscriminate. A new edition in 30 volumes, begun in 1954, has been undertaken by the Academy of Sciences of the U.S.S.R. To judge from the six volumes already published, it promises to be the fullest and most definitive edition. It is similarly provided with many commentaries, which, together with the material contained in *Literary Heritage*, have been of the greatest assistance to me in the writing of this section. Other important sources of information are to be found in the memoirs of a number of Herzen's contemporaries of which the following are the most important: *Vospominanya* ("Reminiscences"), 3 vols., Petersburg, 1905, by Tatyana Passek, Herzen's cousin and the wife of his great friend during his student days, Vadim Passek; the already quoted *Reminiscences* of Natalie Tuchkova and Annenkov's *The Remarkable Decade*; also *P. V. Annenkov i evo druzya* ("P. V. Annenkov and His Friends"), Petersburg, 1892, and *Memoiren einer Idealistin*, Berlin, 1910, by M. von Meysenbug, who was for a time in charge of Herzen's children and was largely responsible for the estrangement between him and his daughter Olga. The memoirs of Meysenbug (whom Bakunin described as "that frightful Germano-Wagnerian Pomeranian Virgin") are almost as unreliable as those of Tuchkova, her great enemy in the Herzen household.

Among the few existing full-length biographies of Herzen the most helpful are by Y. Elsberg, *A. I. Gertsen, Zhizn i tvorchestvo* ("A. I. Herzen, Life and Work"), Moscow, 1951, and by R. Labry, *Alexandre Ivanovic Herzen*, Paris, 1928; for the period after 1847 see E. H. Carr, op. cit.

² See *Memoirs*, Part I, chs. ii and v, where Herzen draws a vivid picture of his father and of his life at home. Herzen's mother (Henriette Louise Haag) was a German of apparently Jewish origin whom Yakovlev married in Stuttgart in 1811. As he failed to repeat the marriage in the Orthodox Church, their son was illegitimate in Russia. Yakovlev is said to have given him his surname Herzen, because he was the "child of his heart".

³ On Ogarev see Carr, op. cit., chs. vii and xvi; and especially M. Gershenzon, *Obrazyproshlovo* ("Images of the Past"), Moscow, 1911, as well as his already quoted *History of Young Russia*. Gershenzon has also published and edited Ogarev's poetry (Moscow, 1904). See also Ogarev's voluminous correspondence, of which there is a full bibliography by L. and R. Mandelstam in the *Literary Heritage*, no. 61. For the early relations between Ogarev and Herzen see the former's *Confession, Literary Heritage*, no. 61, pp. 687 ff., which is an important addition to the account given by Herzen in his memoirs.

⁴ His brilliant University career ended in what he chose to regard as failure: he did not obtain the expected distinction (a gold medal) because his thesis on the Copernican system "contained too much philosophy".

⁵ *Memoirs*, vol. I, p. 178.

⁶ The following sentence from a letter by Herzen loomed large during the enquiry: "All constitutional parties lead to nothing; they are contracts between a master and his slaves; the problem is not to make things better for the slaves, but to put an end to their being slaves." Cross-examining Herzen the president of the Court of Enquiry asked for an explanation.

"I see no obligation", Herzen observed, "to defend constitutional government, and if I had defended it, it would have been charged against me."

"A constitutional form of government may be attacked from two sides", remarked a member of the Court (Prince Golitsyn); "you do not attack it from the point of view of the monarchy, or you would not talk about slaves."

"In that I err in the company with the Empress Catherine II, who ordered that her subjects should not be called slaves."

"You seem to imagine that we are assembled here to conduct scholastic arguments, that you are defending a thesis in the University."

"With what object, then, do you ask for explanations?"

"You appear not to understand what is wanted of you."

"I don't understand."

Later in the proceedings Herzen was made to understand that if, in the words of the priest who took part in the original investigation, he did not persist in "the sin of concealing the truth before persons appointed by the Tsar" and "realized the uselessness of such duplicity, considering the all-hearing ear of God"; or if, as Golitsyn put it more plainly, he were to write a letter admitting guilt and saying he had been "carried away by his youth", and naming "the unfortunate, misguided men who led him astray", he, Herzen, "would be given his future and his father's life". "I have not a word to add to my evidence", was Herzen's reply.

[7] *Memoirs*, ibid., ch. xii.

[8] The association with Vitberg expressed itself also in Herzen's interest in architecture (see *Works II*, vol. I, pp. 325 ff.) and in their joint authorship of *A. L. Vitberg's Notes* (ibid., pp. 380 ff.).

[9] Herzen's two main philosophical works, published in the *Annals of the Fatherland* in 1843 and 1845-6 respectively, were *Diletantism v nauke* ("Dilettantism in Science"), designed as an introduction to philosophy, and *Pisma ob izuchenii prirody* ("Letters on the Study of Nature"), which are an unfinished survey of the history of philosophy. See *Works II*, vol. III.

[10] According to the *ukaz* of Nicolas I about passports (March 15, 1844) no person under twenty-five years of age was allowed to go abroad; a tax of 700 roubles a year was payable for absence; no wife could leave without her husband. Passports were issued only in Petersburg after protracted enquiries and interrogations.

[11] The *Letters* (or rather the first four of them) were first published in the *Sovremennik* ("The Contemporary") in the teeth of the censorship. There is a French and German version of them, published in 1871 and 1850 respectively. *From the Other Shore* was first published in German (without the last three parts but including two letters, to Herwegh and to Mazzini, which have been omitted in the final version), later in French, and still later (in 1855, from London) in Russian. An English version, with a very good introduction by I. Berlin, has appeared in the "Library of Ideas", London, 1956. See *Works II*, vol. V.

[12] See also Herzen's important letter (first published in *Literary Heritage*, no. 61, pp. 325 ff.) to Maria Reichel (*née* Ern), whom he knew from his exile in Vyatka and who was, after Ogarev, probably his most intimate friend; as well as his at the time much publicized letter to Ernst Haug (an Austrian follower of Garibaldi and a General of the Roman Republic), who took up Herzen's defence. The letter to Haug is reproduced in full in the *Memoirs*, vol. IV, pp. 118 ff. See also E. H. Carr, op. cit., chs. iii and iv.

[13] See Natalie's letters to Natalie Tuchkova. Some of these are reproduced in Herzen's *Memoirs* (vol. IV), others are extensively quoted by Professor Carr, op. cit., ch. ii. The already quoted *Reminiscences* of Tuchkova contain the following portrait of Natalie: "I have never seen so attractive a woman as Natalya Alexandrovna. A beautiful open forehead, thoughtful, deep, dark blue eyes, dark thick eyebrows, something quiet, rather proud in her movements and, with it all, so much womanliness, tenderness, gentleness. . . . I am astonished that most of our acquaintances thought Natalie cold; I found her the most passionate, burning nature in a gentle, delicate frame."

[14] Though privacy dissolves with time, and a time comes when anyone may be told anything, this Herwegh-inspired publicity seems to be the simplest

explanation why Herzen—unlike Herwegh, an extremely reserved person as far as his private life was concerned—saw fit or was driven to speak and write about it in public.

[15] *Memoirs*, vol. IV, pp. 23-4.

[16] Madame Haag and her grandson were travelling via Marseilles; from there they took a boat to Nice. During the night the boat collided with another ship near Hyères and sank within a few minutes with nearly a hundred passengers on board.

[17] Here are some of the political leaders included in Herzen's portrait gallery (most of them members of various democratic, socialist, or revolutionary committees whose seats were in London): the Frenchmen Louis Blanc, Ledru-Rollin, Hugo, Barbès, Caussidière; the Italians Mazzini, Garibaldi, Orsini; the Poles Worcell, Bernacki, Mickiewicz; the Hungarian Kossuth; a few insignificant Germans, and many more significant and insignificant Russians.

[18] See, e.g., *Filosofya revolyutsii i sotsializm* ("The Philosophy of Revolution and Socialism"), *Polar Star*, 1855, 1856. Of the other works by Herzen during this period the most important are: *Le Peuple russe et le socialisme* (the famous letter to Michelet); *Kreshchennaya sobstvennost* ("Baptized Property"), of which an English version appeared in *The Leader*, nos. 189-91, London, 1853, under the title "Russian Serfdom"; *Du développement des idees révolutionnaires en Russie*; *Staryi mir i Rossiya* ("The Old World and Russia"); *Russkie nemtsy i nemetskie russkie* ("The Russian Germans and the German Russians"); *Pisma k protivniku* ("Letters to an Adversary"), and others.

[19] The story of the personal, familial and domestic difficulties and unhappiness caused by this episode in Herzen's life will be found in *The Romantic Exiles* which should be complemented by the brief account in Elsberg's biography.

[20] *Memoirs*, vol. VI, p. xl.

[21] See the last chapter of this section where these important differences are discussed at greater length.

[22] See, e.g., *Works II*, vol. I, p. 330.

[23] See, e.g., *Works II*, vol. II, pp. 204, 205, 212-13, 226, and elsewhere.

[24] *The Remarkable Decade*, pp. 79-80.

[25] "Yesterday", Herzen entered in his Diary on December 21, 1842, "—a protracted dispute between myself and Khomyakov about contemporary philosophy. An astonishing gift of mental fascination, quickness, sagacity, extraordinary memory, breadth of understanding, consistency; never loses the *arrière pensée* at which he is driving. Remarkable ability. I was glad of this opportunity: it enabled me to test my own powers. To measure one's strength with such a fighter is worth any lesson. But we parted each having his own way, without surrendering an iota." See also *Memoirs*, vol. II, pp. 284 ff. More will be said about this dispute in the next chapter.

[26] See also Belinsky's appraisal of Herzen's literary talent in his frequently quoted letter to Herzen about *Who Is Guilty? Letters*, vol. III, pp. 108 ff.

[27] Among the works on Herzen's philosophical views the most important are: Shpet's *Filosofskoe mirovozrenie Gertsena* (" Herzen's Philosophical Outlook"), Moscow, 1920; S. Bulgakov's *Dushevnaya drama Gertsena* (" Herzen's Spiritual Drama"), Plekhanov's essays on Herzen, *Collected Works*, vol. XXIII, Moscow, 1926; D. Chesnokov's *Mirovozrenie Gertsena* ("Herzen's Outlook"), Moscow, 1947, and Elsberg's monograph, cited above. See also the relevant chapters in Kotlyarevsky's *Kanun osvobozhdenya* ("The Eve of Liberation"), Petrograd, 1916, in Ivanov-Razumnik (op. cit., vol. I), Massaryk (op. cit., vol. I), Chizhevsky (op. cit), as well as Koyré's "Herzen" in *Le Monde Slave*, nos. I–IV, Paris 1931. For the early Herzen see Florovsky's *Iskanya molodovo Gertsena* ("The Searchings of the Young Herzen") in *Sovremennye Zapiski* ("Contemporary Annals"), nos. XXXIX, XL, Paris, 1929.

[28] *Memoirs*, vol. I, p. 189; *Works II*, vol. III, p. 297, 232; *Works I*, vol. III, pp. 433 ff.; *Works II*, vol. III, pp. 249–50.

[29] *Works I*, vol. IX, pp. 351 ff.; vol. XXI, pp. 1 ff. Alexander was studying natural science in Geneva under Herzen's friend Karl Vogt, with whom he made scientific expeditions to Norway and Iceland. Like his teacher, he was a materialist of the kind who believes in the peculiar doctrine that the brain secretes thought as the liver secretes bile. In 1862 Alexander published a small book entitled *The Physiology of the Will*, which Herzen criticizes in the second of the letters in question. From 1863 to 1881 Alexander lived in Florence with his Italian wife, and later became a professor of physiology at the University of Lausanne. He died in 1906. His son Pyotr (Herzen's grandson) went to live in Russia and was still alive during the last war. He was a well-known surgeon and then occupied a Chair of Surgery at the University of Moscow.

[30] *Memoirs*, vol. I, p. 121 (italics in the original). See also Diary, September 15, 1844, and the conclusion to the last section of *Dilettantism in Science*.

[31] He coined a term, which he often employed even long after his Hegelian preoccupations: *odeystvorenie* (probably a literal translation of the German *Verwirklichung*), meaning "actualization" rather than "realization". It was designed to convey the idea of the philosopher's task as not merely one of seeing things as they are, but of imposing his vision on them and re-creating them (see *Works I*, vol. III, pp. 434 f.; *Works II*, vol. III, pp. 71, 297, 301). This idea, to which, as we have seen, Belinsky and especially Bakunin have similarly given expression, recurs throughout the whole history of Russian thought and can be found in thinkers very different from these three, e.g., in Khomyakov, in Soloviev, in Fyodorov and Berdyaev.

[32] See, e.g., Diary, December 16, 1844, for early evidence of this.

[33] *Works II*, vol. III, p. 129; vol. VI, pp. 32, 35–6; also *Memoirs*, vol. VI, p. 95.

[34] The most important evidence for these ideas is to be found in *From the Other Shore*, especially in the chapter entitled "*Omnia mea mecum porto*".

[35] See *Memoirs*, vol. III, pp. 240, 241.

[36] *Works II*, vol. VI, pp. 118–19, 131–2; *Works I*, vol. XXI, p. 4. See also the important essay *Neskolko zamechany ob istoricheskom razvitii chesti* ("Some Observations on the Historical Development of Honour"), published in a censored version in *The Contemporary* in 1848, *Works II*, vol. II, p. 151 ff.

[37] See *Works II*, vol. II, pp. 97, 168; vol. VI, p. 131.

[38] Ibid., vol. II, p. 99.

[39] Ibid., p. 79.

[40] See *Works II*, vol. IV, pp. 96 ff.; vol. VI, p. 57.

[41] *Memoirs*, vol. V, p. 230.

[42] See *Memoirs*, vol. II, pp. 300, 339; *Works I*, vol. V, pp. 244, 281.

[43] *Memoirs*, vol. III, p. 133.

[44] *Works II*, vol. II, p. 154; see also *Works I*, vol. VII, p. 260; vol. VIII, pp. 493–4.

[45] *Works II*, vol. II, p. 394; vol. III, pp. 156–7.

[46] *Memoirs*, vol. III, p. 135. It is interesting to see how this dualism expressed itself in Herzen's most idealistic phase, as reflected especially in his correspondence from Vyatka. "I am now extremely preoccupied with the religious idea of Lucifer's fall", he wrote in April 1836: "it is an allegory of immense significance"; and later, in the same year, he wrote, in a Byronic or Lermontovian vein, of mankind as "a fallen angel". "The warring instincts within man which poison and destroy him" are "the direct legacy of Lucifer". But, subsumed though he is by the world of care, man lives by a strange desire to return to and forestall the lost Paradise. At that time Herzen could still speak ecstatically of love and beauty which remove "the seal of anguish and despair" from the face of man and

Nature, and throw open the gates of all the ways of glory. See *Works I*, vol. I, pp. 271, 367, 409, 479, 484.

[47] *Memoirs*, vol. IV, p. 16.

[48] *Memoirs*, vol. III, pp. 137, 138, 139.

[49] They include, to mention only a few, Merezhkovsky's picture of Herzen as "a mystic", Bulgakov's view of him as "a herald of religious revival", Plekhanov's as an atheist "on the threshold of materialism", the current estimate of Soviet scholars to a similar effect (with greater emphasis on materialism than on the threshold), and Zenkovsky's well-meaning if clumsy attempt to run with the hare and hunt with the hounds: "the decisive elements in Herzen's later outlook", he writes, "are defined through and through by Christian ideas. Nevertheless [!] Herzen has at bottom abandoned the religious world-view and completely accepted the tenets of atheistic naturalism" (op. cit., vol. I, p. 282).

[50] See, e.g., *Memoirs*, vol. III, pp. 195–6.

[51] The chronology is provided by Herzen himself. "Until 1834", he wrote to his future wife, "I had no particular religious ideas; in that year, which marks the beginning of a new period in my life, the thought of God began to preoccupy me: the world appeared to me somehow incomplete and un-self-sufficient" (*Works I*, vol. I, p. 407). A full discussion of this period with many quotations from Herzen's letters will be found in Florovsky's study cited above.

[52] *Memoirs*, vol. I, pp. 340–1; vol. II, p. 122.

[53] See *Memoirs*, vol. II, chap. xxxii, and Annenkov's *The Remarkable Decade*, chap. xxvii.

[54] *Memoirs*, vol. II, pp. 284–7.

[55] That Khomyakov was a crypto-rationalist is shown by Berdyaev in *Khomyakov*, Moscow, 1912—the most illuminating and imaginative study of the great Slavophil leader.

[56] "Two or three months later", Herzen wrote in an account of his last exile in Russia, "Ogarev passed through Novgorod. He brought me Feuerbach's *Wesen des Christentums*; after reading the first pages I leapt up with joy. Away with the trappings of masquerade, no more muddle and equivocations! We are free men and not the slaves of Xantos, there is no need for us to wrap the truth in myth." *Memoirs*, vol. II, p. 126.

[57] Herzen's meeting with Vladimir Pechorin in the Catholic monastery of St. Mary's Chapel in Clapham, London, is rather illuminating in this connection. Pechorin (1808—probably late 'eighties), one of the most tragic figures in nineteenth century Russia and one of the first *émigrés* from Nicolaian oppression, abandoned a brilliant academic career at the University of Moscow, wandered for many years throughout Europe and eventually became a Roman Catholic monk of the Redemptorist Order. Later he renounced monasticism but remained a priest. Two years after the meeting the news reached Herzen that Pechorin had been brought up for trial in Ireland for publicly burning a Protestant Bible. Pechorin's long spiritual and physical pilgrimage began in a mood of intense hatred of his native land and, as he wrote at the time, "eager expectation of its ruin", and finished in a pathetic nostalgia for Russia and profound disillusion in Catholicism, to which, however, he remained tenaciously loyal to the end. Herzen was greatly interested in Pechorin's fate (see his letter to M. Reichel, March 18, 1853), and the hero of an unfinished short novel of his (*Dolg prezhde vsevo* ["Duty above All Else"], *Works I*, vol. VIII, p. 498 ff.; and *Literary Heritage*, no. 61, p. 32 ff.) appears to have Pechorin as his prototype. On Pechorin see M. Gershenzon, *History of Young Russia*.

[58] Yury Samarin (1819–76), the eminent Slavophil and disciple of Khomyakov, was known to Herzen already in Russia, and, while disagreeing with him, Herzen regarded him as "a very intelligent and very honest man". On learning of Samarin's proposed visit to England, Herzen expressed a "passionate desire"

to see him. The meeting took place in London in 1864, where Herzen arrived hastily from his Bournemouth summer residence. To Herzen's disappointment, however, Samarin was on his guard, and evidently considered it to be his first duty to ventilate his condemnation of Herzen's views and activities. "He bored me", Herzen complained, "by arguing and arguing that no grass can grow without *la question religieuse et la question polonaise*." A few days after the meeting Samarin sent Herzen a long contentious letter, full of denunciations and even insults. Amongst other things, he accused him of "revolutionary lust", of materialism, and of inability to understand the problem of freedom, which he himself defended on the familiar forensic basis as a means of establishing man's guilt. Herzen replied in a series of letters, published under the title of *Pisma k protivniku* ("Letters to an Adversary") in *The Bell* (November 15, 1864, January 1, 1865, February 1, 1865).

[59] *Works I*, vol. IX, pp. 509, 511; *Memoirs*, vol. II, p. 123; *Works II*, vol. I, p. 330.

[60] *Memoirs*, vol. III, pp. 193-4, 198.

[61] *Works II*, vol. VI, p. 104.

[62] The essay appeared in English in *Man and the Machine*, London, 1933.

[63] *Works II*, vol. V, pp. 33, 35.

[64] *Ends and Beginnings*, Letter I passim (*Works I*, vol. XV).

[65] See *Works II*, vol. VI, pp. 37, 39, 56, 78, 98; *Memoirs*, vol. V, pp. 230, 258; vol. VI, p. 59.

[66] *Memoirs*, vol. IV, p. 15.

[67] *Memoirs*, ibid., p. 6. It should be noted that the "disillusionment" was not due, as is currently held, in the first place to the unsuccessful outcome of the revolution of 1848. The sobering, rather than, perhaps, disillusion, began before 1848. *Letters from France and Italy* were written before the revolution, and so was the first section of *From the Other Shore*.

[68] *Memoirs*, ibid., p. 7. This was written in London in 1852.

[69] Unless otherwise stated all quotations are from the final edition (eight sections) of *From the Other Shore*.

[70] *Works I*, vol. X, p. 14. "Laughter", he wrote in the fifth *Letter from France and Italy*, "has something revolutionary about it. Until men believed in Christianity there was no laughter. No one laughs in church or at court—at least not openly. People in serfdom have no right to smile in the presence of their master. Only the free and the equal laugh. Voltaire's laughter destroyed more than Rousseau's weeping."

[71] *Works II*, vol. II, p. 167.

[72] It should be noted, however, that Herzen never shared the Jacobin tendencies of these socialist thinkers. Herzen's early political alignments are most adequately discussed in the already mentioned series of essays by Plekhanov. For his relations with Proudhon see *Herzen et Proudhon*, Paris, 1928, by R. Labry. This important question cannot be dealt with here in detail. We have seen in the section on Bakunin that Herzen was rather appalled by the completed picture of Proudhon's doctrine. Proudhon's greatest merit was, in his view, to have "sacrificed the idols and the language of revolution to the true understanding of it, and to have put morality on its true basis—the inner man, admitting of no idols, nothing but reason, 'if it' " (*Memoirs*, vol. III, p. 227). It is known also that Herzen sympathized with a group of Proudhonists in the First International known as the *mutuellistes* and contributed to their journal *Association*. He shared their opposition to centralized political and economic power, but repudiated their views on the family as the essential basis of society, their glorification of patriarchal principles, and their hostility to the equal rights for women. On Worcell, see *Memoirs*, vol. IV, ch. IV.

[73] The *Letters* were occasioned by one of Bakunin's brochures at the time of

his infatuation with Nechaev (*The Statement of the Revolutionary Question*) in which he appealed to revolutionary brigandage. Ogarev, who, with some reservations, supported Bakunin's policy, criticized the original draft of the *Letters*, and Herzen's reactions to this is an important factor in assessing their true meaning.

[74] Lenin's *Collected Works*, Moscow, 1937, vol. XV, pp. 465, 469. Lenin's quotations are from Herzen's *Letters to an Old Comrade*.

[75] B. Nikolaevsky, *Gertsenovedenie v Rossii* ("The Study of Herzen in Russia"), *Novyi Zhurnal* ("The New Review "), no. X, New York, 1945, pp. 379 ff.

[76] A number of confusions arose because until recently the available versions of Herzen's *Letters to an Old Comrade* were incorrect. This has now been remedied by the publication in Russia of the authentic version and by the additional textual material with which it is provided. In particular, it is important to take into account Herzen's correspondence with Ogarev at the time when the *Letters* were composed, as well as Herzen's notes to Ogarev's criticisms in which he explicitly rebuts the charge of advocating the principle of social and political evolutionism. All this material is to be found in *Literary Heritage*, nos. 39–40, 61; see also *Works I*, vol. XXI, pp. 451 ff.

[77] *Works I*, vol. XX, p. 100.

[78] The occasion was provided by Michelet's book *Légendes démocratiques* in which he made a virulent attack on Russia, about which he evidently knew very little. As a result of Herzen's letter Michelet reconsidered his views and, in due course, became his friend and admirer. The letter was first published in French in 1852, but only circulated in Piedmont and Switzerland, as the French seized almost the whole edition in Marseilles. The other important works in this connection are *On the Development of Revolutionary Ideas in Russia* (published at first in German in 1851) and the series of letters to Turgenev (*Ends and Beginnings*), written some ten years later. The quotations that follow are from the version in *Izbrannye filosofskie proizvedenya* ("Select Philosophical Works"), 2 vols., Moscow, 1948, vol. II, pp. 138 ff.

[79] The study of the Russian village commune as an original form of social life was initiated by August von Haxthausen (1792–1866), to whom Herzen refers on many occasions, although, rightly, he does not regard him as an entirely safe interpreter. Some have detected an analogy between the *mir* and the modern Russian Collective Farm (*kolkhoz*), where agriculture is conducted in common and the produce divided according to number of days and work done by each partner (not counting deliveries to the State and capital investment). To discuss the relation between the village commune and the post-revolutionary collective organization of agriculture in Russia would require a special study. There is no doubt, however, that Herzen's idea of the coincidence of Russian peasant communism and western European revolution corresponds in some important respects with the current Leninist estimate of the rôle of the village commune in Russia. As is well known, the Marxist doctrine, attended as it is by the difficulty of applying it where no *bourgeois* revolution had occurred and by his failure to provide a revolutionary rôle for the peasant, was modified by Lenin and Stalin to meet Russian needs (see, however, section on Bakunin, note 41). To this extent, Herzen's idea may be regarded as an important link between pre- and post-revolutionary social thought in Russia.

[80] *Pisma K. D. Kavelina i I. S. Turgeneva k A. I. Gertsenu* ("Letters of K. D. Kavelin and I. S. Turgenev to A. I. Herzen"), Geneva, 1892, pp. 170 ff.

[81] This declaration of loyalty was occasioned by an incident in the course of which Turgenev was summoned, while abroad, to appear before the Russian Senate to give an account of his association with Russian political *émigrés*. A notice by Herzen about the affair appeared in *The Bell* of January 28, 1864: "We are informed by a correspondent", he wrote, "that a certain grey-haired Magdalene (of masculine gender) was very worried that the Emperor was not aware of

her repentance, which made her sever all relations with the friends of her youth. She therefore wrote a letter to the Emperor in which she declared that she had been robbed of her strength, her appetite, her peace of mind, her grey hair and her teeth."

[82] *Works I*, vol. V, p. 110.

[83] Earlier formulations of the same ideas appeared in *The Bell* of 1859 (especially nos. 32–3 and 59). For a more extensive discussion of Herzen's populist social doctrine and of his influence on the later populists, see Venturi, op. cit., vol. I.

[84] It is worth noting here that, at this stage at any rate, Herzen was not at all averse to approving, in the Bakuninist manner, of the peasant axe and the "Red Cock" (to use the popular Russian expression for arson) as a means of liberation.

[85] Kavelin (1818–85), whose memoirs have been mentioned in another connection, and who has written a number of interesting essays on ethics, is chiefly known as an active partner in the preliminary plans for the emancipation of the serfs and for educational reform, and a collaborator of Nicolas Milyutin, who became a Minister entrusted with the task of drafting the emancipation edict.

Kavelin's relations with Herzen present a knotty point for the historian of Russian social thought. He and, in some measure, Turgenev were responsible for a campaign to dissociate in the mind of the public Herzen from Ogarev, whom they regarded as Herzen's evil "radical" genius, and without whose shadow Herzen could, in their opinion, be ranked among the liberal moderates. Whatever minor disagreements there may have been between Herzen and Ogarev, their fundamental unanimity at the relevant time can be questioned only at the price of serious misrepresentation. Herzen, as is well known, did his best to confute and silence the campaign. Nevertheless the game continued. Its signs are clearly visible in Annenkov's *The Remarkable Decade* and, later still, in Lemke, whose commentaries to the complete edition of Herzen's works are marred by an unmistakable anti-Ogarev bias which would have been harmless if it did not result in a misrepresentation of Herzen's position (see, e.g., *Works I*, vol. XV, pp. 550–5).

[86] The best study of Chicherin known to me is N. Alexeev's essay *Religiozno-filosofskie idei i lichnost B. N. Chicherina* ("The Religious-Philosophical Ideas and Personality of B. N. Chicherin") in *Put*, no. 24, Paris, 1930. See also Chizhevsky, op. cit., ch. V. Chicherin's legal writings have earned him the reputation of the most eminent jurist in the history of Russian thought. In the context of Russian political history he can be regarded as the forerunner of the Constitutional Democratic Party (the so-called Cadets), which played such an important rôle in the First Duma, although he did not live to see it formally organized. His unfinished memoirs, mentioned earlier on, provide a somewhat more human picture of him than his utterances on political, philosophical, legal and religious matters.

[87] Herzen's *Works I*, vol. VIII, p. 323.

[88] See Chicherin's *Puteshestvie za granitsu* ("Journey Abroad"), Moscow, 1932, p. 49; *The Bell*, November 1 and December 1, 1858; January 1 and December 15, 1859; Herzen's *Memoirs*, vol. II, pp. 399–400, 401; and *Works I*, vol. IX, p. 417.

[89] The movement, embodying a great variety of views and attitudes, has been fully examined by Venturi (op. cit.). It had little success, despite the wonderful heroism and sacrifices shown by its individual representatives. The failure was due in some measure to the reaction of the peasants themselves, many of whom were bewildered and confused, and did not know what to make of these new helpers, fellow-sufferers, educators and agitators in their midst. As has been noted before, the failure issued eventually in the adoption by the populists of active terrorist techniques in the fight against the existing order. The populist

motto "Going among the people" is not, however, Herzen's invention: it appears to have been first used by Bakunin, who applied it to Ogarev as early as 1846 or 1847.

[90] "Nihilism", Herzen wrote in an account of his own position, "is logic without structure, it is science without dogmas, it is the unconditional submission to experience and the ready acceptance of all consequences, whatever they may be. ... Nihilism does not turn something into nothing, but shows that nothing which has been taken for something is an optical illusion, and that every truth, however it contradicts our fantastic ideas, is more wholesome than they are, and is in any case what we are in duty bound to accept. Whether the name is appropriate or not does not matter. We are accustomed to it; it is accepted by friend and foe, it has become a police label, it has become a denunciation, an insult with some, a word of praise with others. Of course, if by nihilism we are to understand . . . barren scepticism, . . . haughty passivity, . . . the despair which leads to inaction, then true nihilists are the last people to be included in the definition, and one of the greatest nihilists will be Turgenev, who flung the first stone at them. . . . When Belinsky, after listening to one of his friends, who explained at length that the 'Spirit' attains self-consciousness in man, replied indignantly: 'So, I am not conscious for my own sake, but for the Spirit's. . . . Why should I be taken advantage of? I had better not think at all; what do I care for its consciousness?'—he was a nihilist. When Bakunin convicted the Berlin professors of being afraid of negation, and the Parisian revolutionaries of 1848 of conservatism, he was a nihilist in the fullest sense. . . .' *Memoirs*, vol. VI, pp. 208–9.

[91] *Memoirs*, vol. III, pp. 261–2.

[92] See, e.g., the seditious article *Vivat Polonia!* in *The Bell* of March 15, 1861, i.e. *before* Bakunin arrived in London. This should be taken into consideration when reading Herzen's own subsequent account of the Polish affair (see chapter on Bakunin in *Memoirs*, vol. V).

[93] A full examination of the facts is to be found in *Gertsen, Ogarev i molodaya emigratsia* ("Herzen, Ogarev and the Young Emigrés") by B. Kozmin in *Literary Heritage*, vols. 41–2.

[94] *Memoirs*, vol. III, pp. 58–9.

[95] As for his own emigration, Herzen came to regard it as one of the greatest mistakes in his life. He was prepared to return to Russia in case of an amnesty "such as the last one in Austria" (i.e. the amnesty of 1867 for all participants of the revolution of 1848) (*Literary Heritage*, vol. 61, p. 428; see also Herzen's letter to Ogarev, August 1868.) It is noteworthy that during the Crimean War Herzen, who, together with many of his compatriots, eagerly expected an end of the Nicolaian *régime*, scrupulously refrained from any attempts to cash in on the then prevailing anti-Russian feelings in England. As for the proclamations of a holy war by the Archbishops of Paris and Canterbury, as well as by the Orthodox crusaders on the Russian side, these evoked only a feeling of nausea in him, quite apart from the fact that none, and the western European crusaders least of all, had lived up to their promise of a holy war. The rumour, spread at the time, that Herzen was responsible for the leaflets distributed by the allies among the Russians in Crimea is completely unfounded.

[96] Cf. *Literary Heritage*, vols. 41–2, pp. 24 ff. "Land and Liberty", referred to at the beginning, was a populist slogan coined by Herzen. It was adopted by a secret populist society founded in Petersburg and closely connected with Herzen and *The Bell*; its object was to bring about a revolution from below by violent methods.

Index

(References to Notes are shown by italicized Roman figures followed by Arabic figures, indicating chapter and number of Note respectively. Under V. Belinsky, M. Bakunin and A. Herzen will be found only those references which occur outside the chapters dealing specifically with these men.)